CRISIS MANAGEMENT DURING THE ROMAN REPUBLIC

The Role of Political Institutions in Emergencies

"Crisis" is the defining word for our times, and it likewise played a key role in defining the scope of government during the Roman Republic. *Crisis Management during the Roman Republic* is a comprehensive analysis of several key incidents in the history of the Republic that can be characterized as crises and the institutional response mechanisms that were employed by the governing apparatus to resolve them. Concentrating on military and other violent threats to the stability of the governing system, this book highlights both the strengths and weaknesses of the institutional framework that the Romans created. Looking at key historical moments such as the Second Punic War (218–201 BC), the upheavals caused by the Gracchi (133 and 121 BC), the conflict between Marius and Sulla (88 BC), the conspiracy of Catiline (63 BC), and the instability following Caesar's assassination in 44 BC that marked the end of the Republic, Gregory K. Golden considers how the Romans defined a crisis and what measures were taken to combat them, including declaring a state of emergency, suspending all non–war-related business, and instituting an emergency military draft, as well as resorting to rule by dictator in the early Republic.

Gregory K. Golden is an assistant professor in the Department of History at Rhode Island College in Providence, Rhode Island. His research interests center on the political institutions of the Roman Republic and Empire and the roles they played in maintaining Roman power over a diverse and multicultural Mediterranean world. His current research focuses on the use of mass media, such as they existed in ancient times, by the Roman governing structures to communicate political messages as part of the means of maintaining control over their vast network of allies and subjects. He is the author of entries on "states of emergency" and "senatus consultum ultimum" for the forthcoming *ABC-CLIO Encyclopedia of Conflict in Greece and Rome*.

CRISIS MANAGEMENT DURING THE ROMAN REPUBLIC

THE ROLE OF POLITICAL INSTITUTIONS IN EMERGENCIES

Gregory K. Golden
Rhode Island College

CAMBRIDGE
UNIVERSITY PRESS

CAMBRIDGE UNIVERSITY PRESS
Cambridge, New York, Melbourne, Madrid, Cape Town,
Singapore, São Paulo, Delhi, Mexico City

Cambridge University Press
32 Avenue of the Americas, New York, NY 10013-2473, USA

www.cambridge.org
Information on this title: www.cambridge.org/9781107032859

© Gregory K. Golden 2013

First published 2013

Printed in the United States of America

A catalog record for this publication is available from the British Library.

Library of Congress Cataloging in Publication data
Golden, Gregory K.
Crisis management during the Roman Republic : the role of political institutions in
emergencies / Gregory K. Golden, Rhode Island College.
    pages cm
Includes bibliographical references.
ISBN 978-1-107-03285-9 (hardcover)
1. Rome – Politics and government – 265–30 B.C.   2. Crisis management in government –
Rome.   3. Punic War, 2nd, 218–201 B.C.   4. Gracchus, Gaius Sempronius, 154–121
B.C. – Assassination.   5. Gracchus, Tiberius Sempronius – Assassination.   6. Rome –
History – Mithridatic Wars, 88–63 B.C.   7. Rome – History – Conspiracy of Catiline,
65–62 B.C.   8. Caesar, Julius – Assassination.   I. Title.
DG241.G65   2013
937'.02–dc23   2012042738

ISBN 978-1-107-03285-9 Hardback

For my parents

CONTENTS

ACKNOWLEDGMENTS

The work before you has its origins in a doctoral dissertation written at Rutgers University, *Emergency Measures: Crisis and Response in the Roman Republic*. I wish to thank the faculty, my fellow graduate students, and the staff of the Department of Classics for the stimulating environment I found there while undertaking this task. Many fruitful hours of research were spent in the Alexander Library, and I wish to convey my thanks to the staff there as well.

The present work has been significantly altered from that version, as substantial additions and revisions were made in the following years at Rhode Island College, helped especially by the generous granting of time released from teaching by the dean of the Faculty of Arts and Sciences, Earl Simson, in the fall of 2010 and the fall of 2011. I particularly wish to thank my chair, Robert Cvornyek, and all of my colleagues in the Department of History for their warm and generous support of my work.

My dissertation adviser, T. Corey Brennan, provided very useful guidance and advice throughout the long process from dissertation to book, and I owe him my deepest thanks. I wish to express my gratitude to many other scholars who have read and provided some feedback or comments on an earlier version of the work: Thomas Figueira, Arthur Eckstein, Sarolta Takács, and Fergus Millar.

Of course, a great many people help to contribute to the long formative period of a young scholar. My earliest debts are owed to two great scholars who are no longer with us, Robert E. A. Palmer and A. John Graham, who first introduced me to the intricacies of the ancient world. In more recent times, in addition to all of those named above, I would like to thank Gary Farney, who has been very generous with his advice and encouragement.

At Cambridge University Press, I would like to thank my editor, Beatrice Rehl, who has been very supportive of the project, and her assistant Asya Graf, who helped to guide it through the usual process. I also wish to thank the two anonymous readers for the Press, whose comments have been very useful in helping to refine the work.

None of this would have been possible without the constant support of my family over the years, especially my parents, Peter and Sylvia Golden. Therefore, I dedicate this work to them.

ABBREVIATIONS

Briscoe, *Livy* 1	John Briscoe, *A commentary on Livy, Books* XXXI–XXXIII (Oxford, 1973).
Briscoe, *Livy* 2	John Briscoe, *A commentary on Livy, Books* XXXIV–XXXVII (Oxford, 1981).
Briscoe, *Livy* 3	John Briscoe, *A commentary on Livy, Books 38–40* (Oxford, 2008).
*CAH*²	*The Cambridge Ancient History*, 2nd ed.
Greenidge and Clay, *Sources*²	A. H. J. Greenidge and A. M. Clay, *Sources for Roman history, 133–70 B.C.* 2nd ed. rev. by E. W. Gray (Oxford, 1960).
MRR	T. R. S. Broughton, *The magistrates of the Roman Republic*, 3 vols. (New York, vols. I and II: 1951 and Atlanta vol. III: 1986).
Oakley, *Livy* 1–4	S. P. Oakley, *A commentary on Livy, Books* VI–X, 4 vols. (Oxford, vol. 1: 1997, vol. 2: 1998, vols. 3–4: 2005).
Ogilvie, *Livy*	R. M. Ogilvie, *A commentary on Livy, Books 1–5* (Oxford, 1965).
RE	A. Pauly, G. Wissowa, and W. Kroll, *Real-Encyclopädie der classischen Altertumswissenschaft* (Stuttgart, 1894–1980).
SB	D. R. Shackleton Bailey, *Cicero's letters to Atticus*. 7 vols. *Epistulae ad Familiares*. 2 vols. *Epistulae Ad Quintum Fratrem et M. Brutum* (Cambridge, 1965–1980).
St. R.	Th. Mommsen, *Römisches Staatsrecht*, 3 vols. (Leipzig, 1887).

Walbank, *Polybius*   F. W. Walbank, *A historical commentary on Polybius*, 3 vols. (Oxford, vol. 1: rev. 1970, vol. 2: 1967, vol. 3: 1979).

All dates relating to persons and events in the text are BC except where noted.

PROLOGUE
The Winter of Discontent

Following the assassination of Caesar the Dictator on the Ides of March 44, the Roman ruling class was thrown into grave uncertainty. Into the vacuum would step the consul Mark Antony, but he was not in full control of Caesar's faction and forces. Young Gaius Octavius, calling himself C. Julius Caesar (as was his right, having been adopted in his great-uncle's will), appeared and made overtures to Caesar's friends and veterans for support, even though he was an untested youth who had not yet completed his nineteenth year. The two would-be heirs of Caesar then embarked on a dangerous rivalry for control of the Roman state. That rivalry would draw in others, including those few senior members of the Roman ruling class who hoped that the Caesarian faction might be dislodged completely and the old political *libertas* of the senatorial class could be restored. Antony, however, had the advantage in armed force at his disposal; in the dying days of his consulship, he attempted to entrench himself by seizing the province of Gallia Cisalpina (northern Italy), putting him in a position to menace Rome and its leading men with his army as a means of assuring his political supremacy after his term as consul came to an end.

His attempt to control the Cisalpine territory was not unopposed. D. Brutus, the governor of Gallia Cisalpina, resisted Antony's attempt to take control of the province, as both men had legal claims to it. By the winter of 44/43, a strange coalition of conservatives who desired a return to the old ways, combined with moderate Caesarian elements and Caesar's heir – the young adventurer whom we call Octavian for convenience – had been melded together by the strong and sharp oratory of the senior consular M. Tullius Cicero into an alliance determined to remove Antony from political life.

In the depths of that winter that saw the beginnings of the ultimate crisis of the Roman Republic, the final threat to the "free" workings of the institutions by which the Roman people had been governed for (allegedly) almost five centuries, the senior consular Cicero turned to the established tools of state for emergency situations, which the crisis created by Antony's armed attack on D. Brutus triggered, in order to rally the Republic against its own former consul and still proconsul. He proposed a full range of measures: the declaration of a *tumultus*, a state of emergency, combined with a suspension of all non–war-related business (*iustitium*) and an immediate emergency military draft with no exemptions from service (*vacationes*) being honored. In addition, he pushed for the passage of a political resolution that would signal that the very safety and existence of the state were at stake, the so-called *senatus consultum ultimum*.

All of these measures had long histories as Roman responses to crisis situations, although in the early days of the Roman Republic, another response mechanism was the favored means of reacting to a serious, and often survival-level, threat. This was the extraordinary (*extra ordinem*, as it was outside of the normal rungs on the ladder of offices that comprised the *cursus honorum*, the normal magistracies of the Roman Republic) office of *dictator*. From the earliest days (according to the historical accounts that the Romans wrote for themselves), the Roman ruling class, when faced with a sudden invasion or menaced by internecine strife at home, handed over all executive authority to a single man, the dictator, who was appointed to have full charge of affairs during the emergency. More often than not, this remedy served the Romans of the early Republic well, as one problem with the Roman system of government in terms of rapid and focused governmental response was its deliberate policy of dividing authority and placing checks and balances on those who wielded power within the system. Assigning one man to govern in times of extreme pressure and stress removed the problems sometimes caused by disagreement between decision makers and different policy aims on the part of different groups.

Over time, however, the Romans began to resort to the use of a dictator on fewer and fewer occasions. We shall discuss the reasons later. In general, it was a reflection on the growth and development of the Roman state itself. Handing over all authority to a single man when we are speaking of a small city of 10,000 or so is one thing. When Rome expanded in the course of the fourth and third centuries BC, however, new conditions needed to be faced – new crises that called for more than the simple expedient of appointing one man to deal with it all. Although the use of states of emergency – the *tumultus* and the *iustitium* – did not change (for they had proven their usefulness and did not require single leadership as a prerequisite for their being put into effect; we will discuss these two measures in full detail later), the ruling class – the men who comprised the Roman Senate – began to take upon themselves the task of directing the state in crises under the leadership of regular magistrates. The Roman state had greater resources available to itself now, as it had created new means of placing men in charge of armed force, prorogation, and there was a need for greater flexibility than the limited office of dictator could supply.

Thus, during two of the major wars of the third century, the war against King Pyrrhus and the first war against the mighty trading empire of Carthage, the Romans did not make great use of the dictatorship even in situations where they had suffered a major reverse at the hands of the enemy. The dictatorship as an emergency response mechanism would reappear briefly when the Romans faced the most dire of threats to their very survival in the dark days of the Second Punic War. After two occasions on which the Carthaginian general Hannibal Barca had annihilated a Roman army in the field, killed a consul, and left the Romans back home trembling in fear for their very lives (Trasimene and Cannae), the Romans would again resort to the appointment of a dictator to lead the state in crisis.

After the long, nearly twenty-year emergency that was the Second Punic War, the Roman ruling class did not resort to the irregular office of dictator again. When it was later revived, it was done in a completely unprecedented manner, and the dictatorships of Sulla and then Caesar bear no true resemblance and have no claim to descent, other than in name, from the constitutional, although *extra ordinem*, office of dictator from earlier centuries. Instead, the ruling senatorial oligarchy preferred to rely on regular magistrates and prorogation to meet their immediate military needs, with states of emergency being instituted as necessary through the normal methods. And some crises that challenged the ruling group of decision makers within the Roman state would require measures other than those designed to meet immediate emergencies.

This state of affairs could have continued indefinitely, were it not for the expansion of the Roman state and the consequent problems that empire brought in its wake. The senate could function as an effective decision-making body when the state was small and the ruling class as a group had largely the same goals and same intentions. As the state grew, so did its population, and so did those who aspired to become leaders within the state. The military requirements also grew as it was no longer just a small patch of land that needed to be held but a large overseas empire. As military manpower began to be squeezed, calls for government action to increase available military manpower were made by members of the ruling elite. But instead of the ruling class as a whole sharing similar interests now, these calls for changes were met with fierce opposition. It resulted in a split within the ruling class that broke the senate as an effective body for resolving internal political disputes, a role it had managed to fulfill successfully for many centuries.

From this point, the last decades of the second century BC, the Roman state would be beset more by internal crises than external ones. When two brothers from a very prominent family, Tiberius and Gaius Sempronius Gracchus, decided to bypass a senate that they saw as intransigent in order to appeal directly to the Roman people for changes that would restock the pool of available military manpower, both brothers would be met with violence on the part of the senatorial factions that were most opposed to their plan for increasing the number of men eligible for conscription, which involved reclaiming public lands that had fallen into private hands, largely the hands of senators and their allies. In the case of the latter Gracchus, the consul L. Opimius in 121 passed a new type of senate decree, one that called on him to "defend the state and see that it received no harm." This new decree represented both a departure from current practice while at the same time bringing back an older sensibility in the handling of internal crises. For the so-called *senatus consultum ultimum* passed the baton of decision maker from the senate back to a single executive officer. This did not make L. Opimius dictator, but it expressed the decision of the senate to pass full decision-making authority to Opimius to handle the matter in whatever manner he felt justified.

The expansion of the Roman state also resulted in unprecedented growth in the number of slaves that the Romans acquired, initially through military conquest but later through trade. This, too, presented an increasing internal threat to the Roman state, as greater numbers meant the threat of revolt increased as well. Slave revolts in the provinces, such as the two great slave rebellions in Sicily (in the 130s and 104–100), would occupy Roman minds and affect commodities prices, but slave revolts on Italian soil were a much more serious matter, as they threatened the safety of the state itself. Normally, a state of emergency and the quick call-up of a militia force could see to the suppression of such local threats, as occurred near the beginning of the second century when a group of Carthaginian prisoners of war bound for slavery rose and seized the Italian town where they were being held, and later near the end of the century when a young man who had put himself too far into debt over a beautiful slave girl attempted to raise a slave revolt to escape his self-made predicament. In both of these cases, the hastily improvised militia was enough to overcome the threat. The normal method of response, however, proved inadequate when a much more grave slave uprising occurred in the 70s under the leadership of Spartacus. The normal tumultuary measures there did not suffice; long years of warfare were required to end the threat to Rome. And again, Rome turned to a single executive official to handle the crisis.

Rome in the time of Spartacus's revolt, however, was markedly different from the Rome of the second century. The body of citizens had expanded dramatically after the failed revolt of the Italian allies, who were also incapable of being suppressed by quick tumultuary measures but instead had to be won over by a political as much as a military solution. The place of these new citizens within the Roman governing structure, however, provided a new issue over which members of the Roman senatorial elite could struggle in the attempt to gain an advantage over their peers. Personal rivalries came to the fore that proved to be incapable of settlement either through political compromise or the employment of emergency measures. Brute armed force decided the issue, as L. Cornelius Sulla twice marched on the city of Rome with a formally constituted army and twice conquered Rome. On the second occasion, the regime in Rome passed the *senatus consultum ultimum* against Sulla, but it made no difference as the faction in Rome lost on the battlefield. Sulla would march into Rome and install himself as Rome's dictator in the modern sense of the word. When another man, C. Julius Caesar, moved toward Rome with an army and the same intention, again, the prime emergency response mechanism of the late Republican government, the passage of the *senatus consultum ultimum*, availed them not.

This, in outline, is the history of governmental response to crises that presented the potential to do lasting harm to the Roman state. In the following chapters, we shall first discuss what exactly constituted crises, ones that required the use of the emergency measures that have been briefly described, and then others that did not. After this introductory chapter, the next several chapters will focus on the specific emergency response mechanisms separately in detail to demonstrate continuity and change in their employment over time. Next, situations that clearly were crises but where the Roman decision makers did not, as far as the historical record informs us, employ the use of the emergency measures examined before will be discussed. Then we shall return to the year 43, when two crises led directly to the end of the free functioning of the Roman Republic. Finally, from the vantage point of the final crises of the Roman Republic, we can gauge Roman attitudes toward crisis response throughout the Republic and observe what the study of crisis response by the Roman government has to tell us about the very nature of the system the Romans used to govern themselves.

1

CRISIS AND THE SOURCES FOR
CRISIS AND GOVERNMENTAL
RESPONSES

WHAT MAKES A CRISIS?

Crisis is the one of the defining words of our times. The news media constantly fire the word at us, declaring one situation after another a crisis. In the realm of political interaction, crisis is ever present. As one modern political scientist has stated:

> [C]risis is among the most widely-used verbal symbols of turmoil in the politics among nations. Statesmen often portray their tenure in office as a daily confrontation with crises. Journalists and scholars, too, write about disputes, incidents, riots and rebellions as crises. In sum, crisis is a universal term for disruption and disorder in the global arena."[1]

In the modern study of Roman history, the word is well worn. An entire volume of the *Cambridge Ancient History* was given the title of "The Crisis of the Roman Empire."[2] Recent works such as J. D. Grainger's *Nerva and the Roman Succession Crisis of AD 96–99*[3] and the collected volume *Crises and the Roman Empire*[4] demonstrate that the word has had popularity among ancient historians to the present day. Therefore, a study of crisis situations and the responses of the Roman government to them fits well with the current mindset.

Although popular, the use of the term can be somewhat hazy in modern scholarship. Because crisis is a matter of perspective, it depends on whose viewpoint one is approaching matters from when designating a situation a "crisis." To tackle a famous example, one of the most common usages of

---

[1] Brecher (1993) 2–3.
[2] *CAH*[2] XII, published in 2005.
[3] Grainger (2003).
[4] Hekster, de Kleijn, and Slootjes (2007).

the term by Roman historians today is in treatments of the so-called Crisis of the Roman Republic. In the volume of the *Cambridge Ancient History* that covers the final century of the Roman Republic,[5] the first chapter is titled "The Crisis of the Republic: Sources and Source-Problems."[6] Whole works, including K. Christ's 1979 monograph[7] and a selection of journal articles assembled by Robin Seager,[8] have taken the "crisis of the Republic" for their titles. Interestingly, none of the authors of the aforementioned works have felt it necessary to address two important matters: (1) the definition of what, exactly, makes the situation being described a crisis and (2) a statement of who or what is *in* crisis. Concerning the first matter, I will not take the writers to task because the word *crisis* is used so commonly – albeit uncritically – in the modern world that many readers will not even feel the need for it to be more sharply defined when they encounter it. For most scholars, it has been acceptable to assume that people can recognize a crisis when they see one. However, the tools exist to deploy the word in a much stricter and more refined sense because there has been extensive work by modern political scientists in the realm of crisis as a phenomenon of interstate relations, and some modern ancient historians who have chosen to restrict the use of the term.[9]

Many works will merely call a situation a crisis and assume that readers will nod their heads without further thought. For example, Lintott, in his opening chapter to *CAH²* IX, states: "By the end of the second century before Christ the Romans faced a crisis as a result of their mastery of the Mediterranean."[10] After that, the discussion turns mainly to the nature of the source material, as to be expected from the title of the chapter, and then to discussing the theories of various modern ancient historians about the "downfall" of the Republic.[11] However, what exactly was the "crisis" mentioned at the beginning of the chapter? And who or what is facing this crisis? From the rest of the chapter, it seems clear that he means the potential overthrow of the institutions of government commonly referred to as the Republic, caused by the inability of a "constitution" meant for a

---

[5] *CAH²* IX.
[6] Lintott (1994).
[7] Christ (1979).
[8] Seager (1969).
[9] I very strongly recommend reading Eckstein (2006) 1–36 (who uses the word "crisis" in a much more sophisticated manner than many other works), which has references to many of the more important political science works dealing with interstate interaction, situations that often, but not always, give rise to crises.
[10] Lintott (1994) 1.
[11] Lintott (1994) 1–15.

small city-state to regulate the political dealings of what became, without question, a multiethnic, large territorial empire. That is certainly a threat that would constitute a crisis, but is the destruction of the Republic what he is really talking about? Lintott states that it was a crisis for "the Romans." But were the Roman people as a whole threatened with serious harm by the potential overthrow of the Republic?

No. The continued existence of the common people of the city of Rome and its peripheral territory was not extinguished by the fall of the Republic. Even the fall of the Roman Empire several centuries later did not result in the sudden death and disappearance of the Roman people, even if it marked their complete and lasting political eclipse as Roman political institutions were gradually dismantled throughout the territories once ruled by the Caesars (and the "Romans," of course, were a very different people by that time). Nor was the senatorial order (the ruling class of the Roman Republic) as a whole threatened with annihilation by the fall of the Republic. If the downfall of the Republic that Lintott is discussing is neither the absolute destruction of the state nor the annihilation of its citizens, then what was threatened and who felt that threat?[12]

It appears that he is talking about a segment of the ruling group within the Roman aristocracy: the fall of the Republic meant the end of their continuing hold on the levers of power in the Roman state that the Republic gave them. If this is so, then it should be stated clearly and not left to assumption. Therefore, from the perspective of this narrow elite at the top – and this is the perspective similarly adopted by many works that focus on the so-called crisis of the Republic – this crisis was not so much a crisis of the Republic as it was a crisis for certain ruling elements within the Roman senatorial order. If scholars wish to call it a crisis, they should name it "The Crisis of the Roman Ruling Class" or the "The Crisis of the Elite Roman Families." However, this is not done.[13] In the end, of course, the Republic fell because as a system of government, it could not be separated from the individuals who wielded the most power within it.[14]

---

[12] These are the most important questions in defining a crisis.

[13] The title "Crisis of the Republic" continues to be used. See recently von Ungern-Sternberg (2004).

[14] One need look no further than the fact that the civil war of 49 was centered on the person of Caesar himself and eventually devolved into a contest between "Caesarians" and "Pompeians," not "rebels" vs. "loyalists." Argument continues to rage over the nature of the Roman Republic and where power resided within it. The most recent assessment of current theories on the subject is Hölkeskamp (2010), an interesting work but one that suffers from bias and apparently personal animus against one of the major proponents of the opposing position.

However, the crisis was not a threat to the existence of the Republic itself but a threat to the entrenched power of the ruling element within the senatorial order. The process of their dislodgment from a favored position in running Rome's affairs began when Julius Caesar (*cos.* 59) crossed a small stream in northern Italy in January 49. Although Caesar's invasion of Italy and the events that followed certainly were a crisis, the perspective being employed by many scholars does not entail looking at the crisis from the perspective of the survival of the system of government – a system that, in theory, could have survived (and if you are willing to believe Augustus, it did survive) the displacement of certain "noble" Romans whose families had dominated it for more than four centuries.

In this examination of crisis situations and the response mechanisms employed to face them, our focus will be on the perspective of the governing institutions of the Roman state – that is, when the Roman governmental institutions themselves were placed in crisis. That phrase, "the governing institutions of the Roman state," of course, refers to the Roman Senate, the magistrates, and the Roman People all together. The official name of the government was *Senatus Populusque Romanus* ("the Senate and the Roman People"). In this work, we will be concerned with situations that posed a crisis for the decision-making authorities within the Roman state: those persons or groups who were authorized to take action (a response) in the name of the Roman state in the face of a critical situation. Because "the Roman decision makers" is a rather long and unwieldy phrase, let it be noted here that when I make reference to "the Romans," I am speaking specifically about the decision makers among the Roman ruling class, and the term, unless it is clear I am discussing the Roman people as a whole, should be understood in that vein.

DEFINING CRISIS

Because I have spent some time chiding others for their loose usage of the term "crisis," it is only right that I provide a clear and precise definition of how the term is used in this work and what specific types of crises are discussed. A crisis, to put it in its simplest terms, is a situation in which a decision maker, or a group designated as the decision makers within a community, perceives a threat to itself or to things upon which the decision maker places very high value (core values). If a response is not made to the threat within a limited time frame, the expectation is that core values will be negatively impacted, possibly to the point of destruction.[15] As is immediately apparent, the highest core value is continued existence, and the threat perceived often includes the prospect of temporary or lasting harm to the state if the threat is not dealt with in time. This does not mean that all crises are sudden and must be responded to immediately, but rather that a response must be made within a certain amount of time before certain expected negative consequences will occur. A crisis can resolve itself with no response made, although in this case, it can be argued that *inaction* was the response decided upon, and it happened to lead to a successful resolution of the situation. For our purposes, the decision maker is the governmental institutions of the Roman state that we commonly refer to as the Roman Republic, with authority delegated to those officials and official bodies of the Republic that can make binding decisions for the entire community.

As for the specific types of crises (including specific kinds of threats that are perceived), there are many variations in our modern understanding of the term, ranging from military-security crises to societal, economic, social, and mental crises. My primary concern will be with military-security crises – that is, situations in which physical harm threatened the core values of the Roman state up to and including the free functioning of the governing institutions of the Roman Republic. At times, I also discuss political crises: incidents in which the political machinery of the Republic was under threat of being rendered inoperative because of competing forces within the governing structures. In almost all cases, the Roman members of the governing class – and especially those currently in office as representatives of the government – would have perceived a crisis situation that threatened temporary or lasting harm to the governing institutions or physical harm to those who were charged with the Republic's defense. The line between the two types is not so easily drawn, however, because political crises often gave rise to violence and physical harm; the Romans, as becomes very clear from the discussion to follow, found it difficult to agree to political solutions to end political impasses. Instead of compromise, some men tried methods of "gaming the system" to end the stalemate. When such methods were unavailable, Romans of the upper class often preferred to resort to force to resolve political impasses in their favor.

[15] For this very simple definition, I have benefited from reading a large number of political science works that study crisis as a political phenomenon, especially the theoretical treatment of Brecher (1993). My own definition is not original, representing a simplified rephrasing that best suits the purposes of this study.

Other types of crises that might today evoke a government response did not always produce such from the Romans during the period of the Republic. In general, the Roman authorities were not greatly concerned with societal "crises" such as those that garner media headlines and anguished handwringing from politicians today. It is true that certain prominent Romans took an interest in these types of issues: the most prominent societal "crisis" the Roman upper class seemed to be concerned with was the apparent decline in the numbers of freeborn native Italians, both among the well-to-do and the masses. The biographer Suetonius reports that Emperor Augustus read out to the senate a speech by a Q. Metellus *de prole augenda*, concerned with increasing reproduction among the upper classes.[16] Further, there were the schemes for providing feeding allowances to Roman children throughout the cities of Italy, the *alimenta*; although started by private individuals (the most famous, but not the earliest, established by the younger Pliny),[17] the allowances were eventually put on a state-sponsored basis by Emperors Nerva and Trajan.[18]

Again, one trying to make the case that the Romans considered these types of issues to be public matters could point to the rules and regulations that were established governing the behavior and responsibilities of the upper classes (the senators and the equestrians),[19] created in response to the perception by the Romans among themselves that the ruling order was in some sort of moral swan dive. "It had been the fashion at least from the time of Cicero to describe Rome as a bilge, sink or cesspool into which flowed all that was most depraved and corrupt from Italy and the provinces."[20] It should be noted, however, that these governmental responses to societal crises took shape under the emperors, when what constituted the Roman government was a very different animal entirely, and emperors had their own agendas to pursue. During the Republic, the period under study here, the Roman ruling class spoke a great deal about addressing societal issues but appears not to have employed governmental action to do anything about them.

---

[16] Suet. *divi Aug.* 89. 2; attributed to Q. Caecilius Metellus Macedonicus (*cos.* 143) by Malcovati, *ORF*⁴ p. 107, following a statement by Livy (*Per.* 59). It is wrongly attributed by A. Gellius *NA* 1. 6. 1f. to Q. Caecilius Metellus Numidicus (*cos.* 109).

[17] See Pliny *Ep.* 7. 18 (cf. 1. 8. 10).

[18] For a good summary treatment, see *OCD*³ *alimenta* p. 63.

[19] For example, the SC from Larinum of AD19: see Levick (1983) 97–115. Also the marriage legislation passed at the behest of the Emperor Augustus; for a good account, see Treggiari (1991) 60–80.

[20] Earl (1967) 96–97. As a side note, the first apparent notice of an official ban on senators appearing in the arena comes from the domination of Caesar the Dictator; see Levick (1983) 105–106.

The Sources: A Very Brief Overview

A short word about the sources available for this examination: for the student of crisis situations and the Roman governmental response, the ancient sources are to a certain extent more helpful than they can be for other subjects of inquiry. For the period under study, from the era of historical myth (the early Republic) to 43, we are fortunate that the ancient historical sources are rich in material for an examination of crises and the actions of government officials in response to those situations. Writing about Hellenistic history, Eckstein notes that "the historical writers were intensely interested in crises between significant states."[21] The situation is the same for Roman history, where the main narrative accounts practically read like one recounting of a crisis followed by another. Although the viewpoint is outdated, being much too negative about the possibility of recovering other perspectives from our ancient informants,[22] the general tone of Earl's summation of what kind of information is available to us from the ancient authors only encourages the student of crisis response:

> Since the sources from which we must work were produced by the upper class, the history we can write must mirror the pretensions and interests of this class. Since the concern of the upper class at Rome was almost exclusively with politics and statecraft, military and political history is the only history we have enough information to write, in the sense of being able to trace processes and developments in some detail over extended periods of time.[23]

This is not to say that the sources present us with *all* of the information that we might want to know. What interested the authors of histories and historical works (such as biographies) does not always match our concerns. For example, we might want to know *why* the consul L. Opimius (*cos.* 121) had a body of Cretan archers ready and at his disposal for his showdown with Gaius Gracchus in that fateful year. Did the Romans regularly have armed bands of foreign *auxilia* just sitting nearby Rome? Did Opimius plan on using force from an early time in his term of office? We can do nothing more than make educated guesses as to the nature of their presence, but Plutarch, who informs us of this important and intriguing detail, offers no further information about them, other than that they were of great use to Opimius on that bloody day.[24]

---

[21] Eckstein (2006) 99 n. 81.
[22] Earl (1967) 11.
[23] Earl (1967) 12.
[24] Plut. *C. Gracchus*, 16. 4 [37. 4].

For the earliest period, we are most reliant upon Livy and Dionysius of Halicarnassus. A detailed discussion of Livy, his sources, and his methods is unnecessary here. There is a large body of literature on the subject, including general works,[25] detailed scholarly commentaries on several books,[26] and recently more specialized studies on particular aspects of Livy and his history.[27] For our purposes, he is a wealth of information, but we must, of course, be careful with that wealth; especially for the early period, there is significant room for error and conflation. For some of the early crisis situations that faced the Roman Republic, the information presented by our sources likely tells us more about what the author and his readers would accept as a plausible reconstruction of Roman behavior in the past when responding to such crises rather then providing us with firm, factual material.

Two notable examples are the wrangling over the Licinian-Sextian Rogations (of 370–367) and the grave threat to Rome presented by the coalition of Etruscans, Umbrians, Samnites, and Gauls against the Romans, which would only be relieved by the Roman victory at the Battle of Sentinum (295). For the former, we have a full narrative from Livy, but one plagued with problems.[28] As for Sentinum, again, there are serious source problems, including an account of consular activities that is heavily interpolated with anachronism and rhetoric inspired by the "Struggle of the Orders." Livy himself, on numerous occasions, mentions that his own sources were confused and in disagreement with each other.[29] I shall take this occasion to discuss these episodes but more in terms of what they can tell us about first-century expectations than fourth- and third-century reality.

This is not to say that Livy is untrustworthy. He has many doubters, and it is undisputed that errors and anachronisms appear in his work. Still, we do not have much else to work with on occasion, and regarding the authenticity of the material contained in Livy's history, I am, in general, in broad agreement with the position taken by Cornell: despite the embellishments and errors, "our sources do depend ultimately on a hard core of

---

[25] Walsh (1961); Dorey (1971); Luce (1977).

[26] Including Ogilvie, *Livy*; Oakley, *Livy*; Kraus (1994); Briscoe, *Livy*; the list is merely a sampling of the large number of commentaries on Livy's work.

[27] D. Levene (1993), (2010); Miles (1995); M. Jaeger (1997); Feldherr (1998); Chaplin (2000). This list is not exhaustive.

[28] For the full account, see Livy 6. 34. 1–42. 14. There are serious doubts about the truth of Livy's narrative, for which see the detailed discussion with bibliography and notes by Oakley *Livy* 1. 645–724 (esp. 645–660).

[29] For details, see Oakley *Livy* 4. 268–294, esp. 272–274, 283.

authentic data, much of which is readily identifiable."[30] In the main, we may place a great deal of trust in the information given to us by him.

Of course, the lack of Livy's second decade and all of his books following book 45 is a great loss, as there are incidents of which we only have shortened and not very satisfying accounts (such as the revolt of M. Lepidus in 78), where Livy's full narrative would have been indispensable. As for Dionysius, because his history becomes fragmented far earlier, it is of less value for most of the incidents studied here.[31] Of the other major narrative histories, Polybius is again a wealth of information, but sadly, we do not have his complete work after 216.[32] Except at the very end of the Republic, Cassius Dio, sadly, largely consists of mere fragments, with Zonaras' summary providing some idea of what Dio might have said.[33] Appian's various histories, especially the one treating civil wars in Rome, are sometimes our sole source for important episodes.[34] Occasionally, the history of Diodorus Siculus provides crucial information.[35]

Of other sources, the biographies of Plutarch[36] – and to a much lesser extent Suetonius[37] – provide useful information that is not preserved in our existing narrative accounts. Late epitomes such as those of Florus, Orosius, and others will be noted, but they rarely provide information that is truly valuable. As for inscriptions, they generally do not provide us with much direct information, but they do occasionally give us items for comparison with the narrative histories (for example, Livy's treatment of the "Bacchanalian" conspiracy can be measured against the surviving *senatus consultum de Bacchanalibus*). And of course, especially for the very end of the Republic, the speeches and letters of Cicero are invaluable, albeit providing only one man's view of matters.[38]

Overall, when dealing with the subject of crisis, our source materials are quite good for the aforementioned reasons. They are not, however, as comprehensive as one could wish. For the early sections of Livy, we have

---

[30] Cornell (1995) 16–18; a position followed by Oakley, *Livy* 1. 102 (although he cites Cornell's earlier statement of this position, which Cornell made in *CAH*² VII. 2 249).

[31] For Dionysius, Gabba (1991) is very useful.

[32] The literature on Polybius is immense. A good starting point is Walbank (2002).

[33] On Dio, see Swan (2004) 1–36; Millar (1964) is old, but still worth consulting. See also Gowing (1992).

[34] There does not seem to be a more recent monograph dealing with Appian than Gowing (1992). For some of the problems with Appian as a source, see Badian (1984).

[35] See Green (2006) 1–34 for a good summary treatment with references to previous studies.

[36] The literature on Plutarch is vast. Pelling (2002) is a starting point.

[37] Only the lives of Julius Caesar and Augustus provide major information related to this study.

[38] The literature on Cicero is too large to even suggest a starting point. For the letters, at least, we have the invaluable commentary editions of Shackleton Bailey (1965–1970, 1977, 1980).

to be careful because the reconstruction of crisis behavior sometimes reads more like what appeared to be a reasonable course of action to a first-century Roman than a genuine reflection of the actions of a fourth-century reality.[39] Polybius, although justly praised by many, could occasionally get things wrong, as when he stated that when a dictator was in office, all other magistrates were removed from office (when in actuality they stayed in office but were subordinate to the orders of the dictator).[40] Yet the focus of the sources on crises, as noted in the beginning of this section, compensates for all of the shortcomings of the sources. The greatest problem is actually the lack of detailed source materials for certain events. Plutarch's biographies fortunately tell us much about Pyrrhus and Marius' campaigns against the Cimbri-Teutones, but we do not get the same wealth of institutional or administrative information about those events that we might have gotten from Livy's books had they survived. We are fortunate that some of the gravest crises faced by the Roman Republic – the invasion of Hannibal and the coup of Julius Caesar – have full narrative accounts, and for the latter, the letters of Cicero provide us with an almost daily commentary for certain stretches of time.

[39] Livy also had his own agenda for including or excluding certain events in order to make specific points. For Livy's deployment of certain *exempla*, for example, see Chaplin (2000).
[40] Error noted with citations of other ancient authors who copied the mistake by Walbank, *Polybius* i. 422 on Polyb. 3. 87. 8.

2

THE ROMAN DICTATOR

If we take the Romans at their word (which many do not), from ancient times their primary response mechanism to severe crises that threatened the safety and stability of the state was to hand over all power to a single, extraordinary executive official: the *dictator*.[1] This most unusual Roman magistracy figured prominently in the early Roman Republic's response to military-security crises during the first three centuries of the Republic.[2] During the early life of the Roman state, this extraordinary magistracy was instrumental in providing a means of dealing with severe threats, both external and internal. The very first dictator recorded was T. Larcius Flavus in 501.[3]

EXTERNAL THREATS

In the early history of Rome, it was regular for a dictator to be appointed in response to a severe threat from the outside. To give a good example of how the Romans believed the dictatorship worked in their distant past for these types of situations, I will recount briefly the classic literary example

---

[1] The most recent full-scale, detailed (although with some limitations on its scope) monograph on the subject of the Roman dictatorship is an unpublished dissertation: Hartfield (1982). Then there are the collected volume of Duverger (1982) and the work of Valditara (1989), which is not solely focused on the Roman dictatorship. Kunkel (1995) 665–717 provides a detailed view but includes the anomalous dictatorships of Sulla and Caesar. There is no more recent book-length treatment in any language. There has been little, if any, detailed work done on the dictatorship in the past decade. A fairly detailed, but brief, treatment of the office in relationship to the development of the later office of praetor can be found in Brennan (2000) 38–43.

[2] I will not discuss the role of dictators who were named for other reasons, such as holding elections or fulfilling certain religious duties.

[3] There are, of course, problems with the exact date. Precision is not to be expected in this case. For a detailed discussion, see Hartfield (1982) 310–312.

of the office in action during a crisis, the famous tale of L. Quinctius Cincinnatus, dictator in 458.[4] I call it a "tale" because of doubts about the authenticity of the narrative (further discussed in this chapter). Still, a brief recounting of his activity, drawn from Livy,[5] is helpful in demonstrating the dictator in action during a crisis. When the consul L. Minucius was trapped by the Aequi, the other consul (Nautius) was thought unequal to the task of coming to his colleague's rescue. Therefore, the Romans (3. 26. 6: *consensu omnium*) decided to have Cincinnatus named dictator. A delegation from Rome met him hard at work on his farm, informing him that he had been named dictator and that a Roman army and consul were in danger. They returned to Rome immediately. The next day, Cincinnatus appointed L. Tarquinius[6] as his *magister equitum* (Master of Horse) and appeared before an assembly to announce his orders:

> iustitium edicit, claudi tabernas tota urbe iubet, vetat quemquam privatae quicquam rei agere; tum quicumque aetate militari essent armati cum cibariis in dies quinque coctis vallisque duodenis ante solis occasum in Campo Martio adessent; quibus aetas ad militandum gravior esset, vicino militi, dum is arma pararet vallumque peteret, cibaria coquere iussit. (3. 27. 2–4)

> He proclaimed a *iustitium*, ordered the shops to be closed throughout the city, (and) forbade anyone from undertaking private business of any sort; then anyone who was of military age was to be present, under arms, in the Campus Martius before sundown with cooked rations for five days and twelve wooden stakes; to those who were over the age for military service, he ordered them to cook the food for their neighbors who were to serve, while they were readying their arms and seeking out stakes.

The army was mustered and marched out of the city that night under the command of Cincinnatus. To make a long story short, Cincinnatus managed to approach the Aequian positions besieging the Roman army under Minucius and succeeded in surrounding them. Caught between the two Roman armies, the Aequians had to accept a humiliating surrender, being forced under the yoke. Cincinnatus returned to triumph, and abdicated after only fifteen days in office as dictator, even though the appointment was for six months.[7]

Although there is little doubt that the whole narrative, including the wonderfully picturesque image of Cincinnatus drawn from his plow to

---

[4] For full references, consult MRR 1. 39, or Hartfield (1982) 324–326.
[5] Livy 3. 26. 3–29. 7.
[6] His name is also given as Tarquitius, accepted by some (Broughton MRR), rejected by others (Ogilvie Livy 442); see both for further references.
[7] Livy 3. 29. 7.

save the Roman state, is largely legendary,[8] the details that were used in its construction exhibit very well a script that nearly all dictators who were named to deal with military crises followed. In short, a dictator performed a play in three acts. Act I was to appoint a *magister equitum*. Act II saw the dictator lead the Roman army out to battle. Act III described the dictator returning to abdicate his office, his task completed.[9] Cincinnatus followed the script to the end. What is of greater interest is the series of orders that he gave to the citizens in Rome. As previously stated, the dictator declared a *iustitium* and ordered the enrollment of all men of military age in the city to assemble for action by the end of the day, thus establishing that this important declaration of emergency is believed by the Romans to have existed from a very early era.[10] He further gave very specific instructions for the men to provide stakes for entrenchment and rations for a fixed number of days, details that are meant to inspire confidence in the accuracy of the account. Embellished or not, this account probably reflected actual practice (and may very well have been derived from real events). Therefore, it is useful in helping to establish what became normative expectations among later generations for the dictatorship in its crisis response role.

THE GALLIC SACK

In one very famous case, a crisis was severely mishandled by not immediately appointing a dictator; once a dictator was appointed, things were put back to right – so the literary tradition would have us believe. This, of course, is the story of the Gallic Sack of Rome, which was traditionally thought to have taken place in the year 390 by Varro's reckoning but has been, on Polybius's evidence probably derived from Timaeus, placed more firmly around 387/386.[11] That the account of the events leading to the Gallic march on Rome as we have it in Livy is "not very satisfactory," as Cornell put it,[12] is a view with which I believe most scholars would agree. The run up to the crisis has inspired particular doubt among commentators. Concerning the events at Clusium, Ogilvie considered the whole story a "romantic explanation, typical of the Hellenistic age,"[13] whereas the Clusines' appeal to Rome and the embassy of the Fabii brought out the

---

[8] Ogilvie *Livy* 441.
[9] This almost standard formula is the observation of Hartfield (1982) 19.
[10] The *iustitium* will be treated in greater detail in Chapter 4.
[11] See Walbank, *Polybius* 1. 48; 184–185.
[12] Cornell (1995) 314.
[13] Ogilvie, *Livy* 699.

deepest skepticism in the commentator: "The whole story is baseless."[14] A recent view of the matter would disagree in part, as "Given Rome's military operations as far north as Volsinii in 392 and 391 B.C., Clusium's appeal to Rome, as well as to other states in the region, is certainly plausible, whereas the tale of the Roman ambassadors taking the side of Clusium in the fighting is a later invention."[15]

This episode in Roman history is filled with the kinds of inventions and distortions that do much to deflate confidence in any of the information presented to us by seemingly informed and suspiciously detailed accounts. Many events appear to be mere "romantic" creations, the most prominent example being Camillus's heroic "ride to the rescue."[16] So what can we gain from reviewing this episode when so much of what we are presented can be considered fiction rather than history? Although significant parts of the story are cut from whole cloth, a careful look at the tailoring can confirm for us what the Romans of the late Republic believed to be normative response in a crisis situation and what constituted successful, and unsuccessful, crisis response in their past.

The historical core of the tale, what most historians are willing to consider credible, is the short summary given by Polybius, who mentions the event as merely a minor detail in his larger account of the fractious relations between the Romans and the Gauls.[17] Polybius 2. 18. 1–3 sets out with minimal details that the first invasion of the Gauls (which took place not very long before the attack on Rome in 387/386 by Polybius's reckoning, a date not given in this section but only in passing at 1. 6. 2 as part of his synchronization of important events) resulted in the subjugation of many peoples, including the Romans, whom they defeated in a pitched battle not too long after the Gauls invaded northern Italy. Three days later, they had occupied all of Rome excluding the capitol. After occupying Rome for seven months (noted not here but at 2. 22. 5), the Gauls were distracted by an attack on their own lands by the Veneti. Therefore, a treaty was made with the Romans, and they returned home. Factual and believable but also devoid of any details we might want to know. Did the

---

[14] Ogilvie, *Livy* 716. See also 699–700, where Ogilvie lays out his reasons for doubting the role of Clusium entirely in the matter.

[15] Forsythe (2005) 252.

[16] Most scholars are in agreement that the Camillus legend is a later accretion, probably invented by the late annalists of the first century BC. See Forsythe (2005) 255–256; Cornell (1995) 316–317; Ogilvie, *Livy* 727–728. Hartfield (1982) 351 state: "The dictatorship is a fabrication entirely."

[17] Whereas the Greek sources call them "Celts," for the sake of consistency, I will refer to them as Gauls throughout this section.

Romans take any special measures to counter the Gallic threat? Did they declare a *tumultus Gallicus*, the normal method of responding to Gallic invasions in later times? Sadly, we get no information of that nature from Polybius's brief account.

A somewhat fuller and slightly more detailed version of the episode is found in Diodorus Siculus 14. 113–116, which I will recount here, but I intend to revisit certain important details later when I discuss the accounts of Livy and Plutarch. After briefly noting the conquest of northern Italy from the Etruscans by the Gauls, he notes that one particular group, the Senones, were unhappy with their allotted territory, and in 387, they made a move to find new lands, attacking the Etruscans again, including Clusium (and here is where Clusium enters the tale). Apparently, Roman ambassadors were present at Clusium: Diodorus reports that they were sent specifically to spy on the Gauls (14. 113. 4), which is interesting in that this is a classic example of crisis-related behavior, as decision makers often attempt to seek out more information when a threat is perceived.[18] What may not have been intended was for them to take part in the battle against the Gauls, during which an important leader of the tribesmen was killed (τινα τῶν ἐνδοξοτέρων ἐπάρχων ἀποκτείναντος) by one of the Roman ambassadors. In response, the Gauls sent envoys to Rome to demand the surrender of the unnamed Roman. According to Diodorus, the senate first tried to persuade the Gauls to accept money in compensation, but when this was refused, they voted to hand over the man (113. 6). The man involved was the son of one of the military tribunes with consular power, the alternate heads of state at times during the early Republic,[19] and he appealed to the people to stop the surrender. He apparently succeeded.

The Gauls, naturally, were greatly angered by these events and marched on Rome with an army of 70,000 soldiers. The consular military tribunes, by virtue of their own authority, armed all the men of military age and then led out their troops to fight the Gauls. A battle took place on the right bank of the Tiber. The Romans had stationed their weakest soldiers on a line of hills, opposed by the strongest troops of the Gauls. After the Romans were driven off the hills, the stronger Roman forces in the plain were thrown into confusion and fled. Those who survived the rout fled to the ruins of Veii, which the Romans had recently conquered, fortifying the place for

---

[18] The search for more information is one of the major coping mechanisms during a crisis. See Brecher (1993) 45, 83–117, 126–129, 363–367.

[19] For an account of this office, with discussion and full bibliography, see Forsythe (2005) 234–239.

their own protection. A few survivors made it back to Rome to report their army slaughtered. Some private citizens fled to neighboring cities, while the magistrates (ἄρχοντες) prepared for a siege on the Capitoline hill. For three days, the Gauls, suspecting a trap, did not enter Rome. After entering the city, they pillaged it and placed the capitol under siege.

Meanwhile, the Romans who had fled to Veii fought off an Etruscan raid and, from the captured arms from the enemy, armed more of those who gathered with them. As they planned to attempt a relief of Rome, a messenger, Cominius Pontius, was found who would climb up to the capitol and give the besieged Romans the message. After his coming and going, the Gauls noticed the tracks and tried to follow them up to reach the capitol, but their attempt was foiled by the sacred geese of Juno, who raised a racket as the Gauls approached. Here we have mention of Marcus Mallius (Manlius), who killed the first Gaul to reach the top. In the end, however, instead of the force at Veii rescuing Rome, the Gauls accepted a negotiated settlement with the Romans, receiving a thousand pounds of gold in exchange for leaving the city and withdrawing from Roman territory.

Much more detail than in Polybius's story, yet still lacking many important matters that we would like to know about. When the consular tribunes ordered all men of military age to arm, did they follow the common "dictator" script of proclaiming a *iustitium* and a complete levy with no exemptions from service? Did they declare a *tumultus*? If the consular tribunes (χιλίαρχοι) led the army that was overwhelmed at the Allia, who were the ἄρχοντες who then decided to prepare for a siege in Rome? Important details we would like to know, but are not told.

With these two earlier accounts, we have what is commonly considered the factual core of the incident, which itself is certainly a real event. The trauma of the Gallic Sack left noticeable traces on Roman institutions.[20] Nevertheless, the fullest accounts of the incident, filled with embellishments and accretions, are found in Livy (5. 32–50) and Plutarch (*Camillus* 14–32). Although a good deal of the details they add has been dismissed, rightly, as having no factual basis, it is still worth reviewing, if for no other reason than that it represents actions and processes that a later Roman would accept as plausible and reasonable in the face of a crisis. As both represent the latest – and most embellished – tradition, and Plutarch made use of Livy, I will treat them together.

---

[20] Forsythe (2005) 253. A majority of scholars have followed the line of Bellen (1985) that fear of the Gauls was real and influential in Roman thinking, although a recent article argues the *metus* is overstated; see Rosenberger (2003).

That what we have here is more a morality tale than history can already be seen in the bad omens that precede the disaster. First, it was reported that the censor C. Julius Iullus died in office. It was never a good sign for a senior magistrate to die in office; therefore, the Romans did not appoint a substitute censor to take the place of the deceased man. Then, M. Caedicius, a humble man, reported to the consular tribunes that he had heard a voice warning the Romans that the Gauls were approaching.[21] The portent was ignored.

The story begins its opening act with the appeal from Clusium for Roman intervention in their affair with the Gauls (Livy 5. 35. 4).[22] According to Livy, the Roman Senate refused to intervene directly in the matter but agreed to send ambassadors (three Fabii, a detail that may have entered the story quite late[23]) to warn off the Gauls (Livy 5. 35. 5). So far, the account – while containing seemingly believable extra information in comparison to the full, but less detailed, account of Diodorus – is in agreement. Livy and Plutarch's version continues to agree that the ambassadors apparently joined in the battle of the Clusines against the Gauls (and according to Plutarch, they actually incited the Clusines to attack the Gauls (*Camillus* 17. 5), during which one of the Romans killed a prominent Gaul (Livy 5. 36. 7; Plut. *Camillus* 17. 5). So much for the opening stage.

Of course, the Gallic chieftain Brennus, whose name is nowhere mentioned by Polybius or Diodorus, sent envoys to demand satisfaction from the Romans over the violation of the normal rules regarding the behavior of ambassadors (Livy 5. 36. 8; Plut. *Camillus* 17. 6). This ultimatum directed at the Romans presented a serious threat and introduced a qualitative increase in the likelihood of military hostilities if the Romans failed to satisfy the Gallic demand by other means. As there was now a limited time to respond to this demand, clearly a crisis had come into being.

Unlike the fairly brief account of Diodorus, we get a far more embroidered and detailed narrative of the Roman deliberations. We are told that the senate was divided in its opinion. Plutarch mentions that there was significant sentiment among the priests, especially the Fetials, to hand over the Fabii (Plut. *Camillus* 18. 1). Livy omits this detail but states that whereas the senators condemned the actions of the Fabii, they did not wish to hand over men of such high rank. There is no mention at all of Diodorus's notice of a first attempt to resolve the crisis by offering money to the Gauls

[21] Livy 5. 32. 6–7; Cic. *de Div.* 1. 101, 2. 69; Plut. *Camillus* 14. See also Ogilvie, *Livy* 698.
[22] The incident's possible lack of veracity has already been discussed.
[23] See Ogilvie, *Livy* 716.

(Diod. 14. 113. 6). In contrast to Diodorus's aforementioned report that the senate voted to hand over the accused but the majority of senators were forestalled by an appeal by the ambassadors' father to the people, Livy and Plutarch both state that the senate itself referred the matter to the people, Livy asserting the senate wished to attempt to shift blame for the war from themselves to the people (Livy 5. 36. 9–10; Plut. *Camillus* 18. 2). Whatever the motivation, the Roman people apparently chose the course of action most likely to enrage the Gauls: not only were the three Fabii not punished, but they were also elected military tribunes with consular power for the next year (Livy 5. 36. 10; Plut. *Camillus* 18. 2; not in Diod.).

Although the Gauls' march on Rome with a large force is undisputed, we have a sharp disagreement in the sources as to the Roman response. By comparing all three of the major accounts (as I bring Diodorus back in for contrast), as well as what can be gleaned from other sources, we do learn some interesting facts about first-century Roman expectations of how fourth-century Rome was supposed to respond to a severe crisis (which a Gallic horde heading toward the city certainly was). Whereas this would appear to be a crisis of major proportions, the two late sources note with surprise that recourse was not made at this time to the usual expedient of naming a dictator, a fact specifically noted as strange by Livy (as well as by Plutarch [18. 5], perhaps following Livy here[24]):

> Cum tanta moles mali instaret–adeo occaecat animos fortuna, ubi vim suam ingruentem refringi non volt–civitas quae adversus Fidenatem ac Veientem hostem aliosque finitimos populos ultima experiens auxilia dictatorem multis tempestatibus dixisset, ea tunc invisitato atque inaudito hoste ab Oceano terrarumque ultimis oris bellum ciente, nihil extraordinarii imperii aut auxilii quaesivit. 5. 37. 1–2

> Although so great a mass of ill was threatening (thus does Fortune blind minds when she does not wish her assailing force to be checked) a state which against Fidenae and Veii and other neighboring peoples during many crises had appointed a dictator, making use of that final source of support, and when an enemy not seen nor heard of before at the time was stirring up war from the ends of the Earth, [Rome] sought no extraordinary power or help.

Continuing in this vein, Livy, playing up the *temeritas* "rashness" of the military tribunes, further remarks that the preparations for the war were lax, following the minds of the men in charge: *dilectumque nihilo accuratiorem quam ad media bella haberi solitus erat, extenuantes etiam famam*

---

[24] That Plutarch was familiar with Livy, see Pelling (2002) 16.

belli, habebant (Livy 5. 37. 3). "They [the military tribunes] held a levy no more careful than was normal for regular wars, even making light of the reported seriousness of this war." This stands in stark contrast to Diodorus's account, where all men of military age were immediately enlisted. Diodorus explicitly states that οἱ δέ χιλίαρχοι τῶν Ῥωμαίων ἐπὶ τῆς ἰδίας ἐξουσίας ὄντες, καὶ τὴν τῶν Κελτῶν ἔφοδον ἀκούοντες, ἄπαντας τοὺς ἐν ἡλικίᾳ καθώπλισαν (Diod. 14. 114. 1). "The military tribunes of the Romans, hearing of the advance of the Celts [Gauls], using their own authority, armed everyone of military age."

Interestingly, Diodorus's version gains support from other accounts. Plutarch states that the Romans were not inferior to the Gauls in numbers, but that the Roman force was composed of men ἀνασκήτους δὲ τοὺς πολλοὺς καὶ τότε πρῶτον ἁπτομένους ὅπλων "for the most part untrained and even taking up arms for the first time" (Plut. *Camillus* 18. 4). From Dionysius of Halicarnassus, we learn that the Romans led out four legions of picked troops experienced in war (ἐκ μὲν τῶν ἐπιλέκτων τε καὶ κατηθλη-μένων ἐν τοῖς πολέμοις στρατιωτῶν), but that ἐκ δὲ τῶν ἄλλων πολιτῶν τοὺς κατοικιδίους καὶ ἧττον ὡμιληκότας πολέμοις πλείους ὄντας ἀριθμῷ τῶν ἑτέρων "there were also those from the other citizens, the stay-at-homes and those who busied themselves less with wars, who were greater in number than the rest [of the troops]" (Dion. Hal. 13. 12. 2).

From these accounts, it sounds like a state of emergency, a *tumultus*,[25] was declared and a tumultuary levy was held. Support for this idea can even be inferred from Livy's account, where he notes that the Roman army was led out *velut tumultuario* "as if it were an emergency levy" (Livy 5. 37. 7). That the Romans were not lax can further be confirmed by the fact that there were allied contingents at the battle, a fact only preserved by Polybius.[26] The later tradition "may well have preferred to mitigate the disaster by stressing Roman isolation."[27] In any event, the Gallic advance was certainly fast and may have taken the Romans by surprise, which could possibly explain the lack of a dictator because the Romans may not have been in agreement as to whom to appoint in such a situation. Confronted with the Gauls so suddenly, they went to battle with the troops and commanders that they had.

Nothing further need be said about the battle at the Allia (Diod. 14. 114. 2–115. 1; the sole major difference is that Livy 5. 37. 7–38. 10 and Plut. *Camillus* 18. 6–19. 1 put the battle on the left bank of the Tiber). It was

---

[25] We shall discuss the *tumultus* decree later in greater detail.
[26] Polyb. 2. 18. 2 Ῥωμαίους καὶ τοὺς μετὰ τούτων παραταξαμένους.
[27] Walbank, *Polybius* 1. 185; see also Ogilvie, *Livy* 718.

a complete disaster and was followed by the Gallic Sack of Rome.[28] Upon the approach of the Gauls, some last-minute measures were taken to deal with the inevitable taking of the city: men of military age and able-bodied senators were to retreat to the citadel and the capitol with the women and children, storing arms and provisions for a siege; the flamen (of Quirinus, cf. Livy 5. 40. 7) and the Vestals were to remove the sacred objects to safety; and the old men were to be abandoned to the enemy (Livy 5. 39. 9; cf. Diod. 14. 115. 3–4; Plut. *Camillus* 20. 2–3). As previously noted, Diodorus says that the city magistrates made these arrangements, whereas Livy does not explicitly state who was giving the orders, but he uses the verb *placuit*, which might imply the senate, but the point should not be pressed. Plutarch as well does not name anyone in particular as taking charge.

What is clear from this incident so far is that what the later writers, Livy and Plutarch, felt to be lacking from the Roman response was a recourse to what was considered the usual method of crisis management during this period: the appointment of a dictator. Because the earlier accounts of Polybius and Diodorus do not mention the naming of a dictator in these dire circumstances, when one would be expected, it is fairly certain that no dictator was named during this incident, and the events that I am about to relate are cut out of whole cloth. For in the version of Livy and Plutarch, salvation would be at hand as Rome hit its nadir. The low water point for the Romans was reached when the Romans and the Gauls came to an agreement to ransom the city for 1,000 pounds of gold (Diod. 14. 116. 7; Livy 5. 48. 5–9; Plut. *Camillus* 28. 4–5). For Diodorus, this is the end of the matter. The Gauls left and that was that. However, it is during the period of the siege and before the agreement (which even in Polybius's account was a long period of time – seven months) that Rome's savior, M. Furius Camillus, would arise (Livy 5. 43. 6–49. 7; Plut. *Camillus* 23–29). But first, being an exile, he had to look out for himself. When his place of abode, Ardea, was attacked by a band of Gallic raiders, Camillus led the Ardeates against them and won.

This accomplished, Camillus needed a Roman army. That was provided by the refugees at Veii, who in Livy's account successfully drove off an Etruscan raid (which is noted in Diodorus as well). Of course, all of the formalities would have to be observed. Livy's concern to a great extent is to show how the disaster at the Allia and the Gallic Sack were the result of the Romans not behaving as Romans, with proper care and concern for the

---

[28] The annalistic tradition believed that the Citadel held, but it is also possible the entire city was sacked. See Williams (2001) 144–145.

proprieties, especially the religious proprieties. "The defeat at the battle of the Allia had been one of those moments when the connections between the Roman army and the power of the gods was disastrously broken."[29] The story of Cominius told by Diodorus is recast as the army at Veii's request for Camillus to be recalled from exile and then appointed dictator, which is done forthwith, with the senate ordering the Curiate Assembly to recall Camillus and then that he be named dictator. Oddly, despite this wealth of detail provided by Livy (5. 46. 9–10), there is still vagueness and imprecision: Cominius is led before the magistrates *ad magistratus ductus*, although no specific officer (a consular tribune?) is mentioned. Who then named the dictator?

It is only later, when Rome is at the brink and cannot wait for Camillus any longer and the decision is made by the senate to seek terms, that named officials (the military tribunes) reappear, and one of their number, Q. Sulpicius, is specifically recorded as opening negotiations with Brennus (Livy 5. 48. 8). It is curious that Livy chooses not to name which tribune presided over the senate meeting that ordered Camillus's restoration, nor which tribune carried out Camillus' being named as dictator. When it comes to the ignominious attempt to make terms with the enemy, however, we get a name. It is at this moment that Camillus miraculously appears to save Roman honor from disgrace. According to Livy 5. 49. 1: *Sed diique et homines prohibuere redemptos vivere Romanos*. "But gods and men forbade that the Romans live as people ransomed." Camillus, now on the spot with the army from Veii as the Gauls are about to carry away the gold, points out that as the superior official, any agreement made with a lesser magistrate is null and void. When the Gauls object, Camillus orders his army to fight, thus creating the fairy tale ending as the Romans fight off the Gauls and win back their own freedom.

The entire Gallic incident is quite informative in terms of later expectations. For a grave crisis such as this one, where the very existence of the city hangs in the balance, the later accounts of Livy (based upon the annalistic tradition) and Plutarch (who drew on many sources, including Livy) seem almost to be saying that the reason why the Romans were unable to handle the Gallic crisis properly was because they did not hold true to their normal methods of crisis response. Livy especially either assumes or found in his sources an account of the response being mishandled by the consular tribunes. As previously noted, he also places great stress upon the disconnection between the Romans and their divine protectors. All of this would appear to support a line of argument coming from Livy and

[29] Feldherr (1998) 79.

Plutarch that instead of allowing the regular officers of state to meet the threat, a dictator should have been appointed. It is almost as if Roman failure was guaranteed *because* they did not appoint a dictator to counter the threat. It is no surprise, then, that when no dictator is appointed, the military tribunes prove to be unequal to the task, even if, discounting Livy's very negatively painted picture of their behavior, within the normal limits of their power the tribunes did everything that could possibly have been done to face the threat. The lesson is driven home when Camillus is made dictator and there immediately follows a happy ending to the horrible incident.

INTERNAL THREATS

The dictatorship could also be used to face internal threats, but its use in that manner was largely in the very early period, during the so-called Struggle of the Orders when the patricians and the plebeians were fighting over access to office and honors. The most notable occurrence where it is clear that the dictatorship was used to manage an internal crisis happened as part of one of the climaxes of the patrician–plebeian struggle, which I will briefly recount here, although I will focus on the use of the dictatorship as a response mechanism, not the entire episode.

There is no need to give a full account of the struggles that resulted in the Licinian-Sextian Laws because a great deal has already been written about them.[30] Much in the way of laughable sideshow and farce has made its way into the recounting of events. No credence whatsoever should be given to the story of the two daughters of Fabius Ambustus, in which the younger Fabia is allegedly unaccustomed to a lictor knocking on the door of the house.[31] Then comes what Oakley calls the truly "absurd" part of the historical record as Livy presents it – the five-year anarchy. Still, Oakley is willing to accept a single year of *solitudo magistratuum*, drawing upon the notice from Diodorus (15. 75. 1) and the notion that "it is hard to believe that the idea was invented out of nothing."[32] Not everyone is convinced, however, as Forsythe notes that in historical times during the

---

[30] For a critical treatment of the incident, with references to prior scholarship, see Forsythe (2005) 262–267. For those interested in Livy's shaping of the narrative, see Oakley, *Livy* 1. 645–724.

[31] That the story is part of a tradition of ascribing major political changes to the actions of women was already noted by Kraus (1991) 314–323. Her later commentary on the episode points out the highly comic nature of how Livy even frames his recounting of the tale; see Kraus (1994) 273. I fully agree with Oakley, *Livy* 1. 647: "... and one would have expected the daughter of the consular tribune of 381 to have known all about lictors."

[32] Oakley, *Livy* 1. 647–650.

very depths of late Republican political violence, when the Clodian and Milonian rioters dominated the city in 52, there were only seventy-five days that saw the Roman state without a curule magistrate to head it. Livy does little to bolster his credibility when he treats the entire time period of uncertainty in only eighteen words.[33]

Putting the severe historiographical problems with the account aside, there is information of value and one of the more probable facts of the extended episode is the appointment of a dictator in order to attempt some sort of resolution. In 368, P. Manlius Capitolinus was named *dictator seditionis sedandae et rei gerundae caussa*,[34] during the final battles over plebeian access to the consulship.[35] That he was appointed in order to curb the activities of the tribunes is placed in their own mouths. In recounting the impediments placed in the way of enacting their laws, the pair state that after being stymied by other tribunes and the old tactic of declaring war in order to draft the voters out of the city, in the end, they had been faced with the "thunderbolt" of the dictatorship: *postremo dictatorium fulmen in se intentatum* (Livy 6. 39. 7). In the event, we do not hear of any actions taken by the dictator against the tribunes, contrary to their expectations. This is not entirely conclusive in itself because we know little of his activities while in office beyond Livy's noting that he named a plebeian as his *magister equitum*.[36] No ending to the impasse came under his watch. That he did not succeed in settling the protracted dispute between the plebeian tribunes Licinius and Sextius and the patrician senate is unimportant. The fact is that the Roman ruling class of that time, at least as much as their attitudes were understood by later generations, saw the dictatorship as an office they could resort to in order to face an internal dispute. At least, before the *lex Valeria de provocatione* of 300 was passed.[37]

---

[33] See Forsythe (2005) 263 and Oakley, *Livy* 1. 647.

[34] The dictator's title is preserved complete on the *Fasti Capitolini*, although Manlius's name must be restored. Livy provides us with Manlius's name. For the various *causae* that were listed on the *Fasti* and their meanings, see Hartfield (1982).

[35] Livy 6. 39. 1. For full references on Manlius's dictatorship, see Hartfield (1982) 365. This dictatorship is accepted as genuine by all scholars, unlike that of Camillus, which Livy and Plutarch report immediately preceding Manlius's appointment. Hartfield (1982) 361–363 believes that there is reason to accept that Camillus was appointed dictator *rei gerendae causa* to deal with Velitrae this year. However, there are good grounds for doubt. As Oakley, *Livy* 1. 685–686 notes, Camillus was a personal hero for Livy, and as far back as Bandel (1910) 47, it has been noted that there is a tendency for ancient authors to insert Camillus into all of the notable events that took place during his lifetime. I am inclined to doubt the authenticity of the notice about Camillus for this year.

[36] Also in Dio fragment 29. 5.

[37] Regarding the *lex Valeria* on the effectiveness of the dictator in facing civilian troublemakers, see Hartfield (1982) 249f. with notes to relevant literature and earlier discussions. On the *lex*

Perhaps it would help if we moved away from individual incidents and took a broader statistical view, drawing upon the early records of the Roman state as we have them in order to see what role dictators played in crisis response during the early Republic. As can be seen, the evidence points very strongly to the primary role of the use of dictators in the resolution of serious crises or emergencies. Table 2.1 briefly lists the dictators appointed to combat military threats or internal disturbances (thus omitting those appointed for other reasons) just for the period between 390 and 290 (roughly from the Gallic Sack to the end of the Third Samnite War).

On roughly thirty occasions, the Romans appointed a dictator in situations that may be considered crises under the terms laid out in the introduction, even if the threat varied in intensity. On several more occasions, attempts were made to appoint dictators, but there were technical faults in their appointment (*vitio creatus*).[38] Therefore, in just about one out of every three years, the decision-making authority of the Roman state was turned over to a single executive magistrate. That in itself demonstrates the central importance of the office in the functioning of the early Roman state. Very often, dictators were appointed during a *tumultus* (which we will discuss more fully in Chapter 3). Without doubt, the appointment of a dictator was the prime response mechanism to crisis in the early Republic.

It is unfortunate for our analysis that the great majority of dictators who were appointed to deal with military-security crises and internal political impasses were all appointed during the early centuries of the Republic, where our faith in the sources is somewhat impaired. Fortunately, we do have two examples from a period in which we have greater trust in the veracity of the historical accounts handed down to us.[39] This is during the Second Punic War, about which there has been a good deal of scholarly attention.[40] Let us examine the last two dictators who were appointed to deal with an external military threat that rose to the level of menacing the very survival of the Romans as a political community: the dictatorships of Q. Fabius Maximus Verrucosus ("Cunctator," *cos.* I 233) and M. Junius Pera (*cos.* 230).

Valeria in general, see the extensive note of Oakley, *Livy* 4. 120–134 with a comprehensive synopsis of earlier views and a full listing of earlier discussions.

[38] Strict religious regulations had to be followed in the appointment of a dictator. If any error occurred, the augurs could declare the appointment flawed, and the dictator and his Master of Horse would have to abdicate from office immediately. On the appointment of dictators, see Kunkel (1995) 668–670.

[39] For those interested in a detailed analysis of Livy's Third Decade, there is now Levene (2010).

[40] For general works on the entire war, with references to the extensive earlier literature, one may consult Cornell, Rankov, and Sabin (1996); Hoyos (1998); and Hoyos (2003).

Table 2.1. ROMAN DICTATORS 390 TO 290

No.[a] and man appointed	Year	Reason for appointment
(† = *vitio creatus*)		
18. M. Furius Camillus	389	War with Volscians and Latins
19. A. Cornelius Cossus	385	War against Volscians
20. T. Quinctius Capitolinus	380	Attack from Praeneste
21. M. Furius Camillus[†];[b]	368	Internal strife (Licinian-Sextian)
22. P. Manlius Capitolinus	368	Internal strife (Licinian-Sextian)
23. M. Furius Camillus	367	Gallic war
24. L. Manlius Capitolinus	363	*clavi figendi/rei gerendae?*[c]
25. Ap. Claudius Crassus	362	War against the Hernici
26. T. Quinctius Poenus	361	*tumultus Gallicus*
27. Q. Servilius Ahala	360	*tumultus Gallicus*
28. C. Sulpicius Peticus	358	Gallic war
29. C. Marcius Rutilus	356	War with Etruscans
30. T. Manlius Torquatus	353	War with Caere
31. C. Julius Iullus	352	Rumored Etruscan hostility
36. L. Furius Camillus[d]	345	War with the Aurunci, tumultus
38. M. Valerius Corvus	342	The mutiny at Lautulae
39. L. Papirius Crassus	340	War against the Antiates
40. Q. Publilius Philo	339	War against rebellious Latins?[e]
41. C. Claudius Inregillensis[†]	337	War against the Sidicini
43. P. Cornelius Rufinus[†]	334	War against Sidicini and Samnites
45. M. Papirius Crassus	332	Gallic war, possibly a tumultus
48. L. Papirius Cursor	325	War against the Samnites[f]
50. A. Corn. Cossus Arvina	322	War against the Samnites[g]
54. L. Cornelius Lentulus	320	War against the Samnites[h]
56. L. Aemilius Mamercinus	316	War against Saticula, Samnites
57. Q. Fabius Max. Rullianus	315	Continued campaign of Mamercinus
58. C. Maenius	314	Special *quaestio/rei gerendae causa?*[i]
59. C. Poetelius Libo[j]	313	War against the Samnites
61. C. Sulpicius Longus or	312	Etruscan war
62. C. Junius Bubulcus[k]		
63. L. Papirius Cursor[l]	310	War against the Samnites
66. C. Junius Bubulcus	302	*tumultus* caused by the Aequi
68. M. Valerius Maximus	301[m]	*tumultus*, Etruscans and Marsi

[a] These numbers refer to the numbers assigned these men by Hartfield (1982) 309–518 in her catalogue of dictators. You may find a full list of source citations for them in her catalogue entry, as well as more detailed information about that particular dictatorship. The table itself is adapted from a similar listing given by Oakley *Livy* I. 41–42.

[b] Previously, I have expressed doubts about the authenticity of this dictatorship, but include it here for the sake of completeness in noting all recorded dictatorships that are tied to serious crises.

[c] There are serious problems here. It is true that Capitolinus appears to have been named "to drive a nail," the performance of an ancient religious ceremony to ward off pestilence, but he

Table 2.1 (*continued*)

may also have held a levy, which is an indication of service in war. The whole story of the levy may be a fabrication in order to set up the "trial" (another fabrication) the next year. I admit that this example is problematic at best. For discussion, see Oakley *Livy* 2. 72–76; Hartfield (1982) 369–370.

d There is some question over which L. Furius Camillus this is: either Sp.f. M.n. or M.f. L.n. (the son of the famous M. Furius Camillus, the "savior" and second founder of Rome). See Hartfield (1982) 390–392 (opting for Sp.f.); Oakley *Livy* 2. 267 ("almost certainly the son of the great Camillus").

e There are problems with this dictatorship, as there appears to be a disconnect between its avowed reason for being and what Publilius actually did while in office. See Hartfield (1982) 401–404; on the dispute over his legislation, see Oakley *Livy* 2. 522–528 (with references to important earlier discussions).

f In place of an ailing consul.

g There are problems with this appointment as well, as there is a variant tradition, accepted by many, that he was appointed solely to hold special games. See Hartfield (1982) 420–421; cf. Oakley *Livy* 2. 760–772.

h Livy reports this dictator as a variant against the war being handled by the consuls alone. The account, as given by Livy, is not free from problems, but fragments of the *Fasti Capitolini* provide support for Lentulus's dictatorship in this year. See Hartfield (1982) 429–430; for the problems in Livy, see Oakley *Livy* 3. 167–168.

i Maenius was appointed initially to deal with rumors of a conspiracy at Capua. Beyond that, much of what is recorded is likely annalistic invention to provide another colorful episode in the "Struggle of the Orders." The *Fasti Capitolini* records him unequivocally as *rei gerendae*. See Hartfield (1982) 439–442; on the problems with Livy's account for the entire episode, see Oakley *Livy* 3. 304–306.

j Like many of these cases, there are some doubts about this man's exact identity and what he did while in office. See Hartfield (1982) 443–448; on the identity question, cf. Oakley *Livy* 3. 335–336.

k Longus is named on the *Fasti Capitolini*; Bubulcus only is mentioned by Livy. See Hartfield (1982) 452–454; Oakley *Livy* 3. 348–350.

l Hartfield (1982) 455–457 dismisses this dictatorship. Oakley *Livy* 3. 461 accepts it. There is divided opinion on it (see Hartfield and Oakley, *locc. citt.* for references to earlier judgments for and against).

m There are problems with the date. See Hartfield (1982) 464–466. This man's entire career presents difficulties for accurate reconstruction. See Oakley *Livy* 2. 238–240.

During the Second Punic War, following the Carthaginian commander Hannibal's decisive defeat of the Roman forces under the consul C. Flaminius, a severe crisis gripped the Roman state. For this, we fortunately have the parallel narratives of Polybius 3. 85. 7–86. 7, 87. 6–9, 88. 7–9 and Livy 22. 7. 6–8. 7, 9. 6–12. 2.

According to Polybius, when the word of the defeat first reached Rome, the leading men were unable to cover up the fact and were compelled to announce the result. Polybius has an unnamed praetor laconically proclaim from the Rostra "Λειπόμεθα μάχη μεγάλη" "We have been defeated in a great battle" (3. 85. 7). What is interesting, however, is how Polybius describes the reaction of the Romans to this announcement: τηλικαύτην συνέβη γενέσθαι διατροπὴν ὥστε τοῖς παραγενομένοις ἐφ' ἑκατέρων τῶν καιρῶν πολλῷ μεῖζον τότε φανῆναι τὸ γενονὸς ἢ παρ' αὐτὸν τὸν τῆς μάχης καιρόν "it followed that there was confusion of so great an extent that to those who had been present at both of these critical moments, this moment seemed to be the greater by far than the very crisis of the battle."[41] There can be little doubt about a threat perception and the creation of a crisis atmosphere in Rome.

Livy's account has some similarities, but also significant differences, in recounting the immediate result of the news. As might be expected, we do get more detail from Livy. We learn that it was the praetor *peregrinus* M. Pomponius Matho[42] who announced the defeat, which Livy (22. 7. 8) renders *magna pugna victi sumus*, the same as what Polybius states. Livy differs, however, in portraying the crisis atmosphere. He is closer to Polybius in how he depicts the state of Rome before the news of the defeat is publicly announced, as the people suddenly rushed about in terror and tumult when the first reports of the defeat had come to Rome but before the official announcement by the praetor: *cum ingenti terrore ac tumultu concursus in forum populi est factus* (22. 7. 6). Yet after the official announcement, the atmosphere in Rome following the defeat is one more of apprehension and sorrow than crisis. Livy's Romans do not continue to run about in great confusion, as they do in Polybius. Instead, they stand at the gates, expectantly awaiting further news, especially news of loved ones and relatives who had been serving in the army of the consul Flaminius (22. 7. 10–13).

There is no doubt that the Roman state was in crisis. Livy tells us that the senate met in constant session under the presidency of the praetors following the news, deliberating with what forces and what commanders they could resist the Carthaginians (22. 7. 14). Interestingly, at this point, the two sources diverge a bit as Polybius makes no further mention of the role of the praetors in this crisis. He merely reports that the senate, as if it could act on its own, deliberated about how to respond to the threat (3. 85. 10), whereas we see that Livy specifically notes the praetors presiding over the senate. Polybius and Livy both turn their attention to the other Consul, Cn. Servilius Geminus, and Geminus's attempt to join his colleague Flaminius, along with the decision by Geminus to send ahead a

---

[41] Polyb. 3. 85. 8; my translation.
[42] For him, see *MRR* 1. 244.

flying column of 4,000 cavalry under the command of one C. Centenius,[43] with the intention that they would reach the battle in time. The decision would not be a happy one in the end, as the cavalry were destroyed by Hannibal (3. 86. 4–5; cf. Livy 22. 8. 1).

Both authors connect the fresh news of disaster with the choice the Romans make next in order to face the crisis. Polybius states that not only the populace but now even the senate was perplexed at what to do, and this gave the stimulus to turn to the solution of appointing a dictator (3. 86. 6–7). Livy indulges in a metaphor to describe the feelings of the people at Rome, likening the populace's reactions to those of people learning about someone else who is sick (22. 8. 3–4). Livy continues this metaphor when he speaks of the *remedia* that the Romans turn to in their hour of need: the dictatorship (22. 8. 5). To cite the passage in full: *itaque ad remedium iam diu neque desideratum nec adhibitum, dictatorem dicendum, civitas confugit* "And so the community had recourse to a remedy that had for a long time already been neither desired nor called upon – that a dictator be named." It is interesting to note here that while Polybius notes the move to appoint a dictator after discussing the confusion in the senate, Livy states that the entire political community was involved in the move to appoint a dictator.

Concerning the appointment itself, there is some dispute because our main source, Livy, felt that Fabius should be more appropriately styled *pro dictatore* than *dictator* owing to the irregularities of his appointment.[44] According to Livy 22. 31. 8–11, drawing on authority from the annalistic tradition, including a named reference to Coelius Antipater, Fabius was elected dictator by the people. Hartfield[45] agrees with a line of argument descended from Mommsen,[46] with some modifications by others, which asserts that Fabius was formally named by the *praetor urbanus* after the tribal assembly (*comitia tributa*) had voted him to be named dictator. Walbank, in his note to Polyb. 3. 87. 6 states that "[i]n Servilius' absence, the *comitia centuriata* elected Fabius *dictator*."[47] Broughton professes a certain agnosticism about the manner of selection, terming Fabius "appointed

[43] There is some dispute as to what, exactly, his rank and position was. See *MRR* 1. 245, 246–247 n. 9.

[44] On the question, one may look at J. Lesinski, "Quintus Fabius Maximus Verrucosus: A dictator in 217 BC?" in *EUERGESIAS KHARIN: Studies presented to Benedetto Bravo and Ewa Wipszycka by their disciples*, ed. by Tomasz Derda, Jakub Urbanik, and Marek Wecowski. Warsaw 2002.

[45] Hartfield (1982) 495–496.

[46] St. R. 2. 147 n. 4, which she misses; see Hartfield (1982) 496 n. 2 for references to this line of assumption, as well as noting a quite speculative proposal of G. V. Sumner, *Phoenix* 29 (1975) 253–256 that is not worth pursuing further.

[47] Walbank *Polybius* 1. 422.

or elected," although he is strong in his refusal to accept Livy's remarks about Fabius being *pro dictatore*.[48] Unfortunately, we receive no help from Polyb. 3. 87. 6, who blandly states that "the Romans" κατέστησαν Q. Fabius as dictator. The word is clearly used to mean "appoint" in Greek, but Polybius does not offer any detailed testimony here, neither giving us the name nor office of a magistrate who would have made the appointment (according to the speculations of Mommsen and his followers) nor ruling out any other method of appointment. All later sources clearly draw upon what is already extant in Polybius or Livy.

I see no problems with Fabius having been named by the assembly. The normal naming procedure could not be employed. Brennan, viewing the issue from the perspective of the praetors, does not accept Mommsen's hypothesis of a praetor carrying out the ritual *dictio*. Besides the lack of any explicit evidence in the sources stating clearly that a praetor did so, he notes that Caesar, after his successful coup – who clearly was in need of a firm *exemplum maiorum* to bolster his claim to the office – did not cite the case of Fabius as a precedent. Instead, it is more likely that M. Aemilius the city praetor passed a bill through the centuries ordering Fabius to act as dictator, perhaps until the surviving consul could carry out the proper naming procedure.[49] In the end, it really is unimportant whether Fabius was, in legal terms, *dictator* or only *pro dictatore*. The strange designation *interregni caussa* on the Capitoline Fasti is also immaterial.[50] During the depth of severe crisis, the Roman state needed leadership, and the resort to a dictator was long established as a primary response mechanism to just this kind of situation, even if the Romans had been making less use of it in the preceding decades. Fabius was named sole leader to deal with the grave situation caused by the slaughter of one consul and his army and the cutting off from Rome of the surviving consul.

As dictator, Fabius carried out the duties normal for a dictator named to face an external threat. After first settling alleged affronts to the gods (Livy 22. 9. 7–11), Fabius levied supplementary forces and led out an army to join up with the surviving forces under the consul Servilius (22. 11. 1–3), who had in the meantime begun to march around Hannibal and make his way back to defend Rome (22. 9. 6). Fabius also ordered by edict that all those who lived in unfortified towns should take refuge in safe places, with farmers burning their crops and denying Hannibal and his

---

[48] See *MRR* 1. 243 and 245–246 n. 2.

[49] Brennan (2000) 121.

[50] For a defense of the designation, although it is one I do not agree with, see Hartfield (1982) 303–306. For a more recent assessment, see Gusso (1990).

army any useable supplies – an early example of a scorched earth policy (Livy 22. 11. 4–5). Having taken over the consul's army, Fabius dispatched Servilius to take command of a fleet to oppose Punic naval movements in the Tyrrhenian Sea (Livy 22. 11. 5–7). For the remainder of the year, Fabius was in command of war policy (with the exception of the tussle with M. Minucius Rufus, his *magister equitum*) until he handed over the army to the consuls (M. Atilius Regulus had been elected suffect consul in the meantime to replace the dead Flaminius) and abdicated as winter approached (Livy 22. 31. 7; 32. 1). In the very dire situation that Rome found herself in 217, the Romans returned to the use of a dictator in order to provide decisive leadership to face a severe existential threat.

Finally, let us look at the last historical example of a dictator appointed to deal with a serious military-security crisis. For this case, we do not have problems with either his appointment or sphere of command. The situation was the aftermath of Cannae, where the Roman state faced even more starkly the possibility of its extinction. No greater crisis could be possible. The battle of Cannae itself remains a popular topic, with several recent popular works focused on it.[51] For the effects on southern Italy, there is now the study by Fronda.[52] Concerning the status of the prisoners conscripted by Pera during the emergency, one can consult Crifò (1964). Let us look at this episode in some greater depth.

Our information about this most important event of the war is reliant upon two major sources: Polybius 3. 106–118 and Livy 22. 33. 9–23. 14. 4.[53] Rome was already gripped by an atmosphere of crisis following Hannibal's destruction of C. Flaminius's army in 217. Afterward, the clever maneuvering of Q. Fabius Maximus as dictator had only given Rome breathing space, not a complete relief from the threat. We can see how seriously the Romans now took the threat of Hannibal by looking at their preparations for a decisive battle in consular year 216. The Romans were looking for an end to the danger, and the crisis. Whereas the activity of Fabius receives ample praise in the historical accounts, clearly there was a change in strategy in 216.

Although they are largely in agreement, there are significant differences in emphasis between Polybius and Livy in their accounts, so I will treat them separately. Without specifics, Polybius notes that the time for the elections approached, and the Romans elected L. Aemilius Paullus (named first) and C. Terentius Varro. He then states that it is at this point that

[51] O'Connell (2010); Daly (2002); Goldsworthy (2001).
[52] Fronda (2010).
[53] A list of minor sources can be found in Walbank, *Polybius* 1. 441.

Fabius and Minucius laid down their dictatorships,[54] while Cn. Servilius Geminus and M. Atilius Regulus (suffect chosen in place of C. Flaminius) were made *pro consule* by Paullus. Polybius has Paullus consult the senate in order to fill up the numbers of the consular legions in the field with Geminus and Regulus. It is again Paullus who is given the active role by Polybius, as he orders the two proconsuls to have their men skirmish with enemy – while avoiding a general engagement – in order to season them, as the thinking was that the Romans had lost to Hannibal in previous engagements because they had made use of raw troops (3. 106. 1–5).

It is only now at this point that Polybius changes from speaking of Paullus alone to giving both consuls as a pair the active part in affairs. Now, it is the consuls who assign an army to the Praetor L. Postumius Albinus (*cos*. I 234), who is assigned Cisalpine Gaul, with the intention of causing trouble for Hannibal's Gallic allies, who might then leave him in order to protect their own. It is the consuls who make the dispositions of fleets and order supplies for the Scipios in Spain. Geminus carries out his role as expected (3. 106. 6–11). Although he could have told us more, Polybius decides to pass over the petty details and minor events διὸ καὶ τὸ πλείω γράφειν ὑπὲρ αὐτῶν παρήσομεν (3. 106. 10, "Wherefore I pass over writing further about these things"). It is curious that Polybius gives such a prominent role to Paullus for actions that normally, in an account such as Livy's, are often just recorded as the actions of the senate, without any mention of individual movers behind the issuing of orders.

It is at this point that the actual account of the campaign begins. According to Polybius, the two sides remained in camp opposing each other until the spring harvest had already been gathered. This is when Hannibal decided to move on Cannae, an abandoned town about six miles northeast of Canusium (modern Canosa di Puglia in southern Italy), where only the citadel remained, being used as a supply depot by the Romans (3. 107. 2–4). Now, the commanders in the field (presumably Geminus and Regulus, although only Geminus is named) sent repeated messages to Rome asking for instructions, informing the home government that any approach toward Hannibal would result in a battle. At this point, according to Polybius, the Roman senate decided to give battle (3. 107. 7; cf. 108. 2 the "decision of the senate" τῆς συγκλήτου γνώμην)) and ordered Geminus to wait. The new consuls, L. Aemilius Paullus and C. Terentius Varro, were to be sent into the field.

---

[54] As Walbank, *Polybius* 1. 435 rightly notes, "it is improbable that Fabius and Minucius retained office until the elections . . . and Livy's version is to be preferred." We will get to that version later.

The spotlight turns back to Paullus again, as Polybius has everyone look to Paullus, placing their hopes with him because he had fought in Illyria a few years earlier with distinction (3. 107. 8). The unusual seriousness with which the Romans confronted Hannibal is shown by their decision to meet the enemy with eight Roman legions ὃ πρότερον οὐδέποτ᾽ ἐγεγόνει παρὰ Ῥωμαίοις "which had never been done before by the Romans," and these legions were reinforced units of 5,000 infantry, employed in times of crisis (ἐπὰν δέ τις ὁλοσχερεστέρα προφαίνηται χρεία) (3. 107. 9–11; cf. 6. 20. 8). Polybius's further comment that they did this because they were panic-stricken and fearful for the future (οὕτως ἐκπλαγεῖς ἦσαν καὶ κατάφοβοι τὸ μέλλον) is quite telling, speaking to the threat they perceived that sparked this crisis situation (3. 107. 15).

Polybius continues to make Paullus the center of attention. They (not specified, but likely the senators) exhort Paullus, putting before his eyes the magnitude of what will happen, win or lose, to decide the issue (3. 108. 1). Paullus then is the one who assembles the soldiers and informs them of the senate's decision to give battle, followed by a long speech of encouragement, of which Polybius only provides excerpts, mainly dealing with the reasons why the Romans should be victorious this time, as they will have both consuls present, and the soldiers are not raw recruits, having been trained through skirmishes against the enemy during the winter and spring (3. 108. 2–109. 12). Interestingly, Paullus urges his troops to consider this battle one upon which the very existence of the Roman state hinges (οὕτως ἑαυτοὺς παραστήσεσθε πρὸς τὴν μάχην ὡς τῆς πατρίδος οὐ κινδυνευούσης νῦν αὐτοῖς τοῖς στρατοπέδοις, ἀλλὰ τοῖς ὅλοις 3. 109. 9).

In the run up to the battle, Polybius only now remembers that C. Varro is there as well, but his role is to be the villain of the piece. When the Romans come upon Hannibal, Paullus does not like the terrain and wants to choose another site for battle. Varro, owing to his inexperience, wants to fight now. As the commanders were alternating command following custom (probably not the best idea from a military standpoint), Varro when in command moved against the enemy, while Paullus objected. A minor skirmish was fought while Varro was in command, which was inconclusive, but did not result in a victory for Hannibal. As Polybius has it, Paullus is the one who divided the Roman forces into two camps near the Aufidus (3. 110. 1–11). We then turn to Hannibal, who is eager to force a battle that he thinks he is assured of winning (3. 111. 1–11). Two days later, he orders his men out of camp and forms them into line of battle near the river (3. 112. 1).

Paullus was apparently in command this day and refused to give Hannibal what the latter wanted, so Hannibal retired, but sent out the Numidian cavalry to harass the Roman water carriers from the smaller of the two Roman camps (3. 112. 2–4). This spurred not only the consul Varro but also the Roman soldiers (3. 112. 4–5). Therefore, the next day when Varro had overall command again, he led the Romans out for battle (3. 113. 1). We need not be detained by the events of the slaughter at Cannae.[55] It is unfortunate that Polybius chose to end the third book of his history at this point without giving us a detailed account of how the Romans responded to the crisis caused by the massive loss at Cannae. We only have a few brief comments on Roman behavior, which was affected further by the news of the ambush and death of L. Postumius Albinus with his two legions in Cisalpine Gaul. Polybius merely gives us a series of platitudes about the senate encouraging the people, strengthening the city's defenses, and deliberating in a "manly way" (ἀνδρωδῶς 3. 118. 7). For the full details about the response to this emergency situation, with doom threatening Rome, we must turn to Livy.

Livy's account draws upon a different source than Polybius for many details, or he includes details that Polybius chose to ignore or pass over. The difference has already been noted in chronology, where Polybius has the dictators Fabius and Minucius stay in office until the elections, which is highly improbable, because this would make their tenure close to nine months.[56] Livy has Fabius summon Servilius Geminus and Atilius Regulus to him as his six-month statutory term was coming to a close (22. 31. 7) and the consuls took over the armies in the field during the autumn (22. 32. 1). In Livy's account, Geminus and Regulus appear to engage in constant skirmishes with Hannibal's forces not following the orders of Paullus, who is not even consul elect at this point, but from the consuls' own decision to follow the *Fabii artes* while facing the wily Carthaginian (22. 32. 1). We also get some interesting pieces that show Rome had stepped up its internal awareness, carrying out an investigation into the activity of private persons in Rome. We can see this from the report of a captured Carthaginian spy who had eluded apprehension for two years but was caught now. His hands were cut off and he was released (22. 33. 1). The next sign of stricter internal monitoring comes from the next notice, that twenty-five slaves were accused of conspiring in the Campus Martius. They had a less generous (if we can call having one's hands chopped off generous) fate, being crucified, a normal punishment for rebellious slaves. The informer who alerted the authorities, another slave, was given his freedom and a sizable reward (22. 32. 2).

---

[55] For details of the battle, one can consult the works previously listed. See note 51.
[56] See note 54.

Unlike Polybius's streamlined account, Livy provides us a more detailed look at the elections for consular year 216, which proved to be rather fractious. Praetor M. Aemilius, in accordance with a senate decree, wrote to the consuls in the field asking one of them to return to Rome for the elections. They responded that the danger was too grave and that it would be preferable to allow an interregnum to occur, with an *interrex* holding the electoral assembly. The senate then decided to have a dictator appointed to hold the election (a common device in earlier times),[57] and the consuls appointed L. Veturius Philo, but his appointment was *vitio creatus*, and he and his Master of Horse M. Pomponius Matho were forced to resign fourteen days into their term, before the elections were even held, leading to an interregnum (22. 33. 9–12).

It is curious that the consuls are reported as preferring an interregnum, appointing a dictator only when prodded by the senate, but the dictator is forced from office because of a flaw in his appointment. (A wag might suggest that the consul who carried out the ritual *dictio* allowed an error to occur, but this is just amusing speculation not based on any evidence other than the expressed desire of the consuls for an interregnum.) In the end, their preferred method would be the one chosen for holding the elections. The consuls had their *imperium* extended (by the dictator before his abdication? by the *interrex*? This would be an interesting detail, but Livy does not tell us), and an *interrex* was appointed. Following established custom, the second *interrex*,[58] P. Cornelius Asina, held the electoral assembly, but the *comitia*, we are told by Livy, was marked by a great struggle between the senators and the common people (*In eius interregno comitia habita magno certamine patrum ac plebis* 22. 34. 1).[59] The full details of the struggle need not detain us. The end result of the political wangling was that the *interrex* Asina managed to achieve the election of only one consul, C. Terentius Varro, whom Livy represents as the champion of the "popular" party. With Varro's election, of course, the interregnum ceased

---

[57] On *dictatores comitiorum habendorum causa*, see Hartfield (1982) 195–246.

[58] On the operation of an interregnum, see Kunkel (1995) 276–283.

[59] Foster's Loeb translation is anachronistic, calling it a "bitter struggle between patricians and plebeians." He might have been misled by the special usage of *patribus* in the preceding sentence that only refers to the patrician senators, from whose ranks an *interrex* had to be chosen. That this is not an anachronistic struggle between patricians and plebeians is signaled by the targets of the plebeian tribune Q. Baebius Herennius during the contest: the senate, the augurs, and the "nobles" (*nobiles*). "Patricians" as such are not a specific group in his sights. De Sélincourt's translation, while less wedded to a literal rendering of Livy's Latin, gets it exactly right: "The elections aroused the bitterest controversy between the senatorial order and the populace."

to exist (22. 34. 1–35. 2). Varro held the election for his colleague, and L. Aemilius Paullus (*cos.* I 219) was elected (22. 35. 3–4).

Passing over the election of praetors, Livy moves on to the preparations for the coming year. Unlike the compact unity presented by Polybius when recounting the increased size of the army, Livy tells us that the sources he read had differing accounts about just how many and what kind of troops were added to the normal amounts (22. 36. 1). Some of his annalistic sources stated that 10,000 extra soldiers were enrolled; others stated the figure Polybius reported of four new legions in addition to the usual consular levy of four, raising the total to eight (22. 36. 2). Livy notes as well what Polybius reported, that the size of the legions was also increased by 1,000 infantry and 100 cavalry, to make 5,000 foot soldiers and 300 horsemen each. He adds that the allies furnished substantially larger forces as well (22. 36. 3). Clearly, the preparations were exceptional. A further extraordinary measure was that the usual voluntary oath taken by the soldiers after they had been mobilized and assembled not to abandon the ranks and flee from the enemy was formally administered by the military tribunes to the soldiers, a thing "which had never been done before" (22. 38. 2–5).

We need not delay over the maneuvers of the army, or the behavior of Varro or Paullus before the battle because with Varro especially, what we have is likely more caricature than a true account of his behavior and character.[60] It is important to point out a few key differences between Livy and Polybius, however. Polybius has Paullus as the main actor in almost all decisions, including dividing the army into two camps. This is quite different in Livy, where Varro becomes an equally important player in decisions, even if Livy is inherently negative about almost every action Varro takes. Interestingly, Livy records the decision to divide the Roman force into two camps, but he does not assign an author for that plan (22. 40. 5). The immediate events preceding the battle are basically the same as in Polybius, as previously noted.

As most students of Roman history know, the battle was an utter disaster for Rome. I passed over the details before, but as it is the impact of this battle – and the severe crisis for Rome that it posed – that interests us the most, I will briefly recount the reason why the Romans would be driven into such despair following the defeat. Polybius records more than

---

[60] For a discussion of Varro and the stereotypical slots Livy has fitted him into, that of the "rash commander" and the "demagogue," see Levene (2010) 170–172. Varro and Paullus also form a cliché pair of consuls at loggerheads; see Levene (2010) 187–189.

70,000 deaths on the Roman side; a further 10,000 were captured by Hannibal (3. 117. 2–4). Livy states the number as closer to 50,000 (22. 49. 15). The consul Aemilius Paullus along with the consul of 217, Servilius, and the former Master of Horse (and acting dictator) M. Minucius, were among the dead (Polyb. 3. 116. 8–9; cf. Livy 22. 49. 12; Polyb. 3. 116. 11; cf. Livy 22. 49. 16). At least eighty other notables died in the ranks (Livy 22. 49. 17). The other consul, Varro, escaped with a small band of cavalry to Venusia (Polyb. 3. 116. 13; Livy 22. 49. 14). As previously noted, we have very little about the reaction in Rome from Polybius. For that, our earliest and best source is Livy, on whom we will primarily focus for the Roman response to this emergency.[61]

At Rome, the first news was bleak (and inaccurate): that the entire army and both consuls had been utterly wiped off the face of the earth (Livy 22. 54. 7). With this news, there is little doubt that most Romans perceived a qualitative increase in the likelihood of direct violence to the city of Rome, probably manifesting itself in the appearance of Hannibal and his army before the city gates. Livy sums up the reaction thus: *Numquam salva urbe tantum pavoris tumultusque intra moenia Romana fuit* "never was there so great an amount of fear and unrest within Roman walls while the city was as yet untaken" (22. 54. 7). Still, in this absolute crisis, when the very survival of the state was uppermost in Roman minds, Livy presents the Roman ruling class as being up to the challenge. The praetors in Rome, P. Furius Philus (the city praetor) and M. Pomponius Matho[62] (the praetor *inter peregrinos*), called the senate into session to discuss the defense of the city (Livy 22. 55. 1). Although most were at a loss, Q. Fabius Maximus made a series of sensible suggestions: send light horsemen along the Via Appia and Via Latina to gather information,[63] quiet the uproar and lamentation in the city, bring all informants entering the city before the praetors, post sentries at the gates, and prohibit people from leaving the city (Livy 22. 55. 4–8). The senate unanimously approved all the measures proposed by Fabius (Livy 22. 56. 1). Although Livy does not anywhere formally state this, in modern terms, a state of emergency and martial law would seem to have been declared in the city of Rome. Sadly,

---

[61] Plut. *Fabius* 18 does not contain any details not present in Livy, and omits several important matters, such as Pera's dictatorship (to be discussed in this chapter).

[62] There is some uncertainty whether this is the same man as the praetor of 217, M. Pomponius. One of them might be the consul of 231 (for other possibilities, see *MRR* 1. 246 n. 4). Brennan (2000) 106 states that the praetor of 216 is "probably a different character from the *pr.* 217."

[63] As noted once before, the search for more information is one of the major coping mechanisms during a crisis. See Brecher (1993) 45, 83–117, 126–129, 363–367.

the things that would interest us the most – such as whether a formal state of emergency, such as a *iustitium* or a *tumultus*, was declared – are matters that Livy does not choose to address, or does not have in his own sources.

At this point, better, more accurate information began to flow into the city. A letter arrived from the remaining consul Varro informing the senate of the losses and survivors of the battle, as well as Hannibal's position and movements (22. 56. 1–3). Private losses were then reported house to house, and even public religious rites suffered – the annual ritual for Ceres went unperformed because those in mourning were not allowed to celebrate it (22. 56. 4).[64] The senate was worried about private and public rites going unperformed, so a decree was passed that limited mourning to thirty days (22. 56. 5).

With Rome temporarily put back into acceptable public order, the senate reconvened just in time to receive another magisterial letter bearing bad news, this time from T. Otacilius Crassus, the propraetor stationed at Lilybaeum. He reported that Syracuse was under assault by a Carthaginian fleet and that another was poised to strike the Roman areas of the island if Otacilius went to the help of their ally King Hiero (Livy 22. 56. 6–8). With these reports in hand, the senate made the decision to divert the praetor stationed at Ostia, M. Claudius Marcellus (*cos.* 222), from his mission to Sicily to instead take over the army of Varro at Canusium, with Varro coming back to Rome (Livy 22. 57. 1).

The Romans now turned within to see if the cause of their misfortune lay in their own behavior. They discovered cause for disquiet: two Vestal virgins, Floronia and Opimia, were convicted of *incestus* (impurity). One was buried alive *uti mos est* (in accord with ancestral custom), whereas the other killed herself (Livy 22. 57. 2). Floronia's paramour, L. Cantilius, a pontifical *scriba*, was beaten to death (Livy 22. 57. 3). In response, the senate ordered the *decemviri s. f.* to consult the Sibylline Books, and Q. Fabius Pictor was sent to Delphi to consult the oracle there (Livy 22. 57. 4–5). To mark the desperation of the Romans to regain the favor of the gods, an unusual rite (*minime Romano sacro*) was performed again:

---

[64] These were the *Graeca sacra Cereris*, which were performed by married women (*matronae*). On these rites and the Ceres cult in general, one may consult H. Le Bonniec, *Le Culte de Cérès à Rome des origines à la fin de la République*, Paris, 1958. It may be, however, that Bonniec is incorrect about Livy's notice, meaning that the rites were interrupted as they were being carried out. Boyd (*CR* NS10 [1960] 150), in his review of Bonniec's book, points to Plut. *Fabius* 18. 2 as supporting the idea that the rites were omitted entirely, not interrupted while in the middle of being observed.

the burying alive of a pair of Gauls and a pair of Greeks, one male and one female each (Livy 22. 57. 6).[65]

Marcellus handed over his fleet to the *praetor urbanus* Furius and had his naval legion sent ahead to Teanum Sidicinum, which force he then led to Canusium to take command of Varro's army (Livy 22. 57. 7–8). It is here, with Varro's return to Rome, that the longer-term response measures were now decided upon. One reason certainly was that the senate authorized the appointment of a dictator, which would require Varro, the only man now capable of naming a dictator. M. Junius Pera was named (at this point, Pera must have been a rather old man, as he was consul back in 230) with Ti. Sempronius Gracchus (a much younger man who had not yet been consul) as his master of the horse (22. 57. 9). The dictator instituted a host of emergency measures in keeping with the situation (22. 57. 9–11): A new levy was proclaimed, and all were enlisted from the age of seventeen up, including some who had not even put on the toga of manhood; four legions and 1,000 horse were enlisted, and men were sent to collect allied contingents according to the *formula* (the formal listing of troops owed to the Romans by treaty obligations); arms were ordered to be readied, and even spoils (foreign weapons and equipment) seized from enemies were taken down from temples to equip the army; owing to the scarcity of free men, the state treasury took the extraordinary step of buying 8,000 young and strong slaves, who were willing to volunteer as soldiers. Noted a little later in Livy's narrative, one final desperation measure was adopted by the dictator: yielding to dire necessity, Pera issued an edict that offered pardon to convicted criminals, even murderers, if they would serve in the army.[66] In this manner, 6,000 men were enrolled, armed with weapons and equipment from C. Flaminius's Gallic triumph (23. 14. 3–4).

As we can see, the Romans, again in the depth of peril and worried about their very existence, turned to the dictatorship to provide unified, and presumably creditable (Varro was not cashiered, but certainly no one wanted to leave the direction of state affairs completely in his hands) leadership. The emergency levy, which included scraping the absolute bottom of the barrel for recruits – having recourse to slaves and criminals – demonstrates both the level of resolve of the Romans and the dire necessity they found themselves in. In the end, however, the absolute disaster that appeared

---

[65] See Eckstein (1982) for a discussion of the earlier occurrence in 228 as well the latter repetition in 114/113, and esp. pp. 73–75 for this particular episode.

[66] As mentioned before, one may consult Crifò (1964) for further discussion of these special conscripts.

before the eyes of the Romans never came. They did not know this at the time, but they would escape the noose. For after the battle, while the other officers advised Hannibal to rest his men, Maharbal, the commander of the cavalry, urged Hannibal to make an immediate march upon Rome. Hannibal refused. In response, Maharbal said: "You know how to achieve a victory, Hannibal, but you don't know how to make use of one" (*vincere scis, Hannibal, victoria uti nescis*, Livy 22. 51. 4). Livy immediately followed that with his own comment: *mora eius diei satis creditur saluti fuisse urbi atque imperio* "a delay of one day is commonly believed to have saved the city and the empire."

That is not to say that matters began to turn in the Romans' favor. In fact, matters would get much worse before becoming any better. Even though Hannibal did not immediately march upon Rome, he did eventually get moving, after wasting time haggling over the Roman prisoners, whom, in the end, the senate refused to ransom (Livy 22. 58. 1–61. 10). However, with the appointment of a dictator and the proper attendance to divine matters, the Romans had once again placed themselves on a much firmer footing, at the least psychologically. As an endnote, it should be noted that the Roman ruling class very wisely, in the midst of the crisis, did not spiral downward into internecine strife and recriminations. Although the main sources (Polybius and Livy) do their best to vilify the consul Varro, even Livy did not refuse to record a very interesting detail that occurred in the aftermath of Cannae. When Varro had returned to Rome, he was met by a crowd of all ranks and statuses in life and was formally thanked *quod de re publica non desperasset* "because he did not despair over the state of the state" (Livy 22. 61. 14).[67] In a later Imperial-age tradition, seen in Valerius Maximus, there is even notice that the Roman senate offered Varro the dictatorship but that he refused it (Val. Max. 3. 4. 4, 4. 5. 2). Whether true or not, it is in character with the image we have of the Romans "circling the wagons" in this dire situation instead of looking for a political scapegoat.[68]

The psychological assurance that comes with the decisive leadership of a dictator was likely needed in the aftermath of Cannae. Although this may seem a minor point, it should be noted that there were others who were recorded as being potential proverbial "rats leaving the sinking ship." As an example of this, there is the famous anecdote concerning Publius

---

[67] There are other references to this giving of thanks to the consul Varro. See *MRR* 1. 247.

[68] Compare as well the comments of the soon-to-be-dead Aemilius Paullus on the battlefield of Cannae, where he refused to live in order to be tried again or to stand as the accuser of his colleague in order to defend himself (Livy 22. 49. 11).

Scipio (later Africanus), who served as a military tribune at Cannae and survived. With the remaining survivors at Canusium, when word was brought
to him and other loyalists that a group of young noble Romans, led by
M. Caecilius Metellus, were planning on leaving Italy and finding fortune
with some king across the sea, Scipio burst into their meeting and forced
them all to swear not to abandon Rome or else he would use his sword
on them right there and then. The others, cowering, swore (Livy 22. 53.
4–13). In light of this incident, the thanks given to Varro for not forsaking
Rome makes much more sense as yet another measure that was taken in
order to shore up resistance at Rome to the sinking feeling of defeat that
could have led to Rome's capitulation in the face of the extreme defeat
dealt to them by Hannibal at Cannae.

The End of the Dictatorship as a Crisis
Response Mechanism

The appointment of M. Junius Pera, who did not accomplish much himself while in office, marks the final time that the Romans resorted to a
dictator to take charge of the Roman government either in anticipation
of, or in the very throes of, a serious crisis situation. He was not the last
properly appointed dictator; that was C. Servilius Geminus in 202, who
was appointed to hold the elections for the following consular year.[69]
However, it was already clear that increasingly, the Romans, even in the
midst of very serious crises, such as the Gallic tumult of 225 (to be discussed later), turned less and less often to the dictatorship during the third
century, preferring instead to rely on the regular magistrates to lead their
armies during emergencies. Although no dictators would be appointed in
Rome again until the irregular revival of the office by Sulla in 82, that
does not mean that the office was dead in the minds of Romans before
Sulla's arrogation of it. In fact, while recording the tumultuous period of
the Gracchi, the historian Appian at one point remarks with wonder why
the Romans did not appoint a dictator to deal with the threat posed by
Tiberius Gracchus.[70] Even though he seems to be oblivious to the problem posed by a dictator being just as constrained in the use of his powers
within the city of Rome as any other magistrate by the law of *provocatio*,
one wonders if the remark was Appian's own, or did he see comments of

---

[69] For references, see *MRR* 1. 316.
[70] App. *BC* 1. 16. 67.

a similar vein himself when reading the sources he examined in compiling his own history?[71]

Whereas the dictatorship ceased to be used in order to respond to emergencies that threatened Rome with physical harm or existential danger, many of the mechanisms that were tied to the dictatorship in its very earliest days, such as the *tumultus* declaration and the *iustitium* edict, continued to be employed by the Romans as part of their crisis response. Therefore, let us turn to states of emergency and explore how the Romans made use of them.

---

[71] As for why the dictatorship fell into desuetude, Hartfield (1982) 247–264 explains that it was mainly because of the rise of promagistracies (to deal with military needs) and the availability of consuls to hold the elections (the other major use of the dictatorship in the third century) seems most likely to be correct. A rather speculative notion was put forward by Morgan (1991), suggesting that it was related to ranking within the senatorial order and a wish to avoid elevating a man beyond his proper station.

3

STATES OF EMERGENCY
The Tumultus *Declaration*

How to Declare an Emergency in
the Roman State

One very common response to crisis situations in the modern world is to
declare a state of emergency. Unlike the modern English term "state of
emergency," there does not seem to be a single Latin term or phrase that
can refer in general to any period of time during which the enforcement
of ordinary statute law is temporarily suspended – and in certain respects
superseded – by special regulations that remain in effect for as long as
the suspension of normal law is in place. The lack of such a single word
or phrase, however, does not mean that there were no equivalent devices
available to the Romans. For there were decrees and edicts that were
passed in specific circumstances that legally altered conditions to create
what would be for all intents and purposes a "state of emergency" as we
understand the term. How the Romans declared states of emergency has
not been the focus of much modern comment or investigation. The most
recent synthetic treatment specifically dealing with states of emergency
would be that of Lintott, but his discussion is rather limited, being almost
exclusively focused on the question of the legal status of the so-called
senatus consultum ultimum, without a thorough and detailed discussion
of other states of emergency.[1] The *SC ultimum*, a development of the late
Republic, is often treated as a true emergency decree, when in reality it
was no such thing (to be discussed in greater detail in Chapter 5). It has,

---

[1] Lintott (1968) 149–174. His more recent work on the constitution of the Roman Republic
(Lintott 1999) lacks a full-scale discussion of emergency situations, save for an appendix on
the so-called *SC ultimum*.

however, drawn attention away from the two (and there were two) ways of legally declaring an official state of emergency in the Roman state during the period of the Republic. The two actual means of ordering a true state of emergency to come into being were the declaration of a *tumultus* and an edict proclaiming a *iustitium*. To complicate matters, these two measures were not mutually exclusive and could in fact be, and often were, declared at the same time. From the available evidence we have, it seems likely that a *iustitium* was declared in every situation where a *tumultus* was decreed. The reverse, however, does not hold true, and in the next chapter, we will look at the few recorded instances we have where a *iustitium* was declared but not a *tumultus*. Let us begin our look at states of emergency with an examination of the *tumultus* declaration.

TUMULTUS

For the *tumultus* declaration, it is possible – and in some ways preferable – to offer a synthetic treatment, not a chronological one.[2] That is because the conditions that called for the use of the *tumultus* decree and the measures brought into effect by it did not change through time, but remained constant even after the invention of the *senatus consultum ultimum* might be considered to have caused it to be employed in new circumstances where the threat to the state came not from foreign peoples or slaves but from Roman citizens. A closer examination will show that no serious innovation was made. Even if the late Republic saw times where the declaration was used to prepare forces against civil foes, there were still occasions where in the late Republic a *tumultus* could be declared under conditions that exactly mirrored its usage in the middle and early Republic. I will discuss these occasions separately at the end of this chapter. This is not to say that

---

[2] Brief but recent discussions are provided by Oakley, *Livy* 2. 126–128 and Kunkel (1995) 228–229. Lintott (1968) 153–155 gives a very brief discussion of *tumultus*, largely to contrast it with the *SC ultimum*. There exists an unpublished dissertation on the subject: G. Osthoff, *Tumultus – Seditio. Untersuchungen zum römischen Staatsrecht und zur politischen Terminologie der Römer*. Diss. Köln, 1953. Its findings have not made any significant appearance in later scholarship, although they are briefly referenced by Bellen (1985) 10f. in his treatment of *tumultus*.

The Greek translation for Latin *tumultus* (*-ūs*) appears to be ταραχή. The problem is that the Greek sources are just as imprecise and unconcerned with matters such as "formal" declarations of a state of emergency as the Latin sources often are. The only Greek author who clearly states that a declaration of a *tumultus* occurred is Dio: 46. 29. 5 ταραχήν τε εἶναι ἐψηφίσαντο "they voted that a *tumultus* existed." Also at 37. 31. 1 (quoted in full in the text). From no other Greek author do we get such an explicit and clear statement. Polyb. 2. 22. 7, discussing the Gallic tumult of 225, says at one point εἰς φόβους ἐνέπιπτον συνεχεῖς καὶ ταραχὰς but does not mention a formal vote to declare a state of ταραχή.

the institutional measure was monolithic – a single response to a single triggering event. It was a single response but one that could be caused by several different triggering events; therefore, my treatment will discuss the *tumultus* decree organized around the specific sets of circumstances that triggered its use, which can be clearly delineated into certain types.

In extreme cases of sudden danger threatening from nearby areas or from the Gauls to the north, the Roman state (usually through the senate or a dictator, if one was in office) could declare a state of *tumultus*.[3] Yet what, exactly, did this entail? Cicero provides us with an interesting passage from his *Eighth Philippic*, which he believed would provide a corrective for his opponents in the debate over Antony's actions in Cisalpina in 43, who thought that a *tumultus* was lesser than a *bellum*. It is instructive and worth quoting in full for what the word could mean during the late Republic, even if his etymology may be suspect and he may have his own agenda in pushing the distinction between the two words:

> potest enim esse bellum ut tumultus non sit, tumultus autem esse sine bello non potest. quid est enim aliud tumultus nisi perturbatio tanta ut maior timor oriatur? unde etiam nomen ductum est tumultus. itaque maiores nostri tumultum Italicum quod erat domesticus, tumultum Gallicum quod erat Italiae finitimus, praeterea nullum nominabant. gravius autem tumultum esse quam bellum hinc intellegi potest quod bello [Italico] vacationes valent, tumultu non valent.

For it is possible that there be a war that may not be a *tumultus*, a *tumultus* in turn is not able to exist without war. What is a *tumultus* other than a disturbance so serious that a greater than normal fear arises? From which even the name *tumultus* is derived?[4] Therefore our ancestors called a *tumultus* "Italian" because it was nearby, and "Gallic" because it was at the borders of Italy, and none besides [those two]. That a *tumultus*, however, is more serious than a war can be understood from this point, in that during a war, military exemptions are still in force, but they are not valid during a state of *tumultus* Cicero *Phil*. 8. 2–3.

Several important points arise. First, a state of *tumultus* should be considered something even more serious than a normal "war."[5] For whereas

---

[3] Kunkel (1995) 228.

[4] This is a mistake. As Shackleton Bailey (1986) 215 n. 2 points out, the word actually is connected etymologically to *tumere* ("to swell"), not *timere*.

[5] It was not understood as such by everyone at the time, 8.2: *belli nomen ponendum quidam in sententia non putabant: tumultum appellare malebant, ignari non modo rerum sed etiam verborum*. Cicero, however, makes a solid case that *tumultus* is, logically, more serious than *bellum*. For a good analysis of his rhetorical strategy here, see Wooten (1983) 111–115. That there was some sort of distinction between the two terms can be seen elsewhere: for example,

most wars would result in the holding of a *dilectus* (a draft of men liable to military service),[6] we know that normally, certain classes of persons, such as magistrates' servants, had an automatic exemption (*vacatio*) from service but not during a state of *tumultus*. A piece of first-hand evidence exists in a heavily tralatician municipal charter from Spain, the *lex coloniae Genetivae*.[7] In that text, concerning the *apparitores* (a magistrate's staff, consisting of runners [*viatores*], a herald, scribes, etc.) of the *duoviri* and the aediles of the colony, none of them are to be liable for military service *nisi tumultus Italici Gallicive causa*.[8] As noted in the commentary, "the provisions on *militiae vacatio* are clearly lifted from a form of charter appropriate to a community in Italy."[9] We know that public priests were also exempt from military service from the time following the Gallic Sack, if we are to believe Plutarch,[10] as well as old men – except if a Gallic war occurred.[11] From a minor notice related to an officially declared state of *tumultus*, the senate could even "ask" the tribunes of the plebs not to interfere with the levy by inquiring into the cases of soldiers who claimed exemptions from service.[12]

As we have it from the legal and historical sources, there were two common types of *tumultus*: *Italicus* and *Gallicus*.[13] In general, these referred to dangers that threatened from the immediate vicinity of Rome and those from the north, especially the threat of a major Gallic invasion, a specter that continued to haunt the Romans until Caesar's conquest of Gaul. It should be kept in mind, however, that Cicero's statement is very much a reflection of his times. Cicero's *finitimus* is understandable from his perspective, as by his time the Gallic threat had been pushed "beyond" the borders of Italy by Roman action over the past centuries.[14] Nevertheless,

---

the epitomator Florus (2. 7. 2) commenting on the slave uprising of Herdonius the Sabine (see Livy 3. 15. 4f.) said *sed hic tumultus magis fuit quam bellum* " . . . but this was more an uprising than a war."

6 For a detailed discussion of the military levy during the Republic, see Brunt (1971) 625–634. For an examination of what the term *dilectus* itself meant to the Romans, see further pp. 635–638.

7 For the text, translation and commentary, see Crawford (1996) 393–354 Law 25.

8 See Crawford (1996) 400 Law 25 §62 ll. 31–32.

9 Crawford (1996) 432.

10 Plut. *Cam.* 41. 7; *Marc.* 3. 4.

11 See previous note; App. *BC* 2. 150. 627.

12 Livy 34. 56. 11. For plebeian tribunes interfering with the levy, see Taylor (1962) 20–22.

13 This is not to exclude entirely the possibility of a *tumultus* existing on Roman territory outside of Italy: see following discussion on the *tumultus* of 192 for a fully documented example outside of Italy. On the *tumultus Gallicus* especially, see Bellen (1985) 9–19 and Williams (2001) 171.

14 For a thorough treatment of the subject, see Dyson (1985), esp. chs. 1–4.

Oakley correctly notes that "Gallic tumults of the fourth and third centuries were hardly outside Italy."[15] In general, a *tumultus* represented a "clear and present danger" that was also geographically proximate to the city of Rome itself.

As for the mechanics of the process itself, we have another passage from Cicero to provide some guidance. In the context of the crisis caused by Antony's actions in 43 (which we will discuss in great detail near the end of this book), Cicero put this proposal before the senate at the opening meeting of the year: *tumultum decerni, iustitium edici, saga sumi dico oportere, dilectum haberi sublatis vacationibus in urbe et in Italia praeter Gallia tota* "I say that a state of *tumultus* ought to be decreed, a *iustitium* proclaimed, military dress be assumed and a military levy be held in the City and all of Italy except Gaul [*Gallia cisalpina*, northern Italy] with exemptions from service suspended" (Cic. *Phil.* 5. 31). So, a formal decree of the senate, accompanied by a suspension of all public business (more on *iustitium* in Chapter 4), the formal change into military dress by the senate, and a military draft that suspended normal exemptions comprised the basic elements of a state of *tumultus*. In the early Republic, it was not uncommon for the senate to call for the appointment of a dictator. An example of this comes from 332, where Livy reports that the mere *fama Gallici belli* spurred the senate to call for the appointment of a dictator.[16] A stricter than usual levy was held (*dilectus intentius quam adversus finitima bella haberetur*) by the dictator and his master of the horse. In the end, scouts were sent out and found that all was quiet.[17]

In an earlier example, where Livy argues against one of his sources (Licinius Macer) that a dictator appointed in 361 was clearly named *belli Gallici causa*,[18] the dictator proclaimed a *iustitium* and administered the oath of military service to all men of military age (*omnes iuniores*), these actions being done *tumultus Gallici causa* "because of the Gallic *tumultus*."[19] This seems to be the standard operating procedure for a *tumultus*. If we reach back to a likely mythical record of a *tumultus*, there is Livy's description of the actions taken by the dictator Cincinnatus in 458: on the night he entered Rome, the city was placed on alert throughout

---

[15] Oakley, *Livy* 2. 126 n. 2. However, this did lead Oakley originally to make the mistake of dismissing Cicero's correct statement that there were two distinct kinds of *tumultus*. Oakley has noted and corrected his mistake in his Addenda and corrigenda; see Oakley, *Livy* 4. 550.

[16] Livy 8. 17. 6.

[17] Livy 8. 17. 7.

[18] Livy 7. 9. 5.

[19] Livy 7. 9. 6.

the night.[20] The next day, Cincinnatus proclaimed a *iustitium*, ordered all shops in the city to be closed, and forbade everyone from engaging in private business matters (*iustitium edicit, claudi tabernas tota in urbe iubet, vetat quemquam privatae quiquam rei agere*).[21] He then ordered all men of military age to come armed to the Campus Martius with supplies.[22] Although we need not give full credence to the report of Cincinnatus's dictatorship, the measures themselves are not fantastical or mythical but reflect actual practice, at least in a later era. Whereas Oakley rightly points out that the details provided in Livy and presumably the earlier annalists are likely filler material added by them to flesh out the bare mention of a *tumultus* found in the earliest sources,[23] the measures themselves were just as possible in early Rome as they were in the mature Rome of Cicero's era.[24] Regardless, in discussing what a *tumultus* was and how it operated, the records of Livy and his annalistic predecessors can be used alongside the first-hand knowledge of Cicero to establish what a *tumultus* was, at least how one operated in the first-century.

Concerning the levy thus raised during a *tumultus*, Linderski has drawn upon the antiquarian tradition to provide a likely model for it. It would not be the normal recruitment procedure that we know of from Polybius 6. 19–21.[25] A tumultuary levy worked somewhat differently. As in the normal method of constituting a legal force of combatants, the soldiers would be given an oath to swear, but not in the same manner as during a regular levy. Instead, the leader chosen to raise the army during the *tumultus* would call out the available men and say *qui rem publicam salvam esse vult, me sequatur* ("[those] who wish to the state to be safe, follow me"), and the men assembled would swear at the same time.[26] The soldiers themselves were termed *tumultuarii*, and unlike the usual term of

---

[20] *vigilatum est in urbe*, Livy 3. 26. 12.

[21] Livy 3. 27. 2.

[22] Livy 3. 27. 3.

[23] On early dictatorships and *tumultus*, Oakley, *Livy* 2. 127 (on Livy 7. 9. 6) notes that "... it is ... doubtful how many of the details listed above go back to reliable records: if Cicero knew what measures were appropriate in such a crisis, so did the annalists; and the bare record of a *tumultus* was susceptible to easy expansion."

[24] Oakley, *Livy* 2. 126 notes: "Mass levies might have been recorded; but there is much to be said for the argument that the annalists' notion of Rome putting all her troops in the field was no more than an accurate guess (see Brunt [1971] 629)." It may be entirely right that it was no more than a guess by the annalists, but it also makes rational sense that when faced with a sudden crisis that threatened the safety of the community, the Romans would have armed every able-bodied man they could find.

[25] See Brunt (1971) 625–638 esp. n. 5 for a detailed discussion of the normal levy.

[26] Servius on *Aen.* 8. 1. See Linderski (1984) 76. Cf. Kunkel (1995) 229.

service for regularly raised soldiers who swore the normal military oath, the *sacramentum, tumultuarii* could only be made to serve for the one war.[27] We get confirmation of the last part of what the antiquarians relate from the annalists in their reports of *tumultus* that we have complete. In his account of the Ligurian *tumultus* of 181 (which we will be looking at in detail), Livy reports that when word came to the senate that the emergency was over, the senate instructed the city praetor, Q. Petilius, to write to the consuls – who had already left the city and taken the field – to dismiss all of their emergency troops (*subitarios milites*) that they had enlisted because of the *tumultus*.[28] As the consuls had already begun their regular levy, they also had regularly drafted troops, but these men did not have to be dismissed, unlike the emergency troops, who were only enlisted *ad unum bellum*.

Tumultuary levies were also the normal method of dealing with slave revolts, for which a declaration of a state of *tumultus* was not uncommon. We will look at three slave revolts later in our examination of tumults, where in each instance it was considered a sufficient emergency response to raise a tumultuary force, even inside the city of Rome itself, to put down slave insurrections. Only in the case of Spartacus did a quick emergency levy prove unequal to the task at hand.

ON THE WEARING OF THE *SAGUM*

On numerous occasions, there appear to be notices to the effect that the Romans, at least the senatorial class, changed their clothing during a *tumultus*, not just the notice from Cicero discussing the measures he proposed in January 43, but also on several earlier occasions. For example, during the Social War, Velleius Paterculus comments *utque ad saga iretur diuque in eo habitu maneretur* "[the Roman people] put on military cloaks and remained in this apparel for a long time" (Vell. Pat. 2. 16. 4, my loose translation). We have two more direct references to this specific change in dress from the Social War. Livy's epitomator also records with, alas, all too much brevity "the people put on military cloaks" *saga populus sumpsit* (*Per.* 72). The *sagum* also appears in Orosius, which he calls a *vestis maeroris* "dress of mourning" (Fear's translation), where he notes that following a significant victory by the consul L. Caesar, the senate put aside their *saga* (Orosius 5. 18. 15). Although we do not have an explicit

---

[27] *tumultuarii, hoc est qui ad unum militabant bellum* (Servius on *Aen.* 2. 157). For full discussion, sources, and details, see Linderski (1984) 74–80.

[28] Livy 40. 28. 10.

declaration of a *tumultus* in 90, the massive military preparations, including the enlistment of freedmen, never done before, point strongly in the
direction that a formal state of tumult was declared (this will be discussed
in detail later in this chapter).

Regarding the events in 63, when we have it on record that a *tumultus*
existed, we again get a mention of a change in clothing. After the senate
ordered the consul C. Antonius into the field to face Catiline, he reports
that the Romans "changed their clothing" τὴν ἐσθῆτα μετέβαλον (37. 33.
3).[29] Is this a reference to putting on the *sagum*, the military cloak, in
place of normal civilian dress? Very likely. What exactly does that signify,
however? It has been taken for granted for some time that this was done to
signify a public calamity of some sort. E. Cary in his Loeb Dio notes that
changing the clothing was a "well-known practice on the occasion of a
public calamity,"[30] citing a later mention in 53 when the consuls changed
into the dress of equestrians (ἐν τῇ ἱππάδι) "as on the occasion of some
great calamity" ὥσπερ ἐπὶ μεγάλῳ τινὶ πένθει (Cary's translation, 40. 46.
1). There is an earlier parallel at 38. 14. 7, where Cicero in 58 was opposing
Clodius's attempt to force his exile, where again the specific reference is to
the exchange of senatorial dress for equestrian (καὶ τὴν βουλευτικὴν ἐσθῆτα
ἀπορρίψας ἐν τῇ ἱππάδι περιενόστει). And one could point back to that
Orosius passage.

This might seem to decide the matter, but there is a distinction to be
made. In these later two cases in Dio, the change in dress was done by
individuals on their own, not by the senators or the Roman people as a
group, as changes into the *sagum* are known to have been done. A much
greater difference, however, is in the wording. In these two cases, it is
specifically noted that the change was made from senatorial to equestrian
dress. Was it standard for Roman *equites* to walk around in military
cloaks at all times? On the occasions in 63, Dio merely says that they
changed their clothing, with no details about what specific change was
made. Furthermore, and this is an important distinction, Cicero and the
consuls of 53 changed their dress *after* a "disaster" had already occurred.
In Cicero's case, the bill that pushed for his exile had been passed by
Clodius; the consuls of 53 were expressing their distress at being unable
to elect successors because of the violence in Rome. But in 63, the change
was made *before* any irrevocably negative event had occurred. Instead, the
change of dress must signify something else, as it was looking *forward* to
an event.

[29] Dio notes that they changed again after Catiline was defeated in battle; see 37. 40. 2.
[30] Cary Dio [Loeb] v. 3, p. 153 n. 1.

That we are talking about two different apparel shifts is made more clear when we view the notices about the ending of the changes in dress from the Social War, as reported both by the epitomator of Livy and the sixth-century bishop of Seville. During the course of fighting in the year 90, L. Julius Caesar the consul (the other consul, P. Rutilius Lupus, had died in battle in June) won a significant victory over the Samnites. When news of this reached Rome, the epitome of Livy reports *ob eam victoriam Romae saga posita sunt* "on account of this victory, at Rome military cloaks were put aside" (*Per.* 73). Orosius also records this, noting that L. Caesar was hailed as *imperator* and the senate took off their *saga* and resumed wearing togas (5. 18. 15). At this point, had we not had any further notice, one might assume they had returned to full normal civilian dress, but that was not the case. In the next year, 89, after the new consul Cn. Pompeius Strabo had routed the Picenes, Livy's epitomator records *propter quam victoriam Romae praetextae et alia magistratuum insignia sumpta sunt* "on account of which victory at Rome striped [togas] and the other ornaments of magistrates were taken up" (*Per.* 74). Again, this is echoed by Orosius, who notes the distinction between the two events: *qua victoria senatus laticlavia et caetera dignitatis insignia recepit, cum togas tantummodo victoria Caesaris primum respirans sumpsisset* "After this victory, the senate took back [to using] the broad stripe and the other insignia of respect, while it had resumed [wearing] togas after the victory of [L.] Caesar, merely breathing again for the first time" (5. 18. 17).

I think that the two types of clothing changes confused later authors such as Dio and Orosius. It is true that changes in dress were made as a sign of public sorrow or mourning, much as in modern America the national flag can be flown at half mast. In the case of Roman senators, apparently it was normal for a man to exchange his patrician shoes and purple-striped toga for the less ornamented outfit worn by the *ordo equester* in order to express in public the state's grief or distress. This cannot be the *sagum*. If Cicero was looking for public support against Clodius, what kind of message would wearing a military cloak have sent? Was he going to attempt to use force? This cannot be entirely right. And it is not. We have the evidence from Livy's epitomator and Orosius that there were indeed two different clothing changes that the Roman Senate could order for its members.

As for Dio, one must mention other clothing changes he reports (not noted by Cary), which are telling and directly related to the view that some apparel switches were tied to emergency measures. The first one is part of the coda to the Catilinarian affair. After it appears that everything is over, Dio reports that Q. Metellus Nepos, a tribune of the plebs for 62, tried to have Pompey recalled in order to suppress the disturbances related to Catiline.[31] He was opposed by two other tribunes, the matter devolving into actual physical violence. Because of this, οἱ βουλεταὶ συνῆλθον αὐθημερὸν ἐς τὸ συνέδριον, καὶ τά τε ἱμάτια ἠλλάξαντο καὶ τοῖς ὑπάτοις τὴν φυλακὴν τῆς πόλεως, ὥστε μηδὲν ἀπ᾽ αὐτῆς ἀποτριβῆναι, ἐπέτρεψαν "the senators on that very day came into the senate house and changed their clothing[32] and committed the defense of the city to the consuls, so that no damage might occur to it" (37. 43. 3). In this case, we see without a doubt that the clothing change occurred in conjunction with the passage of the *SC ultimum*, which will be discussed at greater length in Chapter 5. And the clothing change must certainly have been looking ahead to the suppression of Metellus Nepos.

The second instance in which the clothing change occurs is slightly later in Book 40, in a context that again seems closer to looking ahead to an event rather than responding to something that has already passed. When the disorders in Rome in 52 went entirely out of hand, to the point that the *senatus consultum ultimum* was for a second time issued under an *interrex*, here again Dio reports that after the senate had held fresh levies of troops, they then τὰ ἐσθήματα ἀλλάξασθαι "changed their clothes" (40. 50. 1). As this notice comes immediately after the report of new levies, it makes sense that this was tied to the military measures the senate was passing because of the state of disorder that existed in Rome at the time.[33] Dio seems to be unaware of the distinction between the two different types of apparel changes, or unconcerned, expecting his readers to know the difference already.

Coming full circle, returning to the *tumultus* of 43, Cicero notes that the senate was in military dress on account of the perilous situation of D. Brutus in Mutina: "on account of whose danger we went to military cloaks" *propter cuius periculum ad saga issemus* (*Phil.* 14. 1). Here we know that it is the *sagum* – not any other type of dress change – that is at issue, and again, the situation is of the senators in Rome looking *forward* to an event. This was not after D. Brutus's capture or death. They knew that a battle lay ahead of them, and they changed their dress as a result. As for why they changed into military dress, as opposed to using equestrian costume in place of senatorial garb, I can suggest two possibilities. First, it may have been tied to the emergency levies that were

---

[31] For full references, see *MRR* 2. 174.

[32] Although this word, unlike ἐσθής or ἔσθημα, can also refer specifically to a toga or an outer garment, like a cloak (perhaps hinting at *sagum*?).

[33] Was a formal state of tumult declared after the passage of the *SC ultimum*? That is a possibility, and while I am arguing that the change into military dress was tied to the declaration of a *tumultus*, there is no other evidence that one was declared at this specific time.

held after a *tumultus* was declared. It is not that all of those aging senators were going to enlist in the ranks themselves, but it was a public display that the state was on a war footing, and every able-bodied man was expected to serve. The other possibility, which does not exclude my first suggestion, is that it was a public show of resolve. The senators were displaying openly their determination to do whatever would be necessary to put an end to the threatening situation that caused the need for emergency measures, especially the declaration of a *tumultus*.

GALLIC AND OTHER NORTHERN ITALIAN TUMULTS

As already noted, the *tumultus* declaration was made use of in the earliest periods of the Roman Republic, which presumably would have been the *tumultus Italici* spoken of in the municipal law from Spain and in Cicero's speech. For many of these very early uses of the declaration of a state of emergency, the information about them in the annalistic sources is likely to be interpolated with later guesswork and expansion from what may have been original notices that consisted of nothing more than "a tumult occurred."[34] We may not get any direct statement that a *tumultus* decree was passed at all even in cases where we would expect a definitive statement. Instead, we often have to rely on the word echoing in the minds of Roman historians such as Livy, who might see the word in the sources they read, and repeated it, but often using it in its non-technical usage, as it is a very common word to describe any sort of disturbance or commotion.[35]

We can see this clearly in a very brief, but illustrative, event from 296, as the Romans were embroiled in the early years of their third major war with the Samnites.[36] In this year, a large raid by Samnites into Campanian territory was driven off by the consul, L. Volumnius (Livy 10. 20. 1–16).[37] However, the news of "the ravaging of the Campanian territory excited a great commotion in Rome" *magnum ea populatio Campani agri tumultum Romae praebuerat* (10. 21. 1). Here, of course, we have the use of *tumultus* in its non-technical sense, but then, after Livy reports that other peoples

---

[34] If even that much is recorded. When discussing the well-documented *tumultus* of 43 near the end of this book, we will see that the authors could be even more telegraphic in their notices, simply noting only a single aspect of the series of measures instituted during a *tumultus*.

[35] See *OLD* p. 1988 *tumultus* 1.

[36] On the Third Samnite War, see Forsythe (2005) 324–336, with references to earlier discussions and sources.

[37] For Volumnius, see *MRR* I. 176.

(the Etruscans, Umbrians, and even Gauls) were arming for war (10. 21. 2), the Romans were driven to action. The senate, allegedly terrified (*conterritus*) by the news of this combination of peoples rising against them, *iustitium indici, dilectum omnis generis hominum haberi iussit* "ordered a *iustitium* to be proclaimed, and a levy of every type of man to be held" (10. 21. 3). We are then told that the oath of service was administered not only to men who were usually liable for service but also old men who were normally disqualified by age and even freedmen (10. 21. 4).[38] Such a measure would point to a serious shortage of available manpower that was needed immediately – a severe crisis. With the appearance of the word *tumultus* at the beginning of his description of this event, combined with the extraordinary levy described, it is reasonable to assume that a state of tumult was formally declared. However, we get no definitive statement from Livy. The only measure that he records in detail is the declaration of the *iustitium*, which was lifted eighteen days later when word came to Rome that the consul Volumnius had destroyed the Samnite raiding party in Campania, an event significant enough to merit a thanksgiving (10. 21. 5–6).

As we have seen, we have to rely mainly on the notices of military activity and the appearance of the word *tumultus* in its non-technical use. We rarely get a formal statement that a tumult has been officially declared. Another good example of that is the first major Gallic incursion that we have fairly good information about, which occurred in 225. Fortunately, we have something approaching a full and detailed account given to us by Polybius in his Gallic excursus in Book 2.[39]

According to some of the later sources, the Romans were apparently on the watch for war, signaled, as is often the case, by an alleged omen of danger: an oracle from the Sibyl warned them of danger from the Gauls when lightning strikes the capitol near the temple of Apollo, which led to a gruesome and uncommon rite around 228, just before the Gallic rising.[40] As an actual cause, Polybius assigns the blame to C. Flaminius, the later ill-famed general who fell at Trasimene, who was responsible for passing a land bill in 232 against the opposition of the senate, which assigned *viritane* allotments to settlers in the new *ager Gallicus*, a location which the local Gauls perceived as a threat to their holding the parts of northern

---

[38] This was the first time they had ever been enrolled as soldiers; see Oakley, *Livy* 4. 232, who notes a later example in 90 (cf. *Per.* 74).

[39] Polybius is assumed to be drawing his own information for this event from Fabius Pictor, who had taken part in the war: Eutrop. 3. 5, Orosius 4. 13. 6; cf. Walbank, *Polybius* 1. 184.

[40] Dio 12. fr. 50; Zonaras 8. 19, Tzetzes on Lycphron, *Alex.* 603, Plut. *Marc.* 3. 4. Cf. Orosius 4. 13. 3. See Eckstein (1982) 75–81 for this episode.

Italy they had conquered from the Etruscans (2. 21. 8–9).[41] In response
to the Roman "encroachment" (from the Gauls' perspective), the Boii and
Insubres looked to entice Gauls from across the Alps to join them in fighting
the Romans, especially a group called the Gaesatae (the "javelin"[42] men),
whose kings, Concolitanus and Aneroestus, readily agreed to come (2. 22.
1–3). The Romans became alarmed when they heard of these developments
and began to prepare their forces in response (2. 22. 7–8). The seriousness
with which the Romans took this threat was also apparent, according to
Polybius, from their decision to make a treaty with Hasdrubal in Spain
(the famed Ebro Treaty, to be discussed later with regard to the Saguntine
crisis), even though this meant allowing the Carthaginians to expand in
Spain without check (2. 22. 9–11).

The emergency arose when the Romans learned that the Gaesatae
decided to cross with a large host and descended upon the Po region
around 225 (2. 23. 1). The Boii and Insubres joined with them, although
at this point, the Romans scored a strategic and diplomatic victory by convincing other tribes in the area, the Veneti and the Cenomani, to take the
Roman side, forcing the anti-Roman Gauls to leave some of their forces
behind to protect against a threat from their rear (2. 23. 1–3). After the
Gauls began their march toward Etruria, the Romans countered by sending the consul L. Aemilius Papus to Ariminum and an unnamed praetor to
Etruria, while the other consul, C. Atilius Regulus, headed to Sardinia with
his army (2. 23. 5–6). It has been thought odd that Atilius would be sent
to Sardinia, not northern Italy, to face the expected Gallic horde, but Walbank makes the interesting suggestion that the Romans may have expected
the Carthaginians to make some sort of surprise attack while the Romans
were entirely intent upon the Gallic threat, as is evident from the placement
of two legions in Sicily and Tarentum (2. 24. 13); there is also a possible
report of unrest in Sardinia around this time.[43] Why those two places
would need strong garrisons when the threat was from the north would
make little sense unless there was, in Roman minds, danger from the south
(Carthage) as well. In this context, Atilius being sent to Sardinia, another
former Carthaginian possession and a possible area for attack from Spain
as well as Africa, makes greater sense. Not all are convinced by Walbank's
suggestion, as Brennan proposes the legion in Tarentum was intended to
guard against attack from Illyria, always a source of trouble. Further, there
is no evidence to indicate that Hasdrubal in Spain commanded a sizable

---

[41] See Walbank, *Polybius* 1. 193; Dyson (1985) 28.
[42] See Walbank, *Polybius* 1. 194–195.
[43] Walbank, *Polybius* 1. 196.

fleet.[44] Valid points against Walbank, but it does not explain the need to garrison Sicily, which, as even Brennan notes, was open to the possibility of a Carthaginian naval attack.

The Romans were incredibly alarmed by the whole situation (2. 23. 7) and therefore made very thorough preparations, which included stockpiling food supplies and war material in amounts larger than in any instance known before and compiling extensive lists of draft-eligible men – not only among their own population but also among the allies (2. 23. 8–10). Polybius then records the famous list of forces that Hannibal would have to face when he began his war against the Romans (2. 24). Walbank has noted the problems with Polybius's figures, which resulted in nominal totals of 700,000 infantry and 70,000 cavalry, numbers in which we cannot put complete trust.[45] More believable are the reports of some of the individual units and dispositions of forces, although they, too, seem to be round figures. The consuls each commanded two legions that were above normal strength, with 5,200 foot soldiers and 300 horsemen, the same type of "crisis"-strength legions we saw already mentioned in the previous discussion of Cannae.[46] These Roman-citizen forces were accompanied by 30,000 allied infantry and 2,000 allied cavalry each (2. 24. 4). An unnamed praetor had under his command a large force of Sabines and Etruscans (2. 24. 5).[47] A reserve force of 20,000 Roman-citizen infantry and 1,500 Roman cavalry, along with 30,000 allied foot soldiers and 2,000 allied horsemen were stationed at Rome for any contingency (2. 24. 9). As already noted, two normal-strength[48] legions were stationed in Sicily and Tarentum (2. 24. 13).

The Gauls advanced into Etruria, where they met little opposition (2. 25. 1).[49] When they had reached Clusium, three days from Rome, the Roman force stationed in Etruria under the praetor faced the Gauls and were defeated (2. 25. 2–9). The Gauls kept the praetor's force under siege (2. 25. 9–11). Fortunately for the Romans, the consul Papus came down from Ariminum quickly and camped near the besieged force, making

---

[44] Brennan (2000) 93.

[45] For details, see Walbank, *Polybius* 1. 196–199.

[46] Walbank, *Polybius* 1. 199 "these legions are over-strength, an indication of the crisis."

[47] Walbank, *Polybius* 1. 200 supports those who express skepticism at the number recorded (50,000 foot, 4,000 horse), thinking Polybius's source, Fabius Pictor, has confused the full list of those able to be drafted with the actual number who were.

[48] For infantry at least. Walbank, *Polybius* 1. 202 notes that they are slightly under strength in cavalry.

[49] They may, in fact, have expected to find support among some Etruscans, but it did not materialize. See Dyson (1985) 30.

contact with them; he ordered his own forces to march forth to battle the next day to relieve those trapped under siege (2. 26. 1–3). The Gauls, following the opinion of King Aneroestes, decided that they had acquired enough booty and intended to return to their own lands; they could fight the Romans later after they had unencumbered themselves (2. 26. 4–7). Papus joined the surviving forces of the praetor to his own army but chose to follow the Gauls for now rather than force a general engagement, waiting upon an opportune moment to attack (2. 26. 8).

This is where fortuitous timing aided the Romans. The other consul, C. Atilius Regulus, now arrived at Pisa with his army, having left Sardinia, and began to march toward Rome (2. 27. 1). When the Gallic horde was near Telamon in Etruria, foragers from the tribesmen were captured by Atilius's advanced force (2. 27. 2). After being interrogated, Regulus learned that Papus's force was following behind the Gauls, and he had the opportunity to catch the invaders between the two Roman armies (2. 27. 3–4). He immediately put his army into fighting order and advanced toward a hill with his cavalry, thinking it to be an important position to hold in the coming battle (2. 27. 4–5). When the Gauls noticed the Roman cavalry moving toward the hill, the battle of Telamon began, as they sent their own cavalry, although as yet they were unaware that it was a new Roman force, not the one following them, which had begun the engagement (2. 27. 6).

The battle itself was a long and bloody affair (2. 27. 6–31. 10). The Romans won, but not without cost: the consul Regulus was killed in the fighting on the hill (2. 28. 10),[50] and 40,000 were reportedly slain, with 10,000 taken prisoner (2. 31. 1).[51] King Concolitanus was captured, but Aneroestus escaped, only to commit suicide (2. 31. 2). The surviving consul, Papus, collected the spoils, returning property to their owners when possible, and then led his forces into Boian territory, plundering it, before returning to Rome in triumph (2. 31. 3–6). Although the tumult of 225 began as a troubling situation for the Romans, it ended up providing them with the opportunity, and justification, to expand farther in the north against the Gallic peoples.[52]

Still, there is one lingering point that needs to be addressed. Why is this event called the *tumultus* of 225, when at no point does Polybius,

---

[50] Zonaras 2. 20 and Orosius 4. 13. 8 mistakenly state that Regulus died in a separate engagement. See Walbank, *Polybius* 1. 204.

[51] The number of the dead is repeated in later sources (Diod. 25. 13, Eutrop. 3. 5, Orosius 4. 13. 10), but not the amount of prisoners. See Walbank, *Polybius* 1. 206.

[52] See Dyson (1985) 30–31.

our best source, call it one? Neither do the lesser sources (Diod. 25. 13, Livy *Per.* 10, Orosius 4. 13. 5–10, Eutropius 3. 5, Florus 1. 20. 4).[53] Only Walbank confidently names it thus.[54] There is a strong circumstantial case to be made for arguing that a formal *tumultus* declaration was passed. The vast preparations, with extensive lists of men subject to conscription, and the crisis-level legions all point toward a complete draft of available manpower. It is clear that the Romans were on what we would call a state of alert, yet it could be argued that all of this would be possible without a *tumultus* declaration. Nevertheless, we can dismiss that possibility because we have two pieces of positive evidence: one a passing reference in the *Natural History* of Pliny the Elder and the other, nothing more than an aside in a biography by Plutarch. Pliny, while concluding his description of the peoples and places of Italy, recalls the *levée en masse* in the consulship of L. Aemilius Papus and C. Atilius Regulus, cites numbers close to Polybius's figure, and much more importantly for our interests, gives the reason for the draft as *nuntiato Gallico tumultu* "when a Gallic tumult was announced" (Plin. *NH* 3. 138). His usage of the word *tumultus* to refer to the decree is reinforced when we draw upon a short digression in Plutarch's *Life of Marcellus*.[55] In chapter 3 of the biography, Plutarch gives a brief account of the events from 228 to 225, including the unusual sacrifice of two Greeks and two Gauls (as previously mentioned). A bit before that, however, he notes the exemption from military service that Roman priests had πλὴν εἰ μὴ Γαλατικὸς πάλιν ἐπέλθοι πόλεμος "except if a Gallic war should suddenly come up again."[56] As Plutarch goes on to note the extensive preparations the Romans made for this war, it would be reasonable to assume that the reason why he noted the military service exemption for priests except in cases of a *tumultus Gallicus* is because he saw such a notice in the sources he was reading when compiling the life of Marcellus. From these two pieces of evidence, we can state with some confidence that a formal state of *tumultus*, in this particular case a *tumultus Gallicus*, was declared.

Unfortunately, for a number of other Gallic tumults, we are provided with far fewer details beyond a stray notice that signals to us that a *tumultus* was, or might have been, declared. In 201, the consul P. Aelius Paetus

---

53 I have omitted some of the minor sources that are little more than one-line mentions. For the complete list of sources related to the consuls of 225 and the censors, who would presumably have played some role in drawing up the enrollment lists, see *MRR* 1. 230–231.

54 Walbank, *Polybius* 1. 184 et passim.

55 M. Claudius Marcellus (*RE* 220), *cos.* I 222.

56 Plut. *Marc.* 3. 3.

was assigned Italy with two legions.[57] Not surprising, as northern Italy was still a source of trouble for the Romans, especially with anti-Roman Gallic groupings that had some aid from a Carthaginian officer left behind.[58] Later in Paetus's term, we find him in Gaul (Livy 31. 2. 5; by which we should understand *Gallia cisalpina*, no doubt), where Roman allies were being raided by the Boii. Because of the attacks, Paetus decided extra force was necessary to counter the threat, so he ordered two emergency legions to be enrolled and added to them four cohorts from his own force and placed them under the command of C. Ampius, his prefect of the allies (31. 2. 6: *duabus legionibus subitariis tumultus eius causa scriptis*).[59] He ordered Ampius to take this *tumultuaria manus* and invade the territory of the Boii (31. 2. 6). This hastily levied force proved to be unequal to the task (31. 2. 7–9), but its existence and the terms used to describe it seem to indicate that a state of *tumultus* might have been declared.

The next year, an official state of tumult was most likely declared. Even though the Romans had their attention turned toward war with Macedon, a Gallic uprising occurred (Livy 31. 10. 1).[60] This was thanks to the efforts of the Carthaginian officer, Hamilcar, as previously noted.[61] Placentia, an important Roman colony in the region, was destroyed and nearby Cremona placed under siege (31. 10. 3–4). The Roman magistrate in charge of the *provincia*, L. Furius Purpurio,[62] was unable to bring aid from his base at Ariminum because he had only a small force of 5,000 Latins and allies, having been ordered by the senate to disband the larger army that had been assigned to the area during the Punic War. He now wrote to the senate about the state of emergency in the province (31. 10. 5: *quo in tumultu provincia esset*).

When Purpurio's letter reached the senate, immediate measures were taken. The consul, C. Aurelius Cotta,[63] was ordered to mobilize his army

---

[57] Election: Livy 30. 40. 5; *provincia* 30. 40. 16. For full references, see *MRR* 1. 319.

[58] See Dyson (1985) 34–36 for Carthaginian activities in the area during and after the Second Punic War.

[59] This use of *subitarius* in a military context appears to be unique to Livy. See Briscoe, *Livy* 1. 58; cf. Ogilvie, *Livy* 401.

[60] Although some doubt was expressed about this entire episode by Munzer, who believed it was a doublet for the campaign of Cornelius Cethegus in 197. Briscoe, while believing specific details have been interpolated and jumbled, also thinks that the fact of a Gallic campaign by Purpurio can be taken as genuine, and I am inclined to agree. Broughton as well thinks the episode may not be a doublet. See Briscoe, *Livy* 1. 82, 110; *MRR* 1. 326 n. 1. The only other source, Zonaras 9. 15, adds nothing that is not already known from Livy.

[61] See note 58.

[62] On Purpurio, see *MRR* 1. 323 and Brennan (2000) 197–200.

[63] For full references on Cotta, see *MRR* 1. 323.

at Ariminum instead of at Arretium[64] in Etruria, and that the consul should himself, if it were in the best interests of the state, set out to suppress the *tumultus Gallicus*, or when the legions had been assembled at Ariminum and 5,000 allied troops been transferred to Etruria as a garrison, order Purpurio to take the legions and relieve Cremona (31. 11. 1–3). When the consular army was assembled at Ariminum, Purpurio set out to raise the siege of Cremona (31. 21. 1–2). After a night's rest (his troops were weary from the forced march), the Romans and Gauls met in battle, which resulted in an overwhelming Roman victory (31. 21. 3–17). A three-day thanksgiving (*supplicatio*)[65] was voted (31. 22. 1), a sign of the significance of the victory.[66] When the consul Cotta finally arrived on scene, the emergency was clearly over (31. 47. 4).

Although it is fairly clear that a state of *tumultus* was declared in 200, it is not explicitly stated. We get one of those rare cases where it is stated without doubt seven years later. As consular year 193 opened, the consuls, L. Cornelius Merula and Q. Minucius Thermus, were not expecting war (Livy 34. 56. 1).[67] Of course, that is when wars come upon one, and a letter arrived in Rome from the Roman prefect at Pisa, M. Cincius, that the Ligurians were up in arms and had overridden the entire seacoast (34. 56. 1–2). Minucius, who had been assigned the Ligurians as his *provincia*, immediately took steps to mobilize an army, ordering the two city legions of the year before to assemble at Arretium in ten days, while he enrolled two new city legions (34. 56. 3–4). He summoned the leaders of the allies and the Latins and gave them quotas of soldiers to fill immediately, sending them out of the city gate to start the levy immediately (34. 56. 5–7). Men who had served in the city legions the year before started to ask the tribunes if they had met the requirements for exemption (either from having served the required number of *stipendia* or because of illness). As that was occurring, a fresh dispatch from the north, from the consul of

---

[64] Not stated as the mobilization point for Cotta's army until later. See Livy 31. 21. 1.

[65] Usually translated as "thanksgiving," it called for the state to formally thank the immortal gods because of the actions of a Roman (pro)magistrate on behalf of the state, usually for defeating foreign enemies in battle. It was a high honor, and was normally required as a preliminary step for the granting of an ovation or a triumph. See Beard (2007) 191.

[66] Briscoe, *Livy* 1. 115 notes that the victories at the Metaurus (207) and Zama (202) also received three-day *supplicationes*, whereas Scipio's defeat of Syphax and the Carthaginians earlier in 203 was honored by a four-day thanksgiving, which was matched only by two occasions that involved two commanders being honored at the same time (for a victory over the Samnites in 293, and the Gallic victories of the consuls of 197). The only single commander to surpass them all in this general time period was Flamininus, whose victory at Cynoscephalae was celebrated with a five-day *supplicatio*. See Briscoe, *Livy* 1. 115 for full references.

[67] Full references for these men appear in *MRR* 1. 346.

194 Ti. Sempronius Longus,[68] still in the region, reported that the Boii were now also up in arms and attacking Placentia (34. 56. 9–10). With all of these events occurring, here we finally get an explicit notice from Livy: *Ob eas res tumultum esse decrevit senatus* "on account of these matters, the senate decreed that a state of *tumultus* existed" (34. 56. 11).

As a state of emergency had been declared, the senate also asked the tribunes of the plebs not to inquire into any cases brought to them that might prevent soldiers from being drafted according to the edict (34. 56. 11). Furthermore, the senate ordered those who had served in the armies of P. Cornelius Scipio (Africanus) and Longus the year before should assemble in Etruria where the consul L. Cornelius Merula was mobilizing his army (for he had been assigned Gaul), even though they had been discharged (34. 56. 12). That the threat from the Boii was considered the more serious (and the reason for the declaration of a *tumultus*) is evident from the final measure the senate authorized, which was to allow Merula to enlist any man that he met on his line of march into his army whom he thought fit to serve (34. 56. 13).

TUMULTUS OUTSIDE OF ITALY

Whereas most *tumultūs* were declared and had effect on Italian soil, the state of emergency could also be declared in a province by the senate's authority, although the report of the provincial governor, especially if far away from Rome, would be the decisive voice in calling for one. In such cases, it seems that a governor could declare a *tumultus* in his province, which could be recognized by the senate after hearing the report of the situation there. When C. Flaminius, praetor in 193 with Nearer Spain as his province,[69] asked for extra troops (the previous governor, Sex. Digitius, had fared poorly and lost many of his men [Livy 35. 1. 1–2]) so that he might carry out affairs (35. 2. 1–5), the elder members of the senate (*seniores*) responded that they were not about to pass decrees on the basis of rumors spread by friends of a magistrate in order to please him (35. 2. 6). They had more to say, much of which will interest us:

> nisi quod aut praetores ex provinciis scriberent aut legati renuntiarent, nihil ratum haberi debere; si tumultus in Hispania esset, placere tumultuarios milites extra Italiam scribi a praetore. Mens ea senatus fuit ut in Hispania tumultuarii milites legentur.

---

[68] On Longus, see *MRR* 1. 342–343, 348–349.
[69] On Flaminius, see *MRR* 1. 347.

> [U]nless the praetors wrote something [about the situation] from their
> provinces, or legates reported back [in Rome], nothing ought to be con-
> sidered confirmed; if a state of emergency existed in Spain, it pleased [the
> Senate that] emergency soldiers be enrolled outside of Italy by the praetor.
> The intention of the senate was that emergency soldiers be chosen in Spain.
> (35. 2. 6–7)

The interesting sentence is the conditional *si tumultus in Hispania esset*,
as that holds out the prospect that a state of emergency could exist in
Spain, but the formal declaration would have to wait until confirmed
(*ratus*) information was received by the senate. In the end, Flaminius was
apparently authorized to recruit extra soldiers outside of Italy, and Valerius
Antias reports that he recruited men from Sicily and even Africa, as well
as Spain (35. 2. 8–9).

THE DANGER FROM ANTIOCHUS III

We get a much better idea of a provincial tumult from the next year, as
larger world affairs began to impinge on Roman decision making with
greater effect. After the defeat of King Philip V of Macedon in the Second
Macedonian War, a new challenger to the expansion of Roman power
and influence appeared in the person of Antiochus III.[70] While Rome was
focused upon the Antigonid Kingdom, the Seleucid monarch moved to
reclaim his control of the cities and territories of Asia Minor that had
once been under the sway of his dynasty. Livy presents this in the light of
Antiochus taking control of cities that were previously tied to the Ptole-
maic kingdom (33. 19. 6–11). An attempt to stop his advance was made by
Rhodes when Antiochus reached Coracesium, but the news of Cynoscephalae and Philip's utter defeat allowed the two sides to back down for the
moment (33. 20).

   Expressions of fear of Antiochus involving himself in Rome's settlement
of Greece already appear in the immediate aftermath of Rome's defeat of
Philip.[71] T. Quinctius Flamininus (*cos.* 198) was eager to have matters

---

[70] On the subject of Antiochus III and his hostile encounter with Rome, the most recent full
treatment is Grainger (2002), which has full references to earlier important discussions. Considerable attention to Antiochus's activities in Asia Minor before the outbreak of the crisis
can be found in Ma (2000). The diplomatic interchanges between Rome and Antiochus and
why relations broke down and led to war are discussed in detail by Eckstein (2006) 292–306.
Although the best source is Polybius, he is only extant in fragments for this important period.
Fortunately, we have the complete text of Livy for this era.

[71] Eckstein (2006) 305 and n. 206 notes that Harris (1979) 221–223 disbelieves the Roman
tradition of fear about Antiochus. Harris (1979) 222 himself states: "Too much importance

settled after Philip's defeat, as there was already a hint that Antiochus had his eye on a crossing to Europe (Livy 33. 13. 15; cf. Polyb. 18. 39. 3). Again, in another context, the sources portray Flamininus as worried about Antiochus (Livy 33. 27. 5–7; cf. Polyb. 18. 43. 2). In the final settlement and the Isthmian Proclamation, fear of Antiochus again entered the picture, as the reason for Roman reluctance to remove their forces from the so-called fetters of Greece (Livy 33. 31. 8–11; Polyb. 18. 45. 10–11). Clearly, the perception of a threat coming from Antiochus was on the rise among the Romans, and a crisis was brewing.

Following the Isthmian Proclamation, when the ambassadors of Antiochus came before the ten commissioners, the Romans began to take a hard line (Livy 33. 32. 2–4; cf. Polyb. 18. 47. 1–4; App. *Syr.* 2). Diplomacy continued for a while, as a group of the Roman commissioners went to meet Antiochus at Lysimachia in Thrace (Livy 33. 39–41; cf. Polyb. 18. 50–52; App. *Syr.* 3). Again, the hard line, calling for Antiochus's withdrawal from much of what he had reconquered in Asia Minor, was pronounced. Tensions would mount slowly.

The opening of consular year 193 was already one filled with tension, as a state of *tumultus* had been declared in Italy as previously noted. Therefore, the crisis level was already very high when ambassadors came to Rome from Antiochus at the same time T. Quinctius Flamininus, the victor at Cynoscephalae, returned to Rome, his job to settle affairs in the East completed, in order to have his *acta* ratified.[72] After the senate had ratified Flamininus's arrangements for Greece, the ambassadors from Antiochus (Menippus and Hegesianax) were brought before the *patres conscripti*. On both sides the talk – while ostensibly about agreeing on an alliance – was in reality an attempt by each to divine the intentions of the other side. In the end, no agreement was reached and the matter postponed (Livy 34. 57–59; cf. App. *Syr.* 6; Diod. 28. 15). But the senate had made its intentions clear to Antiochus by openly stating that Rome would intervene on behalf of the Asiatic Greeks unless Antiochus agreed to withdraw completely from Europe (mainly from his recent activities in Thrace). Antiochus's ambassadors begged the Romans to allow them time to go back to the king and report the Roman demand. The stage had been set for the potential outbreak of hostilities between the two sides because

has been attributed to Roman fear," discounting the opinions of Walbank (1940) and Badian (1959).

[72] For an attempt to set a clear chronology with approximate correlations to the later Julian (solar) calendar of the entire period preceding the outbreak of hostilities, see Warrior (1996) 356–375. For my purposes, however, events will generally be presented in the order they are related in the sources.

the Romans had practically issued an ultimatum to Antiochus, demanding that he withdraw from Thrace. The Romans had triggered a full-blown crisis for Antiochus, but the reverse held true as well for Rome. For if Antiochus refused to comply, then Rome would be compelled to carry through on its threat to liberate the Asiatic Greeks.

At this point, both sides were slowly heading toward war. Rome's suspicions were only increased when ambassadors from Carthage arrived, informing the Romans that Hannibal had sent an agent to try to stir things up there (Livy 34. 60–1; cf. App. *Syr.* 8). In the winter of 193/192, the Aetolians, dissatisfied with the Romans, began to send embassies around Greece and to Antiochus, openly calling for Antiochus to cross to Greece and push out the Romans (Livy 35. 12–13). The Romans countered with a diplomatic and intelligence-gathering mission of their own, sending envoys that included P. Sulpicius Galba (*cos.* 200) and P. Villius Tappulus (*cos.* 199), former members of the Board of Ten commissioners sent to advise Flamininus in the treaty with Philip, back to Greece to sound out the various groups and gain information (Livy 35. 14–16). There was another meeting between the Roman commissioners and Antiochus, one that settled the king on a course of war with Rome (Livy 35. 17–19; cf. App. *Syr.* 12).

Roman perceptions of danger from the King reached a peak in 192. The senate prepared for any eventuality by assigning both consuls Italy as their *provincia*, but specifying that the consuls should cast lots to see who would hold the elections. The consul who would not hold the elections would prepare to lead legions outside of Italy, if the need arose (Livy 35. 20. 2–3). The consul who might leave Italy was permitted to raise two new legions and substantial (20,000 infantry and 800 cavalry) allied forces (Livy 35. 20. 4). Further preparations were made in respect to the outside possibility that Antiochus could invade Italy or Sicily. The two praetors who were originally designated for Spain, M. Baebius Tamphilus and A. Atilius Serranus, were reassigned (by both decree of the senate and plebiscite[73]) respectively to Bruttium and a fleet that was to operate in "Macedonia" (Livy 35. 20. 9–10). The praetor in Bruttium was assigned the city legions of the previous year, along with substantial allied forces (15,000 infantry and 500 cavalry), while the praetor in charge of the fleet was ordered to build 30 new quinqueremes and launch all available old ships. The consuls were ordered to provide the praetor with 2,000 allied

---

[73] Briscoe, *Livy* 2. 174 thinks that the involvement of the People (through the plebiscite) in the moves against Antiochus from the beginning was to avoid a repetition of what occurred in 200, when the war vote against Philip failed. Perhaps.

infantry and 1,000 Roman infantry for marine service (Livy 35. 20. 11–12). The Romans "said" that these forces were being prepared to move against Nabis, the tyrant of Sparta (Livy 35. 20. 13), but "they were really to be ready in case Antiochus invaded Greece."[74] The mustering of such significant forces showed that Rome was preparing for a serious armed clash with the Seleucid king.[75] The upshot of these preparations, however, was that the Roman commissioners returned from the east, and their report made hostilities seem less imminent, so both consuls were sent to the north against the Gauls and Ligurians, while Atilius was ordered to cross to Greece with his fleet and begin operations against Nabis only (Livy 35. 22. 1–5).

Although the level of perceived fear then abated, the crisis atmosphere in Rome did not die down. As rumors began to swell again in Rome, including one that Antiochus planned to send a fleet to Sicily after he had landed in Aetolia (Livy 35. 23. 3), the senate decided to take certain countermeasures even though the reports were only rumors. First, the senate, although the praetor Atilius had already been sent with the fleet, decided that there was need for *auctoritas* as well as force, so a group of senatorial ambassadors, including Flamininus, was sent to hold fast the minds of the allies; in addition, M. Baebius was to move his army from Bruttium to Tarentum and Brundisium, to be prepared to cross to Macedon (Greece) if necessary (Livy 35. 23. 5). The city praetor, M. Fulvius, was ordered to send a fleet of twenty ships to Sicily to defend the island's coasts, under a commander with *imperium* (Livy 35. 23. 6). Further, Fulvius was instructed by the senate to write to his colleague L. Valerius, the praetor in charge of Sicily to inform him that there was danger of Antiochus crossing to Sicily and that the senate had authorized him (Valerius) to raise an emergency force (*tumultuarii milites*) of 12,000 infantry and 400 cavalry to defend the coast that faced Greece (Livy 35. 23. 8).

---

[74] Briscoe, *Livy* 2. 175.

[75] *Contra* Grainger (2002) 165–167. 167: "The dispositions of Roman magistrates and armies . . . do not provide any support to the theory that the Senate either expected or intended war against Antiochus in 192." Grainger puts forward the theory that the praetor Baebius and his army were in Bruttium to assist in Roman colonization projects in the area. He points out that when Baebius was transferred to Greece, an army of similar strength was sent to replace his force. I am unconvinced. More plausible is the interpretation of Brennan (2000) 202–203, who accepts that Baebius was there to defend against a possible attack by Antiochus but also to watch against any potential revolt among "Rome's reluctant allies." This twofold remit seems much more likely than the idea that Baebius was in Bruttium solely to oversee colonization work. For a discussion that forces were sent to watch after Rome's own subject peoples, see also App. *Syr.* 15.

Here we have the key wording that makes it more than likely that a formal state of *tumultus* was decreed, or at least recognized to exist by the senate, for Sicily. We have a direct parallel to events previously reported concerning Spain in the year prior. In that case, the praetor Flaminius was authorized to recruit soldiers outside of Italy *si tumultus in Hispania esset*. As we likewise have a mention of the senate specifically authorizing the raising of *tumultuarii milites* in Sicily in 192, we can say with confidence that they formally recognized, and very likely declared, a state of *tumultus* for Sicily.

Fuel was added to the flames by the arrival of Attalus, brother of King Eumenes (II) of Pergamum, who brought word that Antiochus was crossing the Hellespont and the Aetolians were preparing everything for his entry to Greece (Livy 35. 23. 10–11). As reports came in to Rome saying that war was imminent, the senate decided that new consuls should be chosen as soon as possible (Livy 35. 24. 1). The senate ordered City Praetor Fulvius to write to the consul L. Quinctius Flamininus,[76] to whom the lot had fallen earlier to hold the elections for 191 (Livy 35. 20. 7), and inform him that the senate wished the consul to turn his army over to his lieutenants and hurry back to Rome, issuing the edict announcing the elections while on the road; Quinctius complied (Livy 35. 24. 2–3). The haste with which the senate demanded that this be accomplished provides convincing evidence that the senate was gripped by a crisis mentality – a high-threat perception and an imminent feeling that hostilities were soon to come. Why else the haste to have the new leadership in position and ready to undertake affairs so far in advance? Even though the state waited for the new magistrates to come into office, the Romans still took some measures: Baebius was ordered to cross to Epirus with his army and concentrate his forces around Apollonia, while City Praetor Fulvius was ordered to build fifty more quinqueremes (Livy 35. 24. 7–8).

We do not know how long the state of *tumultus* lasted in Sicily, for in the end, the *tumultus* of 192 would be anti-climactic (much as the entire war would be). In the end, Antiochus did not invade Sicily or present any real threat to Roman Italy at this time. Without the expected invasion, the war finished two years later with the defeat of Antiochus at the Battle of Magnesia by the Scipios: L. Cornelius Scipio (*cos.* 190) assisted by his elder brother and legate, P. Cornelius Scipio Africanus (Livy 37. 2. 10; cf. App. *Syr.* 30–36). The Seleucid king fled to Apamea and sued for peace. His ambassadors were willing to accept any terms given by the Romans (Livy 37. 44–45; cf. Polyb. 21. 16–17; App. *Syr.* 36–39). We have to assume

---

[76] For full references on L. Flamininus, see *MRR* 1. 350.

that the state of emergency in Sicily, if it had continued beyond 192, was certainly lifted when the war with Antiochus was over.

THE LIGURIAN TUMULT OF 181

When we think of emergencies and crises, however, we often think of sudden events that catch us unaware. While the instances noted before were situations where the danger was long seen to be coming, there are examples that fit more with our expectations. One such event was nothing more than a minor episode in Roman history (Julius Obsequens's terse statement *Ligures proelio victi deletique* may be short on details but says everything that a later Roman might care to learn about the matter), the Ligurian *tumultus* of 181. Minor, perhaps, but of great interest to us as it provides a very detailed example of crisis behavior and response when a sudden crisis hit during the middle Republic. Events such as this episode could well have been more common than reported. Sadly, we do not have accounts of any similar instances. No doubt the later prominence of the general played some role in making this episode worthy of recollection by the historians. There is no specialized treatment of this episode, but it has recently received some discussion in Briscoe's new volume of commentary on Livy, which includes coverage of Book 40.[77] Although there are brief mentions in other sources,[78] we will rely on the earliest and most complete account extant, which is Livy 40. 25–28.

In the spring of 181, L. Aemilius Paullus, consul of 182,[79] now *pro consule* in Liguria commanding the same army he had as consul, led his troops against the Ingauni (40. 25. 1).[80] While he was encamped near the enemy, ambassadors from the Ingauni came pretending to seek peace (40. 25. 2). The ambassadors engaged in deceit, asking Paullus not to allow his men to forage on a nearby mountain, where they claimed that their cultivated lands were; Paullus himself was a little lax in his guard and followed their request (40. 25. 3–4). The Ligurians used the cover of the nearby mountain to mass their forces and then attacked the Roman camp continuously the next day (40. 25. 5–6). According to Plutarch, the Romans were severely outmatched, a mere 8,000 pitted against 40,000

---

[77] Briscoe, *Livy* 3. 471–478.

[78] Frontinus, *Strat.* 3. 17. 2; Plutarch, *Aemilius Paullus* 6. 4–7; Obsequens 6. The battle may have been described by Lucilius in Book 5 of his *Satires*. See Briscoe, *Livy* 3. 472.

[79] For his consulship, see *MRR* 1. 381. His second consulship in 168 and the war he successfully prosecuted against King Perseus of Macedon, of course, brought him much greater fame.

[80] For Roman activity in Liguria in the years before this episode, see Briscoe, *Livy* 3. 25.

Ligurians (Plut. 6. 4; Livy does not provide exact figures for the strength of either side).

After holding against the attack for the day, Paullus sent two cavalry-men with a message for Cn. Baebius (his fellow consul in 182), who was currently in command of an army at Pisa (Livy 40. 25. 7). Unfortunately for Paullus, Baebius had already handed over his army, as he had been ordered to do by the senate (40. 19. 8), to the praetor bound for Sardinia, M. Pinarius; Baebius did, however, take the initiative to write about Paullus's situation to the senate (40. 25. 8), as well as to M. Marcellus (*cos.* 183) in Gaul, who was in command of an army there, urging him, if possible, to march to Paullus's aid (40. 25. 9). Paullus stayed behind his fortifications and waited for relief (40. 25. 10).

The arrival of Baebius's letter caused *trepidatio* at Rome (thus, we have the threat perception made manifest [40. 26. 1]). The budding crisis atmosphere worsened in Rome a few days later when Marcellus arrived in the city and reported that he had handed his own army over to the praetor Fabius Buteo, who had marched against the Histrians (40. 26. 2). At this point, "there was one hope of help, one that itself was slower than the crisis demanded" *una, et ipsa tardior quam tempus postulabat, subsidii spes erat*: the only measure was to urge the new consuls of 181 (P. Cornelius Cethegus and M. Baebius Tamphilus)[81] to take the field with their newly levied armies immediately (40. 26. 4). The senators individually urged this measure, although whether it was formally voted on or not is unclear from Livy's account.

Although the consuls tried to delay this measure, saying that they could not take the field until the levy was completed (40. 26. 5), they eventually gave in to the pressure from the senators and left Rome in uniform (*paludatus*) issuing the standard order to their newly enrolled troops, commanding them to mobilize at Pisa on a fixed day; further, the consuls were permitted to raise emergency troops (*subitarios milites*) wherever they went (40. 26. 6).

In addition, tasks were given to the two praetors in the city: Q. Petilius the city praetor was ordered to enlist two emergency legions (*legiones tumultuarias*) of Roman citizens, enlisting everyone under the age of fifty, while Q. Fabius Maximus the praetor *inter peregrinos* was instructed to call on the Latins and allies for 15,000 infantry and 800 cavalry (40. 26. 7). Also, the Romans elected two naval commanders (*IIviri navales*),

---

[81] See *MRR* 1. 383–384. Broughton corrects Livy's naming Cornelius as Cornelius Lentulus. See *MRR* 1. 386 n. 1.

C. Matienus and C. Lucretius;[82] one of them, Matienus, was assigned the Gallic Gulf and ordered to sail to Liguria and aid Paullus in any way he could (40. 26. 8).

As we can see, the Roman state mobilized considerable resources to attempt to rescue Paullus. Salvation for Paullus's beleaguered army, however, would come from within. Thinking that his messengers had been captured and despairing of relief from outside, Paullus determined on fighting his way out of his plight (40. 27. 1). He marshaled his troops, made a little speech, and attacked the Ligurians, putting them to rout (40. 27. 2–28. 5). Afterward, he even managed to force the capitulation of the entire tribe of Ingauni (40. 28. 6). A slightly divergent alternate account is supplied by Frontinus: he states that Paullus deliberately feigned fear and kept to his camp in order to tire out the Ligurians. After they were sufficiently exhausted, he made his attack (Front. *Strat.* 3. 17. 2).[83]

When the news of the defeat of the Ligurians by Paullus came to Rome, the emergency measures were suspended. Q. Petilius was told to discharge the two city legions he had raised, and Fabius Maximus was instructed to cancel the allied levy (40. 28. 9). Further, the senate ordered the praetor Petilius to write to the consuls, commanding them to discharge their emergency troops (*subitarios milites)* who had been enlisted because of the state of emergency (*tumultus causa conscriptos*) as soon as they could (40. 28. 10). From this last mention, we can be certain that a formal state of *tumultus* was declared. The likelihood of hostilities decreased, and the end of the crisis not only came within sight but also occurred.

As a final note here, we can see how difficult it can be to discover when a *tumultus* was declared, as we so rarely get an explicit and unmistakable notice of a decree being passed declaring a formal state of tumult of the kind that Livy provides (34. 56. 11). In general, we have to infer it from Livy's notice that an emergency levy was held, such as we learn from a minor incident in 178, when it appears that a tumultuary levy was held in response to the report that the consul A. Manlius Vulso and his army had been destroyed by the Istrians.[84] Livy then records "and thus, as is accustomed to be done in a *tumultus*, an extraordinary levy was proclaimed not only in the city, but in all of Italy" *itaque, quod in tumultu fieri solet, dilectus extra ordinem non in urbe sed tota Italia indicti* (41. 5. 4). Forces were hastily gathered and the other consul, M. Junius

---

[82] For full references to them, see *MRR* 1. 386.

[83] Briscoe thinks that the two accounts may be reconciled, if Frontinus's statement is "a garbled version of L[ivy]'s *qui segnius socordiusque oppugnabant.*" See Briscoe, *Livy* 3. 471.

[84] For the sources on Vulso's consulship, see *MRR* 1. 395.

Brutus,[85] was dispatched to Istria. As it turned out, however, Vulso and his army had merely been driven from their camp, not destroyed, and had defeated the Istrians themselves. When Brutus learned of this, he sent word to Rome; the extraordinary levy was cancelled and the men who had been enlisted immediately discharged (41. 5. 11). Note again that it is clear we have a *tumultus*, but nowhere does Livy mention that a state of emergency was formally declared.

We can see the emphasis on troop movements and emergency levies yet again as we get hints of another *tumultus* in 176. In that year, already marked by the death of a consul,[86] an uprising of the Ligurians occurred. The surviving consul, Q. Petilius, after seeing to the election of a replacement, C. Valerius Laevinus, left for his province in uniform (Livy 41. 17. 6). Unfortunately, we have a lacuna here in Livy, so we do not know what happened immediately thereafter, but when the text resumes, we have an interesting series of notices about Roman activity. First, the senate *tumultus eius causa* ordered the third legion to set out to join the proconsul C. Claudius (Pulcher)[87] in Gaul (41. 17. 7). The latter, when he heard about the rebellion in Liguria, began to move toward the region and even enlisted additional emergency soldiers (*subitariis collectis militibus* 41. 17. 9). The consul Petilius, however, fearing that Claudius might finish the war before he even arrived, ordered the latter to rendezvous with him and turn over his force (41. 18. 5). Claudius did as requested and then retired; Petilius waited for his colleague Valerius, and then the two consuls divided their forces and moved against the Ligurians (41. 18. 6–7). Their fates were different: Petilius fell in battle following a bad omen, although his army was victorious (41. 18. 9–14); as for Valerius, we have no details other than that he survived to come back to Rome and became involved in a dispute over who would hold the elections for the consuls of 175, as the priests were opposed to a suffect consul holding the elections when both regular consuls had died in office (41. 18. 16). Because of the missing text, we do not know how the matter was settled.

What we do know is that in the next year, the consuls P. Mucius Scaevola and M. Aemilius Lepidus achieved victories over the Ligurians,[88] for which a three-day *supplicatio* was voted (41. 19. 1–2). Livy ends this section about wars in the north with the comment that *et tumultus quidem Gallicus et Ligustinus, qui principio eius anni exortus fuerat, haud magno*

---

[85] *RE* Iunius 48. See *MRR* 1. 395 for sources on his consulship.
[86] Cn. Cornelius Scipio Hispallus. See Broughton *MRR* 1. 400 for full references.
[87] See *MRR* 1. 397–398 for his consulship, 401 on his proconsulship.
[88] For full references for them, see Broughton *MRR* 1. 401–402.

conatu brevi oppressus erat "and indeed the Gallic and Ligurian tumult, which had arisen at the beginning of this year, was soon suppressed without great effort" (41. 19. 3). Unfortunately, the condition of Livy's text – or rather, the complete lack of it in parts – makes it difficult to reconstruct what level of emergency response Rome made to these outbreaks in the north. The reference to C. Claudius enlisting emergency soldiers, along with the speed with which Q. Petilius left Rome after seeing to the election of his replacement colleague, would point to a formal state of *tumultus* being declared. However, we cannot know when this state of emergency ended, which it likely did; otherwise, C. Valerius would not have been able to return to Rome and contend with men *periti religionum iurisque publici* ("knowledgeable about public law and religion") who sought to block him from holding the elections. Livy's comment from the next year, although he may well be using the word *tumultus* in its less technical meaning of an uprising, leads me to believe that a *tumultus* might have been declared again when we take into account the employment of both consuls again in the north, this time to quell an uprising of both Gauls and Ligurians – one that resulted in a victory significant enough to merit a three-day thanksgiving. Another possibility is that the previous state of emergency in 176 had never been lifted and continued in force until the final suppression of this particular uprising by the consuls of 175.

INTERNAL THREATS: SLAVE TUMULTS

In addition to threats from outside peoples, it appears that the *tumultus* declaration may have been used as well to deal with internal threats of one specific kind of nature, one that would call for emergency measures: a sudden uprising of slaves. Throughout the history of the Roman Republic, there were many occasions when slaves rose up against their masters.[89] On some occasions, the danger to Rome rose to a level that threatened public order within the Roman *imperium*. In some instances, we have an indication that the Romans may have made use of the *tumultus* decree, or at least measures that can be tied to a state of *tumultus*. Sadly, we are not well-informed enough about every major slave rebellion, even for ones where we have detailed information available, to make a determination that a *tumultus* was declared. I present here a few instances where we seem to have enough knowledge to do so. They are all ones that occurred

---

[89] For those interested in the larger subject, there is a very useful collection of the sources in translation by Shaw (2001). For a detailed look at the period between 140 and 70, I recommend Bradley (1989).

on Italian soil. Although the two great Sicilian Slave Wars were large in scale, our sources do not give us as much information about Roman actions to suppress them as we might like. It is hard to judge whether a *tumultus* was declared during either of them.[90]

The first two examples we will look at are cases similar to the tumult of 181, in that they were sudden emergencies that required immediate action, and the emergency response measures tied to the *tumultus* declaration were enough in themselves to counter the threat.

Our first example is slightly odd in that it most certainly looks like a *tumultus*, but from a comment of Livy (our main source), one prominent commentator has not thought it to be a declared one. In the year 198, Livy remarks that Gaul was quiet (beyond expectation) but that Rome itself was almost faced with a slave uprising (*circa urbem servilis prope tumultus est excitatus* [32. 26. 4]). Briscoe comments that *prope tumultus* means "it did not become a *tumultus*, though it was dealt with as if it were."[91] I am not convinced that Livy's wording rules out that a state of emergency was declared. Let us look at the event in greater detail.[92]

Following the conclusion of the Second Punic War, the Romans held a large number of Carthaginians hostage. Many of them were the sons of prominent men at Carthage, and they were accompanied by a large number of slaves. The hostages were kept under guard in the town of Setia.[93] Further, as a great number of enemy prisoners had been enslaved, many people in Italy, including the inhabitants of Setia, had purchased a large number of slaves from the war booty, including many who were from Africa. As one could reasonably imagine, having so many slaves from a single region being allowed to be in contact with prominent men from their homeland proved to be an invitation to plot some mischief. In 198, a conspiracy was formed by the slaves (perhaps with some direction or leadership from the Carthaginian hostages, but this cannot be proven)[94] to

---

[90] The only bare hint we have that could point to a declared *tumultus* is a reference to a praetor, L. Plautius Hypsaeus, whom Diodorus reports to have led a force of 8,000 Sicilian soldiers (34/35. 2. 18). However, Diodorus does not characterize the force as a sudden or emergency levy of any sort, and the other sources make no mention of his force; see *MRR* 1. 482. cf. Brennan (1993).

[91] Briscoe, *Livy* 1. 216.

[92] The only other significant source besides Livy for this incident is Zonaras 9. 16, but his account is a very brief (two-sentence) notice that does not add any important details.

[93] Modern Sezze, about forty-five miles south of Rome. See Briscoe, *Livy*, 1. 216.

[94] The brief notice in Zonaras, deriving from Dio, is definite on the point, but Dio himself might only have been basing his opinion on what Livy wrote. Unfortunately, Livy's own view cannot be recovered fully because of two large lacunae in the text at 32. 26. 8 and 13. See Briscoe, *Livy* 1. 216–218.

take over the towns of Setia, Cerceii, and Norba, starting with Setia during games scheduled to be held there (Livy 32. 26. 4–7). The slaves rose and managed to seize the town of Setia, although they failed at Cerceii and Norba (32. 26. 8).

At this point, two slaves laid information about what was happening before the city praetor at Rome, L. Cornelius Merula.[95] Merula consulted the senate, which ordered him to investigate and suppress the conspiracy (32. 26. 8–10). Setting out with five legates, Merula conscripted every man he encountered and ordered them to follow him with their arms. From this *tumultuario dilectu*, he raised a force of nearly 2,000 men and proceeded to Setia (32. 26. 12). Arriving at the town, he summarily arrested the ringleaders, leading to a mass exodus of slaves from the town. He then sent his troops into the countryside to round up the runaways (32. 26. 13). The two slave informers and a free man who also provided evidence were rewarded (32. 26. 14). With these actions, the main threat was snuffed out, although some embers still glowed. News came to Rome that the remnants of the same slave conspiracy were planning to seize Praeneste. Therefore, Merula set out again and executed 500 men who were implicated in the plot (32. 26. 15–16). In Rome itself, the continuing worry led to the institution of night watches in the neighborhoods of the city (*vigiliae per vicos servatae*), the minor magistrates[96] were ordered to patrol the neighborhoods of the city, and the *triumviri carceris lautumarium* (the *tresviri capitales*) were ordered to guard the prison more carefully (32. 26. 17).

---

[95] Livy mistakenly refers to him here (32. 26. 8) as L. Cornelius Lentulus when in the election notice and praetorian provincial assignment notice of the previous year, he is listed as L. Cornelius Merula (32. 7. 13, 8. 5). Zonaras 9. 16 also calls him Lentulus in error.

[96] Not specified here, Livy refers to them by the generic title *minores magistratus*. Briscoe, *Livy* 1. 218 seems to think the reference is solely to the plebeian aediles, but Rome in this era was a fairly substantial city, and two officials alone leading patrols would seem rather lax when the entire city was under a state of emergency. Three points can be made to suggest that here, the term refers to a number of minor magistrates, members of the boards that make up what was collectively referred to as the *vigintisexviri*. First, it can be pointed out that Livy was not beyond naming the plebeian aediles specifically when they were involved in emergency actions in the city; cf. 26. 10. 2. Second, the term itself could refer to all magistrates not elected by the *comitia centuriata* (thus, every elected officer apart from consuls, praetors, and censors; cf. Kunkel (1995) 39). With the reference immediately following to the *tresviri capitales*, it seems reasonable to suggest that the other members of the *vigintisexviri* could have been deployed to lead night patrols in the city. Finally, there are two direct parallels to this measure: one, in the handling of the Bacchanalian affair (discussed in Chapter 6), where the *capitales* and the two boards in charge of the banks of the Tiber were ordered to provide patrols to prevent arson, which itself had a precursor in 213; the second during the *tumultus* declared during the uprising in Etruria tied to Catiline (see Chapter 5).

Further, the praetor (likely meaning Merula, the city praetor) sent a letter to all of the Latin communities, ordering them to keep the Carthaginian hostages who were in private custody under house arrest and not allow them to go out into public. Prisoners of war were to be placed under chains of not less than ten pounds of weight and to be guarded in public prisons only, not private houses (32. 26. 18). As we hear nothing further about the incident, we can consider it to have been fully suppressed by Merula's actions.

Now we can return to the question of whether a formal *tumultus* was declared. As previously noted, Briscoe would take Livy's *prope tumultus* to imply that what occurred was just short of a full *tumultus*, yet we have the record of actions taken by the Roman state to judge this matter. After Merula consulted the senate, he was immediately authorized to take five legates and proceeded to give the oath to any man he met in the fields, compelling them to follow him with their weapons (*cum quinque legatis profectus obvios in agris sacramento rogatos arma capere et sequi cogebat* [32. 26. 11]). Livy then explicitly calls this a *tumultuario dilectu* in the next sentence. Later, Livy reports how the fear of a further rising at Praeneste spurred the Romans to put the city under watch with armed patrols (32. 26. 17). From these measures, it seems quite clear that a state of emergency, a *tumultus*, was declared. I think the key to understanding Livy's *prope* is to compare the appearance of *tumultus* in §4 with its later use in §8. There, Livy begins the narrative of the slaves' uprising with *Setia per caedem et repentinum tumultum capta* "Setia was seized through slaughter and a sudden uprising." Here, *tumultus* is not being used as a technical term (the *tumultus* declaration) but in its more common usage to mean a disturbance or uprising, as noted at the beginning of our discussion of historical tumults. I would argue that the use in §4 is the same, non-technical usage. The reason why it is *prope* in §4 is because the rising was crushed before it could fully bloom. Thus, it was *almost* an uprising.

Similar to the rising in 198, but on a much smaller scale, was this odd little incident at the end of the same century. Immediately preceding the Second Sicilian Slave War, there were several minor uprisings in Italy, including this incident that was puzzling even for the ancients. Diodorus calls it "contrary to expectation" παράδοξος. Although unimportant in the grander scale of things, this case illustrates the textbook approach to minor slave revolts that grew too powerful for local authorities to handle. Our only source is Diodorus (36. 2, 2a).

After noting a couple of minor revolts at Nuceria and Capua, Diodorus moves on to the more substantial tale of T. Minucius, an *eques* and son of a very wealthy man.[97] This young man fell in love with a slave woman of exceptional beauty owned by another man. Being desperately in love, he offered an exorbitant amount of money (seven Attic talents) for the girl. Time was given him to make payment, as he was extended credit based on his father's wealth. When he failed to pay, a new deadline for thirty days later was made. When he was unable to pay by the second deadline, Minucius concocted a mad scheme.

He acquired 500 suits of armor, arranging for a delay in payment, naturally, and secretly stockpiled them in one of his fields. He then incited 400 of his own slaves to rise in revolt. One can wonder why anyone would extend to him so much credit, but the fact that he had 400 slaves would seem to answer that question. Interestingly, Minucius then donned a purple cloak and a diadem (the Hellenistic emblems of kingship) and made use of lictors along with the other "emblems of power" (τὰ ἄλλα σύσσημα τῆς ἀρχῆς [36. 2. 4]), proclaiming himself king. In this respect, he was likely making use of the established symbols and rituals of authority in order to maintain his control over his followers.[98] Minucius then proceeded to kill his creditors. He then began to raid nearby estates, drawing more slaves to his banner. With added numbers, he established a palisaded fort and welcomed any who wished to join.

When these matters were reported in Rome, the senate deliberated what to do. It had clearly escalated to a point beyond which the local authorities could handle it, as Minucius's forces continued to grow. They appointed L. Licinius Lucullus, one of the praetors who were in the city (τῶν ... κατὰ πόλιν στρατηγῶν [36. 2. 5]) to apprehend the fugitives.[99] On the very day he was appointed, Lucullus enrolled 600 soldiers in Rome itself. By the time he reached Capua, he had raised a force of 4,000 infantry and 400 cavalry. A battle was fought, and the slaves got the better of it because of superior position. It should also be noted that Minucius's force had grown to around 3,500 men by this time, as slaves from the nearby farms joined his banner.

---

[97] The two passages of Diodorus, 36. 2 and 36. 2a, are parallel excerpts, the first made by Photius, the second is part of the Constantinian collection. The man is called T. Minucius by Photius at the beginning but then later called T. Vettius, which is the name used in the Constantinian excerpt. I opt for Minucius as does Bradley (1989) 72. Walton in his Loeb edition (see n. 1 on p. 144–145) notes that the corruption of the name could have gone in either direction, so absolute certainty, barring new evidence, is not possible.

[98] See Bradley (1989) 123.

[99] Although his title is not given, Broughton MRR 1. 559 lists him as likely the city praetor or praetor peregrinus. Brennan (2000) 465 agrees, but also suggests that he could have been a praetor presiding over the extortion court.

Even though a full legion was employed, the enemy force was nearly equal. Therefore, Lucullus turned to somewhat less heroic, but more effective, means. He suborned one of Minucius's subordinates, a certain Apollonius, by promising him immunity. When Apollonius turned his forces against Minucius, the latter chose to do away with himself rather than face punishment; the rest of his followers also died, except Apollonius. With the death of Minucius and his followers, the uprising was over. Once again in this example, we see what is clearly a *tumultus*, but no mention at all about declaring one is made. However, the activity of the praetor Lucullus is quite clear. He was able to enlist 600 men in Rome on the spot and was authorized to recruit anyone whom he met on his line of march to Capua, the same power granted to the praetor Merula in 198 when the former was dispatched to suppress the rising at Setia. So, we can be fairly certain that the power to hold a tumultuary levy was granted Lucullus, and thus, a formal *tumultus* was declared.

Spartacus

Let us now turn to a well-known episode in Roman history, one for which we have much more information. It is so famous that it hardly needs an introduction at all. Perhaps the largest and most serious of all slave uprisings in Roman history, it has even made its way into the modern popular imagination, especially with Stanley Kubrick's 1960 film. As a sign of the enduring appeal of the legendary figure, a cable television series, *Spartacus: Blood and Sand*, which purports to tell of the life of Spartacus before the great revolt associated with his name, made its debut at the beginning of 2010. There will be no need to recount every last detail; our focus will be on the emergency measures taken.[100] The main source is Plutarch's *Life of Crassus* 8–11, which will be followed here, noting important alternate details from the other surviving sources. Sadly missing is the complete text of Sallust's *Historiae*, of which only scattered fragments survive.[101]

At the gladiatorial school of one Lentulus Batiatus near Capua during consular year 73,[102] 200 of the captives there were planning a rising, but information was given on them before they could act. Being made aware

---

[100] For a good overview of the whole affair with analysis, see Bradley (1989) 83–101. For the roles of praetors in this war, see Brennan (2000) 431–434.

[101] All of the major sources are conveniently collected and translated by Shaw (2001) 130–165.

[102] Cn. Lentulus Batiatus is otherwise unknown. This is not entirely surprising because the profession of *lanista* was held in very low regard. See Bradley (1989) 85.

that their plans were known, they attempted a breakout, and 78 slaves escaped.[103] On the road fleeing from the gladiatorial school, the band came upon wagons bearing gladiators' weapons. They seized them, armed themselves, and took up a strong position. Three leaders were elected, including Spartacus, a Thracian (*Crassus* 8).

The gladiators repulsed an armed force from Capua and exchanged their gladiators' weapons for the arms they seized from the Capuans (9. 1).[104] At this point, Rome had to respond. The praetor Claudius Glaber[105] was sent from Rome with 3,000 soldiers (9. 2). He placed the escaped slaves under siege on a hill with only one road up or down, but the slaves used ladders made from vines to climb down the unwatched side and surrounded the Roman force. They launched a sneak attack and routed the Romans (9. 3). Following this success, they were joined by herdsmen and shepherds in the area (9. 4). Sadly, Plutarch's account is somewhat lacking here, as we wonder why the Roman government would now choose to send a praetor with a full legion to deal with a mere group of bandits on a hill, even if they now had better weapons from the Capuan force they had defeated earlier. Here, we have to draw upon the other sources: Appian, Florus, and Orosius.[106] From them, we learn that Spartacus and his band were no longer a small group but had grown considerably in size and had established themselves on Mt. Vesuvius as their base for raiding the local area (although the number 10,000 that Florus estimates [2. 8. 3] as the figure Spartacus had already attracted before setting up a base on Vesuvius is certainly an exaggeration, as suspected by Bradley[107]). We cannot be certain of the numbers, but the response of sending Glaber and a large force signals that Rome now took the threat of Spartacus and his band seriously.

Returning to Plutarch's account (which is roughly in accord with the other accounts, although with differences as will be discussed), the Romans

---

[103] This is Plutarch's number. The numbers vary. Livy *Per.* 95 says 74 slaves escaped. Yet others such as Orosius (5. 24. 1) and Velleius (2. 30. 5) say sixty-four. Florus (2. 8. 3) has a vague "thirty or more." Bradley (1989) 93 thinks "about seventy." The real number is lost.

[104] This detail is only in Plutarch, but it makes sense that the first response to crushing a group of escaped slaves who had now set themselves up as bandits would be for a local force, if available, to crush it. As Bradley (1989) 162–163 n. 19 notes, there is earlier evidence for a garrison at Capua (Livy 23. 46. 11). Considering the large numbers of slaves being trained as gladiators near Capua, it would make sense to maintain an armed force there.

[105] The confusion of the sources makes a definitive identification difficult. Broughton *MRR* 2. 109 lists him as praetor for 73 (followed by Bradley). Brennan (2000) 431 tentatively accepts this view, but also suggests an alternative: that Glaber was actually an ex-praetor and legate of Varinius, which follows the somewhat muddled epitome of Livy.

[106] App. *BC* 1. 116–121, Florus 2. 8, Orosius 5. 24. 1–8. Livy *Per.* 95–97 lack many details.

[107] Bradley (1989) 93.

then sent the praetor P. Varinius to confront the slaves. His legate Furius, commanding 2,000 men, was the first to engage the enemy and was routed (9. 5). Then Spartacus carefully watched and attacked L. Cossinius, who had been sent to advise and assist Varinius, capturing his camp and killing Cossinius himself (9. 5–6). Finally, Spartacus defeated the praetor Varinius, even capturing his lictors and his horse (9. 7).

Although Appian's account is confused (he calls Glaber "Varinius Glaber" and Varinius "Publius Valerius"), it does have one detail about the two early commanders (Glaber and Varinius) that ties this into the earlier slave uprisings that resulted in a *tumultus*. Appian notes that: οὐ πολιτικὴν στρατιὰν ἄγοντες, ἀλλ' ὅσους ἐν σπουδῇ καὶ παρόδῳ συνέλεξαν οὐ γάρ πω Ῥωμαῖοι πόλεμον, ἀλλ' ἐπιδρομήν τινα καὶ λῃστηρίῳ τὸ ἔργον ὅμοιον ἡγοῦτο εἶναι συμβαλόντες ἡττῶντο "they, engaging in battle, were defeated not leading the citizen army [a regularly levied army], but gathering together whomever they collected by chance and on the road (for the Romans did not yet consider this a war, but some sort of raid and action similar to banditry)" (App. *BC* 1. 116. 541). This notice of troops collected on the road follows a pattern of response we have already encountered in the two earlier incidents in 198 and 104 of which I have already recounted. Therefore, this is likely to be an accurate detail in an otherwise muddled account (at the very least, for Glaber's force). Clearly, these early forces were raised by a tumultuary levy and were not regularly constituted armies. Although none of the sources record the fact, it seems quite likely that a formal state of *tumultus* was declared.[108]

At this point, with two Roman armies defeated, even if they were tumultuary levies, Rome was certainly in a full state of crisis. Plutarch records that the threat perception among the Romans had now reached a peak level, requiring a more serious response: Οὐκέτ' οὖν τὸ παρ' ἀξίαν καὶ τὸ αἰσχρὸν ἠνώχλει τῆς ἀποστάσεως τὴν σύγκλητον, ἀλλὰ δὴ διὰ φόβον τε καὶ κίνδυνον ὡς πρὸς ἕνα τῶν δυσκολωτάτων πολέμων καὶ μεγίστων ἀμφοτέρους ἐξέπεμπον τοὺς ὑπάτους. "It was now no longer the indignity and disgrace of the revolt that harassed the senate, but they were constrained by their fear and peril to send both consuls into the field, as they would to a war of the utmost difficulty and magnitude" (*Crassus* 9. 8; tr. Perrin [Loeb]). What had been a minor affair previously was now a serious crisis for the Roman state.

---

[108] Although we have a reference in Caes. *BG* 1. 40 to this conflict in a speech – *nuper in Italia servili tumultu* "recently in the slave uprising in Italy" – we know the word is often used to mean an uprising without specifically denoting the formal declaration of a *tumultus*; I would not push the significance of this statement very far.

At the beginning of consular year 72, both consuls for the year, L. Gellius and Cn. Cornelius Lentulus Clodianus,[109] were assigned to the war against Spartacus. The consul Gellius fought and won a major victory against a group of Germans who had separated themselves from Spartacuss' main body (9. 9).[110] The consul Lentulus, however, suffered a major defeat (9. 9). After that victory, Spartacus headed for the Alps, where he was met by the governor of the province, C. Cassius Longinus (*cos.* 73). Cassius was defeated with heavy losses (9. 10).[111] Livy further records a praetor Cn. Manlius who was also defeated by Spartacus that year (Livy *Per.* 96). The sources other than Plutarch also record Gellius and Arrius being defeated (Livy *Per.* 96, Orosius 5. 24. 4, Appian *BC* 1. 117. 544).

Faced with multiple defeats and ineffectiveness of the consuls, Plutarch records that the senate ordered the consuls to "keep quiet" and chose M. Licinius Crassus to conduct the war, with many prominent men serving under him (*Crassus* 10. 1). There has been some discussion concerning his exact status at the time of his appointment, but I am in agreement with Brennan's position that Crassus was praetor in 73 and likely holding a promagisterial post (probably *pro praetore*) somewhere in Italy during 72 when he was appointed to the command against Spartacus.[112] As for the actual mechanism, Brennan has put forward that Appian's garbled account of Crassus's election as praetor (*BC* 1. 118. 549) may retain a true notice of a special election for the command.[113]

Crassus took the field and began a series of operations with varying success until he managed to corner Spartacus in the neighborhood of Rhegium (*Crassus* 10. 2–9). He also wrote to the senate to ask them to summon M. Lucullus from Thrace and Pompey (the Great) from Spain to assist him, although Plutarch records that Crassus later regretted the request, as he wanted all of the glory for himself (11. 3). After further desultory operations, Crassus managed to force Spartacus to fight to a finish, which he did. Crassus achieved an overwhelming victory over the slaves (11. 7–10; cf. Livy *Per.* 97; App. *BC* 1. 120. 557–558). With the defeat of the slaves,

---

[109] For sources on them, see *MRR* 2. 116.

[110] Unless this victory properly belongs to the praetor Q. Arrius, as recorded in the Livian epitome; see Brennan (2000) 432.

[111] Plutarch records that Cassius escaped with difficulty, whereas Orosius 5. 24. 4 states that Cassius was killed. Florus 2. 8. 10 puts the battle site at Mutina but mistakenly names him as Publius (no word about his fate). Livy *Per.* 96 merely notes that Cassius was defeated.

[112] Brennan (2000) 432–434.

[113] Following a suggestion made to him by Prof. Christopher Mackay. See Brennan (2000) 433 and n. 390. Cited there is the special election of Marius in 88 to command the Mithridatic War, but another (and perhaps more auspicious) precedent was the special election in 211 that named P. Cornelius Scipio to the command in Spain *pro consule* (Livy 26. 18. 1–9).

all that remained were mop-up operations. Soon after the battle, Pompey, freshly arrived from Spain, encountered a large body of fugitives from Spartacus's forces and slaughtered them (*Crassus* 11. 10–1; *Pompey* 21. 1–4). According to Appian, Crassus himself captured 6,000 slaves and crucified them along the Appian Way from Capua to Rome (App. *BC* 1. 120. 559).

We have to assume at this point that if a formal state of emergency had been in effect since at least 73, now, in 71, it was lifted. The major threat from the servile forces was over, even though the Romans were still rounding up alleged remnants of the slaves as late as 60, when the senate ordered the praetor C. Octavius[114] (bound for the governorship of Macedonia) to round up runaway slaves near Thurii, leftovers from the revolts of Catiline and Spartacus (Suet. *div. Aug.* 3. 1).

Non-slave Tumults in the Late Republic

The massive slave uprising led by Spartacus was not the only probable tumult from the first decades of the first century. We have good evidence that earlier in the century there was another *tumultus* declared when Rome found itself assailed by its own strong source of military support, the *socii Italici*. This, of course, was the event that we call the Social War, the war of the allies (*socii*).[115] As a full narrative can be found elsewhere,[116] I will concentrate on the major events and the evidence we have that a *tumultus* was declared, following Appian for the most part as he is our most complete source. The cause of the crisis was the rising expectations of the Italian peoples who had been allied with Rome now for centuries. The triggering event that brought their dissatisfaction to a head was the murder of M. Livius Drusus, tribune of the plebs for 91, whose extensive legislative program included an attempt to extend the Roman citizenship to all the Italian peoples.[117] The failure of the attempt at enfranchisement followed by the death of Drusus led to the revolt.[118]

The Romans were not ignorant of events. Initially, the Romans absorbed themselves in internal squabbling. Appian's account has the equestrians

---

[114] Father of the future triumvir.

[115] On the Social War, see Ridley (2003) and Gabba (1994).

[116] For a full narrative of events, see Gabba (1994) 104–128.

[117] For Drusus, see Livy *Per.* 71; Diod. 37; Vell. Pat. 2. 13; App. *BC* 1. 35. 155–36. 164; Florus 2. 5–other minor references in *MRR* 2. 21.

[118] There has been some debate over what, exactly, the aims of the Italians were: whether they merely wished for Roman citizenship or desired to break away and be free from Rome entirely. For a balanced and detailed discussion, see Sherwin-White (1973) 134–149.

and senators at loggerheads over Drusus's legislation, with the equestrians "retaliating" against Drusus by having prominent senatorial supporters of Drusus put on trial for trying to help the Italians (App. *BC* 1. 37. 165–168). Unrelated, but indicative of internal political strife, Plutarch records the rather silly (but to them important) spat between Marius and Sulla over the monument that Bocchus, the king of Mauretania, had erected in Rome, which seemed to magnify Sulla's role in capturing Jugurtha, while removing Marius from the picture (Plut. *Marius* 32. 5; *Sulla* 6. 2). The Romans, however, began to notice that something was afoot, which prompted them to send out agents to observe the actions of the now wavering Italian allies (App. *BC* 1. 38. 169–170). What is interesting is that they did not engage in ham-handed action but instead tried a "softly, softly" approach, sending men who were well acquainted with the individual towns to obtain information. The key word in Appian's account is ἀφανῶς "secretly" (App. *BC* 1. 38. 170). Of course, they also had less secretive surveillance as well, as Appian notes that ἦσαν γάρ, ὡς ἔοικε, τότε καὶ τῆς Ἰταλίας ἄρχοντες ἀνθύπατοι κατὰ μέρη: "for there were, so it seems, proconsular magistrates at the time distributed among the parts of Italy" (App. *BC* 1. 38. 172). This is a rather extraordinary measure, considering the fact that up to this point, there is no indication in the sources that a state of emergency of any sort or any state of war was extant in Italy.

The flashpoint for the conflict occurred at Asculum (App. *BC* 1. 38. 171, 172–174; cf. Diod. 37. 13. 2; Livy *Per.* 72; Vell. Pat. 2. 15. 1).[119] A Roman agent saw what appeared to be a good-faith hostage being transferred from Asculum to another town and informed the praetor Servilius (probably *pro consule* now in late 91/early 90),[120] who was nearby. The praetor came into the town and attempted to menace the populace but ended up getting killed along with his legate Fonteius. Other Romans in the town were massacred, and the war was on. A last-minute attempt at negotiation proved futile (App. *BC* 1. 39. 175–177). With the murder of Servilius, the Romans surely perceived the seriousness of the threat, which marks the beginning of the crisis.

According to Appian, both consuls marched to war, leaving the defense of Rome to others, the usual case in matters that were nearby and involving Rome's neighbors (App. *BC* 1. 40. 178). The unusual step of assigning a large number of prominent men, including C. Marius and L. Sulla, as legates to the consuls for the year 90 P. Rutilius Lupus and L. Julius Caesar, further demonstrates that the Romans took this war very seriously

---

[119] For other, minor references, see *MRR* 2. 20.
[120] See Brennan (2000) 371–372 and n. 122.

(App. *BC* I. 40. 179). It seems more than likely that the Romans declared a *tumultus*. Although this is not explicitly recorded in the sources, there was a very public action taken that we know was tied to a later *tumultus*: Velleius's comment *utque ad saga iretur diuque in eo habitu maneretur* "[the Roman people] put on military cloaks and remained in this apparel for a long time" (Vell. Pat. 2. 16. 4, my loose translation). The wearing of the *sagum* was already noted at the beginning of the chapter as one of the measures that is often associated with a formal state of *tumultus*. Livy's epitomator also records with, alas, all too much brevity *saga populus sumpsit* (*Per.* 72). Another reference to the *sagum* appears in Orosius, which he calls a *vestis maeroris* "dress of mourning" (Fear's translation), where he notes that following a significant victory by the consul L. Caesar, the senate put aside their *saga* (Orosius 5. 18. 15). We have already noted how this betrays a likely misunderstanding by Orosius. Considering the magnitude of the preparations and these multiple references to the *sagum*, a *tumultus* was in all likelihood formally declared.

As for how long this state of emergency lasted, it is possible to point to a potential ending point in 90. Interestingly, two sources, the epitome of Livy and the later work of Orosius, record when the Romans began the switch back to civilian dress, from the wearing of *saga*,which was our indication that a *tumultus* was in effect. During the course of fighting in the year 90, L. Julius Caesar the consul (the other consul, P. Rutilius Lupus, had died in battle in June)[121] won a significant victory over the Samnites. When news of this reached Rome, the epitome of Livy reports *ob eam victoriam Romae saga posita sunt* "on account of this victory, at Rome military cloaks were put aside" (*Per.* 73). Orosius also records this, noting that L. Caesar was hailed as *imperator* and the senate took off their *saga* and resumed wearing togas (5. 18. 15). Later, there was another apparel change noted. In the next year, 89, after the new consul Cn. Pompeius Strabo[122] had routed the Picenes, Livy's epitomator records *propter quam victoriam Romae praetextae et alia magistratuum insignia sumpta sunt* "on account of which victory at Rome striped (togas) and the other ornaments of magistrates were taken up" (*Per.* 74). Again, this is echoed by Orosius, who notes the distinction between the two events: *qua victoria senatus laticlavia et caetera dignitatis insignia recepit, cum togas tantummodo victoria Caesaris primum respirans sumpsisset* "After this victory, the senate took back [to using] the broad stripe and the other insignia of respect [worthy of their status], while it had resumed [wearing]

---

[121] For full sources on both men, see *MRR* 2. 25.
[122] For full references to him, see *MRR* 2. 32.

togas after the victory of [L.] Caesar, merely breathing again for the first time" (5. 18. 17). As we have discussed,[123] these two apparel choices should be considered separate matters, with only the wearing of the *sagum* tied to a formal state of tumult. So, it would appear that the *tumultus* came to an end after Caesar's victory, but as the state was still in the midst of major calamity, full senatorial dress, with magistrates using their full regalia, was not restored until the situation had markedly improved.

As a final note about the seriousness of the episode, we know from Appian's narrative and from the epitomator of Livy that the Romans were pushed to make use of an extraordinary measure: they drafted freedmen for army service for the first time (Appian *BC* 1. 49. 212; cf. Livy *Per.* 74). They were used to garrison the sea coast from Cumae to Rome, the Romans making use of them because of a shortfall in manpower (δι ἀπορίαν ἀνδρῶν). This clearly indicates that the Romans had already carried out a levy without honoring military exemptions (a tumultuary levy), as they only went to extraordinary lengths, such as this, when all other sources of manpower had been exhausted.

OTHER TUMULTS OF THE LATE REPUBLIC

Having looked at the Social War and the famed revolt of Spartacus and their probable examples of a formal state of tumult being declared, let us turn to other events from the late Republic, a period where a greater number of contemporary sources are available, although they do not always tell us everything we would wish to know. Because of their tendency to omit or pass over information that was not considered important for their readers, but which we would be greatly interested in reading, it can be difficult to find other instances where a formal declaration of a state of emergency, a *tumultus*, was instituted. Following the Social War but preceding the uprising of Spartacus, we have a likely situation where a *tumultus* was declared: the revolt by the consul M. Aemilius Lepidus in 78.[124] The problem is that this is nothing more than a supposition. We do not have an explicit statement that a *tumultus* was decreed, and we do not have reports of an extraordinary levy being held. There are nothing more than linguistic echoes in the sources. For example, Dio, when recounting Lepidus's uprising in a later time period, says that he gathered a faction καὶ πᾶσαν ὀλίγου τὴν Ἰταλίαν ἐτάραξεν "and stirred up almost all of Italy" (44. 28. 2). The word ταράσσω, of course, comes from the same root as ταραχή, the Greek

---

[123] See pp. 48–52.
[124] For this man's career, see N. Criniti (1969).

translation for *tumultus*. The echo is there in earlier works as well. In the fragments of Sallust's *Historiae*, we see the word *tumultus* appear in two important places, although in both cases the word is probably being used in its less formal, more general meaning of an "uprising." We also have *Etruria omnis cum Lepido suspecta in tumultum erat* "It was suspected that all of Etruria was in an uprising with Lepidus" (fr. 1. 69). And in the lengthy speech of Philippus (fr. 1. 77), at one point he says, speaking of the followers of Lepidus, *Hi tumultum ex tumultu, bellum ex bello serunt* "These men sow disturbance from disturbance, war from war" (fr. 1. 77. 7). In this last case, perhaps *tumultus* could be used in the more restrictive sense of a state of unrest – a formally declared *tumultus* – but we cannot in any way be certain. Therefore, whether a state of tumult was declared on this occasion or not can, as I said, only be a supposition, not a fact. What we are quite sure about, however, is that the so-called *senatus consultum ultimum* was passed during this event, so we will discuss Lepidus and his revolt further in Chapter 5.

We have one unmistakable declaration of a *tumultus* in 63 in response to the danger posed by Catiline and his armed following. There is firm documentation for the existence for a state of tumult, consisting of a passage from Sallust and a passage from Dio. The earlier author notes: *Ille cohortes veteranas, quas tumulti*[125] *causa conscripserat, in fronte, post eas ceterum exercitum in subsidiis locat* "He [M. Petreius] placed the veteran cohorts, which he had enrolled because of the state of emergency, in the front, and the rest of the army behind them in reserve." From Dio, we have an explicit reference to the passage of the decree: καὶ ἐπ᾽ αὐτοῖς δόγμα ἐκυρώθη, ταραχήν τε εἶναι "and on account of these things a decree was passed that a state of *tumultus* was in existence" (37. 31. 1). This is a rarity to find in any of the sources, as we have previously noted.

This use of a declaration of a tumult in order to raise an emergency force to deal with a threat to the state (the purpose of the decree, after all) would seem to be a departure from all earlier known occurrences. For as one may note, in no previous case had the *tumultus* declaration been made in response to a threat posed by Romans to the Roman state.[126] Did this reflect a true change in the use of the decree? I do not believe so, for two important reasons. First, analogous to the use of the *tumultus*

---

[125] The reading adopted by Reynolds in his OCT, using the archaic genitive singular ending in *−i*, rests upon a later grammarian, Nonius (489. 34). The manuscripts have the normal fourth declension ending in *-us*. Ramsey (1984) 231, noting problems with Nonius, expresses some reservation about the reliability of the grammarian's testimonium.

[126] We just mentioned the possibility with regard to Lepidus in 77, but again, I stress we have no firm evidence a *tumultus* was ever declared.

declaration to respond to sudden uprisings of slaves or unexpected risings of Gauls, it was not at all unusual for the magistrates in Rome to call for a declaration of tumult when a sudden danger appeared. We have no documentation that the *tumultus* declaration was intended exclusively to be employed against external foes or non-Romans in the case of slaves. It was intended to provide an emergency means of raising armed forces outside of the normal yearly levy authorized by the senate at the beginning of the magisterial year. Second, this episode is more prominently tied to the use of the so-called *senatus consultum ultimum*, which provided the more visible response mechanism employed to resolve the crisis brought on by the threat the consul Cicero perceived to be coming from Catiline and his associates both within and without Rome. Once the *senatus consultum ultimum* was passed, the consul Cicero would have considered himself free to employ any measure he considered useful in suppressing the threat, and the *tumultus* declaration is one he might immediately have thought of when it was reported that Catiline and Manlius had taken the field with an army. As this entire incident is more closely tied to the use of the "last" decree, we shall discuss this event, along with the analogous situation in 49, where a *tumultus* also occurs after the passage of the *SC ultimum*, in much greater detail in Chapter 5.

Moving on to further instances, we are hard pressed to find another occasion where it is clear that a formal *tumultus* was declared. Part of the difficulty stems from our sources themselves. For example, in the usage of Cicero and Caesar, the word *tumultus* is used only in the more general meaning to refer to unrest, commotion, or disturbance[127] and on occasion to a foreign rising, but without any indication that a formal state of tumult is being noted.[128] On a few occasions, we have references that might point to the use of *tumultus* that is of interest to us, but not necessarily meaning that a formal state of emergency was declared. For example, in the year 43, a letter from C. Asinius Pollio to Cicero has the governor report to the elder statesman: *et ego hercules longe remotus ab omni suspicione futuri civilis tumultus penitus in Lusitania legiones in hibernis conlocaram* "Far

---

[127] This less technical use of the term has been discussed (see n. 35). For example, Caes. *BG* 2. 11:...*Ea re constituta, secunda vigilia magno cum, strepitu ac tumultu castris egressi nullo certo ordine neque imperio.* There are many other examples: cf. 6. 7, 6. 37, 7. 47, 7. 60; *BC* 1. 7, 3. 18, 3. 64, 3. 69, 3. 106. Likewise in Cicero, see Cic. *Fam.* 8. 10 [SB 87], 9. 7 [SB 178], 15. 4 [SB 110], 16. 7 [SB 127]; *Cat.* 1. 5; *Mur.* 10; *S. Rosc.* 6; *Deiot.* 7; *Ver.* 2. 1. 63; *Agr.* 2. 37; *Pis.* 12; *Red. pop.* 3. cf. Sall. *Cat.* 43, 45; *Iug.* 12, 38, 53, 57, 60, 66, 72, 99.

[128] Caes. *BG* 5. 26:...*Diebus circiter XV, quibus in hiberna ventum est, initium repentini tumultus ac defectionis ortum est ab Ambiorige et Catuvolco;* Cic. *Att.* 5. 21, 14. 1; *Fam.* 15. 1[SB 104], cf. Cic. *Sul.* 5; Caes. *BC* 2. 25

removed as I certainly was from any suspicion of a coming civil upheaval, I had stationed my legions in winter quarters in the interior of Lusitania" (trans. Shackleton Bailey, Cic. *Fam.* 10. 33 [SB 409]). In this case, the use assuredly is tied to the formal state of emergency declared in 43, which we know about for certain, and which we will focus on in Chapter 7.

More often than not, we have to tease out the existence of a *tumultus* from indirect mentions or linguistic echoes again. We can say with certainty that a *tumultus Gallicus* existed in the year 60, when C. Pomptinus was governing Transalpine Gaul.[129] The situation became so serious by March of that year that we get this mention of what actions the senate had decided to take from a letter of Cicero to Atticus dated firmly to the Ides of March of that year (*Att.* 1. 19). After noting the setback to the friendly tribe of the Aedui and the likelihood that the Helvetii had taken up arms and would invade Roman territory, Cicero recounts the measures passed in the senate: *senatus decrevit ut consules duas Gallias sortirentur, dilectus haberetur, vacationes ne valerent, legati cum auctoritate mitterentur qui adirent Galliae civitates darentque operam ne eae se cum Helvetiis coniungerent* "the senate decreed that the consuls should cast lots for the two Gauls [Transalpine and Cisalpine], that a levy be held, that exemptions should not be in force, that envoys be sent with authority who would set out for the Gallic communities and see to it that they did not join themselves with the Helvetii" (1. 19. 2).

The immediate decision to send the consuls into the field brings to mind the situation in 181, when the senate urged the consuls to mobilize at once to rescue L. Aemilius Paullus. The next measure, however, brings us greater certainty: an immediate levy with no exemptions from service tells us that there is little doubt that a state of emergency is in effect here. Yet we must note, of course, that Cicero does not state that the senate decreed a state of tumult. Then again, that may not have been necessary. He was writing to Atticus, a close friend and member of the upper class who was well-informed about the Roman political system even if he did not involve himself directly in it. There would be no need to spell out to him that an emergency response was being employed to deal with the danger from the north. Atticus would likely have understood that from the measures that were brought into effect.

As it happened, however, the uprising in the north that led to a state of emergency being declared would be handled by the governor Pomptinus largely on his own. That the consul, in this case Q. Caecilius Metellus Celer, did not go to the province is confirmed by another letter of Cicero's

---

[129] His title is not preserved. Pomptinus was praetor in 63. Full sources in *MRR*.

to Atticus (*Att.* 1. 20), sent sometime after the middle of May, where he relates that *Metellus tuus egregius consul; unum reprehendo, quod otium e Gallia nuntiari non magno opere gaudet. cupit, credo, triumphare* "Your friend Metellus is an outstanding consul; I fault him for only one thing, that he does not take particular joy that peace is announced from Gaul. He desires to triumph, I believe" (1. 20. 5). There was a realistic prospect of that for Celer. The main threat turned out to be a rising of the Allobroges, who were defeated in a campaign that was directed, if not personally fought by, Pomptinus.[130] Had Celer been able to achieve the success that Pomptinus did, he (not the former praetor) might have eventually returned to Rome to hold a triumph, although he may have a hard time getting to that point.[131]

---

[130] Dio 37. 47. 1–48. 2. See Brennan (2000) 578.

[131] Pomptinus did not have an easy time gaining recognition for his victories. The vote for a *supplicatio* was evidently opposed by Julius Caesar and his friends, and then later the usual suspects (especially the younger Cato, see Cic. *Att.* 4. 18. 4; compare this to Cicero's own experience with Cato the obstructionist later in 50, see Cic. *Fam.* 15. 4. 11–16; 15. 5) tried to prevent Pomptinus from entering the city in triumph. See Brennan (2000) 578–580 for the full tale.

4

STATES OF EMERGENCY

The Iustitium *Edict*

IUSTITIUM

A *iustitium*[1] was a complete cessation of public business, preventing all government activities not related to war. Kleinfeller makes a list of the usual actions that followed a proclamation of a *iustitium*: the assumption of military dress (*saga sumere*) in preparation for the entry of the *populus* into military service; the complete call up of available men of military age (*dilectus omnis generis hominum*); the suspension of meetings of the senate and all public business; the closing of the shops; a complete ban on private business; a suspension of the courts; a stoppage of the holding of auctions.

A *iustitium* was normally proclaimed by edict (the normal verb is *indicere* or *edicere*) by a consul (P. Scipio Nasica in 111, Cic. *Planc.* 33; Sulla and Q. Pompeius in 88, Appian *BC* 1. 55. 244; cf. Plut. *Sulla* 8. 3; *Marius* 35. 4)[2] or dictator (Livy 3. 27. 2, 7. 9. 6). The senate might order one to be proclaimed (Livy 10. 21. 3), but keep in mind that the senate required a magistrate to call it into session, and on this occasion in 296, the praetor P. Sempronius would have been presiding. In a later instance, where one might have been proclaimed with the senate described

---

[1] Most recent is the interesting article of Scalia (1999). See also Kunkel (1995) 225–228. Although old, many still reference Kleinfeller's useful treatment in *RE* (v. 10 coll. 1339–1340). Unlike *tumultus* and ταραχή, it is hard to demonstrate that there was a single Greek word for *iustitium*. The ordering of a *iustitium* often goes unnoticed in Greek sources. In a rarity, we get a possible word for it from Appian: ἀργία *BC* 1. 55. 244. Plutarch, *Sulla* 8. 3, *Marius* 35. 4, chooses a different word: ἀπραξία. Both, however, are isolated usages, but these are the only times we get a term that would seem to translate what a *iustitium* was. Not all, however, are convinced that these words are a translation for *iustitium*. This will be discussed in full detail in this chapter.

[2] There is some debate about the instance in 88. We shall discuss this in detail.

as the prime mover, it is said that the praetors were forced (*cogerentur*) to suspend the courts (Livy 39. 18. 1). So it seems clear that the edict had to be put into effect by a magistrate.

The *iustitium* could only be cancelled by the authority that ordered it (the consul Sulla was forced to cancel the *iustitium* he ordered in 88 under duress from Marius and Sulpicius, App. *BC* 1. 56. 248, Plut. *Sulla* 8. 3, *Marius* 35. 4). The normal terminology for its termination was *remittere* or *exuere*. Shiemann in the *New Pauly* makes the bold statement that "by the late Republic this order [proclaiming a *iustitium*] had to be preceded by a resolution of the Senate" and cites as evidence Livy 3. 3. 6.[3] The example mentioned comes from the 460s but obviously relies on the fact that Livy's account was shaped by what was customary in his day. Yet in historical cases of which we are aware, there is no notice that a senate decree was required, and Sulla's action in 88 canceling the *iustitium* that he and his colleague Q. Pompeius had proclaimed without any consultation with the senate or his colleague would strongly point to its being entirely within a magistrate's own competence and authority to declare or cancel a *iustitium* he had announced. For that matter, when the *iustitium* was proclaimed in the first place, there was no notice of a senate meeting beforehand.

Although not always mentioned in conjunction with a declaration of a state of *tumultus*, it seems rather obvious that the proclamation of a *iustitium* would naturally follow a declaration of *tumultus*. Cicero's linking of the two in the prior passage, along with its pairing in other contexts (the *tumultus* of 361 already noted), strongly points in that direction. But the opposite does not hold true, as the proclamation of a *iustitium* did not necessarily mean that a *tumultus* was declared. From two examples previously noted – that of Nasica in 111 and Sulla and Q. Pompeius in 88 – a *iustitium* could be proclaimed in the absence of a declaration of *tumultus*, which complicates our understanding of what kind of situation justified the declaration of a *iustitium*, but not a *tumultus*. We shall now discuss this in greater detail.

We have no evidence of any other authority being able to issue a proclamation of a *iustitium*. Whereas Tiberius Gracchus's blanket obstruction in 133 – where he issued an edict announcing that he would forbid all the other magistrates from handling business (διαγράμματι τὰς ἄλλας ἀρχὰς

---

[3] *BNP* 6 1142 [English edition]. He is following Kunkel (1995) 227 here, but Kunkel just notes that Livy always mentions a preceding *senatus consultum* when recording *iustitia* proclaimed by consuls and praetors and further notes that there were no notices when dictators issued them, leading him to believe that a *senatus consultum* was necessary before a consul or praetor could proclaim one.

ἁπάσας ἐκώλυσε χρηματίδειν) until his law was voted on – may have had the effect of a *iustitium*, it is clear that it was not one.[4]

Concerning the issue of the wearing of military dress, it was already discussed[5] that I believe reports of changes of dress appear to be tied to times when a *tumultus* was formally declared. Kleinfeller (see beginning of this chapter) associated the change in military cloaks with the *iustitium*, but every time we get a notice, it appears to be in conjunction with a situation where a *tumultus* was in effect. What complicates this matter is that that does not exclude the possibility that it was tied to the proclamation of a *iustitium* because in general, it happens that most declarations of *tumultus* were concurrent with or followed by the proclamation of a *iustitium*. However, the two occasions where a *iustitium* was declared independently of a *tumultus* decree, there are no references to any change in dress. The matter cannot be settled decisively.

As we have seen, the *iustitium* edict was normally employed in situations where a *tumultus* was in effect and in those contexts does not need further elaboration. Its purpose on those occasions was obvious: to facilitate the emergency draft and prevent anything that could distract the government from dealing with the military emergency. We have seen that already in the emergency that gripped Rome in 296, where we have a definite record of a *iustitium*, but one that was likely proclaimed following the declaration of a *tumultus*.[6] It remains, therefore, to examine cases where a *iustitium* was employed independently of a *tumultus* declaration in order to get a clearer picture of what was involved.

INDEPENDENTLY DECLARED *IUSTITIA*

Sadly, for the first of these events, we lack defining details in the very brief notice of the *iustitium* that we have, although the general historical context can be reconstructed fairly well, as it involved an incident that has received detailed treatment in antiquity. In Cicero's *Pro Plancio*, as nothing more than an aside, the orator recalls a witty vignette involving an auctioneer and P. Nasica (P. Cornelius Scipio Nasica, *cos.* 111),[7] which occurred *edicto iustitio* "when [Nasica] had announced a cessation of public business"

---

[4] Although Mommsen and his followers called it one, and some, such as Lintott (1999) 125 leave the question open ("Whether this should be termed technically a iustitium or not …"), Scalia's assessment of the case of 133 clearly demonstrates that there was no iustitium in 133. See Scalia (1999) 685–695.

[5] See pages 64–69.

[6] See p. 70.

[7] For full references, see *MRR* 1. 540.

(*Planc.* 33). By itself, it is nothing more than an isolated notice, puzzling perhaps. Cicero was not interested in the suspension of public business in and of itself. The point for him was the witty comment from Granius the auctioneer, an indication of the level of freedom of speech men were able to exercise in days gone past.

In the year 111, of course, Rome was involved in something more momentous than a consul and an auctioneer trading words during the suspension of business. There was the reason why that *iustitium* was instituted: the war declared against Jugurtha, King of Numidia. Full details can be had from Sallust's monograph on the war, but just to provide the background in brief: after the Second Punic War had ended, Rome's most faithful ally in Africa was the King of Numidia, Masinissa, friend to Scipio Africanus, the conqueror of Hannibal. When Massinissa ended his life in 148, he was succeeded by his son Micipsa. Micipsa had two sons, Adherbal and Hiempsal. In addition to his two sons, he also raised a nephew, Jugurtha, son of Mastanabal, who did not hold princely rank because his mother was a concubine (*Jug.* 5. 4–7). As Jugurtha was more capable than his own children, Micipsa sent Jugurtha to lead the Numidian allied force sent to aid P. Cornelius Scipio Aemilianus at Numantia in 134, the intent being he should die in battle. Instead of his falling to an enemy's weapon, however, Jugurtha proved himself quite capable, although he also made some less savory Roman friends, men who told Jugurtha that his merit might well make him the best qualified to succeed Micipsa as king. He would not need to worry about Rome's sanction to the change in succession, as Sallust puts in their mouths what has become a famous saying: *Romae omnia venalia esse* "at Rome, everything is for sale" (8. 1).

Jugurtha made such a mark in his time with Scipio that the latter sent a glowing letter to Micipsa. Micipsa was impressed enough to decide to adopt Jugurtha and make him joint heir with his own two sons (9. 1–3). But in his declining years, Micipsa realized the danger in store for his children and tried to urge Jugurtha and his own sons to keep harmony between them or else risk ruin to the kingdom (9. 4–10. 8). Long before Shakespeare wrote *King Lear*, we can see what the outcome would be when three heirs were left to take over the kingdom. Micipsa, however, was more fortunate than Lear to the extent that he did not live to see the aftermath. The three heirs, Jugurtha, Adherbal, and Hiempsal, decided to divide the kingdom, but on the way to the meeting to divide the royal treasure, Jugurtha had Hiempsal treacherously murdered (11. 1–12. 5). Adherbal tried to raise an army to defend himself, but Jugurtha had the better soldiers of the kingdom on his side and drove Adherbal out; the latter then fled to Rome (13. 1–4). Jugurtha, now being afraid of what the Romans might decide, followed the advice of his old friends from Numantia and sent envoys to Rome who bribed as many as they could, which had the intended effect (13. 5–8). After speeches from Adherbal and Jugurtha's envoys, the senate, largely won over by Jugurtha's bribes, sent a commission of ten senators to divide the kingdom. It was led by L. Opimius (*cos.* 121), who earned fame and influence through his suppression of Gaius Gracchus (which we will discuss in detail in Chapter 5). Opimius was bought by Jugurtha, along with the majority of the commission, which divided the kingdom in a manner that ultimately favored Jugurtha over Adherbal (16).

Jugurtha, however, was led on to covet the entire kingdom and began raids in order to start a war. Adherbal held off as long as he could but eventually had to turn to arms. Jugurtha launched a sneak attack on Adherbal's camp at night (20. 1–21. 2).[8] Adherbal fled to the town of Cirta, which was then put under siege by Jugurtha. The main defense of the town was a large number of Italians who lived in it (21. 2). Jugurtha was in a hurry to take the town and kill Adherbal because he knew that envoys had been sent to Rome, and Rome would soon be responding (21. 3). The Romans first sent a low-level embassy of three younger senators (*tres adulescentes*), who informed Jugurtha (they were unable to meet Adherbal) that the senate ordered both kings to stop fighting and settle the matter by law (21. 4–22. 5). After they left, Jugurtha increased his efforts to take the town, leading Adherbal to send two of his most trusted men to sneak out of Cirta and make their way to Rome with a letter from him (23). The letter was read to the senate and spurred some members to call for an army to be sent to aid Adherbal. Jugurtha's friends were able to block that proposal, but another set of envoys was sent, this time headed by M. Aemilius Scaurus (*cos.* 115), who was also the *princeps senatus* (25. 1–4).[9] While Jugurtha was afraid of this embassy, especially Scaurus, he delayed for a while, continuing in his attempts to take Cirta. When he could not delay any longer without angering the senatorial ambassadors, he met them and heard their threats but wasted quite a lot of time (25. 5–11).

This is when matters turned against Adherbal. The Italians in the town, trusting in the name and prestige of Rome, believed that they would be

---

[8] Paul (1984) 80 commentary on 20. 3 places these events in 112, with the siege of Cirta beginning sometime around April.

[9] The *princeps senatus* was the first man listed on the censors' roll of the senate, a position of some honor usually bestowed upon the senior living patrician ex-censor, although Scaurus was not *censorius*, but there was possibly no living patrician ex-censor at the time. For this man, see Paul (1984) 64–66 commentary on 15. 4, with full references to earlier studies of this important figure and his career.

able to escape any harm in the event of surrendering the town. They therefore advised Adherbal to surrender and ask only for his life, allowing all other matters to be handled by the senate. Although Adherbal had no faith in Jugurtha, he was under something close to compulsion because the Italians in the town were the main strength of the town's defense. Thus, he followed their advice, surrendered, and was promptly tortured to death by Jugurtha, an event that preceded the general massacre of the townspeople and all Italian traders who were found armed in Cirta (26). At this point, one might imagine that the Romans would finally be roused to arms, but there were many in the senate who still pleaded Jugurtha's case (27. 1). However, now Sallust brought onto the stage C. Memmius, tribune of the plebs elect, who started to draw attention to the attempt to cover up what Jugurtha had done (27. 2). This changed matters decisively.

When the end of 112 came around, the senate, in accordance with the *lex Sempronia*, designated the *provinciae* for the consuls of 111 as Numidia and Italy (27. 3).[10] This itself would signal to informed readers that war was to be waged against Jugurtha by one of the consuls of 111. Sallust apparently saw no need to mention that war was officially declared, although we know that it was from other sources.[11] The elections were held,[12] and P. Cornelius Scipio Nasica and L. Calpurnius Bestia were created consuls, with Numidia falling by lot to Bestia (27. 4). We now have the direct tie-in to the declared *iustitium*, as this Scipio Nasica was the P. Nasica whom Cicero was referring to in his speech. It should come as no surprise that our seemingly best and more detailed account – the historical monograph of Sallust – does not record every detail we might be interested in. We have seen before how the sources routinely do not record formal votes of a state of *tumultus* when all other signs point to one being in existence. We are fortunate that we have Cicero's offhand remark, as it reveals something important. A *iustitium* could be declared independently of a *tumultus* or the appointment of a dictator entrusted with the handling of a crisis, who often declared one shortly after taking office. It makes sense that one would be declared now. A major campaign was about to be undertaken; the provinces had already been allotted. An army needed to be enrolled, provisions and material gathered, transport arranged. It

[10] One law of Gaius Gracchus (*tr. pl.* 123) not repealed was his law that ordered the senate to determine the consular provinces in advance of the consular elections.
[11] Omission noted by Paul (1984) 89 commentary on 27. 3 "Numidia." Orosius 5. 15. 1 and Val. Max. 7. 5. 2 both date the declaration of war specifically to the consulship of Nasica and Bestia. Livy *Per.* 64 also notes the declaration of war and the assignment of it to Bestia.
[12] Late in the year, perhaps October or November, possibly December; see Paul (1984) 89 commentary on 27. 4.

would be natural to temporarily suspend all other business to carry out the preparations necessary for the war. Sallust does record precisely those things: the enlistment of the army and the collection of supplies (27. 5).

It is unfortunate that we have to rely upon a chance remark by Cicero to know that a *iustitium* was declared around the same time that war was officially declared against Jugurtha in 111. No other source records the fact. It would be very valuable to our knowledge if we could know whether it was standard procedure to declare a *iustitium* immediately after a major war was declared. It would make some sense, as a means of setting aside all other business in order to focus on war preparations. Otherwise, if we could know that it was unusual for this to occur, then that would mean that this declaration was a special occasion in 111, and we might inquire further what was special about it.

SULLA AND SULPICIUS IN 88

Much better documented, but subject to debate, is a *iustitium* that was declared in 88 by the consuls L. Cornelius Sulla and Q. Pompeius Rufus, already noted in the introductory section. I believe that it was a *iustitium*, but that has not been the universal verdict of all scholars. Let us first provide some background and take a look at the three major accounts we have of the event that record the declaration but that also present potential contradictions that can be resolved, partially through the use of notices from fragments and lesser sources. Rome in the year 88 was already a city that had been through severe crisis. It had surmounted the survival-level threat of the Social War, which we have already discussed in Chapter 3 regarding *tumultus*. Although the Romans had presented a strong united front against the threat to their survival from the revolt of the Italian allies, internal dissension and more menacing signs of internal strife had not disappeared. As a bad omen for the health of the state, in 89, a Roman praetor, A. Sempronius Asellio, was killed by a mob of moneylenders in the forum because he dared to try to allow the law to help debtors who were suffering from the effects of the Social War (Appian *BC* 1. 54. 232–239; Livy, *Per.* 74; Val. Max. 9. 7. 4). The murder of the city praetor in Rome, with the apparent encouragement of a tribune of the plebs (one L. Cassius, according to Valerius Maximus), did not bode well for Rome. The senate offered rewards to informers, but no one came forward (Appian *BC* 1. 54. 239). A bad omen indeed.

If we continue to follow the account of Appian, the next year, 88, saw the Social War now on the path to suppression, although there was still unfinished business remaining. The consuls chosen for this year were

L. Cornelius Sulla, who had distinguished himself in the Social War, and Q. Pompeius Rufus.[13] Despite the fact that the Social War was not at an end and the city was in internal ferment,[14] the consuls Pompeius Rufus and Sulla drew lots for the command in Asia, the conflict with Mithridates receiving higher priority, and Sulla received the command (Appian *BC* 1. 55. 241; cf. *Mithr.* 22. 84).[15] Appian then brings onto the stage C. Marius, the former hero against the Cimbric-Teutonic menace (to be discussed later in Chapter 6), who desires the eastern command for himself, and his ally, the tribune of the plebs P. Sulpicius Rufus,[16] with whose help the war could be reassigned to Marius. There was also a proposal to rework the arrangements for the newly enfranchised Italians, who had been deliberately "gerrymandered," to use the modern term, in order to reduce their influence in Roman elections (*BC* 1. 55. 242). Sulpicius then immediately brought a bill to redistribute the newly enfranchised Italians into all of the Roman voting tribes, a move that would greatly increase the influence of Marius and Sulpicius, who would benefit from the gratitude of the Italians (*BC* 1. 55. 243). This was opposed fiercely by the "old" citizens, as Appian calls them, with the fighting turning into literal violence as the two sides fought with sticks and stones, which finally led to the intervention of the consuls (*BC* 1. 55. 244).

The measure the consuls took was the following: δείσαντες οἱ ὕπατοι περὶ τῇ δοκιμασίᾳ τοῦ νόμου πλησιαζούσῃ προύγραψαν ἡμερῶν ἀργίας πολλῶν, ὁποῖον ἐν ταῖς ἑορταῖς εἴωθε γίγνεσθαι, ἵνα τις ἀναβολὴ γένοιτο τῆς χειρο-τονίας καὶ τοῦ κακοῦ "the consuls, being afraid concerning the approaching assembly for the approval of the law, gave public notice of a cessation of work for many days, such as is customary in times of religious festivals, so that there might be a delay of the vote and of the evil" (*BC* 1. 55. 244). Sulpicius, however, would not wait for the cessation of work to end but instead ordered his supporters to arm themselves and be prepared for any-thing. He then confronted the consuls, ordering them to lift the ἀργία, claiming that it was illegal, so that he could proceed to the approval of the law (*BC* 1. 56. 245–246). They refused, so Sulpicius resorted to violence, which led to the consuls' retreat. During the violence, the son of Pompeius

---

[13] For full details of these two men's consulship, see *MRR* 2. 39.

[14] Not in his *Civil Wars*, but this is how Appian characterizes the time in *Mithr.* 22. 83: ἀσχολού-μενοι στάσεσιν ἀτρύτοις ἐν τῇ πόλει καὶ οἰκείῳ πολέμῳ χαλεπῷ "[the Romans] were occupying themselves with wearisome internal strife in the city and a difficult civil war."

[15] For the outbreak of the war with Mithridates, see Kallet-Marx (1995; now Morstein-Marx, but to avoid confusion, I will reference him by the name the work was published under), Tamura (1990) and McGing (1986).

[16] For full references, consult *MRR* 2. 41.

Rufus, who was married to Sulla's daughter, was killed (*BC* 1. 56. 247). Sulla then revoked the cessation of work and went to his army at Capua, intending to begin his march to the east to confront Mithridates, as he was as yet unaware of Sulpicius and Marius plotting against his retaining the command (*BC* 1. 56. 248). Sulpicius was then able to pass his law, and Marius was given command of the war against Mithridates (*BC* 1. 56. 249). In reaction to this, Sulla suborned his army and marched upon Rome (*BC* 1. 57. 250–252).

If one takes Appian's account as the authoritative one, we are not dealing with a *iustitium* here, but instead, a declaration of *feriae imperativae* – the announcement of days devoted to religious observances, such as *supplicationes*, which do not have fixed dates. This is the position of Levick, following Valgiglio, also agreeing with the earlier pronouncement of Lintott.[17] The use of this device would indeed have been effective in stopping the vote on the law, as it brought into play not only religious scruples but also a possible breach of the *leges Aelia et Fufiae*, as Lintott notes, whereas infringing a *iustitium* might not invoke any automatic penalty.[18] If this were the only account that we had of the incident, it might be decisive. However, we have two other closely related accounts that might cast some doubt on this judgment.

These are the accounts of Plutarch in his separate lives of *Marius* and *Sulla*. Unfortunately, they do not provide the clean, complete, historical narratives that would help to establish an uncontested chronology of events, but they contain valuable information about this incident that gives a different spin to the whole affair. As a brief aside, we may note that Plutarch provides us with an otherwise unattested piece of information regarding the relations between the two men *before* they attempted to employ violence upon each other. Long before they had wrangled over the Mithridatic command, Marius and Sulla demonstrated that they had no love lost for each other. A few years before, just prior to the outbreak of the Social War, the two nearly came to political (if not literal) blows over a monument erected in Rome by Bocchus, the king of the Moors (Plut. *Marius* 32. 4–5; cf. *Sulla* 6. 2). The monument recounted Bocchus's role in capturing Jugurtha and paid great attention to Sulla, while apparently

---

[17] Levick (1982) 508 (citing Valgiglio); Lintott (1971) 444 n. 4. However, Levick notes (n. 43) that Emilio Gabba, in his commentary on Appian *BC* Book 1 (Firenze, 1967), believed that Appian was mistaken in his interpretation of the situation, not outside of the realm of possibility with this ancient author.

[18] Lintott (1971) 444–445 n. 4; for a *iustitium* not making the man who infringed it liable to automatic penalty, he notes that Mommsen (*St.R.* i³ 265) first made the observation.

making little to no mention of Marius. As one might expect, the latter fumed at the idea.

In his *Life of Marius*, Plutarch apparently places the dispute over the Asian command after the Social War was nearly finished. When many (πολλοὶ) were contending for the right to lead the war against Mithridates with the help of the "popular leaders" (διὰ τῶν δημαγωγῶν), contrary to all expectation, Sulpicius brought forward Marius as a candidate for the command, specifically as a proconsul (34. 1). Plutarch then remarks how the people were divided in their opinion, some in favor of the idea, others favoring Sulla and telling Marius that he should go to the spa villa near Baiae that he owned (34. 2–3).[19] Perhaps in response to that jibe, Marius then began to show how fit he was physically, exercising in the Campus Martius with the young men, which some though well of but others regarded with pity (34. 5–6). It is at this stage that Plutarch gives us the first of several important pieces of information. For at this time when who would have the right to command was being disputed, it was not as yet a major war that was envisioned. Although it contradicts what he said about the war being against Mithridates, he goes on to note that part of what people pitied was the prospect that he (Marius) was desiring to set out for Cappadocia and the Euxine Sea to fight against Mithridates' satraps Archelaus and Neoptolemus (34. 6). This would strongly suggest that in Rome at this time, the war was not yet seen as a major undertaking. Marius's reputed reason for wishing to lead the expedition, reported next by Plutarch, was not taken seriously by anyone but makes greater sense if one considers that the war was not yet regarded as a major conflict: Marius claimed that he wanted to oversee his son's military training (34. 7).

Plutarch now reintroduces Sulpicius, whom he claims Marius found to be a useful instrument for achieving his goals, and it is further claimed by Plutarch that Sulpicius was an admirer and imitator of Saturninus,[20] although the latter did not go far enough in his (Sulpicius's) mind (35. 1). Sulpicius is portrayed as having an armed guard of 600 equestrians, and with them he proceeded to attack the consuls, although no reason is given why. In the mêlée, the son of the "other consul" (Pompeius Rufus) was killed as Sulla himself fled, forced to take refuge in the house of Marius, to evade Sulpicius's armed thugs (35. 2). Sulla was allowed to escape

---

[19] For Marius's property at Baiae, see D'Arms (1970) [2003] 37–42.

[20] We shall discuss L. Appuleius Saturninus in much greater detail in Chapter 5. There is no other evidence that Sulpicius was a genuine admirer of Saturninus, and it may well be nothing more than part of Plutarch's attempt to paint Sulpicius as some troublemaker. Powell (1990) 459: "Plutarch's version of Sulpicius is far too much the conventional portrait of the seditious tribune."

through another door by Marius and then went straight to his army, although Plutarch distances himself from the report as he terms it λέγεται (35. 3). Plutarch now quotes another version, directly from the memoirs of Sulla, where Sulla claimed that he went to Marius's house in order to consult Marius about Sulpicius's demands and then afterward returned to the forum where he rescinded the decree suspending public business, as Sulpicius and his gangs desired: ἄχρι οὗ προελθὼν ἐκεῖθεν εἰς ἀγοράν, ὡς ἠξίουν ἐκεῖνοι, τὰς ἀπραξίας ἔλυσε (35. 4). Notice the term that Plutarch uses is ἀπραξία, not the ἀργία of Appian. There is no notice at all of any religious festivals, rites, or celebrations involved. Then Sulpicius proceeds to the passage of the law transferring the command to Marius, who sent out two military tribunes to take command of Sulla's army (35. 5). Following this, Sulla suborned his army and marched against Rome, killing the military tribunes Marius had sent (35. 6). Of course, this entire account is fragmented and difficult to understand without knowing the basic story from other accounts. Its defective nature lowers its worth.[21] Therefore, let us turn to the slightly better and fuller account Plutarch gives in his *Sulla*.

The *Sulla* provides a fuller narrative, although one perhaps flawed as well. While the Social War was yet being fought, Plutarch states that Sulla, while still commanding soldiers in the field, was already desirous of being appointed general to fight Mithridates, for which reason he indulged his soldiers even after serious misdeeds (6. 9). After his election as consul with Pompeius Rufus, Plutarch then mentions Sulla's marriage to Caecilia, daughter of Metellus Delmaticus (*cos.* 119), the Pontifex Maximus (6. 10). Passing over a digression on his wife, we return to Sulla, who continues to be portrayed, even though now consul, as desiring to hold command in the Mithridatic War. In this, he was rivaled by Marius (7. 1). When Sulla set out for the army camp,[22] Marius apparently plotted (7. 2). We may pass over the prodigies Plutarch then recounts and return to the main narrative. Marius is now presented as making an alliance with Sulpicius, who again is presented as a wicked tribune (8. 1). Interestingly, Plutarch – while also mentioning the armed bodyguard, this time a more impressive 3,000 swordsmen in addition to the equestrians who accompanied him – tells us now of a law Sulpicius proposed and carried that no other source mentions: a law setting a limit on how much debt a senator might incur (8. 2). This one apparently passed without violence, because it is only after

---

[21] Powell (1990) 455 calls this sudden mention of the cessation of business, not noted before, "a fairly typical example of Plutarchean incompetence."

[22] At Nola, still a holdout from the Social War. We must assume this from other sources' reports: Diod. 37. 2. 13; Vell. Pat. 2. 18. 4; cf. Orosius 5. 19. 3.

mentioning this law that Plutarch relates that Marius and Sulpicius turned to force in order to pass other laws, especially a law appointing Marius to the command of the war against Mithridates (8. 2). Contrary to the account of Appian, Plutarch then ties the consuls' suspension of business to their attempt to block this measure, the one transferring the Asian command (here again, he uses the term ἀπραξία 8. 3). Sulpicius then led a mob to attack the consuls while they were holding an assembly near the Temple of Castor and Pollux, which led to the fatal riot where Pompeius Rufus's son was killed and Sulla was forced to retreat to the house of Marius. Sulla was then forced to come out and rescind the cessation of business: ἠναγκάσθη προελθὼν τὰς ἀπραξίας λῦσαι (8. 3).

Plutarch proceeds to add the rather extraordinary details that although Sulpicius had Pompeius removed from office, he did not abrogate Sulla's magistracy because Sulla had lifted the ἀπραξία. Sulpicius punished Sulla only by transferring the command against Mithridates to Marius, and then sending military tribunes immediately to Nola to take command of the army and hand it over to Marius (8. 4). Most accounts have Sulla win over his soldiers and march on Rome quickly, but here, Plutarch makes it appear that events were more drawn out. Sulla escaped Rome, got to his army first, and suborned it. The soldiers, won over to his side, stoned to death the military tribunes sent by Sulpicius (in this account). In return, Marius killed several friends of Sulla (9. 1). There was an exchange of persons, as some fled the city for Sulla for others fled Sulla's camp for Rome, and when the senate, under control of Sulpicius and Marius, learned that Sulla was marching toward Rome, two praetors were sent to intercept him and stop his advance (9. 2). We will stop here for the moment.

Clearly, we are dealing with problematic accounts here. The *Marius* is patchy and fragmented, mentioning the cessation of business ἀπραξία when it was revoked but not mentioning when it was first put in place. The *Sulla* seemingly presents a full narrative, but contains details that strain belief. The notice that Sulpicius removed Q. Pompeius Rufus from office is particularly unbelievable.[23] Plutarch clearly seems to be telescoping events, attributing the consuls' obstruction to the more controversial bill Sulpicius proposed, transferring the command against Mithridates rather than the bill to reorganize the enfranchisement of the new citizens, which Appian is probably correct in tying to this event.[24] And yet we get details that

---

[23] Lintott (1971) 443 rightly notes that this would be an unparalleled incident in Roman history, and suggests that Sulpicius instead worked to prevent Pompeius Rufus from exercising his authority, which he could do by constant personal obstruction through his tribunician powers.

[24] Powell (1990) 451–452.

are lacking from Appian's report that are likely correct. Sulpicius did not just have two bills but a full legislative program, and Plutarch provides us with an example of another law he passed (we will learn of a further one in a moment). Most importantly for our concerns, Plutarch makes no mention of any religious context for the cessations of business that the consuls announced in order to prevent Sulpicius's law from being passed at the assembly. There is not much that can be argued from the Greek terminology used. Both basically mean a work stoppage of one sort or another, and Lintott, although he opts for *feriae*, does not believe the case can be made based solely upon the Greek word choices.[25] How then do we decide which this was – *feriae* or *iustitium*?

Other sources do not mention the period of idleness at all, although they give us more and potentially intriguing details. Livy's epitome is extremely bare and goes straight from mentioning the "pernicious" laws of Sulpicius (passed with Marius's help), straight to the riot and Sulla marching on Rome with his army (Livy *Per.* 77). The only new detail he adds is that Sulpicius also proposed a law to recall exiles, further proof of the incompleteness of both Appian and Plutarch's accounts. The account in Velleius Paterculus is light on specifics but does have a surprise or two. After Sulla is elected consul (2. 17. 3), the Mithridatic War arrives, and Velleius notes that the province came to Sulla by lot (2. 18. 3). He has Sulla, however, set out for Nola, which was still under siege, a holdout from the Social War (2. 18. 4). It was at this point, when Sulla was out of Rome, that Sulpicius passes his "pernicious" laws, including a bill that abrogated Sulla's command and transferred the war against Mithridates to Marius (2. 18. 5–6). Velleius also has Sulpicius send men specifically to kill Pompeius Rufus's son. It is after this that Sulla returns to Rome with his army (2. 19. 1). So, either Velleius is omitting details (very likely) or Sulla was not even in Rome when Sulpicius was engaged in his legislative activity.

The key factor in understanding the situation is being able to place where Sulla was in relation to the activities of Sulpicius. One thing is clear: at some point, Sulla left Rome. From other sources, we get further confirmation of this. Orosius, although not very helpful otherwise, tells us that Sulla was outside of Rome dealing with the remnants of the Social War in Campania while still in his consulship. He was involved in this immediately before his intention to proceed to Asia (5. 19. 3). Diodorus, sadly only preserved in excerpts, records that Sulla, at some point after Marius had contended with C. Julius Caesar Strabo[26] for the Mithridatic

[25] Lintott (1971) 444 n. 4.
[26] For him, see *MRR* 2. 26.

command,[27] set out for Nola and forced the surrender of several places that were still held by Italian rebels (37. 2. 13). Taking all of the information thus laid out, I would like to present a possible reconstruction of events, one that might, when we compare this to the *iustitium* in 111, support the notion that it was indeed a *iustitium*, not *feriae*, which was proclaimed by the consuls.

Following his entry into office and the dispute with Caesar Strabo at either the very end of 89 or early in 88, P. Sulpicius Rufus proceeded to promulgate his bills. The first bill, concerning the debt limit for senators, apparently passed without violent opposition. He then proceeded to promulgate two bills that caused a greater stir: one recalling certain exiles and the other redistributing the new citizens into all thirty-five Roman tribes. This latter law met with fierce opposition from those whose existing political supremacy might be challenged by any further changes to the system (the extension of Roman citizenship to a great number of Italians had already created a sea change). At some point, we cannot be certain of exactly when, Sulpicius turned to C. Marius for political support to help with the passage of his bills. In exchange, Marius, who desired that the war with Mithridates be given to him, wanted Sulpicius's support in that endeavor. It would appear that the news of the danger from the East had not yet reached a point where there was need for the immediate dispatch of an army, as we have the notice from Plutarch regarding the minor nature of the affair so far, and the fact that Sulla did not set out immediately for Asia but instead was busy with the siege of Nola. It may even be that Sulla was not allotted the province of Asia until after he had already set out to stamp out the remains of the Social War in Campania.[28] At the moment, the war was against Mithridates's satraps. It had progressed beyond the competence of the Roman commissioners sent out in 90 (whom we will discuss in greater detail in Chapter 6) but did not yet require the immediate dispatch of a commander of consular rank with a large army to supersede the praetorian governors of Asia and Cilicia. It is not beyond the realm of possibility that the sources, when they speak of Sulla operating in Campania as something he only did while on the way to Asia, are speaking

---

[27] A tangled issue. As we have from other sources, Caesar Strabo attempted to be elected consul despite the fact that he was only an ex-aedile and had never run for, let alone held, the praetorship. His candidacy was opposed successfully by Sulpicius. Most date this event to the very end of 89 or very early in 88. See Powell (1990) 452–453; Levick (1982) 507; Mitchell (1975) 198–203; and Lintott (1971) 446–449. For a possible way to explain the connection to the Mithridatic command, see Mitchell *op. loc. cit.*

[28] This is the suggestion of Mitchell (1975) 202–203.

in deliberate error, in hindsight, or telescoping events by ignoring the fact that the Asian campaign had not been decreed yet.[29]

The bill to change the terms of enfranchisement of the Italians, however, provoked serious violence. Perhaps Pompeius, worried about it, called his colleague back to Rome to aid him in tamping down the ferment. It could be that Sulla heard what was occurring, discovered that Marius was involved (for whom he had no love lost, as we know from Plutarch), and came back on his own to aid in obstructing the latter's goals. It is also possible that Sulla returned to Rome at this time because this is when the sortition of provinces occurred, when the senate decided to change the consular *proviniciae* for the consuls of 88 and assign Asia to one of them, in response to the greater alarm occasioned by Mithridates's successes against Roman forces in Asia. It was in the midst of these events, which also saw the violence at the assembly for discussing Sulpicius's law about the redistribution of the new citizens, that the consuls declared the ἀργία/ἀπραξία. Although this is nothing more than a possibility, when one looks to the events of 111 – when a *iustitium* was declared after the consuls had drawn lots to see who would lead the Roman army against Jugurtha – it could be that following the assignment of the war to Sulla now, a *iustitium* was declared in order to focus all government activity on preparing for the war. If it had the beneficial (from the perspective of Sulla and Pompeius and others who shared their political opinions) side effect of preventing Sulpicius's law from causing further trouble (and possibly delaying its passage long enough to cause Sulpicius's political support to wither away), that was only a bonus. Violence, however, forced Sulla (and the sources seem clear that it was Sulla who revoked the cessation of public business) to end the *iustitium*, after which he proceeded to his army.

In the end, however, it is not possible to express full certainty on the matter. Whereas the passage of Appian might be considered definitive by some, if we follow his interpretation, another question can be raised: is there any other example of *feriae*, which are dedicated to the gods, being cancelled? Whereas consuls had discretion in when to announce *feriae imperativae*, the decision to have them (by voting to grant *supplicationes* and such) was originally made by the senate. Could the consuls revoke dates already announced without the senate's permission? In this case,

---

[29] If Asia had been allotted to Sulla before the consuls entered office, then we can assume that Pompeius Rufus was given Italy as his *provincia*. If so, then why was Sulla, not he, in Campania dealing with the remnants of the Social War?

considering the context of war, a context where a *iustitium* would fit much better, it is my belief that one was called on this occasion.

We have no other reports of a *iustitium* edict being announced outside of the context of either a *tumultus*, whether declared or suspected or a situation where war or military hostilities seemed imminent. We do, however, have an incident from later in the first century where a reference is made to a proposed *iustitium*, one that would have been unprecedented and unusual in every respect. There is a curious report made by Cicero in a speech he gave to the senate in 56, the *de Haruspicum Responsis*.[30] After an earthquake and other bad omens had been reported, the senate, following normal procedure, consulted about the proper means of expiation.[31] The *haruspices* were consulted and, among other things, claimed that a sacred site had been profaned. Apparently, P. Clodius Pulcher, who had a personal feud with Cicero,[32] attempted to take advantage of this situation to attack Cicero, claiming in a public meeting that the profaned site was Cicero's house, which Clodius had tried to consecrate into a shrine to Liberty during Cicero's exile.[33] Cicero responded with the speech to the senate that gave his own interpretation of the priests' pronouncements. What interests us specifically is a section where Cicero claims *monent enim eidem "ne occultis consiliis res pvblica laedatur." quae sunt occultiora quam eius qui in contione ausus est dicere iustitium edici oportere, iuris dictionem intermitti, claudi aerarium, iudicia tolli?* "For indeed they warn 'that the state should not be harmed by secret plots.' What are more secret than [the plots] of this man [Clodius], who in a public meeting dared to say that a *iustitium* ought to be declared, the administration of justice suspended, the treasury to be closed, the courts to be pushed out of the way?" (*Har.* 26). Although this is only a reference to a proposed *iustitium*, not one that was actually put into effect, it is notable that we have here a proposal for a *iustitium* that does not in any way appear to be tied to the declaration or conduct of a war. In all of the instances related to *tumultus* and in the two independent occurrences discussed in this chapter, war was

---

[30] For the background and full context of this speech, see Lenaghan (1969). For a very brief summary with references to earlier discussions, see Mitchell (1991) 190.

[31] On the normal procedure, see J. A. North, *The Interrelation of State Religion and Politics in Roman Public Life from the End of the Second Punic War to the Time of Sulla.* Diss. Oxford, 1967. More recently on prodigies, consult D. Engels, *Das romische Vorzeichenwesen (753–27 v. Chr.). Quellen, Terminologie, Kommentar, historische Entwicklung.* Stuttgart, 2007.

[32] It stemmed from the events of the "Bona Dea scandal" in 61. For a brief summary from Cicero's viewpoint with full references to the sources, see Mitchell (1991) 83–86. The feud had graver consequences earlier for Cicero, to be discussed in the context of Clodius's successful effort to exile Cicero in 58 (see the discussion of the Catilinarian crisis in the next chapter).

[33] Dio 39. 20. 3.

related to the announcement of a *iustitium*. Of course, Cicero is here trying to emphasize the lawlessness of Clodius, who was calling for an emergency measure, a war-related measure, to be instituted when no emergency requiring it was in existence. The passage is interesting nonetheless in that it confirms what effect a *iustitium* had, closing not only the courts but even the public treasury.

5

THE SENATUS CONSULTUM ULTIMUM

The History and Development of the So-called *Senatus Consultum Ultimum*

What complicates our discussion of states of emergency in the last century of the Roman Republic is that a new development occurred in emergency response, although this change was more a political change than anything else. This is the appearance of the so-called *senatus consultum ultimum* (*SC ultimum*).[1] It was Caesar the Dictator who coined the phrase "the last decree of the Senate."[2] Attempts that have been made to displace it with a more accurate descriptive moniker, such as the *senatus consultum de re publica defendenda*, have not gained much in the way of broad acceptance so far.[3] There is no special Greek term or usage for the *senatus consultum ultimum*. For example, in one of the best documented cases, when it was passed by the senate on the motion of M. Tullius Cicero as consul in response to the threat he perceived to the state from L. Sergius Catilina and his adherents in 63, Dio (37. 31. 2) records that καὶ προσεψηφίσαντο τοῖς ὑπάτοις τὴν φυλακὴν τῆς πόλεως καὶ τῶν ὅλων αὐτῆς πραγμάτων, καθάπερ εἰώθεσαν· καὶ γὰρ τούτῳ τῷ δόγματι προσεγράφη τὸ διὰ φροντίδος αὐτοὺς σχεῖν ὥστε μηδεμίαν ἀποτριβὴν τῷ δημοσίῳ συμβῆναι "and they voted further both the protection of the city and all of its affairs to the consuls, as they were accustomed [to do]; for it was written in addition in

---

[1] The most recent detailed discussion is Lintott (1999) 89–93, which is largely a restatement of his discussion in Lintott (1968) 149–173. Oakley, *Livy* 1. 554 provides a very good collection of references to the major discussions of the subject up to when his work was published.

[2] For the phrase *senatus consultum ultimum*, see Caes. *BC* 1. 5. 3.

[3] This was the formula preferred by Plaumann, noted by Lintott (1999) 90 n. 5. It is also adopted by H. Last, see *CAH¹* 9. 84–89 and Last (1943) 93–97.

this decree that they should have care that no harm was suffered by the state." Dio, thankfully, was far more attentive than Appian, who does not even mention that a decree of the senate was passed.[4] It is only from the specific wording that Dio uses, which is almost an exact translation of how the decree is referred to by Latin authors, that we can even guess that he is referring to an *SC ultimum*. Those same Latin authors, other than Caesar, who were not likely intending to give the decree that specific name, also do not have any shorter name for it, always referencing it by quoting what was obviously its opening advisory statements to the magistrate who had it passed. Without any other candidates for an official designation for the decree coming forward and gaining broad support, the label derived from Caesar's characterization of the resolution seems to have stuck.

So, what exactly was it? In its own words, it was a decree in which the senate exhorted the magistrates – generally the consuls as chief magistrates of the state – to defend the *res publica* and take whatever measures they thought necessary to see that the state did not suffer any harm. To cite one specific example, here is Caesar's description of the *SC ultimum* that was passed against him: *dent operam consules, praetores, tribuni plebis quique pro consulibus sint ad urbem, ne quid res publica detrimenti capiat* "[the senate advised] the consuls, praetors, tribunes of the plebs and those who held *imperium pro consule* in the environs of Rome that they should make it their business that the state not take any harm."[5] This reflected in many ways the later, fully developed, version. From Cicero, attempting to rally the senate against the threat that he saw from Catiline in 63, we have a view of the original version, as he told the senate: *decrevit quondam senatus uti L. Opimius consul videret ne quid res publica detrimenti caperet* "The senate once decreed that L. Opimius the consul ought to see to it that the state not take any harm."[6] Much later in 43, Cicero refers to Opimius again by citing what would seem to be the actual wording of the *relatio*[7] put forward by Opimius and voted upon by the senate in 121: *Quod L. Opimius consul verba fecit de re publica, de ea re ita censuerunt uti L. Opimius consul rem publicam defenderet* "In regard to what L. Opimius the consul said concerning the state, concerning this matter thus [the senate] resolved: that L. Opimius the consul should defend the state."[8] In the earliest version, we should note that only the consul,

---

[4] *BC* 2. 3. 8–6. 22. In all, Appian is not a very good historian, as he does not even get Catiline's praenomen correct, calling him Gaius instead of Lucius: see *BC* 2. 2. 4.

[5] Caes. *BC* 1. 5. 3.

[6] Cic. *Catil.* 1. 4.

[7] The motion put forward by the presiding magistrate to the senate for a vote.

[8] Cic. *Phil.* 8. 14.

presumably the one who presided over the senate session where the decree was passed, is mentioned as the one charged with defending the state.

From these notices, however, we can piece together what was the basic wording of the decree and what were the root concerns that it addressed. A presiding magistrate presents the senate with information that the state is in imminent danger, and the senate votes to advise the magistrate to defend the state and take whatever measures they think necessary to see that the state is not harmed. The later development of including other magistrates and even tribunes of the plebs (an irony, considering that the first two passages of the decree were intended to support action *against* particular tribunes of the plebs) arose from the different circumstances in later instances that the decree was meant to address.

If we can trust his view (which one should take *cum grano salis*), this decree was, so Caesar tells us, only passed as a last resort (thus, why he called it *ultimum*), when the city of Rome itself was already practically in flames and there was despair over the safety of everyone in the state.[9] Cicero, in the passages previously noted from *Catil.* 1. 4 and *Phil.* 8. 14–15 cites several earlier occasions when it was used: during the uproars caused by Gaius Gracchus, Saturninus, and Catiline. These were obviously the precedents that he thought merited mention in trying to have the decree passed. The decree, however, was passed on more occasions than Cicero sees fit to mention and would be used again with increasing frequency, if little effect, at the end of the Republic. Perhaps it would be useful to list here all of the historical instances of the passage of the decree, along with the "threat" that was seen as making it necessary for extraordinary measures to be undertaken by the magistrate(s) in office: Gaius Gracchus (121), Saturninus (100), [Sulla (83)],[10] M. Lepidus *cos.* 78 (77), Catiline (63),[11] the Clodian rioters (52), Caesar (49), Dolabella and Trebellius (47), Antony (43) and Octavian (43).[12]

Before proceeding further, we may ask the important question whether this decree was a true way of declaring a "state of emergency" or not. For during true states of emergency, such as a *tumultus* or a *iustitium*, we know that the enforcement of the regular statute law was to some degree curtailed for a limited time period, or at the very least normal legal procedures or privileges were not honored. During a *tumultus*, men who

---

[9] Caes. BC 1. 5. 3 *quo nisi paene in ipso urbis incendio atque in desperatione omnium salutis ... numquam ante discessum est.*

[10] This instance is problematic in two respects, which we will discuss in detail.

[11] And if we accept the lone notice from Dio 37. 43. 3, it was passed again in January of 62.

[12] This list is mainly taken from Oakley, *Livy* 1. 554, but he missed the final usage of the decree, against Octavian in the summer of 43. We will discuss this event later.

normally were exempt from being drafted into the army were not allowed to remove themselves from the levy. When a *iustitium* is proclaimed, the law courts are closed and even private business transactions appeared to be forbidden. What, however, changed following the passage of an *SC ultimum*? Were there any laws, any customs that had the same force as law, which the *SC ultimum* could render temporarily unenforceable?

The main theories fall into several camps.[13] I will give only a very brief overview, as more detailed discussions with full citations of the previous literature have already been mentioned. The early theory of Mommsen was that in a grave crisis, the notion of "self-help" overrode the need to follow the normal law. In such conditions, the passage of the "last" decree was relatively superfluous because necessity trumped the niceties of law. Regardless of whether such a concept of "self-help" was important or not in Roman minds,[14] we are concerned with whether the decree had any legal consequences. In this respect, Mommsen would hold that it would not because in form, a *senatus consultum* was only a recommendation to a magistrate, which could only be given effect by that magistrate and did not have any power of its own.[15]

Although not holding with Mommsen's views, the next group, represented by Hugh Last and G. Plaumann, hold that the decree was without any binding force of its own, but relied on the magistrates' own discretion to determine what course of action to follow. While referring back to his discussion in *CAH¹* IX in a later book review, Last states that the *SC ultimum* was:

> in effect an intimation to the magistrates of the Senate's opinion that a situation might shortly arise in which the public interest would require them to ignore some of the legal limitations on the use of their *imperium*, and to act in accordance with the maxim expressed by Cicero in the words 'salus populi suprema lex esto' (*de legg.* iii, 8).[16]

However, that "intimation" did not in any way actually remove the constraints of the law from the magistrate. Plaumann lays greater stress on the decree as providing the magistrate(s) who wished to resort to unusual measures with the senate's support and authority in the actions that he

---

[13] Lintott (1999) 89–93 provides a useful summarizing of earlier positions, but he seems hesitant on firmly adopting one. Lintott (1968) 149–173 is actually more detailed and informative even though it is thirty years older.

[14] Lintott (1999) 90 and n. 10 would argue that the concept was accepted by the Romans under the Republic, although he does not go so far as to state that this supports Mommsen's position.

[15] Mommsen *St.R.* 3. 2. 1025f., followed by Lintott (1999) 90 and n. 7.

[16] Last (1943) 94.

was about to take. Both men felt that the decree was there to support the magistrate in taking measures that went beyond the normal law.

Finally, there is a third camp in which two differing versions of a doctrine of "senatorial supremacy" have been put forward. First was that of von Lübtow, who held that the senate had a latent *imperium* that could be transferred to the consuls in an emergency. As Lintott notes, this view runs contrary to all of the evidence that we have about the nature of *imperium*, and finds no support among modern scholars.[17] Later, T. N. Mitchell advocated that the senate formed some sort of supreme deliberative body that the magistrates and people were bound in some way to support.[18] Basing himself upon Cicero's writings related to his defense of Rabirius and his suppression of Catiline, Mitchell thinks that "the Senate was recognized to have a certain power of initiative in dangerous crises."[19] He asserts that "Cicero held that the Senate had the power to decide when the public safety demanded the suspension of normal procedures in dealing with dangerous citizens"[20] and further proposes that "Cicero held that the *senatus consultum ultimum* was an extraordinary machinery of government whereby, in dangerous internal crises, sovereign power in the state was temporarily assumed by the Senate."[21] Such assertions are rather extreme and have not found any support in later scholarship, and with good reason. Such a position, that the senate had actual sovereignty of any sort, is frankly unsustainable.

So, what status did the decree have in terms of law? Most scholars, whatever their position, would agree that unlike the *tumultus* declaration or *iustitium* edict, the *SC ultimum* did not and could not stop the normal legal process from functioning. The clearest proof of that comes from Cicero and his experience after making use of the decree. For the passage of the *SC ultimum* in response to the threat created by Catiline and his associates in 63 did not render Cicero immune from future prosecution for the subsequent actions he took as consul to respond to the crisis. Cicero would face an immediate attempt to bring him to account right after his consulship, as the tribune of the plebs Metellus Nepos publicly denounced Cicero for killing Roman citizens without the consent of the Roman people, but on this occasion, the senate stepped in to save him by passing an amnesty. Whatever the status was of the amnesty passed

[17] Lintott (1999) 92.
[18] Mitchell (1971) 47–61.
[19] Mitchell (1971) 48.
[20] Mitchell (1971) 53.
[21] Mitchell (1971) 55.

in 62, it apparently had no deterrent effect on the next man who tried to prosecute Cicero for his actions in his consulship, P. Clodius Pulcher, who successfully had Cicero exiled. From the outcome of this attempt, it is clear that the *SC ultimum* conferred no permanent legal immunity by itself upon a magistrate who went beyond the normal law in order to suppress a supposed or even a real threat. We shall discuss the attempts to call Cicero to account in greater detail later in this chapter.

So much for the theories about the nature of the decree. In what manner did it serve as an emergency measure, a means by which to respond to crises? In order to answer this question, we must trace the creation and development of the decree, focusing on its use as a response mechanism to critical situations. There are some false forerunners to these historical occurrences, invented appearances placed far back in Rome's near-mythic past in the annalistic tradition. In 464, according to Livy 3. 4. 9, the *SC ultimum* was passed owing to a dire situation during the Second Aequan War, with a consul trapped by the enemy. Unusually, this situation does not involve an internal enemy, as all historical uses of the senate's "final" decree do. This in itself made Ogilvie suspicious: "It might be expected that such a resolution would have its origins in a military emergency before it was adapted to political circumstances, but if there were any earlier precedents Cicero must have invoked them." Following from this, he concludes: "The present passage is therefore an invention by the post-Gracchan annalists to supply a pedigree for the actions of 121;" Ogilvie even nominates Piso (the annalist L. Calpurnius Piso, *cos.* 133[22]) as the originator of this episode, although Valerius Antias has been put forward more recently.[23] Whoever was the inventor, it is agreed that this incident is surely an anachronism.

Another alleged usage occurred in 384 during the reported sedition of M. Manlius Capitolinus.[24] Whereas its usage in this case would be for suppressing a supposed internal threat, again, there is serious doubt as to its authenticity. Oakley notes Ogilvie's position on Livy 3. 4. 9 as being equally applicable to this incident, but he thinks it is more likely that "the aim was to provide a plausible account of the suppression of a revolution: just as the *s. c. u.* was used in the late Republic, so the annalists tried to help readers by inserting it into their tale of Manlius."[25] Regardless of the

---

[22] For the man and his historical work, see Forsythe (1994).

[23] Ogilvie, *Livy* 399; for Antias as inventor, see Forsythe (2005) 207.

[24] Livy 6. 19. 3.

[25] Oakley, *Livy* 1. 553–554; he even notes a "curious attempt" to defend the tradition – see his note. Concerning this whole episode, Forsythe (1994) 302 would follow the line of Ogilvie that the insertion of the *SC ultimum* here was mainly meant to serve "a later political agenda," that of justifying the senate's use of the decree in the late Republic.

explanation, we should put no faith in the historical veracity of these two early appearances of the SC *ultimum*.

The First "Last" Decree of the Senate

Let us therefore turn our attention to the first real occasion on which a decree ordering the consul to defend the state and see that it took no harm was passed and acted upon. This is, of course, when Rome was in serious ferment owing to the actions of Gaius Sempronius Gracchus during his tribunate. As a great deal of scholarship has already been devoted to this study of this important figure in Rome's history, there is no need to recount his political program or aims here in any detail.[26] Let us move swiftly to the crisis that marked his final days. Our main informant is Plutarch, who wrote a biography of the two Gracchi brothers, supplemented by Appian and notices elsewhere.[27]

The actual crisis created by Gaius Gracchus only comprises the end of his "career." The entire period leading up to that point, the two terms as tribune he served and the legislation he passed can be considered, in some ways, the long, slow build-up to that final crisis. The situation started to become more ripe for the outbreak of a crisis when L. Opimius was elected consul for 121, largely with the intent of revoking the laws that had been passed by Gaius (Plut. *C. Gracchus* 34. 1).[28] He also worked with a group of tribunes to start undoing Gracchus's legislative work, intending to provoke Gaius into a violent reaction.[29] While trying to bear with it at first, Gaius was convinced by his friends, especially M. Fulvius Flaccus (*cos.* 125), to contest matters (*C. Gracchus* 34. 1).

---

[26] Stockton (1979) provides a comprehensive introduction to the main themes and issues with reference to discussions up to 1979. More recent examinations both of the Gracchi and the issues involved can be found in Thommen (1989) and Perelli (1993). Currently, there is some debate about how the death of the Gaius Gracchus is portrayed, whether it is influenced by dramatic considerations that might interfere with the historical truth involved or not; see Wiseman (1998); Beness and Hillard (2001); Keaveney (2003).

[27] For a complete list of sources and cursory references, see Broughton, *MRR* 1. 513–514, 517–518, 520. Sadly, Diodorus and Dio only exist in "patchy excerpts," Stockton (1979) 1.

[28] Stockton (1979) 115–161 has a quite comprehensive account of Gaius's legislative program.

[29] This is the interpretation of Stockton (1979) 195 of Plut. *C. Gracchus* 13. 1, which I am inclined to support. Plutarch's Greek is much more euphemistic: ὡς ἂν αἰτίαν ὀργῆς παρασχὼν ἀναιρεθείη "so that he (Gracchus), furnishing a reason for anger [against himself] might be removed." Perrin's Loeb "that he might furnish ground for resentment, and so be got rid of" captures the sense fairly well. Note that there is no explicit mention of Opimius desiring a violent reaction, but it is not hard to imagine that provoking the Gracchans to violence, in order to justify using violence against them, was the goal of his maneuvers.

In this case, the trigger for the crisis was the fractious legislative meeting on the capitol where the tribune Minucius Rufus[30] attempted to repeal Gracchus's law authorizing a colony on the site of old Carthage in North Africa, with encouragement from Opimius (*C. Gracchus* 34. 1; cf. Appian *BC* 1. 24. 106). Although violence was not unexpected by both sides, matters got out of hand as Q. Antullius, one of the consul's attendants, was killed by Gracchus's supporters. There are two versions of this event. In Plutarch's account (*C. Gracchus* 34. 3–5), Opimius and his adherents had intended to annul the laws of Gaius Gracchus that day and had occupied part of the capitolium, as had Gracchus and a number of his supporters. After the consul had offered sacrifice, Antullius apparently insulted the supporters of Gracchus, telling them to clear the way for him ("Δότε τόπον ἀγαθοῖς, κακοὶ πολῖται" "give way to good men, o base citizens" *C. Gracchus* 34. 4) and perhaps making an obscene gesture with his arm. A group of Gracchus's supporters killed Antullius on the spot with giant writing styluses. The act created confusion among the crowd, with opposite reactions from the leaders of the two factions. Gracchus was grieved by it (ἤχθετο), as it furnished cause for Opimius to lay charges against them all, whereas Opimius himself was elated (ἐπῆρτο), having gotten what he wanted (*C. Gracchus* 34. 5).

According to Appian, the senate summoned a voting assembly to repeal the law on the African colony, based on an alleged omen that called for the colony to be reconsidered on religious grounds (*BC* 1. 24. 105).[31] Gracchus and Fulvius then claimed that the senate was lying about the wolves and went to the capitolium, where the assembly was being held to repeal the law, with their supporters armed with daggers (*BC* 1. 24. 106). Fulvius then began to address the crowd, but Gracchus turned aside and walked into a portico (στοά), and here it was that Antullius ('Αντύλλος in Appian) – identified as a common plebeian, not an attendant of the consul Opimius – saw him while he was engaging in a sacrifice (*BC* 1. 25. 107–109). Antullius then approached Gracchus and placed his hand on Gracchus, either because he suspected something or because he wished to speak to him, and begged him to spare his country (*BC* 1. 25. 109). Gracchus was apparently startled by Antullius and gave him a sharp look (ἐνέβλεψεν αὐτῷ δριμύ *BC* 1. 25. 110). One of Gracchus's supporters then took his leader's reaction, even though no signal had been given, as a sign that something should be done; he rushed forward and stabbed Antullius

---

[30] For full sources on him, see *MRR* 1. 521.

[31] It was reported that wolves had torn out and scattered the boundary makers placed by Gracchus and Fulvius, which was taken as a bad omen.

with his concealed dagger, which led to the confusion and dispersal of the crowd outside the temple (*BC* 1. 25. 110–111). Gracchus tried to explain what happened to the crowd, but no one listened (*BC* 1. 25. 111–112).

The circumstances may be slightly different in the two accounts, but it does not make any significant difference in terms of the crisis, for a crisis had now come into existence. The fact is that Antullius was killed by Gracchan supporters during the assembly being held to repeal the law that authorized the colony in Africa. Whether he was killed by daggers or extra large styluses does not change the fact of his demise at the hands of followers of Gaius Gracchus. If Opimius was looking for a reason to work up anger against Gracchus, he had found the perfect one.

If we continue to follow Appian's account, Gracchus and Fulvius returned to their homes while Opimius ordered an armed force to gather on the capitol at dawn, as well as sending heralds to announce a meeting of the senate, taking his place in the Temple of Castor and Pollux (*BC* 1. 25. 112–113).[32] The next day, the senate summoned Gracchus and Fulvius to come and defend themselves; instead, they decided to seize control of the Aventine, intending to hold it with an armed force to pressure the senate into coming to terms with them, offering freedom to the slaves, and sending Fulvius's son Q. Fulvius Flaccus to negotiate with the senate (*BC* 1. 26. 114–115). The senate ordered the Gracchans to lay down their arms and for Gracchus and Fulvius to come to the meeting and tell them what they wanted or else send no more messengers (*BC* 1. 26. 115). When Quintus was sent again, Opimius had him seized, saying he had been warned and was no longer an ambassador and sent his armed force against the Gracchans (*BC* 1. 26. 116). There followed, of course, a rout. Gracchus fled and committed suicide, whereas Flaccus was betrayed after trying to hide in a workshop (*BC* 1. 26. 117–118). Their heads were given to Opimius, who offered those who brought them the heads' weight in gold (*BC* 1. 26. 119). Others were imprisoned and executed (*BC* 1. 26. 119).

Appian's account seems detailed, but it is not in certain respects, as we will see later. It is completely lacking, especially in one particular area: where is the record of the *SC ultimum* being passed? You will not find it in Appian. For that, we must turn to the account of Plutarch.

Going back to the day of the riotous assembly, it was dismissed on account of rain, so Plutarch tells us (*C. Gracchus* 35. 1). Opimius called the senate to meet early the next morning, while others placed the body

---

[32] The one in the forum, not the one near the Circus Flaminius. Appian himself specifies ἐν μέσῳ πάντων.

of Antullius on a bier, uncovered, and had it paraded past the senate house[33] wailing and lamenting (*C. Gracchus* 35. 1). Opimius pretended to be surprised by this (he, however, had arranged it beforehand), and the senators then went out into the Forum to behold the spectacle. The senators now began to complain angrily that Antullius's death was a terrible and great misfortune (ἐσχετλίαζον ὡς ἐπὶ δεινῷ καὶ μεγάλῳ πάθει), although the majority of the people gathered in the area were not impressed, recalling the harsh treatment that Tiberius Gracchus had earlier received from the oligarchs (called specifically that by the many people gathered there as Plutarch records it), while Antullius was mourned over by the senate, the goal being to overthrow the last champion of the people (*C. Gracchus* 35. 1–2). After this little dog and pony show, we get to the important point: the senate then reconvened inside the senate house ἐψηφίσαντο καὶ προσέ-ταξαν Ὀπιμίῳ τῷ ὑπάτῳ σώζειν τὴν πόλιν ὅπως δύναιτο, καὶ καταλύειν τοὺς τυράννους "and then voted and enjoined upon Opimius the consul to save the city however he might be able to and to put down the tyrants" (*C. Gracchus* 35. 3).

Here we have the *SC ultimum* quite clearly, including the injunction on the consul to defend the state.[34] For the denouement, let us continue with Plutarch's superior version of events. After the passage of the decree, Opimius ordered the senators and the equestrian order to assemble with armed retainers the next morning. Fulvius made counter preparations, but Gaius Gracchus was despondent (*C. Gracchus* 35. 4). Plutarch presents a sharp contrast between those at Fulvius's house, who were drunken and boastful of what they would do on the next day, while those with Gracchus were anxious and watchful (*C. Gracchus* 35. 5–6). Fulvius and his followers armed themselves with the weapons and armor stored in his house as trophies from his victory over the Gauls while consul and then seized a position on the Aventine Hill near the Temple of Diana, a place with long-known associations with the plebeians and their fights

---

[33] Here, a minor, but interesting, divergence from Appian, who seems to indicate that the senate meeting took place at the Temple of Castor, on the south end of the forum, whereas the Curia Hostilia stood on the northern end. For the locations, see Haselberger et al. (2002) 83–84 (Castor) and 123 ("Felicitas," site of the old senate house). Cf. Richardson (1992) 74–75 (Castor) and 102–103 (Curia Hostilia).

[34] Livy *Per.* 61 records that Opimius called the people to arms and put down Gracchus *ex senatus consulto* but does not give any further details. It comes as no surprise that we do not get a direct reference to the *SC ultimum*, as the epitomator only once mentions it explicitly, in *Per.* 109, where the passage of the decree against Julius Caesar is recorded. We cannot say at all whether this accurately represents the number of times Livy made explicit reference to the decree or not.

against the "nobility"[35] (*C. Gracchus* 36. 1). Gracchus, however, went forth dressed in his toga, armed with only a dagger. His wife Licinia tried to stop him, making an impassioned speech pointing to the fate his brother Tiberius suffered, but Gaius did not stay home that day, leaving Licinia in tears until she was taken to her brother Crassus's house (*C. Gracchus* 36. 2–5).

We may quickly summarize what happened that day. Gaius Gracchus prevailed upon Fulvius to talk instead of fight, so they sent Fulvius's younger son to speak on their behalf (*C. Gracchus* 37. 1). A majority of the senate was not opposed to the peace feelers sent out, but Opimius demanded that they come in person and surrender themselves for trial. The younger Flaccus was to come back on those terms or not come back at all (*C. Gracchus* 37. 2). Gracchus was willing to come to the senate meeting to plead his case, but no one else among his supporters agreed with the idea, so the younger Flaccus was sent again (*C. Gracchus* 37. 3). Opimius, however, was σπεύδων μάχην συνάψαι "eager to join battle," so he placed the younger Fulvius in custody and took the offensive with many heavily armed men and a body of Cretan archers (*C. Gracchus* 37. 4). The Gracchans were easily thrown in confusion and routed, especially as Opimius had that unit of Cretan archers, whose volleys were instrumental in dislodging the Gracchans and Fulvians from their positions on the Aventine (*C. Gracchus* 37. 4). Fulvius and his elder son hid in a bath, where they were found and slain (*C. Gracchus* 37. 5). Gracchus had not taken part in the battle, withdrawing into the Temple of Diana, where he contemplated suicide but was stopped by two of his closest supporters, Pomponius and Licinius (*C. Gracchus* 37. 5–6). Opimius did not rely solely on brute force, as he also got many of Gracchus's common supporters to change sides by proclaiming immunity to those who did so (*C. Gracchus* 37. 7).

Gracchus now fled across the Tiber on the wooden bridge; there, his two friends (probably the Pomponius and Licinius mentioned by Plutarch before) held off his pursuers until they were both killed (*C. Gracchus* 38. 1). Gracchus himself now had but a single servant as his companion, named Philocrates, and the two of them continued to flee, but their pursuers were gaining (*C. Gracchus* 38. 2). The pair managed at last to hide in a sacred grove dedicated to the Furies, where Philocrates killed Gracchus, and then slew himself over his master's body. An alternate version is that both were caught alive, but the slave shielded Gracchus and had to be killed before their pursuers could get to Gracchus (*C. Gracchus* 38. 3). There followed

---

[35] See Stockton (1979) 196–197; Richardson (1992) 47.

the beheading and barbaric reward offered by Opimius (*C. Gracchus* 38. 4–5).

The aftermath was horrific, as upwards of 3,000 Gracchan partisans had been killed, their bodies – along with Gracchus's and Flaccus's – thrown into the Tiber (*C. Gracchus* 38. 6). Plutarch may have included in this number people whom Opimius arrested and killed after the slaughter, as related by Appian (*BC* 1. 26. 119).[36] Even the women-folk – especially Licinia, the widow of Gaius Gracchus – were financially punished (*C. Gracchus* 38. 6).[37] And as Plutarch notes "most cruel of all," the younger son of Fulvius (named Quintus by Appian), who had taken no part in the fighting, was executed by Opimius (*C. Gracchus* 38. 7; cf. Appian *BC* 1. 26. 120). After these events, as a final insult to the Gracchans, the senate entrusted the construction (refurbishing) of a temple of Concord to Opimius, which led to a notable piece of graffiti written underneath the dedicatory inscription: ἔργον ἀπονοίας ναὸν ὁμονοίας ποιεῖ "a deed of discord makes a temple of Concord" (*C. Gracchus* 38. 8–9; cf. Appian *BC* 1. 26. 120).

In this first instance of the passage of the *SC ultimum*, one thing is clear: the prime mover behind the state's reaction to the actions of Gaius Gracchus, M. Fulvius Flaccus, and their supporters was L. Opimius. This makes perfect sense, of course, because he was the senior magistrate in Rome (his colleague Q. Fabius Maximus was campaigning in the north).[38] We can then, with some assurance, point to Opimius as the author of this specific decree. Opimius would also be the man charged with breaking the law in relation to the suppression of the Gracchans. In the next year (120), P.[39] Decius, a tribune of the plebs, brought an accusation against Opimius for having thrown men into prison without trial and for having killed Gracchus against statute law.[40] From Cicero's mentioning of the senate decree in relation to Opimius's actions, we can assume that his defense rested on the facts that he had killed Gracchus in order to "save" the state from peril and in accordance with a decree of the senate. All of

---

[36] See Stockton (1979) 198.

[37] Flower (2006) 69, 76–81 discusses the effects on the public memory of Gaius Gracchus and sanctions against his family after his death.

[38] For the sources on Fabius, see *MRR* 1. 520–521.

[39] Livy *Per.* 61 has Q, but Cicero and the much later *de viris illustribus* both have P. See *MRR* 1. 525 n. 4.

[40] Livy *Per.* 61 records the charge as *quod indemnatos cives in carcarem coniecisset* whereas Cic. *De Or.* 134, who phrases it as a question for a rhetorical exercise, says *qui civem ex senatus consulto patriae conservandae causa interemerit, cum id per leges non liceret*. It seems reasonable to assume that Decius made as many charges as he thought might have any chance of success, and both of these actions taken by Opimius were against statute law.

this, however, was a matter of contention as far as Decius was concerned, as Cicero sums up his position on that as *at id ipsum negat contra leges licuisse Decius* "but Decius says that that very thing is not permitted, (as it is) in violation of statute law" (Cic. *De Or.* 2. 132). For the moment, however, the legality of the actions taken by Opimius, if not the ability of the senate's decree to shield a magistrate from prosecution afterward, was validated by Opimius's acquittal.[41]

It is important to note that it was only in retrospect, after the trial and acquittal had occurred, that a viable procedure that could be used as a later precedent was established for handling internal political controversies. For Opimius had been engaging in innovation, something the Romans generally did not approve of, as they preferred in all things for matters to be handled *more maiorum*. A precedent, however, is only recognized as being one when a similar situation arises later in time and the people of that time resort to the same measure. The occasion for making use of this precedent would come a little over twenty years later, when again there was an armed insurrection in the city of Rome itself, this time led by a tribune of the plebs and a praetor.

THE PRECEDENT IS FOLLOWED: THE SECOND USE

The figure of L. Appuleius Saturninus has been recently re-evaluated along with his close collaborator, C. Servilius Glaucia.[42] His extensive legislative program does not concern us directly and has been treated in detail by other scholars.[43] What is important is the clash that occurred in 100, when for the second time the "last" decree of the senate was passed. Although there are problems with his account,[44] our main source is Appian, so we shall draw mainly on him. Despite the drawbacks, Appian may in fact offer a better account than some other testimonia. For instance, he may be correct in separating the death of L. Equitius, the would-be son of Gracchus, from the death of Saturninus and his main adherents.[45] Regardless of the problems in chronology, a basic outline of the crisis can be constructed.

Whereas a clash between the majority of senators and Saturninus was long in coming, the actual crisis that led to the suppression of Saturninus

---

[41] Livy *Per.* 61.
[42] Evans (2003). Not everyone has been convinced by the new view. See Tatum (2004).
[43] References to earlier work can be found in Evans (2003).
[44] See Badian (1984).
[45] For discussion, see Beness and Hillard (1990).

and his supporters began with the elections for the consulship of 99.[46] Saturninus's close ally, C. Servilius Glaucia, who was praetor in 100, was illegally seeking to become consul the next year. Another one of the candidates was C. Memmius, once a "troublesome" tribune himself in 111 (where he led the attack on the foot-dragging commanders in the early years of the Jugurthine War) but now seen as a threat by Saturninus and his supporters to the success of Glaucia. The electoral assembly had already elected M. Antonius to one place when Glaucia and Saturninus sent men, while the election was still in progress, to beat Memmius to death with clubs (*BC* 1. 32. 142). The assembly was broken up amid uproar; the next day, the people gathered to kill Saturninus, but he, along with his confederates Glaucia, the quaestor C. Saufeius, and all of their supporters, seized the capitol (*BC* 1. 32. 143).

There has been debate about the exact date of this insurrection and its crushing. The date accepted by many scholars is December 10. The date has been questioned by Emilio Gabba in his commentary on Appian, and other scholars have accepted his challenge to this late date, based on a series of arguments.[47] Whereas Seager, as noted by Broughton, has refuted many of the points raised by Gabba (who is followed by Badian and Gruen), I find myself drawn to the detail that caught Broughton's eye that Seager cannot explain away: the matter of Saturninus's supporter, C. Saufeius the quaestor. If the date is December 10 and the consular elections had not been completed, it is more than likely the praetorian, curule aedilician, and quaestorian elections had not even been held yet. Nevertheless, the quaestors of 100, if Saufeius was among them, left office on December 5. Therefore, it is quite possible the date is before December 5.[48]

Following Memmius's murder and the seizure of the capitol, a clear and present danger to the Roman government was likely perceived by not just the dominant element within the senate but also the consul C. Marius. The senate was roused to anger and called on the consul C. Marius to put down the tribune. According to Appian, the senate voted for the arrest of the rioters (*BC* 1. 32. 144: καὶ αὐτοὺς τῆς βουλῆς ἀναιρεθῆναι ψηφισαμένης). According to Cicero (*Rab. perd.* 20), the senate decided that the time had come for even stronger measures: *Fit senatus consultum ut C. Marius L. Valerius consules adhiberent tribunos pl. et praetores, quos eis videretur,*

---

[46] The sources for the riot at the consular *comitia* are conveniently collected in Greenidge and Clay, *Sources*[2] 108–109.

[47] See *MRR* 3. 21–22 [however, there is an error in the reference to Seager, it should be *CR* 17, 1967 not *CR* 18, 1968] and Badian (1984) 101–106 for full arguments and the references to both sides in the debate.

[48] *MRR* 3. 22.

operamque darent ut imperium populi Romani maiestasque conservaretur.
Loosely: "A decree of the senate was passed that advised Gaius Marius
and Lucius Valerius the consuls to employ the tribunes of the plebs and
praetors, those whom seemed good to them, and give their attention so
that the power and majesty of the Roman People be preserved." Although
the wording here is a little different from the norm, it is taken that this
was equivalent to an emergency decree, the so-called *senatus consultum
ultimum.*[49] Two other Ciceronian works affirm that the *SC ultimum* was
passed at this time.[50] It is much later in date, but the traditional wording
is cited in the anonymous *de viris illustribus.*[51] If the Ciceronian quotation
is correct in its language, it may be a sign that the senate was still finding
its way along the path to institutionalizing the use of the "ultimate"
decree. There were few precedents to draw upon, the situation with Gaius
Gracchus being the most recent, and perhaps it may have taken some
deliberation before deciding to follow the method used in that earlier
episode, where the safety of the city was entrusted to the consuls.

The consul Marius may have hesitated at the beginning, as Appian
reports (*BC* 1. 32. 144), but this was likely owing to the novelty of the
circumstances.[52] Appian is not as forthcoming with details about how the
armed force was raised to put down Saturninus, merely commenting that
Marius armed some people (ὥπλιζέ τινας *BC* 1. 32. 144). It is from Cicero
that we learn some sort of emergency levy was held, as Marius distributed
arms to the people hastily enlisted in the city itself, weapons being taken *ex
aedificiis armamentariisque publicis* "from public buildings and armories"
in response to the senate's decree (*Rab. perd.* 20). There is no mention at
all about any state of emergency, such as a *tumultus* or *iustitium* being
proclaimed. Orosius adds the minor detail that the other consul, Valerius
Flaccus, was sent to hold the Quirinal with a guard (5. 17. 7). A battle of
some sort occurred in the Forum, driving Saturninus and his supporters
to take refuge on the Capitol (Appian *BC* 1. 32. 143; cf. Plut. *Marius* 30;
Florus 2. 4; Orosius 5. 17. 7–8).

---

[49] Badian (1984) 108 and following always refers to it as "the Senate's emergency decree," but
then compares it to 121 explicitly (p. 118) and notes that others (see esp. note 41) take it that
way as well.

[50] *Catil.* 1. 4 states that a decree "similar" to the one Opimius had was passed, whereas *Phil.*
8. 15 has C. *Mario L. Valerio consulibus senatus rem publicam defendendam dedit*, which
accords with what he said immediately before in §14 of that same speech, which seemingly
reproduces the *relatio* made by Opimius in 121.

[51] Auct. *de vir. ill.* 73. 10: *Marius senatusconsulto armatus, quo censeretur, darent operam
consules, ne quid respublica detrimenti caperet,...*

[52] On this point, I am in agreement with Badian (1984) 117–120.

After Saturninus and his supporters were placed in a virtual state of siege on the capitol, Marius decided to cut the water supply to force a surrender. This had an effect, as Appian reported that the quaestor Saufeius ὑπὸ δίψης ἀπολλύμενος "was dying of thirst" (*BC* 1. 32. 144). It may be that the day was rather warm, pointing to a date earlier than December, but the evidence is not assured.[53] At this point, the "rebels" surrendered and were placed under arrest in the senate house by Marius. The senators and their allies then put a full stop to any chance of recurrence by massacring Saturninus and his followers in the senate house, with Glaucia possibly dying separately, and Equitius likely at another time.[54]

For a second time, the "last" decree was passed and acted upon. Its validity would not be challenged at the time, although it would be in future (as already noted) and would be discussed again later.

Unusual Measures for Unusual Times

Thus far, we have seen what could be considered the "exemplary" instances of the passage of the so-called final decree. These two previous examples were referenced by Cicero. There were, however, other occasions upon which we have evidence that the *senatus consultum ultimum* was passed, ones that Cicero conspicuously avoids mentioning; in one case, perhaps it was because in later times the passage would have been considered invalid. In the other, it may be that the situation, a very strange one, did not provide an *exemplum* that he thought would do anything to strengthen the case he was making when he cited precedent.

The first of these two instances where Cicero deliberately takes no heed of the passage of the *SC ultimum* was in 83, when we have a single notice that it was passed by the Marian-Cinnan regime's senate in Rome. As one digs deeper into this occasion, it may be that Cicero had good reason *not* to mention it, for there are two notable issues that merit discussion about the validity of the report. First, one can raise the question of whether this example should be accepted as an "official" passage of the decree. For at the time, the Roman political world was in the midst of civil war. Since the end of 87, the "government" in Rome was under the control of a faction, originally headed by C. Marius (*cos.* I 107, d. 86) and L. Cornelius Cinna (*cos.* I 87, he had himself "elected" consul for the next several years until his

---

53 Auct. *de vir. ill.* 73. 10 mentions *maximo aestu*, but this is an emendation of a clearly faulty manuscript. See Seager (1967) 9–10, who dislikes this suggested reading and proposes another that he thinks makes better sense.

54 See Beness and Hillard (1990) 270–272 for full sources and discussion.

death in 84), but in 83, the leadership had devolved upon others, including Cn. Papirius Carbo (*cos.* I 85) and Q. Sertorius (*pr.* 83) in addition to the consuls C. Norbanus and L. Cornelius Scipio Asiaticus.[55] Broughton's magisterial work, extremely useful as it is, is slightly misleading in one respect. During these years of civil unrest and open civil war, the recording of Sulla as a promagistrate, alongside those who were put in post by the Marian-Cinnan faction, papers over the fact that the two sides did not fully recognize the legitimacy of each other and saw the other side as usurpers who had to be destroyed in order to "save" the Republic. In the eyes of the faction that currently controlled Rome, L. Cornelius Sulla was a dangerous renegade at the head of a powerful army.[56] From Sulla's perspective, the reverse was true.[57]

The members of the faction controlling Rome were hardly models of upright government either. When Cinna and Carbo were gathering resources for the coming war against Sulla during the course of the year 85, Sulla started corresponding with prominent members of the senate, who now wanted to avoid further bloodshed and wished to reconcile the two sides. The senate therefore ordered Cinna and Carbo, who were traveling throughout Italy recruiting soldiers, to stop the levy. The pair pretended to follow the message from the senate, but then proclaimed themselves consuls for the next year (84) and continued to recruit soldiers.[58] Although there certainly was precedent for the immediate reelection of consuls during a period of deep crisis – such as during the Second Punic War and the consecutive consulships of Gaius Marius during the Teutonic-Cimbric menace – in this case, the enemy was not foreign but domestic. And one wonders how the "election" was carried out.

The second questionable matter is the source we have to rely upon. None of the major surviving sources record the passage of the *SC ultimum*. Neither do any of the minor ones. For this notice, we are reliant upon Julius Exuperantius, a late (possibly fourth-century AD) writer who put together a "brief and muddled" epitome that extracted its information

---

[55] For full references on all these men, consult *MRR* 2. Although the younger Marius (*cos.* 82) can be counted as a leader of the group, he did not rise to a visible leadership role until his (illegal) election to the consulship.

[56] He had been voted a public enemy (*hostis*) at Cinna's request, according to App. *BC* 1. 81. 370; cf. *BC* 1. 77. 351. Afterward, his house was destroyed and his family forced to flee. See Flower (2006) 86–87 and 304 nn. 2, 5 with full references to important earlier discussions.

[57] Sulla, after seizing Rome in 88, had Marius, Sulpicius, and their supporters declared *hostes*. It was the first time, in fact, such a declaration had been made; see Appian *BC* 1. 60. 271. See Bauman (1973) and see also previous footnote.

[58] App. *BC* 1. 77. 350–354.

from the lost *Historiae* of Sallust.[59] The short report we get states that during the consulship of Norbanus and Scipio, it was Sertorius who had the decree passed that "the state should not receive any harm" in response to the return of Sulla from Asia, which threatened great suffering for everyone as the leaders of the two sides would inevitably clash (Iul. Exup. 43). This account seems to raise more questions than it answers. Although Sertorius, as praetor during the year 83,[60] could convoke the senate, why would he be the one to do it and not one of the consuls? Then there is the potential problem created if we follow an interesting suggestion put forward by Konrad that Sertorius's praetorship might have been earlier than 83, if he ever held the post to begin with.[61] If Sertorius was in fact *pro consule*, not a praetor in his year of office, then the matter becomes even stranger. For we are then asked to imagine that Sertorius, a promagistrate temporarily carrying out government business in Italy, called the senate into session outside of the *pomerium* and then asked them to pass the *SC ultimum*, calling upon the consuls to take measures to defend the state.

Still, we cannot rule out entirely the possibility that the decree was passed around this time. Some admittedly weak support for it might be found in the account of Appian. After Sulla landed in Italy, the historian reports that the people in the city were terrified, remembering what it had been like the last time Sulla entered Rome with an army (*BC* 1. 81. 371). Therefore, "thinking that there was nothing for them in the middle, either victory or utter destruction, they united with the consuls against Sulla, but with fear" καὶ οὐδὲν σφίσι νίκης ἢ πανωλεθρίας μέσον εἶναι νομίζοντες συνίσταντο τοῖς ὑπάτοις ἐπὶ τὸν Σύλλαν μετὰ δέους (*BC* 1. 81. 372). The mention of the people in the city (certainly referring to the upper classes) joining with the consuls can be interpreted to refer to the passage of a *SC ultimum*, but this is only an interpretation, not a definitive statement of confirmation. The state of the sources can bring us only so far.

---

[59] I have cited here Konrad's characterization of Exuperantius; Konrad (1994) xliv.

[60] As he is styled in *MRR* 2. 63, but this is not certain.

[61] Konrad notes that it is only "nearly" certain that Sertorius held the praetorship. It is possible that he was sent to Spain in 83 as a *privatus cum imperio*; that is, he was made *pro consule* by act of the Assembly, not through prorogation after holding office. Konrad thinks this unlikely, but then moves onto his main argument that the sources make it more likely that Sertorius was praetor before 83, as early as 85, and then was designated to command Nearer Spain afterward. He remained in Italy for a long time because of the coming crisis brought on by the expected return of Sulla. See Konrad (1994) 74–76. Brennan (2000) 379 terms him "*pr.* by 83," and of his actions in Italy that year notes "almost certainly conducted all those activities in Italy in 83 with consular *imperium*." On p. 503, he notes Konrad's suggestion and says that the latter makes "a reasonable case," although he believes the evidence might rule out an early (certainly 86 is out, possibly 85) date.

Whereas the use of the *SC ultimum* by the Marian-Cinnan regime to shore up support against Sulla and his adherents is one that Cicero would likely wish to pass over without notice (because Sulla won and his legacy still had effect in Cicero's own day), the next time the measure was passed was one that Cicero likely approved of but perhaps decided not to mention as it involved a highly anomalous situation (not one he would probably wish to cite as precedent). Later in 43, he would surely be at pains *not* to refer to this event, as it involved the father of an important man he was trying desperately to keep on the side of the Republic.[62] This was the revolt of M. Aemilius Lepidus, the consul of 78.[63] Interestingly, Lepidus owed his election as consul to the support of Pompey, so Plutarch tells us (*Sulla* 34. 4–5; *Pomp.* 15), but he was not enamored of the new order imposed by Sulla. Among his first acts was to try to prevent Sulla from receiving public burial honors, although Pompey made sure that it happened (*Sulla* 38. 1; *Pomp.* 15. 3). In Plutarch's rather brief account (*Pomp.* 16), Lepidus immediately takes to arms and because his co-consul, Q. Lutatius Catulus, was not his equal in military affairs, the Sullan faithful turned to Pompey, who was given the command against Lepidus (16. 2). He spent a long time laying siege to Mutina, which was being held by Lepidus's deputy M. Brutus, who had been sent by Lepidus with an army to hold Cisalpine Gaul (16. 3). When Lepidus then marched on Rome to demand a second consulship, it was the arrival of a letter from Pompey announcing the end of the siege (Brutus had apparently surrendered himself to Pompey) that ended the fear of those in Rome (16. 4). Plutarch then takes the occasion to digress about this Brutus, the father of the later assassin, before briefly coming back to Lepidus, informing us that Lepidus was driven out of Italy and then died in Sardinia (16. 6). Plutarch's account, of course, gives star billing to Pompey and leaves out many details. For those details, we must turn to Appian, Florus, and some important fragments of Sallust.

Let us first dispose of Florus's account. Lepidus begins by trying to have Sulla's new dispensation rescinded (2. 2), including revoking the Sullan land grants and recalling the survivors and children of those whom Sulla formally had proscribed (2. 3).[64] He then went to Etruria and readied an army against Rome (2. 5). In response, Catulus and Pompey raised

---

[62] This, of course, is M. Aemilius Lepidus (*cos.* 46), who in 43 commanded a sizable army in Gaul. See *Fam.* 10. 27 [SB 369], 10. 34 [SB 396], 10. 34a [SB 400].

[63] For the man and his career, see Criniti (1969).

[64] For a good recent discussion of the proscriptions with references to earlier scholarship, see Flower (2006) 90–96 and 305 n. 13. The only other measure we know of was a grain dole, which passed unopposed. This is preserved only in a fragment of Granius Licinianus (36. 34–35C).

an army and held the Mulvian Bridge and the Janiculum to oppose him (2. 6). Lepidus was driven back and then formally declared a *hostis* by the senate after he had fled back to Etruria; he would eventually go to Sardinia, where he died (2. 7). Although much fuller than Plutarch's account and more balanced (the spotlight does not shine solely on Pompey), we still are left wanting to know more about what exactly happened.

Even though he is not the best historian,[65] we get a slightly different account from Appian that contains many important pieces of information. He notes the enmity between Catulus and Lepidus from the very start, calling them members of opposing groups, Catulus of the Sullani (τῶν Συλλείων) and Lepidus from the "opposite" group (τῶν ἐναντίων). He adds that they hated each other bitterly (*BC* 1. 105. 491). After Sulla's death, Appian also records that Lepidus was among those who tried to prevent Sulla from receiving a public funeral, but Catulus "and the Sullani" prevailed (*BC* 1. 105. 493–494).[66] There follows a detailed description of the elaborate funeral procession and burial (*BC* 1. 105. 494–106. 500). It is in the immediate aftermath of the funeral that Appian places the attempt by Lepidus to repeal the acts of Sulla, although the only specific measure he notes is the attempt to return lands to those whose property was confiscated by Sulla (*BC* 1. 107. 501). The contention between the two sides frightened the senate enough that they made both swear they would not decide the matter by war: ἄμφω μὲν οὖν ἡ βουλὴ δείσασα ὥρκωσε μὴ πολέμῳ διακριθῆναι (*BC* 1. 107. 502).

We then learn that Lepidus was allotted the province of Transalpine Gaul, after which Appian signals that Lepidus was already thinking ahead to future hostilities because he would be able to make war against the Sullani when the year passed without any fear with regard to the oath, which only bound him during his year of office (*BC* 1. 107. 502). Now the senate, being made aware of this, called him back to Rome,[67] but Lepidus returned with an army. When he was prevented from bringing his army into the city, he called his men to arms, and Catulus, inside of Rome, did the same (*BC* 1. 107. 503). A battle was fought not far from the Campus Martius, and Lepidus got the worst of it. Afterward, he left for Sardinia, where he died (*BC* 1. 107. 504).

---

[65] For problems with Appian as a source, see Badian (1984).

[66] Note how there is no mention at all of Pompey here, who figures so prominently in Plutarch's account of the affair.

[67] A fragment from Sallust, *Hist.* 1. 66M *Uti Lepidus et Catulus decretis exercitibus maturrime proficiscerentur*: "That Lepidus and Catulus set out with the armies decreed [to them] most quickly." would seem to support the idea that they had departed for their provinces. There is possibly some further corroboration from Granius Licinianus (36. 38–41C).

As one can see, there are contradictions in the accounts. Florus is wrong when he places Pompey with Catulus during the battle at the Campus Martius, as we know that he was in the north, attempting to overcome Brutus.[68] Although it is otherwise of little help, the three brief sentences in the *Periocha* of the lost ninetieth book of Livy that cover this event assign Lepidus's defeat and expulsion from Italy to Catulus, while Pompey is mentioned only in the context of Brutus's murder in Cisalpine Gaul. Orosius as well references Pompey only in the context of his fight against Brutus (5. 22. 16). There is, of course, one issue of much greater concern for this survey of instances where the *senatus consultum ultimum* was passed. As one can see, there has been no mention at all of the decree in any of the sources noted so far.

We find our evidence for that in a source that sadly does not come to us complete: the fragments of Sallust's *Historiae*. We have already noted that this same source gives us our only indication that a *tumultus* was possibly declared during the course of this situation, which clearly was a crisis, as it threatened violence and bloodshed in the city of Rome itself.[69] So it is from the remains of Sallust again that we discover that the *SC ultimum* was passed, although in very unusual circumstances, thus why Cicero might have also been loath to cite this instance when giving a list of precedents. In a lengthy preserved speech (*Hist.* 1. 77M), L. Marcius Philippus, a leading member of the Sullan group,[70] made a lengthy tirade against Lepidus but, more importantly, ended his speech by proposing that because Lepidus was leading an army against the city, *ut Ap. Claudius interrex cum Q. Catulo pro consule et ceteris quibus imperium est urbi praesidio sint operamque dent ne quid res publica detrimenti capiat* "that Appius Claudius the *interrex*, with Q. Catulus the proconsul and others who hold *imperium* defend the city and see to it that the state takes no harm" (1. 77. 22).

Unlike the first two instances, where it is a consul who is clearly the main mover behind the passage of the so-called final decree, here we have a senior senator proposing that the senate ask an *interrex*, who, it must be remembered, is only a temporary official,[71] in addition to a proconsul and any other officials with *imperium*,[72] to undertake the defense of the

---

[68] Although he may have been right to associate Pompey with Catulus, in that Pompey may have only been legally empowered to command troops as a legate of Catulus. See Brennan (2000) 430, following Criniti.

[69] See Chapter 3.

[70] For a very brief sketch of his career and his ties to Sulla, see McGushin (1992) 132.

[71] On the *interrex*, see see Kunkel (1995) 276–283.

[72] The praetors from 78 who were now *ex magistratu* and had been given provincial assignments would have fallen into this group. See Brennan (2000) 430.

city and the state. Of course, it is probable that the *interrex* is mentioned solely because he was the chief magistrate of the Roman government, even if only for five days, and it is likely that the meeting of the senate was taking place in Rome under his presidency. It would be hard to imagine an *interrex* taking the field with an army, as his term would end too quickly to exercise effective command, even if it were only to guard the city of Rome. Sadly, we only have the speech preserved, not the context of exactly when and where the meeting of the senate took place at which the decree was passed. This was also the first time that others besides the consul(s) who saw to the decree's passage were mentioned in the charge to defend the state.[73] This situation may have had one antecedent: during the Second Punic War, when Hannibal made his sudden march on Rome in 211, owing to the fear and disturbance the report of his approach created in Rome, the senate took the unusual step of granting *imperium* to all previous dictators, consuls, and censors who were in the city. They were to hold *imperium* "until the enemy had withdrawn from the walls" (Livy 26. 10. 7–10). As a matter of practicality, it would be necessary to ask someone other than the *interrex* to be able to take command of an army to defend the city and the government. Nevertheless, one can see how this situation is very different from the first two "canonical" passages of the *SC ultimum* and how Cicero, who himself made use of it as a consul in office, may not have considered this episode to provide a good precedent for later times.

CATILINE

This brings us to the next instance where the "final" decree was passed, one where Cicero would claim it was put to its intended use – naturally he would because he was the consul who called for its passage. We are, of course talking about the Catilinarian Crisis of 63. I will not make any attempt to go through the massive bibliography that has accrued over the years concerning this matter. For the subject of Sallust's monograph devoted to Catiline alone, there is a large and continually growing corpus. In addition to the classic treatments by Büchner, Earl, La Penna, and Syme,[74] there is a useful, recently revised commentary in English by

---

[73] Although Cicero reported that in 100 the consuls Marius and Valerius were to call for aid from those praetors and tribunes of the plebs they saw fit, the charge to defend the state was still entrusted solely to the consuls.

[74] For full citations, and useful commentary on the past several decades of Sallustian scholarship, see Ronald Mellor's foreword (xxxiv–xlvi) to the recent paperback re-publication (2002) of Syme's *Sallust* (1964).

J. T. Ramsey,[75] which also has an updated bibliography to bring it up to the present. Further, Pagán has provided a new examination of Sallust's narrative technique and how he creates continuity in his account of the Catilinarian affair.[76]

Opinions about the severity of this crisis have varied over time. In the Prefatory Note to his 1937 Loeb edition of *In Catilinam I-IV, Pro Murena, Pro Sulla,* and *Pro Flacco,* Louis E. Lord stated: "Six of the seven orations contained in this volume are connected with one of the best known and least significant episodes in Roman history – the conspiracy of Catiline." That is surely a bit harsh, but perhaps it is not as harsh as the extremist position taken by K. H. Waters, who would like to make Cicero his personal piñata, if not for the fact that Mark Anthony had already beaten him to it approximately 2,000 years before.[77] For him, the affair was a "storm in a tea-cup."[78] Much more reasonable diminutions of its importance in history come from other scholars. Zvi Yavetz, in an important article on the question of where Catiline's support came from, notes that it "is possible that the importance of Catiline's conspiracy is over-estimated by some modern historians."[79] Erich Gruen sums it all up best: "It is evident, in retrospect, that the event did not shake the foundations of the state. The government was in no real danger of toppling; the conspiracy, in fact, strengthened awareness of a common interest in order and stability. It is not, however, to be dismissed as a minor and meaningless episode."[80] Granted, in the end, the Catilinarian Crisis was hardly the straw that would break the proverbial camel's back (that would come in 49), but it is still worthy of close inspection if for no other reason than that it is a very well-documented affair[81] and one where we can learn much about how the Roman government dealt with a crisis. Pagán

---

[75] Ramsey (1984), revised 2007.

[76] Pagán (2004) 27–49, esp. 32–49.

[77] Waters (1970) 195 "Not only has its importance been greatly exaggerated; the scale, extent, duration and aims of the conspiracy, perhaps its very existence, have all been vastly over-stated; only in the fertile imagination of Cicero himself could many of the alleged facts have had their origin."

[78] Waters (1970) 195.

[79] Yavetz (1963) 485–499; quote is from p. 497.

[80] Gruen (1974) 431–432.

[81] Excluding casual mentions and highly fragmentary works, we alone have Cicero *In Catilinam* 1–4; *Pro Sulla; Pro Murena;* Sallust *De coniuratione Catilinae;* Livy *Per.* 102, 103; Dio Cassius 37. 24–36, 39–43; Plutarch *Cicero* 10–23; *Caesar* 7. 3–8. 4; *Crassus* 13. 2–4; *Cato min.* 22–24. 2; Suetonius *div. Iul.* 14; Appian *BC* 2. 2–7 [4–25]; Diodorus 40. 5, 5a; Velleius 2. 24–25; Florus 2. 12; and Orosius 6. 6 to draw upon, although as Pagán (2004) 28 notes "from a historiographical standpoint, the Catilinarian conspiracy is unique" because we have one contemporary (Cicero) and one near contemporary (Sallust) source for information.

has provided a very good summary sketch of the conditions that led to the incident.[82] In brief, L. Sergius Catilina, better known as Catiline to English speakers, was from an old patrician family, but one that had become relatively impoverished. This was a serious drawback to any man who wished to ascend to the highest tiers of the Republic's magistracies, as impressing the electorate at each stage required significant financial outlay. In 66, Catiline attempted to run but was rebuffed, as he faced a charge of extortion from his term as governor of Africa the year before. Passing over the so-called first Catilinarian conspiracy,[83] Catiline managed to escape conviction for extortion and was a candidate for the consulship again in 64 (for the year 63), with the other major contenders being C. Antonius and M. Tullius Cicero. Catiline did not succeed as Cicero and Antonius were preferred to him by the voters. Let us now proceed to the event itself, drawing from Cicero and Sallust, with supporting references from later sources. Following the defeat in the year 64 for the consulship of 63, Catiline was reported by Sallust already to have been gathering weapons and money (borrowed, of course) (*Cat.* 24. 2), but Catiline had not yet embarked on any overtly treasonous act, deciding to stand for the consulship again in 63 for the year 62 (*Cat.* 26. 1). Therefore, there may be reason to doubt Sallust's report.[84] Before the election, Cicero had already tried to alert the senate to the "threat" posed by Catiline, but it had fallen on deaf ears (Cic. *Mur.* 51; cf. Dio 37. 29. 3). The trigger to the crisis that arose was Catiline's defeat in the elections for 62, the one where Cicero, as consul presiding at the *comitia*, ostentatiously appeared wearing a breastplate for his own protection (a detail not in Sallust; see Cic. *Mur.* 52; Dio 37. 29. 4; Plut. *Cicero* 14. 5). It was after this second consecutive defeat in the polls that Catiline decided to use violence to achieve his ends (Sall. *Cat.* 26. 5; cf. Dio 37. 30. 1). Sallust reports that Catiline had already sent agents to various points in Italy to serve his cause (*Cat.* 27. 1).

A true crisis did not emerge until firm evidence of Catiline's plotting came to the attention of Cicero, along with even graver news. Not the story of Fulvia, picturesque as it is, but the letters that were brought to Cicero by Crassus and other important men in the state, which purported to reveal that a plot was in motion to massacre leading citizens in Rome (Dio 37. 31. 1; Plut. *Cicero* 15; *Crassus* 13. 3). A meeting of the senate was held the next morning, possibly October 21, and the letters were read

---

[82] See Pagán (2004) 28–30.

[83] Which has engendered a long trail of doubt for over a century. See Pagán (2004) 142 n. 10 for the history of scholars who have expressed deep skepticism and doubt about this event.

[84] See Ramsey (1984) 16.

out.[85] According to Dio, at this point, after the letters had been read καὶ ἐπ'αὐτοῖς δόγμα ἐκυρώθη, ταραχήν τε εἶναι καὶ ζήτησιν τῶν αἰτίων αὐτῆς γενέσθαι "... and concerning these matters, a decree was ratified that a state of *tumultus* was in existence and that there would be a search for the causes of this thing" (37. 31. 1). As noted earlier in the section on *tumultus*, here we have the evidence that a formal *tumultus* was declared, and we can have some confidence in Dio's information as we have confirmation of the state of emergency from a passing remark by Sallust, where he records M. Petreius's dispositions of the army that met Catiline's forces at Pistoria: *Ille cohortes veteranas, quas tumultus*[86] *causa conscripserat*, "He [stationed] the veteran cohorts, which he had conscripted because of the *tumultus*" (Sall. *Cat.* 59. 5). Interestingly, Sallust does not give an explicit notice of when the declaration of a *tumultus* was put into effect.

The sources are all a little jumbled and provide some variations in detail, but around the same time as the letters addressed to Crassus and others, news came in of Manlius's activities in Etruria. Plutarch (who names the informant, Q. Arrius, an ex-praetor–see *Cicero* 15. 3) and Dio place the news from Etruria after the letters were read out. Sallust, however, is deliberately vague about matters, referring only to generic "plots" (*insidiis*), although he is more specific about the threat from the *exercitus Manli* (*Cat.* 29. 1). Those "plots" however, likely refer to the letters and the alleged plan to carry out a massacre in Rome (although one wonders why Sallust chose not to include this particular detail in his narrative). In direct response to these events – in particular, the news from Etruria about Manlius's attempt to raise an armed force – the senate now passed the "last" decree, which according to the sources basically gave Cicero full authority to respond to the crisis as he saw fit (Sall. *Cat.* 28. 4–29. 3; Dio 37. 31. 2; Plut. *Cicero* 15. 3–4). All of this occurred around October 20–22. The one firm date that we have, one that marked a sure, further escalation in the crisis, was the verified report that Manlius had taken up arms at Faesulae on October 27 and reports began to come in of slave insurrections at Capua and in Apulia (Sall. *Cat.* 30. 1–2).

---

[85] For the chronology and exact dates of events, see Ramsey (1984).

[86] Reynolds in his 1991 OCT (following earlier editors) prints the alternate form *tumulti*, an archaic form of the genitive ending in *-i*, which rests solely on the testimony of the third/fourth-century AD grammarian Nonius. The MSS tradition, however, without divergence has *tumultus*, thus leading Ramsey (1984) 231 to note that "perhaps this testimony should be treated with caution." Whatever the proper form, the meaning of the passage is not in dispute and provides testimony for the declaration of a *tumultus* at some point preceding the consul C. Antonius's army taking the field.

In response to this, Sallust records (*Cat.* 30. 3–5) that Cicero and the senate began to make their own countermoves to put down the threat posed by armed insurrections. Proconsuls awaiting triumphs who had armed soldiers under their command were dispatched: Q. Marcius Rex[87] was sent to Faesulae, whereas Q. Caecilius Metellus Creticus[88] was sent to Apulia. The praetors Q. Pompeius Rufus and Q. Caecilius Metellus Celer[89] were sent to Capua and Picenum, respectively. They were given permission to raise an army if the situation required: *iisque permissum uti pro tempore atque periculo exercitum conpararent.* As a state of *tumultus* had already been declared, it comes as no surprise that the praetors would be allowed to hold tumultuary levies if needed. The senate, as usual, also promised rewards to informers, ordered the troops of gladiators to be distributed among Capua and other free towns (thus separating them from joining into a larger grouping), and ordered night watches to be kept by the minor magistrates[90] (*Cat.* 30. 6–7).

Catiline was as yet not able to be held personally liable for what was occurring. That changed when messages came in from Etruria confirming his ties to the uprising, which led to his indictment by L. Aemilius Paullus under the *lex Plautia de vi* (*Cat.* 31. 4; cf. Dio 37. 31. 3). It was around this time in early November (probably the night of November 6) that Catiline called a meeting of his chief supporters at the house of M. Porcius Laeca, where he encouraged someone to make an attempt on the life of Cicero; two of his supporters did, but their attempt the next morning failed (*Cat.* 27. 3–28. 3; cf. Dio 37. 32. 3–33. 1). Later that day, or perhaps during the next,[91] Cicero addressed the senate with his withering attack, *In Catilinam* I (*Cat.* 31. 6). Catiline tried to respond with abuse of Cicero but was shouted down and left; he resolved now to join Manlius and the army (*Cat.* 31. 7–32. 1).

Sallust reports that Catiline made his way to Manlius's army, and once there, he assumed the fasces and other symbols of authority (*Cat.* 36. 1; cf. Dio 37. 33. 2). This provoked an immediate response from Rome, as the senate declared Catiline and Manlius *hostes* and offered an amnesty to anyone in their following not under a capital sentence who surrendered (*Cat.* 36. 2; cf. Dio 37. 33. 3, who states Catiline was convicted of *vis*

---

[87] See *MRR* 2. 169.
[88] See *MRR* 2. 168.
[89] For these two men, see *MRR* 2. 166.
[90] Notice that this particular measure exactly parallels what occurred during the slave *tumultus* of 198 (discussed in Chapter 3) and during the Bacchanalian affair (see Chapter 6).
[91] Pagán (2004) 31 says Cicero made his first speech against Catiline on November 7, whereas Ramsey (1984) 151 says Cicero allowed another day's interval.

[βία] upon receipt of the news he had made himself consul). The senate also formally authorized the consuls to hold a levy and that C. Antonius should immediately proceed against Catiline while Cicero guarded the city (*Cat.* 36. 3; cf. Dio 37. 33. 3). At this point, Dio supplies for us the curious notice that the Romans at this point changed their clothing, which has already been discussed at length.[92] Sallust does not mention this at all.

Had matters ended here, with Rome preparing for war and a consul about to take the field with a tumultuary levy, we could end discussion now, for all of this was in keeping with both the previous uses of the *SC ultimum* and the *tumultus* declaration. However, matters did not end here. For Cicero, left in charge of the defense of the city of Rome, had to face the plot of Lentulus and the involvement of the Allobroges that resulted in the incident at the Mulvian Bridge (Sall. *Cat.* 39. 6–41. 5, 43. 1–45. 4; Plut. *Cicero* 17–18; Dio 37. 34. 1–2). Of the former, P. Cornelius Lentulus Sura,[93] one of the praetors, was not your ordinary praetor. He had been consul in 71 but had been expelled by the censors of 70, forcing him to win election again to a magistracy to reenter the senate. It is hardly surprising that he was also not satisfied with the current state of affairs and was actively helping Catiline. He is now presented by Sallust as the chief of Catiline's associates in the city, entrusted by the latter with issuing orders to others and plotting ways of helping their cause. It was he who decided to try to bring in the Allobroges, a Gallic tribe that was not entirely happy with Roman hegemony.

This turned out to be a mistake, however. The ambassadors from the Allobroges decided that the safer course was to reveal everything to the government, and they approached their patron Q. Fabius Sanga with the details. Cicero was informed and then used the envoys of the Allobroges as double agents, intending that they would speak to as many members of the conspiracy within Rome as they could, so that all of them could be uncovered. The plotters, led by Sura, gave oaths signed by seal to the Allobroges, who were to take them back to their people as proof of good faith from the plotters. There was a letter for Catiline as well. When the Allobroges left Rome, it had been prearranged by Cicero that their party, which included T. Volturcius of Croton, a personal envoy from Sura, would be ambushed. The praetors L. Valerius Flaccus and C. Pomptinus lay in wait and seized the party, the Gauls giving up immediately, and Volturcius surrendering when it was clear that there was no escape.

---

[92] See the discussion on the *sagum* in Chapter 3.
[93] See *MRR* 2. 166 for references to his praetorship.

Cicero then brought Lentulus, Cethegus, Statilius, and Gabinius before the senate in the Temple of Concord (*Cat.* 46. 3–5). Another man, Caeparius of Terracina, managed to escape before capture (*Cat.* 46. 3–4). He then convened the senate there to hear the testimony of T. Volturcius and see the dossier of letters taken from the Allobroges (*Cat.* 46. 6). After a grant of immunity, Volturcius revealed all he knew, and the letters were opened, the seals confirmed. Sura, Cethegus, Statilius, Gabinius, and the recently captured Caeparius were then handed over to prominent men for custody, Sura first being forced to resign his magistracy (*Cat.* 47. 2–4; cf. Dio 37. 34. 2).

The plotters were arrested around December 2–3. What occurred next is where Cicero apparently overstepped his bounds, leading to his exile discussed in the opening section of this chapter. Around December 4, there was an abortive attempt to free the prisoners. In the wake of this threat, the senate met to debate about the punishment of the plotters. After the famed senate debate that Sallust records as pitting Julius Caesar against M. Porcius Cato, Cicero acted in accordance with the decree of the senate issued on December 5,[94] which followed Cato's *sententia* that the conspirators be immediately executed (*Cat.* 46–55; cf. Plut. *Cicero* 19–22; Dio 37. 34. 2; Appian *BC* 2. 5. 17–6. 22). At the news of the execution of the Catilinarian plotters, support fell away from Catiline's army (Sall. *Cat.* 57. 1; Dio 37. 39. 2). Although there were some remnants remaining afterward, the defeat and death of Catiline at Pistoria early the next year (Sall. *Cat.* 57–61; cf. Plut. *Cicero* 22; Dio 37. 39–40) marks the end of the Catilinarian crisis.

Catiline may never have presented a serious threat to the Roman Republic, but the full range of emergency measures were employed in response to the events, so perhaps some scholars have been unfair in their judgment of the affair. A *tumultus* was declared (if one wants to categorize it, it was a *tumultus Italicus* certainly) and the "last" decree of the senate was passed, which the sources for this episode represent as granting the consul full and unchallenged authority to act. Later events would show that this was not the case. Although the military measures – the use of armed force acquired from a tumultuary levy – would be in keeping with previous uses of the "final" decree, in no previous case had a consul summarily executed Roman citizens without trial, who had not been caught with weapons in their hands and with only a decree of the senate to provide justification. It was one thing for Gracchus, Flaccus, or Saturninus to be murdered: they had either taken up arms themselves or been in the midst of armed men.

---

[94] We have an explicit mention from Cicero: *Att.* 16. 14. 4.

Catiline died on the field of battle, and it would be hard to claim Cicero had acted without cause or justice in exposing him. It was a different story with Lentulus Sura, Cethegus, and the others. They may have been part of a conspiracy, but they were not taken with weapons in hand and were, by law and custom, entitled to a trial before execution.

The consul Cicero, as we already have noted, would later have to pay his own price for exceeding statute law when not all Romans believed that the *SC ultimum* gave a consul the ability to act with impunity. A tribune of the plebs for the next magisterial year, Q. Caecilius Metellus Nepos,[95] tried to call Cicero to account for executing Roman citizens without the consent of the people (Dio 37. 42. 2). The attack might have succeeded, had not the senate, according to Dio, granted immunity to all who were involved with managing affairs during the period and threatened anyone who brought a case against them with being voted a public enemy (37. 42. 3). This did not necessarily make Cicero's actions in executing Cethegus and the others legal, for it is a question whether the senate could confer such blanket immunity, but the threat of being declared a *hostis* worked to frighten off anyone who wished to prosecute him under the existing laws. Nepos backed off and would soon be out of Rome for other reasons, to be noted in a moment. The next attempt would be more successful.

The senate's threat to vote anyone a public enemy who attempted to prosecute Cicero or other officials acting in defense of the state in 63 applied to laws currently on the books. To get around this, P. Clodius Pulcher, Cicero's personal enemy, passed a new law in 58 that proclaimed a sentence of exile (*aqua et igni interdictio*) on anyone who put to death a Roman citizen who was not tried and found guilty by the Roman people.[96] The law succeeded in its purpose, with Cicero yielding before the threat. From this outcome, it is clear that the *SC ultimum* conferred no permanent legal immunity by itself upon a magistrate who went beyond the normal law in order to suppress a supposed or even a real threat. A new statute law could always trump a decree of the senate. Cicero apparently thought that he could use his powers without worry about strict adherence to statute law since in two previous uses of the decree, the ones that he cited as precedent for his own actions, in 121 and 100, the consul in charge did not suffer any serious consequences immediately attributable to his arbitrary use of power in suppressing an internal foe. Even though the

---

[95] About him, see *Att.* 16. 14. 4, p. 164.
[96] For the full narrative, see Dio 38. 12–17. Cf. Vell. Pat. 2. 45. 1; Cic. *Sest.* 25, 53; *Dom.* 62; *Att.* 3. 15. 5; App. *BC* 2. 15. 54–58; Plut. *Cic.* 30–32. 1. This will be discussed again later in this chapter.

consul L. Opimius, the first consul to make use of the decree, was brought to trial for his actions, he was acquitted.[97]

Cicero thought that he would be afforded the same protection as Opimius, strengthened further by the vote in 62 that granted him some sort of immunity. We do not know, however, for how long that grant of immunity was meant to last. It could not trump the new law that was passed by Clodius, and the senate did not step in again to save the orator. In any event, Cicero should have been on his guard long before Clodius passed his law, taking notice from the outcome of the trial of C. Rabirius, whom he tried to defend in 63 against the charge of treason (*perduellio*) for having taken part in the suppression of Saturninus in 100. Rabirius was already condemned by a special court and was likely to be condemned again by the people, so his supporters had to resort to a procedural trick to save him.[98]

THE CRISES OF THE 50S, CAESAR'S COUP D'ÉTAT, AND THE CIVIL WAR OF 49

During the next decade and a half, the Roman political system would veer far away from the vision that Cicero had in 63 of a "unification of all orders in defense of the Republic under the resolute leadership of the Senate."[99] The formulation may be Mitchell's, but the statement is most certainly one that Cicero himself would have cited as his own. Cicero expressed the idea numerous times in relation to the Catilinarian conspiracy. As just one of many examples and variations on the theme, *Catil.* 4. 18: *omnes ordines ad conservandam rem publicam mente, voluntate, voce consentiunt* "all groups join together in mind, will and voice to save the state."[100] Whereas there may have been a consensus against Catiline once he had taken the field with armed men, there was never such unanimous feeling about how Cicero handled those who had not been caught with weapons in hand but only signed statements that showed they had been plotting harm against the state. Cicero's coalition of "all good men" was a mirage. It disappeared almost immediately, if we believe what Dio alone records before Catiline

---

[97] Livy *Per.* 61; Cic. *de Or.* 2. 106, 132–134; *Part. Or.* 104; *Sest.* 140.

[98] The praetor Metellus Celer pulled down the warning flag from the Janiculum, which forced the adjournment of the *comitia centuriata*, which was hearing the appeal, Dio 37. 27. 3.

[99] Mitchell (1991) 11.

[100] See Mitchell (1991) 11 n. 5 for a full list of passages where Cicero's coalition *omnium bonorum* united under senatorial leadership against those who would destroy the state is mentioned or referenced.

had even been defeated in battle: that the "last" decree was resorted to yet again just as the year 62 began, when the tribune Metellus Nepos, failing to hit at Cicero, next tried to call for Pompey to be summoned to suppress the disturbances in Rome. The *SC ultimum* was passed when Nepos, unable to get his way, resorted to violence to attempt to pass his measure (Dio 37. 43. 3). Garments were also changed that very day, a sign perhaps of a *tumultus* or a *iustitium*. We hear nothing of an emergency levy, however, so the evidence for those are thin, but the passage of the *SC ultimum* is definite. As Nepos chose to slink away instead of fight, the matter was settled quickly. However, it was a sign that the consensus Cicero had built was fragile.

The man who would help to disperse fully the mirage of everyone united in harmony to protect the state would be C. Julius Caesar, son of Gaius, a patrician from a family that had had some recent prominence (a distant relative had been consul in 90 and another in 64) but whose immediate family was not quite as successful, as his father had only been a praetor. The study of Julius Caesar, as he is more simply known to most laymen, is an industry in itself. A recent addition is concerned solely with the "reception" of Caesar in Western culture.[101] A quick electronic search at any major research library will turn up pages of listings.[102] He lives on as well in popular fiction, from the novels of Colleen McCullough to the recent HBO/BBC cable television series *Rome*. Major modern biographies of Caesar exist in C. Meier's rather popularizing *Caesar* (Berlin, 1982; also in English translation, New York, 1995) and the more scholarly M. Gelzer's *Caesar: Politician and Statesman* (6th ed., Wiesbaden, 1960; tr. P. Needham, Oxford, 1968). The past decade alone has produced two new contenders for the position of definitive biography of Caesar.[103] To mention works that touch upon the man and his work would be to list much of the bibliography of the entire late Republic.

So, it is Caesar who begins to take center stage, not Cicero, although at first he shared that stage with Pompey "the Great." In many ways, the decade of the 50s can be considered a long series of crises that finally culminated in the last one that brought an end to the Republic as "revised" by Sulla the Dictator. It is perhaps ironic that it would be overturned by another man who would be commonly referred to by that same title, Caesar the Dictator. Although Sulla destroyed the Roman Republic, after he had

---

[101] Wyke ed. (2006).

[102] For example, a simple search for the exact phrase "Julius Caesar" in JSTOR returned more than 5,000 hits at the time of this writing.

[103] Goldsworthy (2006) and Billows (2009).

defeated all of his domestic enemies he set about recreating the Republic, or at least recreating what he liked about the old system, while bringing in innovations (such as removing most of the powers of the tribunate) that he felt would stabilize the system. The Sullan regime did not last long, however, before opposition arose. We have already recounted how in 78, one of the consuls of the year following Sulla's death, M. Aemilius Lepidus, led an insurrection that required the use of the *SC ultimum* to aid in its suppression. The later conspiracy of Catiline saw it employed again within fifteen years. The wait for the next passage of the resolution would not be as long after 63 (and the next fifteen years would in fact see two occasions where the decree was invoked), although in order to understand how matters arrived at that point, we must look at specific aspects of this crucial time period closely. As the events of this decade are so well known and have been dissected in many works, I will limit myself to facts that are necessary for discussing the emergencies that occurred and will keep references to a minimum.[104]

The origins of the Crisis of 50 and the civil war begun in 49, however, follow close on the heels of Catiline as we turn the clock back to 60, where we find Julius Caesar, ex-praetorian governor of Spain (Lusitania), waiting patiently outside the *pomerium* for a chance to enter the city in triumph (literally, in a triumphal procession). At the same time, Caesar had made sure to arrive in time for the elections for 59, so that he could place himself before the voters, fresh from the glory of his triumph. In addition, he tried to get permission to canvass for votes before he had even entered the city, a move that brought the immediate opposition of that alleged stickler for the observation of the rules of the Republic, M. Porcius Cato. Cato's opposition to Caesar was successful, to the point where Caesar had to make a choice between obtaining a triumph or being allowed to stand for the consulship, so Caesar chose the latter and entered the sacred boundary, which terminated his *imperium*, but allowed him to begin canvassing for office. Although these matters about *imperium* and the *pomerium* and such are not too important at this moment, they will come back later into the discussion when we come to the Crisis of 50. (Appian *BC* 2. 8. 28–30; Dio 37. 54. 1–4; Plut. *Caesar* 13. 1–4; Suet. *div. Iul.* 18. 2; Plut. *Cato min.* 31. 3–6).

As the main accounts of the period have it, Caesar gained the political friendship of Cn. Pompeius (Pompey the Great, hereafter, simply "Pompey") and M. Licinius Crassus, the former consuls of 70, who each

---

[104] In addition to the biographies of prominent figures such as Caesar, Pompey, and Cicero, classic treatments such as Syme (1939) and Gruen (1974) will provide more detailed overviews of the entire time.

wielded considerable clout, but who were often at loggerheads with one another. Winning the support of these two men, the "three-headed monster" was born, so christened by Terentius Varro (Appian *BC* 2. 9. 31–33; Plut. *Crassus* 14. 1–4; *Pompey* 47. 1–3), which some modern scholars have erroneously and highly misleadingly called the "First" Triumvirate. Caesar would win the consulship for 59.

I pass over the events of Caesar's consulship.[105] Needless to say, none of his actions won the plaudits of the so-called optimate faction in the senate. While Caesar was away in Gaul as proconsul, however, a new and powerful player in the Roman political scene arose, one of Caesar's own making: the "patrician tribune," P. Clodius Pulcher.[106] Clodius had a long-standing feud with M. Tullius Cicero, the orator, and now got the upper hand against him by orchestrating his banishment in 58.[107] Then Clodius began to become a thorn in the side of Pompey, who, in turn, engineered the recall of Cicero the following year, partially through the tribune T. Annius Milo. What made things somewhat different is that Clodius and Milo played the familiar game of getting matters pushed through the popular assemblies by new rules. When trying to bring the recall vote before the assembly, Clodius disrupted matters by using gladiators who had been gathered by his brother App. Claudius Pulcher for funeral games for a relative (Dio 39. 7. 1–2). Milo tried to get Clodius indicted (for causing the violence at the assembly), but the court process was blocked by maneuverings of Clodius (Dio 39. 7. 3–4). In response, Milo collected his own armed gang, and the two men engaged in street skirmishes (Dio 39. 8. 1).

So, we already have a context where street brawling was becoming more a norm than an anomaly. The basic stability of the state, however, was not threatened by the actions of ruffians and thugs. The leadership at the top – the coalition of Caesar, Pompey, and Crassus, balanced against the so-called optimates – was still able to skirmish over control of the levers of power within the system without bringing it down around them. However, this relied to an extent on a balance – a balance that could be upset. In many ways, the Crisis of 50 has its initial origin in a sad event that occurred in 54. In that year, Julia, wife of Pompey and daughter of Caesar, died in childbirth, the child dying as well (Appian *BC* 2. 19. 68; Dio 39. 64; Livy *Per.* 106; Plut. *Pompey* 53. 4; *Caesar* 23. 5). Appian notes that δέος "fear" gripped everyone, as they were afraid that with the

---

[105] Those interested in that somewhat tumultuous year can consult Gelzer (1968) 71–101.

[106] With apologies to Tatum, whose book title I have appropriated here and whose work should be consulted on this notable figure: Tatum (1999).

[107] Full references already noted before in n. 96.

end of the marriage link between them, Caesar and Pompey might come into conflict. The death of their political ally Crassus the next year would also contribute to the eventual clash, but other events in 53 and 52 would portend that trouble lay ahead.

In 53, the first seven months of the year passed without any regularly elected magistrates for the Roman state, the tribunes of the plebs officiating at state games in place of the praetors (Dio 40. 45. 3). The normal process of dealing with an interregnum, the appointment of patrician *interreges*, one of whom would eventually see to the election of at least one consul, was apparently unable to function properly. Unusual remedies were proposed by the tribunes. Dio reports that one such suggestion was the appointment of χιλίαρχοι in place of the consuls, dredging up practice from over three centuries ago, suggesting the appointment of *tribuni militum consulari potestate*, to give them their proper Latin title (Dio 40. 45. 4). A more serious proposal followed: the naming of Pompey as dictator (Dio 40. 45. 5; Plut. *Pompey* 54. 2). Although this did not come to pass (Pompey publicly refused the offer and instead brought about the election of consuls), the incident indicates just how unsettled the situation had become.

The virtual anarchy of 53 would spill over into 52, as the consuls were incapable of getting their successors elected (Dio 40. 46. 1).[108] What made matters worse, two of the candidates for office for 52 were Milo (seeking the consulship) and Clodius (aiming for the praetorship). The almost-guaranteed violence, however, did not take place at the voting enclosure but instead occurred outside of Rome on the Appian Way near Bovillae. When the two bitter rivals and their entourages encountered each other on the road, a servant of Milo took it upon himself to stab Clodius in the back, although the blow was not fatal. Milo, feeling certain that he would be punished for the act, decided that if he was "in for a penny" he would certainly be "in for a pound." Following Clodius into the inn where he had been brought, Milo finished the deed (Appian *BC* 2. 21. 75–76; Dio 40. 48. 2; Livy *Per.* 107).

The reaction at Rome was predictable, with Clodius's partisans baying for blood, while Milo attempted to avoid punishment.[109] In perhaps a portent of what was to come for the Sullan regime, the Curia Hostilia, the senate house that had been restored by the late dictator himself, was burned to the ground by the partisans of Clodius, who used it as the crematorium for their dear leader (Appian *BC* 2. 21. 78; Dio 40. 49. 2).[110]

[108] Alluded to before when discussing a change of dress by these consuls. See pp. 64–69.
[109] For a recent treatment of this tumultuous episode, see Sumi (1997).
[110] On the senate house, see previous discussion in footnote 33.

According to Appian, Milo attempted to stage a show trial for himself through the friendly tribune Caelius, but his attempt failed when armed thugs loyal to Clodius stormed in and broke up the assembly by violence (Appian *BC* 2. 22. 80–82). Faced with violence and bloodshed in the streets while there were still no magistrates in office, the senate, meeting on the Palatine (we can only assume under the presidency of a tribune of the plebs), apparently voted for an *interrex* to be chosen, and for him, the tribunes, and Pompey to see to the guarding of the city, so that it should not come to harm ὥστε μηδὲν ἀπ᾽ αὐτῆς ἀποτριβῆναι (Dio 40. 49. 5). For the second time in this final decade of the Republic, the *senatus consultum ultimum* was passed, and the state's protection was entrusted to an *interrex* and a proconsul who technically could not command armed forces within the city of Rome, although it must be assumed that an enabling resolution, or perhaps just the *SC ultimum* itself, was sufficient to grant him that ability. The situation was very different from 77. There was no hostile proconsul leading an army against the city. It was civil unrest – what would be a police, not military, matter for a modern state – that plagued Rome. Whereas the Romans had methods of clamping down on public disorder,[111] they required a united leadership, or at least a sizable group of the ruling class that was united and resolved. For the moment, there was too much division and indecision to form such a group.

Milo apparently came out of hiding and began to press his claims for the consulship again, which led to more violence (Dio 40. 49. 5). In response, according to Dio, the senate called in Pompey and authorized him to make fresh levies of troops and ordered a change of dress (Dio 40. 50. 1). This last notice could possibly indicate the declaration of a *tumultus* (this we will have to assume was done under the presidency of the *interrex*). Considering the seriousness of the situation, this is not impossible. The senate then met under armed guard at Pompey's theater, located outside of the *pomerium* (Dio 40. 50. 2). Passing over minor details (what should be done with Clodius's remains, the rebuilding of the *curia*), talk moved to what the next step should be. What was clear was that the common members were eager to honor Pompey and Caesar as much as possible (Dio 40. 50. 3–4).

The small group of long-established families who thought of themselves as the natural leaders of the Roman state apparently were alarmed at the prospect of Caesar and Pompey both gaining greatly from the crisis. There was talk again of Pompey being named dictator, while Caesar's supporters put forth the suggestion that he be made consul, neither prospect being

---

[111] See Nippel (1995) 47–60.

palatable to the powerful senatorial group attached to Cato. Faced with no "good" choice, they decided on what might seem to them the least of all evils. On the motion of either Cato (Appian) or Bibulus (Dio), a completely "novel" proposal was made and accepted: Pompey would be named sole consul (Dio 40. 50. 4; Appian *BC* 2. 23. 84; cf. Plut. *Cato min.* 47. 3–4; *Pompey* 54. 4–5; *Caesar* 28. 7–8; cf. Livy *Per.* 107; Suet. *div. Iul.* 26. 1). As Dio notes, this was done specifically ὥστε μὴ δικτάτορα αὐτὸν λεχθῆναι "so that he [Pompey] could not be chosen dictator." Furthermore, they kept Caesar from being named his colleague. Pompey brought in his soldiers to reestablish order. There followed strictly controlled trials, and many, including Milo, were condemned (Appian *BC* 2. 24. 89–94; Dio 40. 54–55).[112] The *SC ultimum* had been again successfully employed. Although matters changed once Pompey was named consul, the state of disorder was still in effect, and Pompey had been charged even while still only proconsul to employ any means necessary to protect the state; making him consul in this situation merely brought matters back into line with previous usages of the decree.

While the troubles caused by the rioting following the murder of P. Clodius had been suppressed, the gap between occasions where the senate resorted to the "final" decree now grew even slimmer. A little over twenty years separated the first two instances. The next two somewhat unusual episodes came after intervals of seventeen and six years, respectively. If we put aside the use in 83 as irregular – the act of a government that was not considered completely legitimate after Sulla's victory in the civil war – then there had been another gap of over twenty years. Fourteen years separated the suppression of Lepidus and that of Catiline, and eleven intervened before the need for it again.[113] But there would be no break of a decade or two this time. The next situation that merited the passage of the decree would come a scant three years later, although the crisis that caused it had a long build-up.

The earliest indications of the Crisis of 50 (which actually stretches into early 49) came in 51, when the consul M. Claudius M. f. Marcellus (curse the voters of the *comitia centuriata* for giving us three Marcelli at the end of the Republic)[114] started to make noises about having Caesar replaced before his term as governor of Gaul expired. For this, we even

---

[112] Cicero, apparently, attempted to defend Milo but ended up doing little but splutter – Plut. *Cicero* 35. The *Pro Milone* we have is little more than the speech Cicero would have delivered, had he had the courage.

[113] If we count the decree issued against Metellus Nepos as still part of the Catilinarian affair, albeit not tied to Catiline personally but as part of the aftermath.

[114] For this Marcellus, see *MRR* 2. 240.

have a firsthand account (a real rarity) in the letters sent by the young M. Caelius Rufus to Cicero while the latter was governor of Cilicia from about summer 51 to summer 50 (Cicero *Fam.* 8. 1, 2, 4, 5, 8, 9, 10). Especially important are the copies of the proposals made in the senate that Caelius records in Cicero *Fam.* 8. 8. Another (brief) contemporary account comes from A. Hirtius (Hirtius [Caesar] *BG* 8. 53).

Matters really came to a head, however, during the next year, when C. Claudius C. f. Marcellus, consul with L. Aemilius Paullus for 50,[115] made a renewed attempt to oust Caesar, only to be countered by the tribune of the plebs C. Scribonius Curio, who had allegedly been won over to Caesar's side by an obscenely large bribe.[116] Unlike many of the previous crises and emergencies discussed in this work, from this point forward, we can provide a somewhat more precise timeline of events because we have Cicero's correspondence, and those letters sent to him to provide rough, and sometimes exact, dates. The summer of 50 saw a marked increase in hostile actions between Caesar and his opponents, when C. Claudius C. f. Marcellus and C. Curio sparred in the senate over how to handle Caesar and Pompey. Although Marcellus succeeded in getting the senate to pass his motion to have Caesar superseded (which Curio vetoed), Curio's countermotion that both Caesar and Pompey should lay down their extraordinary commands (it should be remembered that they both owed their current positions to acts of the assembly, not to the usual distribution of provinces at the discretion of the senate) passed overwhelmingly. Marcellus then attempted to pass a decree to pressure the tribune to withdraw his veto, but when it came to a formal division of the chamber, the senate voted his proposal down overwhelmingly (Cic. *Fam.* 8. 13. 2, Caelius's letter of c. June 50; cf. Appian *BC* 2. 30. 118–119; Plut. *Pompey* 58. 4; *Caesar* 30. 2–5).

It is somewhere in the vicinity of the fall of 50 that matters started to come to a head. We may take a statement from a letter of Cicero as a good indicator of when men of his station began to fear that a major threat against the safety of the state was arising from the contention of Caesar and those arrayed against him. Cicero, of course, is not the senate, but he is a fairly good example of a middle-of-the-road senator, who would have preferred that matters not be decided on the battlefield. From a letter to Atticus firmly dated to the Kalends of October, we learn that he had heard things from one Batonius and from a certain Lepta that were *spero*

---

[115] For full references to both men, see *MRR* 2. 247.
[116] Some firsthand notices in Cic. *Fam.* 8. 6. 5, Cic. *Att.* 6. 3. 4. Cf. Appian *BC* 2. 27. 102–106; Dio 40. 61–62; Livy *Per.* 109.

falsa sed certe horribilia "[which] I hope are false, but certainly horrifying" (Cic. *Att.* 6. 8. 2). He had heard that Caesar would not dismiss his army (in early 49), and that three praetors,[117] the tribune of the plebs Q. Cassius (Longinus), and the consul Lentulus (L. Cornelius Lentulus Crus, designate for 49 with C. Claudius M. f. Marcellus) would all take the part of Caesar. Fifteen days later, on the Ides, Cicero heard a report (which turned out to be false) that Caesar would winter in Placentia with four legions (Cic. *Att.* 6. 9; cf. *Att.* 7. 1. 1 [Oct. 16, 50]). The rumor turned out to be false, but it contributed to the air of crisis that continued to build among Romans of the ruling class.

The specter of the political battle turning into something far more serious appeared in December, when Cicero in a letter notes *sic enim sentio, maximo in periculo rem esse* "as far as I feel, the whole thing is in the greatest danger" (Cic. *Att.* 7. 3. 5 [Dec. 9, 50]). When Cicero met Pompey at Cumae sometime during the middle of that month, Cicero's report was not positive: *de re publica autem ita mecum locutus est quasi non dubium bellum haberemus: nihil ad spem concordiae* "about affairs of state, however, he spoke to me as if without doubt we would have a war; he said nothing relating to hope for an agreement" (Cic. *Att.* 7. 4. 3). The notices of fear would only build (granted, Cicero was rather timorous, but these notices are worth noting): *Att.* 7. 5. 4: *de re publica cotidie magis timeo*; *Att.* 7. 6. 2: *de re publica valde timeo*. Without question, the atmosphere among those at the top was becoming filled with trepidation. January 1 presented a hard deadline for either Caesar or the influential faction opposed to him to compromise. The alternative was open warfare.

A major escalation occurred when another false rumor was circulated sometime during December that Caesar had crossed the Alps and was marching on the city. The consul Marcellus proposed that the army at Capua (the two legions taken from Caesar, see Hirtius [Caesar] *BG* 8. 54; Appian *BC* 2. 29. 114–115; Dio 40. 65) be turned against Caesar, but Curio intervened (Appian *BC* 2. 31. 120). Marcellus then stated that if he were hindered from taking measures to protect the common safety (through a senatorial decree, it must be assumed), he would do so by virtue of his own consular authority: "εἰ κωλύμαι ψήφῳ κοινῇ τὰ συμφέροντα διοικεῖν, κατ᾽ ἐμαυτὸν ὡς ὕπατος διοικήσω" (Appian *BC* 2. 31. 121). The consuls and possibly the consuls-elect left the city and presented Pompey with the command of the army at Capua, as well as the authority to raise whatever extra levies he wished (Appian *BC* 2. 31. 121–122; cf. Dio 40. 66. 1–3; Plut. *Pompey* 59; *Caesar* 30. 6). It is interesting that there is

---

[117] This is Shackleton Bailey's Teubner reading.

no word about declaring a state of emergency, a *tumultus* or a *iustitium*, which would have facilitated the levying of forces. It would appear that the consuls were taking this action on their own without the official approval of the majority of the senate. It may be that they could not get a majority of the senate to approve the measures they were undertaking.

The tribune Curio, meanwhile, unable to effect anything further, fled to Caesar (Appian *BC* 2. 31. 123). Before he left office, so about December 9, 50, Curio delivered an accusing address before the people condemning the actions of Pompey and the consuls-elect (Dio 40. 66. 5). After the new tribunes took office, Mark Antony kept up the attack, as he gave a strong speech on December 21 attacking Pompey all the way from boyhood to the present, especially complaining about Pompey's court proceedings in 52 (Cic. *Att.* 7. 8. 5 [c. Dec. 25/26 50]). Here would seem to be an echo of tribunes past, calling into question the actions of a consul taken following the passage of a *senatus consultum ultimum*.

At the very end of 50, Caesar was at Ravenna with 5,000 infantry and 300 cavalry (one legion, the Thirteenth). Curio came to him, and Caesar sent him back to Rome bearing a letter for the consuls who would take office on the first of January. Here we have the opening of Caesar's own account, his *commentarii* on the Civil War to provide a source, although one that should be viewed with a critical eye.[118] As the outgoing governor of Gaul tells it, his letter was read only after the intervention of the tribunes Antony and Q. Cassius. The contents of the letter are passed over by Caesar. We have to seek them in another source. Dio tells us that Caesar offered to disband his army and lay down his command – if Pompey would do the same. Apparently, there was even more to this letter that Dio recorded, as Appian notes that it also contained an implied threat of armed force if his proposal were refused.[119] Returning to Caesar's account, the consuls (Caesar makes out Lentulus as the more forceful of the pair) brought forward a *relatio de re publica*, which drew different responses. M. Marcellus, the consul of 51, thought that no decree regarding the matter should be passed until levies had been held throughout Italy and armies raised to protect the senate's ability to pass a decree freely. One M. Calidius proposed that Pompey leave Rome for his designated provinces (Spain) so that there would be no cause for hostilities. M. Rufus proposed a measure

---

[118] Although not *the* source. Caesar's narrative, of course, reflects Caesar's political ambitions and was not above providing an *apologia* for his actions. For various essays on the political intentions of his war commentaries, see Welch and Powell (1998).

[119] Obviously, not in Caes. *BC* 1. 1, and as noted, absent from Dio 41. 1. 3–4. Appian *BC* 2. 32. 128 provides us with this important detail, which has contemporary support from Cicero's description of the letter as *minacis ad senatum et acerbas litteras*–Cic. *Fam.* 16. 11. 2.

similar to Calidius's. Lentulus the consul refused to put Calidius's motion to a vote, and Marcellus withdrew his.

The resolution that was passed was the one put forward by Metellus Pius Scipio (Pompey's father-in-law) that Caesar should disband his forces by a fixed date, but it was vetoed by Antony and Cassius. Pressure was placed on the tribunes to withdraw their vetoes. The senators apparently also met with Pompey outside the city (Caes. *BC* 1. 1–4). Turning to another source, Dio again, we have an interesting notice that makes sense: it appears that the senate at this time may have tried to declare a state of *tumultus*, as the later Greek senator records that the senate voted to change their apparel, but this was vetoed. The senate ordered the *sententia* recorded, and many senators apparently went ahead and changed from normal senatorial dress anyway (Dio 41. 3. 2).

At some point between January 1 and 7, it is clear that severe pressure was placed on the tribunes Antony and Cassius, perhaps even to the degree where threats to their personal safety were made if they did not leave Rome. The point of no return was January 7,[120] when the senate, in Caesar's words:

> decurritur ad illud extremum atque ultimum senatus consultum, quo nisi paene in ipso urbis incendio atque in desperatione omnium salutis latorum audacia numquam ante discessum est: dent operam consules, praetores, tribuni plebis quique pro consulibus sint ad urbem, ne quid res publica detrimenti capiat.

> There was recourse to that last and final decree of the senate, having never been voted before except in the imminent threat of destruction of the city and in despair over the safety of all due to the audacity of proposers [of inimical laws], by which [the senate ordered] the consuls, praetors, tribunes of the plebs, and those who were near the City *pro consule*,[121] to take care that the state should not be harmed (Caesar BC 1. 5. 3).

Whereas on the surface it would appear that the "final" decree was passed in order to intimidate the tribunes, it would appear that even Caesar knew who its real target was. Thus, his insistence that the decree was never previously invoked except when an armed force was threatening the state with imminent destruction because the tribunes posed no such threat of violence. As we know from previous instances, however, this portrayal of the circumstances leading to the passage of the *SC ultimum* is not the

---

[120] Caes. BC 1. 5. 4: *Haec senatus consulto perscribuntur a. d. VII Id. Ian.*

[121] Promagistrates returning from their *provincia*, like Cicero, who had not yet entered the *pomerium* and were therefore still in possession of *imperium*, particularly *imperium pro consule*.

entire story. Sulla was far away when the decree was passed against him in 83. The threat to Rome was largely from the prospect of Etruria up in arms when Cicero successfully passed the resolution in 63. In Caesar's favor, however, were several of the historical invocations of the decree. If we keep in mind the most recent use, during the riots in Rome of 52, as well as its employment against Lepidus in 78, and especially the first two times the decree was invoked (121, 100), the "canonical" usages in Cicero's mind, the characterization that Caesar gives to the "last" decree is not significantly misleading. Regardless, the tribunes Antony and Cassius, along with the Caesarian supporters Curio and M. Caelius Rufus, left Rome and headed for Ravenna, Caesar ascribing their departure to the passage of the SC *ultimum* that was followed by decrees that affected the tribunes (Caes. BC 1. 5. 1–5).

We learn from the other, and perhaps less biased, contemporary witness, Cicero, that Caesar is at least telling the truth that the Caesarian-leaning group left when the "final" decree was passed, but that no violence was offered them (Cic. *Fam.* 16. 11. 2). Cicero was in a position to know about the decree and the time of Antony and friends' departure, being himself in the vicinity of Rome then, although he may not have known exactly what kind of threats or pressure were placed on Antony and Cassius Longinus. Dio Cassius notes that after the senators changed their dress, they reconvened to debate punishing the tribunes (41. 3. 1). Appian states that the consuls of 49 ordered Antony and friends to leave the senate, lest they be harmed, tribune or not (BC 2. 33. 131). Of course, we do not know where they gained this information, so the absolute truth about the matter concerning a physical threat to the tribunes is difficult to uncover.

Thanks to the contemporary sources, Caesar and Cicero, we can note many major events with exact dates. Events moved rather quickly. After the passage of the final decree on the seventh, the senate met again on the next day outside of the *pomerium*, so that Pompey could attend. A levy was ordered throughout all of Italy at this meeting, according to Caesar (BC 1. 6). Among other measures discussed at that meeting was certainly the decision to divide Italy into supervisory districts,[122] which Cicero reports in his letter of January 12, where he also records the flight of the tribunes, the SC *ultimum* and his own appointment to superintend Capua and the Campanian coast (Cic. *Fam.* 16. 11. 2–3). The next two weeks would see a flurry of activity, as Cicero in a letter dated around the twenty-first records the defection of T. Labienus, one of Caesar's legates, which did nothing to

---

[122] Similar, perhaps, to the situation in 91 right before the Social War, when regions of Italy were also placed under watch by holders of *imperium*.

slow down Caesar's advance into Italy as he took Cingulum and Ancona. Cicero himself was assigned to conduct the levy along the Campanian coast (*Att.* 7. 11). Pompey at this point had decided that his forces were not sufficient to stop Caesar, so he ordered Rome to be abandoned, all senators leaving with him or being considered enemies (Cic. ad *Att* 7. 11; Plut. *Pompey* 61. 3–4; *Caesar* 33. 6; Dio 41. 6. 1–2; Appian *BC* 2. 37). It is also likely that at this time a state of *tumultus* was in effect, perhaps one of the measures passed during the meeting of the senate back on January 8.[123]

If there are any who believe the senate's decree was aimed solely at the tribunes, the actions of the consuls and Pompey in the days following argue strongly against that position, for they immediately began to act as if Caesar were an enemy in the field, poised to invade Italy. If the decree had been aimed solely at the tribunes, then its goal was fulfilled the moment the tribunes left the city. Instead, the consuls moved ahead as if the state were still in a state of emergency. In this case, however, in the face of an external invasion, as occurred from Sulla over thirty years before, the *senatus consultum ultimum* was ineffectual. It is not that it was the "wrong" measure to take. What else could Pompey and the senate do in the face of Caesar's armed force other than pass the "final" decree, declare a *tumultus*, raise an army, and prepare to meet Caesar in battle? The only thing they did not do is meet Caesar in battle yet, as Pompey felt that his forces were not capable of facing Caesar's battle-seasoned soldiers. Instead, Pompey and the senate played for time, ceding northern Italy to Caesar for the most part while negotiating with him. Cicero in several letters (*Att.* 7. 14, 7. 15, 7. 16, 7. 17) records that an interim agreement was even made with Caesar agreeing to all of his demands if he withdrew his army from northern Italy. By this time, around the end of January, Cicero (*Fam.* 16. 12) reports that Caesar already was in firm control of Ariminum, Pisaurum, Ancona, and Arretium.

That this was merely playing for time is clear from what transpired later. Cicero, expecting that a real agreement was going to be worked out, reported that a meeting was set for the consuls and others to convene at Capua on February 5 (*Att.* 7. 16. 2, 7. 17. 5, 7. 18. 1), but when he got there, only the consul Lentulus appeared, while C. Marcellus did not (*Att.* 7. 20. 1, 7. 21. 1). After the meeting that was not, the consuls were ordered to return to Rome, not yet in Caesar's hands, to remove the

---

[123] See Dio 41. 3. 3 and cf. Suet. *div. Iul.* 34. 1, which notes on L. Domitius *Lucio Domitio, qui per tumultum successor ei nominatus Corfinium praesidio tenebat*. This clearly refers to a formal state of *tumultus*, see Butler and Cary (1982) 86.

sanctius aerarium, but they failed in that mission (*Att.* 7. 21. 2; cf. Caes. *BC* 1. 14. 1). Throughout the rest of February, Pompey began his plans for evacuating Italy. Caesar took control of most of the Italian peninsula. It had not been a successful usage of the "final" decree or any other emergency measures that the senate had passed. The Republic had fallen; the crisis for the Roman state was over. The civil war to see who would get to rebuild it had begun.

SUPPRESSING URBAN RIOTS IN 47

The Republic may have fallen (yet again), but the use of the decree did not come to an immediate end. In the year 47, we have indications that the senate, what there was of it in Rome at the time (as this was during the Civil War, when a sizable number of senators were outlawed or even in open rebellion against Caesar and his faction, which controlled Rome) were forced by the deterioration of security in Rome to entrust the defense of the city to Mark Antony, Caesar's master of the horse, who was holding Rome for Caesar. The cause of this breakdown into mob violence was owing to the activities of two tribunes of the plebs, P. Cornelius Dolabella and L. Trebellius.[124] Dolabella was championing debt relief (much to the horror of his father-in-law Cicero, who was relieved when the family connection would soon be ended with the divorce of Dolabella and Cicero's daughter Tullia; see *Att.* 11. 23. 3[125]) and faced forceful opposition from Trebellius. The two tribunes clashed in Rome with armed gangs, reminiscent of the era of Clodius and Milo.

Matters came to a head apparently (according to Dio, who provides a thorough account at 42. 29–33) when the murders and arson caused by Dolabella's and Trebellius's followers threatened the safety of the holy vessels tended by the Vestals who carried them out of the temple of Vesta for safekeeping (42. 31. 3). After this incident, the senators voted that the master of the horse should keep a stricter guard over the city (αὖθίς τε οὖν φυλακὴν οἱ βουλευταὶ τῆς πόλεως ἀκριβεστέραν τῷ ἱππάρχῳ ἐψηφίσαντο 42. 32. 1). Still intent on passing his bill, Dolabella and his supporters barricaded themselves in the forum. Antony then employed armed force to drive the tribune and his supporters out of the forum, smashing down the

---

[124] For full references, see *MRR* 2. 287. Dolabella came from an old patrician family, but had transitioned to the plebs, as P. Clodius had done before him. Trebellius came from a relatively new family in the senate, probably the son of L. Trebellius *tr. pl.* 67; see Wiseman (1971) 267.

[125] Although undated, we get the date of this letter as July 9, 47, as Shackleton Bailey notes [SB *Att.* vol. 5. 291] that the matter discussed here in this letter to Atticus [SB 232] was mentioned in a letter to his wife Terentia, which also touches upon Tullia's divorce.

tablets that contained the law.[126] In a rather dramatic detail, Dio states that Antony had some of those engaged in the disturbances (ταραχώδεις) thrown from the capitolium (42. 32. 3).

Plutarch provides a slightly different version of the time at which the passage of the decree was made, omitting any reference to the danger to the Vestals. In his version, he goes straight to Dolabella and his supporters occupying the forum in order to force the passage of his law abolishing debts, at which point Antony marched an armed force against Dolabella after the senate had voted that arms were needed against the tribune (καὶ τῆς βουλῆς ψηφισαμένης ὅπλων δεῖν ἐπὶ τὸν Δολοβέλλαν *Antony* 9. 4). His soldiers forcibly dispersed Dolabella's supporters. From his account, it makes it appear as if the decree was in reaction to Dolabella's seizure of the forum. The two versions are not irreconcilable: the incident with the Vestals may have given Antony the leverage to push the senate into passing the decree, whereas both sources agree that armed force was not employed until Dolabella and his supporters had barricaded themselves in the forum. The difference between the two accounts seems to be in the emphasis on who was directly responsible for causing the situation that called for the passage of the *senatus consultum ultimum*. Dio's account of the passage of the decree makes it seem that Antony intended to suppress the violence and unrest caused by both Dolabella and Trebellius, whereas Plutarch's account paints Dolabella as the greater troublesome tribune, which is supported somewhat by the laconic account in the epitomator of Livy. Livy *Per.* 113 does not mention Trebellius at all but does record the unrest caused by Dolabella and his attempt at debt relief, which led Antony to bring in the troops, which led to the slaughter of 800 commoners.

Regardless of the outcome, the decree did not have the effect of completely suppressing the troubles caused by the two tribunes. As Lintott rightly notes: "The vagueness of the *relatio* and the decree had embarrassing results in 47. M. Antonius invoked the decree to repress Dolabella and Trebellius, but they were still able to act 'as if they themselves had been delegated some sort of command by the senate.'"[127] In the longer term, the return of Caesar to Rome put an end to all of the disorder, which had itself given rise to the violent disputes, since neither tribune believed that

---

[126] These would be the tablets that would contain the draft version of the law, required to be displayed for three *nundinae* (market days) before the formal vote on passage could be held. See Meyer (2004) 97.

[127] Lintott (1968) 152, including a translated quote from Dio 42. 29. 4 ὥσπερ τινὰ καὶ αὐτοὶ ἡγεμονίαν παρὰ τῆς βουλῆς εἰληφότες.

Caesar would return from Egypt (Dio 41. 30. 3). This would be the last example available to the Romans of the effectiveness, or not, of employing the so-called last decree when they debated matters in January of 43.

The *Senatus Consultum Ultimum* as an Emergency Measure

So, what exactly did the *SC ultimum* do in terms of emergency powers? From the historical examples examined, it has been demonstrated that the decree itself was largely "superfluous" to the extent that magistrates had all the authority they needed in their *imperium* to take whatever measures were necessary during a severe internal crisis. They had the ability regardless of the decree's passage to call upon the senate to declare a *tumultus* or other official state of emergency, which would grant them the ability to hold an extraordinary levy and employ soldiers to suppress armed threats to the state. The senate could not grant an executive official any further powers outside of those that were already sanctioned by statute law.

Basically, the *senatus consultum ultimum* was a public statement by the senate that an emergency existed. In a sense, its passage marked the *declaration* of a state of emergency, but beyond serving as a public signal, it could not actually grant magistrates any further powers, nor did it confer any special immunity on magistrates who used extra-legal means of accomplishing their task of suppressing internal dissent. Its main force was largely to provide political cover for a magistrate who went beyond the law in order to deal with a crisis. As noted previously in the incidents involving Opimius and Cicero, a consul could be brought to trial later for the actions undertaken by him during the course of the emergency. The senate could use its influence to get the man acquitted (as would seem to be the case with Opimius) or provide some sort of limited immunity (as happened with Cicero, although the real protection the senate offered may have been the threat to declare anyone who attempted to prosecute Cicero a public *hostis*). It could not, however, protect a former consul from being subject to the operation of statute law, as Clodius's law would certainly have led to Cicero standing trial for unlawfully killing Roman citizens without trial, a trial at which it is not impossible he might have been condemned. Clodius may have had to pass a new law because of the earlier measure granting Cicero "immunity," but note that that immunity could not affect future laws passed. There was the example of Roscius from only a few short years before, who had to be saved by an extreme procedural maneuver.

In terms of the law, however, it was not actually a formal declaration of a state of emergency, as a *tumultus* or a *iustitium* certainly was. Yet it does belong in this discussion of emergency response mechanisms to crisis because it had the practical effect of signaling that a state of emergency was thought to exist by the presiding magistrate who put it to the senate to pass the decree, which may in itself have cleared the way for a consul to call for the declaration of a *tumultus*, which otherwise would seem to have been intended mainly to deal with armed threats from external sources. In some respects, however, the *SC ultimum* was more an affirmation of magisterial power than an expression of senatorial authority because it marked the executive's request that the government be put into a state of emergency and signaled that the executive was to be given full discretion in countering the threat to the government. The vague wording of the decree in itself indicates that a magistrate was being given wide discretion by the present senators.

6

CRISES RESOLVED BY OTHER
MEANS

Not every crisis was an emergency – that is, it did not call for an immediate suspension of normal government activity, with all state resources being redirected to meeting the perceived threat. Not every emergency was met with the responses that have been discussed in detail in the previous chapters. The use of the *dictator* in the early Republic, the declarations of states of emergency (*tumultus, iustitium*) and in later times the senatorial decree that signaled a high state of alert (the so-called *senatus consultum ultimum*) were the primary means of emergency response. This does not mean that they were the sole methods of responding to a crisis. There are a number of episodes that are most clearly crises by our definition: events that threatened serious impairment to the Roman state, including the prospect of its destruction, where the sources do not provide us with clear and convincing evidence that the specific emergency measures examined so far were employed. In some of the following events that we will look at, there are good reasons why the measures discussed before would not be of particular use: although these events were certainly crises, the measures discussed previously would not have provided any practical help. In other cases, the situations would appear to be ones where the emergency measures discussed would be of use, but the sources do not give us explicit or even firm circumstantial evidence that would point unquestionably to the deployment of the crisis response measures discussed in the previous chapters.

THE SAGUNTINE CRISIS

The first crisis we will examine began in 220, as the Roman state found itself faced with the possibility of renewing war against a powerful and troublesome foe. This was the crisis triggered by Hannibal, the Carthaginian commander in Spain, when he started a dispute with the town of

Saguntum, an ally of Rome.[1] The chain of events that lead to the Saguntine Crisis cannot be separated from the general chain of events that led to the Second Punic War. Therefore, let us very briefly recount the causes, as noted by the best source for the opening stage of the conflict, Polybius.

The Achaean statesman and historian mentions a series of reasons that he thinks were the causes of the Second Punic War, and it is worth mentioning at least two of them here, as they certainly were triggering events that made the showdown over Saguntum inevitable. First, there was the Roman annexation of Sardinia, the circumstances of which certainly left a bitter taste in the mouths of the Carthaginians (Polyb. 1. 88. 8–12; 3. 10. 1–5, 28. 2–3). Occurring in 238,[2] just a few years after the end of the first conflict and following the horrific Mercenary War that bled Carthage even drier after the First Punic War, the incident inspired the Carthaginian general Hamilcar Barca all the more to create and expand Punic power in Spain (3. 10. 1–5). Polybius follows with his account of Hamilcar's endeavors to make that dream a reality. It was, in Polybius's opinion, the expansion of Punic power in Spain that became the final enabler of the resumption of hostilities between Rome and Carthage (3. 10. 6–7; for the rise of the Barcid "empire" in Spain, see 2. 1. 5–9, 13. 1–7, 36. 1–7).[3]

Even though the Romans did not do much to counter Carthaginian expansion in Spain, they were neither entirely ignorant nor inactive in regards to it. At some point just before the major Gallic *tumultus* of 225, the Romans made a treaty with Hasdrubal, Hamilcar's son-in-law and successor as commander-in-chief of Carthaginian forces in Spain, which limited Punic military activity to the areas south of the Ebro River (Polyb. 2. 13. 7).[4] For the moment, this agreement was acceptable to both sides, as Hasdrubal had not yet reached this area, and the Romans did not have a free hand to impose an arrangement more to their liking.

The complication – the beginning of the chain of events that would lead to the crisis – was Rome's relations with a little town called Saguntum.

---

[1] There is substantial bibliography for this event. Especially useful is Hoyos (2003) and (1998). On the outbreak of the war, see also Schwarte (1983) and Rich (1996). On Saguntum as a potential source of economic competition, see Domínguez Pérez (2005).

[2] There is some debate whether the seizure occurred in 238 or the next year. See Walbank, *Polybius* 1. 149–150 for a brief discussion. For our purposes, it is not important whether it was 238 or 237. For the episode and the later moralizing discussions of how the Romans behaved based on the judgment of Polybius, see Carey (1996).

[3] There is need for a full treatment of Punic Spain. Most of the very limited bibliography on the subject currently extant is largely archaeological: for example, see Untermann and Villar (1993), Devijver and Lipinski (1989), Peacock (1986).

[4] With multiple later references. See Walbank, *Polybius* 1. 168 on §7.

Although there has been longstanding debate and discussion related to the status of Saguntum in relation to the Ebro Treaty and the rights and wrongs of both parties, the Romans and the Carthaginians, it is not directly relevant to this discussion about crisis and the Roman response to it.[5] It is enough to state the basic facts. Saguntum was a town in alliance with Rome (Polyb. 3. 30. 1), acknowledged by the Carthaginians. Whether it was north or south of the Ebro, included or not in the Ebro Treaty, covered or not covered by the Treaty of Lutatius that ended the First Punic War, are inconsequential; all are important issues, but blame and legality are not our concerns here, only the triggering of the crisis and the Roman response to the situation. It is not a matter of dispute that Hannibal, shortly after he took command of Punic forces in Spain, decided to attack the town. He did not do so immediately, as Polybius informs us (3. 14. 10). The Saguntines, alarmed by Hannibal's activities, sent messages to Rome (3. 15. 1).

When the message from Saguntum arrived, it sparked a crisis for Rome. An ally of Rome was in danger from the Carthaginians. In this situation, the Romans acted in accordance with normal crisis behavior: they sought more information.[6] Polybius reports that a senatorial embassy was sent to Spain late in 220 to investigate (3. 15. 2; Livy 21. 6 wrongly places these events in 218). There is some slight divergence in the sources here, as Polybius states that the ambassadors were received by Hannibal and debated with him before setting off for Carthage (3. 15. 4–9, 12). The annalistic tradition, represented best by Livy (21. 6. 5–8, 9. 3–11. 2; cf. Appian *Iber.* 11; Zonaras 8. 21), has a different view, stating that Saguntum was already under siege and that Hannibal refused to see the ambassadors, who then went to Carthage immediately. The ambassadors received a hearing at Carthage, but it did not effect any resolution, as Hannibal began the siege of Saguntum while the Romans were busy with affairs in Illyria, attempting to "clean their plates" for the inevitable (to them) war with Hannibal in Spain (Polyb. 3. 16–19; cf. Livy 21. 10–15).

The immediate crisis ended when news of the fall of Saguntum reached Rome (Polyb. 3. 20; cf. Livy 21. 16). It ended badly for the Romans, as a Roman ally had been forcibly conquered without the Romans' ability to intercede successfully. The Romans now exchanged this crisis for a tough decision: overlook the blow to their position in Spain and the more

---

[5] For a good brief summary of the long-running debate up to the mid-1950s, see Walbank, *Polybius* 1. 170–172. More recent discussions of the issues can be found in Errington (1970), Sumner (1972), Schwarte (1983), Eckstein (1984), Bender (1997), and Hoyos (1998).

[6] As has been noted before, the search for more information is one of the major coping mechanisms during a crisis. See Brecher (1993) 45, 83–117, 126–129, 363–367.

important blot to their good name in relation to their allies or begin a war with a powerful adversary that would doubtless lead to the expenditure of much blood and treasure. This new situation was not exactly a full-blown crisis, for time was not as pressing an issue in this matter. Hannibal was not yet at their gates, and there was no limited temporal window for response. Yet the Romans made an almost immediate response: prepare for war while also sending a high-level embassy to Carthage to deliver an ultimatum to either surrender Hannibal or accept war (Polyb. 3. 20. 6–8, 33. 2–4; Livy 21. 17: Roman war preparations included a formal vote of the Roman people for war (21. 17. 4); the embassy and its ultimatum (21. 18). Although the time for diplomacy had not yet passed, the Romans did not intend to open lengthy negotiations, employing the compellence diplomacy practiced by most ancient states.[7]

That the Roman Senate was serious in their resolve can be demonstrated by the high-level status of the embassy they sent: both outgoing consuls of 219, two other ex-consuls (including the lead envoy, Fabius[8]), and a member of the previous embassy to Hannibal at Saguntum the year before (219).[9] The tense standoff had not yet expanded into an unavoidable clash at this point, as there was still a choice for Carthage (it would, in fact, be Carthage's turn to be put into crisis). As Polybius described it, there were two very distinct options: ὧν τὸ μὲν αἰσχύνην ἅμα καὶ βλάβην ἐδόκει φέρειν δεξαμένοις τοῖς Καρχηδονίοις, τὸ δ' ἕτερον πραγμάτων καὶ κινδύνων ἀρχὴν μεγάλων "of which the one, to the Carthaginians choosing it, seemed to bear shame and harm, the other the beginning of great troubles and dangers" (3. 20. 7). The Carthaginians refused to surrender Hannibal, choosing the course of danger.

Of course, with the mutual declarations of war, the crisis that had been sparked by Hannibal's siege of Saguntum had led to greater hostile interaction, as both sides had chosen to settle affairs by war. It may be stating the obvious, but when the crisis was still in existence, which is when Saguntum was under siege, the emergency measures we have discussed in great detail so far would not have been of great use. A state of emergency and an emergency levy would not have provided an army capable of reaching Saguntum in time to raise Hannibal's siege. Even if it could, scratch levies without any time to engage in basic training or establishment of discipline

---

[7] For the term compellence diplomacy and its application to ancient states, see Eckstein (2006) 60–61 esp. nn. 100 and 101; 97–98; in the Roman context, see 121; 155–156, 166–167; 173 (for the ultimatum issued to Carthage to hand over Hannibal).

[8] There is some dispute over whether it was Q. Fabius Maximus Verrucosus or M. Fabius Buteo. See *MRR* 1. 239, 241 n. 7.

[9] The high-level nature of the embassy is noted by Eckstein (2006) 173.

would hardly have availed against the veteran forces of the Carthaginian general. Appointing a dictator would have done nothing to stop Hannibal from taking the city. Time and distance were against the Romans being able to use their existing emergency measures to respond to this crisis. One could argue that war was the only response that they would be able to make to the situation, and war is what they chose once the Carthaginians showed that they, too, had chosen to settle the dispute on the fields of battle.

HANNIBAL'S MARCH ON ROME IN 211

Thus began the war that resulted in serious setbacks for Rome, sparking two major emergencies as noted earlier in Chapter 2, when the defeats at Trasimene and Cannae drove the Romans to make use of the extreme expedient by that time of appointing a dictator. These would not be the only serious intra-war crises that faced the Romans. Another one occurred in 211, when Hannibal, concerned for the position of his ally Capua, closely besieged by the Romans, decided to undertake in that year what many others (especially with the gift of hindsight) thought he should have done in 216 after Cannae, which was to march against Rome.[10]

For this event, our best source is Livy. At the beginning of his twenty-third book, Livy narrates the chain of events that culminated in the revolt of Capua and most of the Campanians against Rome. The first defection to be noted was that of the town of Compsa among the Hirpini (23. 1. 1–3). He continues with the long tale of the rise of Pacuvius Calavius, a Campanian noble who planned to hand Capua over to Hannibal (23. 2–4). Following Rome's defeat at Cannae, the Campanians began to despise Roman power. Yielding to the entreaties of the parents and relatives of Campanian nobles serving as cavalry for the Romans in Sicily, a delegation was sent to see the surviving Roman consul of 216, M. Terentius Varro, whom they met while he was still in Venusia. There, Varro made a rather pitiable speech (Livy again trying to make the least of the man), which only encouraged the Campanians to despise Roman power more (23. 5–6. 1). They decided that an alliance with Hannibal could see them become the rulers of Italy in Rome's stead, so the Campanians sent the same ambassadors who had

---

[10] Beyond general works on the Second Punic War noted before in the discussions about the crises that followed Trasimene and Cannae, there is not much to add specifically about Hannibal's march on Rome in 211 that concerns crisis management. Of what there is, Salmon (1957) traces the route of march, Bassett (1964) is concerned with the site of Hannibal's camp, whereas Davis (1959) and Novara (1982) look at Livy's account of the march.

gone to see Varro to meet with Hannibal (23. 6. 2–5). Terms were agreed on, and Capua and much of Campania switched their allegiance from Rome to Hannibal (23. 7–10).

The revolt of the Campanians put Rome in a very sore spot, although surprisingly, Livy never recorded what the immediate reaction at Rome was to the revolt of some of their nearest allies. One might think that such news would precipitate a crisis, but as the Romans were already beset by so many other problems, it may not be surprising that this did not provoke any immediate response. They had more pressing matters – such as their own survival – to hold their attention. After several years, however, the situation changed. In 212, the new consuls, Q. Fulvius Flaccus and App. Claudius Pulcher, decided that it was time to attack Capua and punish the Campanians for their defection several years before (25. 15. 18–19), even though they had been assigned the war with Hannibal by decree of the senate at the opening of the year (25. 3. 3). There were setbacks and diversions (25. 15. 20–19. 17). Having settled them, the consuls eventually managed to commit themselves to the slow and difficult business of laying siege to Capua (25. 20. 1–4). Despite another serious reverse (the destruction of the praetor Cn. Fulvius's army, 25. 20. 5–21. 10), the Romans persevered, inspired by the continuing success of the consuls (25. 22. 1). The siege was pressed into the next year, although the senate made the decision to offer amnesty to any Campanian who left Capua before the next Ides of March (the beginning of the next magisterial year), taking their possessions with them (25. 22. 5–12). In response to pleas from the Campanians (25. 15. 1–3, 22. 10, 15–16), Hannibal decided that the way to break the siege of Capua was by making a direct assault on the city of Rome itself (26. 7. 3).

The Roman response was energetic. The proconsul Q. Fulvius learned of Hannibal's plans and immediately informed the senate (26. 8. 1). "As usual in so alarming a situation" (*ut in re tam trepida*), the senate was immediately called into session (26. 8. 2). So, here we have the triggering event for the crisis: the report that Hannibal himself was headed toward Rome. The gravity of the situation is clear from the proposal of P. Cornelius Asina, who wanted all of Rome's armies and commanders to drop whatever they were doing and immediately march to the defense of the city. Fabius Maximus (Verrucosus) opposed that move, thinking it shameful to concede Capua, when that was Hannibal's goal in threatening Rome. In the end, the senate chose to follow the opinion of P. Valerius Flaccus (*cos.* 227): to ask the proconsuls at Capua to choose which of them would return to Rome with part of the army stationed there, while the other proconsul continued to press the siege (26. 8. 2–8). As Appius was wounded, Fulvius had to go, so he chose 16,000 men from the army at Capua, and having ascertained Hannibal's route of march (the Via Latina), Fulvius himself traveled by the Appian Way in order to reach Rome before him (26. 8. 9–11).

Hannibal caused devastation along the route of his march (26. 9. 1–5). As alarm spread in Rome, Livy reports some scenes of panic (26. 9. 6–8) but also notes the measures that the Romans took for the defense: the senate sat in constant session in the forum for consultation; men were given assignments for the defense; and guards were posted on the citadel, the capitol, along the walls, and around the city (26. 9. 9). When word came that Fulvius was on his way, the senate quickly decreed that his *imperium* would be made equal to the consuls, thus allowing him to enter the city without the loss of *imperium* that would normally occur (26. 9. 10). Once he arrived, he pitched camp between the Esquiline and Colline Gates (26. 10. 1). The plebeian aediles were in charge of bringing supplies to the army, and the consuls and senate gathered there to discuss the defense of Rome. The consuls and Flaccus met with the senate at Flaccus's camp near the Esquiline Gate to discuss the situation. Among the many measures that were voted by them (under the presidency of the consuls) was that *senatum frequentem in foro contineri si quid tam in subitis rebus consulto opus esset* "that a session of the senate with full attendance be held in the Forum if there should be any need for consultation during such a crisis" (26. 10. 2).

It was decided that the consuls would pitch their camps near that of Fulvius (there is no mention of what forces they had at hand, but we can assume the two city legions "of the previous year" mentioned at the opening of consular year 210 at Livy 26. 28. 4 were included, as well as any volunteers). The city praetor C. Calpurnius took station on the capitol and the citadel. As there was an almost constant state of panic in parts of the city, the senate had to take the unusual step of granting *imperium* to all previous dictators, consuls, and censors who were in the city until the enemy had withdrawn from the walls of Rome so that there would be enough officials with coercive powers to suppress any and all disturbances in the city itself (26. 10. 7–10).

Apparently, Fate or something intervened on the side of the Romans because twice when the two sides had attempted to decide the issue in battle, the heavens broke open and rained on their parade of arms (26. 11. 1–4). Eventually, Hannibal retired and marched all the way back to Bruttium, leaving Rome safe (26. 11. 5–12. 2). Upon Hannibal's departure, the immediate crisis de-escalated and terminated.

Although it may not have been the case with Saguntum, this situation certainly does seem like an emergency – a crisis in which a rapid call up of all available military manpower and a declaration of a state of emergency would be expected. Hannibal was threatening the very existence of Rome. We have a full narrative in Livy that makes clear that the Romans perceived the danger to themselves most keenly. What we do not have, however, is any explicit reference to the main emergency response measures that have been discussed in the previous chapters. The obvious one we should expect to be mentioned is the *tumultus* declaration, but whereas we have many linguistic nods, especially at 26. 10. 1 where Livy presents Fulvius Flaccus the proconsul entering Rome *in hoc tumultu*, we do not get an unambiguous reference to the state of emergency being decreed. Barring that, we also do not have explicit references to an extraordinary levy and the enrollment of emergency soldiers, even though it would seem obvious to us that this was a situation where surely the Romans held a tumultuary levy and an emergency force of *tumultuarii* was enrolled. But we do not have any reference to that, nor the telltale mention of *vacationes*, military deferments, being suspended. It is not that the Romans did not employ "emergency" measures during this situation, which was clearly an emergency if there ever was one. What else can one make of the truly extraordinary senatorial decree that all former dictators, consuls, and censors would be invested with *imperium* until Hannibal had withdrawn from the walls of Rome? Granted, the intention there was to increase the number of "police" magistrates who could stamp out disturbances within the city while at the same time providing a pool of available commanders who could take command of soldiers within the city if it came to street-to-street fighting for the defense of their very homes.

Therefore, while this crisis might very well be placed within Chapter 3 dealing with *tumultus*, I hesitate to do so as we do not have an explicit statement that a *tumultus* was declared. Failing that, we would know that a *tumultus* had been declared if we had notices of enlistment exemptions being suspended and/or an emergency draft of *tumultuarii* being held. We do not have any notices of that kind, however. What we do have are singular notices of extraordinary measures (the grant of military authority to former dictators, consuls, and censors and the continuous sitting of the senate) that do not have parallels elsewhere. I am sure that some would consider this hesitation to state that a *tumultus* was declared at this time as being excessively cautious, but without firmer, clearer evidence, it is nothing more than an assumption, not a likelihood.

THE MACEDONIAN CRISIS OF 200

The beginning of the second century BC saw Rome triumph over Carthage but now no longer able to ignore events beyond Italy and its immediate environs. Circumstances now forced the ruling class of Rome to broaden its horizons. The events that led to the Romans crossing the Adriatic Sea and ending in the defeat of one of the Successor kingdoms of Alexander the Great are intricately tied to the Second Punic War, but they are also intensely intertwined with the larger power transition crisis in the Hellenistic world that began in 207, concerning which one should consult the important recent work of Eckstein.[11] Whereas it is often dangerous to state that an event was preordained, especially as hindsight blinds us to the mentality of the people making decisions at the time, it is not unreasonable to think that a full-scale clash with the Antigonid realm was inevitable, as Macedon had a serious interest in countering the slow encroachment of Roman power eastward, which began in the third century with Roman involvement in Illyria.[12] King Philip V's alliance with Hannibal during the Second Punic War eventually brought him no benefit. Quite the opposite: it brought an even more intensive Roman interest into Greek affairs. Whether Rome did or did not have its own imperial ambitions in the area (a subject with a vast bibliography) has provoked a long-lasting debate but one that has no direct bearing on whether this episode represents a crisis or not.[13] For this episode in Roman history, we are largely reliant upon Livy's narrative, with some fragments of Polybius and Appian, along with Plutarch's life of T. Quinctius Flamininus, to provide important details.

The Romans were not necessarily eager to begin a new major military undertaking, having just completed the titanic struggle against Hannibal.[14] What may have prompted them, as Polybius surmised, was the news brought to the senators by numerous Greek ambassadors that Philip and Antiochus III, the Seleucid monarch, had joined forces and were

---

[11] For the terminology and details of this event, whereby the balance of power among the three Successor kingdoms to Alexander the Great was severely, and irrevocably, disrupted, see Eckstein (2006) 104–116.

[12] For background, see Hammond (1968); Gruen (1984), especially 359f.; Derow (1991); Eckstein (1994); Warrior (1996); and Eckstein (1999), with sometimes diverging views and with references to earlier scholarship in all of these.

[13] The most recent extensive treatment of the scholarship on this episode is by Eckstein (2006) 257–292. Going against the prevailing trend of recent decades, he finds merit in the older "defensive" view of Holleaux (1921), especially 276–331, which has been somewhat swept aside by the influential work of Harris (1979), who (212–218) dismisses the "defensive view" and thinks the Romans gladly embraced the war with Philip. Of recent works, Mandell (1989) follows the Harris line strongly. Earlier followers of Holleaux were noted by Harris (1979) 212 n. 1. Prominent followers of the Harris line (as well as his precursors) are noted by Eckstein (2006) 262 n. 60.

[14] See Eckstein (2006) 266–269.

attempting to dismember the third of the Successor kingdoms, Egypt of the Ptolemies.[15] Rome did not want that to happen. During the turn of the consular year 203/202, envoys from Greece came to Rome to complain of attacks on their lands by the forces of Philip, and Philip's rebuffing of their attempts to receive redress for their complaints (Livy 30. 26. 2). They further reported to the senate that Philip had sent soldiers and money to Carthage to help them in their last stand against Roman forces in Africa (30. 26. 3; cf. 30. 42. 4–5). Modern scholars have taken these troops to be an annalistic invention, as neither Polybius nor Appian mentions them.[16] I am in agreement with those who have taken the charge to be false, but there is also the possibility that it was a contemporary charge, perhaps invented by the Greek states appealing to Rome for help against Philip. There is, however, no strong evidence for this conjecture (and sadly, the sections of Polybius and Appian that concerned the Greek embassies at Rome are no longer preserved).

The response of the senate was to dispatch a senatorial embassy of three (C. Terentius Varro, C. Mamilius, and M. Aurelius Cotta) to visit Philip and warn him that his actions were violating the Peace of Phoenice (Livy 30. 26. 4; cf. Polyb. 16. 27, 34). One year later, during the opening of consular year 201, embassies came to the senate again to argue over Philip's behavior. Philip's ambassadors complained about the actions of the Roman senatorial legate M. Aurelius, who apparently worked with the minor Greek states in raising troops to counter Philip's raiding parties. The Romans, however, responded to Philip's ambassadors by telling them that Philip's actions were violating the treaty and that he was looking to start a war (Livy 30. 42. 1–10). Philip's aggressive behavior toward Greek states that Rome considered to be under its protection heightened the possibility of a clash between the two greater powers. Further embassies would come, this time from the Rhodians and from King Attalus of Pergamum reporting the state of affairs in Asia Minor, as well as news that Athens was being harassed by Philip (31. 1. 9–2. 1). The senate responded by saying that they would look into these matters. That war was already contemplated was indicated by the Romans taking this opportunity to send an embassy of three (C. Claudius Nero, M. Aemilius Lepidus, and P. Sempronius Tuditanus) to King Ptolemy in Egypt, thanking him for his support during the Second Punic War and asking him, in the event of a war between the Roman state and Macedon, to stay neutral (31. 2. 3–4).

---

[15] See Eckstein (2006) 269–276.

[16] See Walbank, *Polybius* 2. 456 (with references to earlier scholarship). But see also Briscoe, *Livy* 1. 55 (with bibliography). Referenced also by Warrior (1996) 102–103 and n. 12.

The Romans themselves took the initiative in escalating the crisis in late consular year 201. Up to this point, neither side had taken any action that required an immediate decision concerning peace or war. Now, the Romans began to press the issue. At a meeting of the senate (a well-attended one: *frequens*), presided over by the consul P. Aelius Paetus (*cos*. 201), the senate instructed the consul to send someone with *imperium* to take over the fleet that Cn. Octavius (*pr*. 205, who had been continuously prorogued to command the fleet supplying Scipio's force in Africa) was sailing back to Rome from Sicily, and to move that fleet to "Macedon" (31. 3. 1–2). As Briscoe points out, this likely meant that the fleet would be moved into the territory of Rome's allies in Illyria near Macedon.[17] M. Valerius Laevinus, the consul of 210, was given the command with *imperium pro praetore* to transfer the fleet to the East. Once there, he consulted with the senatorial legate M. Aurelius, and the two of them planned Roman countermeasures to Philip, with Aurelius writing an alarming report to the senate as to affairs in the area (31. 3. 3–6).

The immediate triggering events to the crisis – what gave rise to the perception that Philip presented a real danger to the Romans and their interests – were the reports at the opening of consular year 200 that came back to Rome from Aurelius and Laevinus, as well as an embassy that arrived from Athens to report that the city was being harassed by Philip (31. 5. 5–6; cf. Polyb. 16. 27). The *patres* were alarmed by events in the East, and that fear provoked a crisis. Now, from a certain perspective on Roman imperialism (that of W. V. Harris), the events of this year should not be seen as a crisis. It cannot be a crisis because in his opinion, the Romans did not feel any fear with regard to Philip.[18] He makes a case for why we should simply disregard Livy's clear notices to the contrary (31. 3. 4–6 [alarming report of the legate Aurelius]; 31. 7. 1–15 [speech of the consul Galba]). Harris's own line of reasoning, however, is grounded upon nothing more than a supposition. He is correct to ask: "What then do we know about Roman feelings towards Philip V in 201 and 200?"[19] What he does next, however, is to make use of mere speculation to counter Livy. For he states that although we do not have Polybius (and we do not for this important point in Roman history), "His [Polybius'] analysis probably gave due prominence to the Roman ἔννοια of world-conquest, a view which Livy naturally rejected."[20]

---

[17] Briscoe, *Livy* 1. 61.
[18] Harris (1979) 212–218.
[19] Harris (1979) 215.
[20] Harris (1979) 215–216.

The foundation of his argument is that the Romans did not feel fear "because Polybius might have said that they did not at this time." That is mere speculation and in itself cannot, in my opinion, trump the extant testimony of Livy, even if Livy himself is writing at a much later date. Furthermore, his reasoning for dismissing Livy is suspect on two further grounds. First of all, Harris seems to think that Livy and the annalists felt the need to justify Roman actions in 200. "Livy or a source of his is attempting to justify Roman actions by making Philip into a serious threat."[21] The question can be asked (and is not answered by him at all), to whom were the annalists and Livy trying to justify Roman actions? To the Greeks? Which Greeks, especially in Livy's time, who could read Latin, would require a justification for Roman actions against Philip? And in an earlier period as well, who of the Latin annalist reading public would require a justification to be made for Roman actions against Philip? Why would the Latin annalists, or Livy if we believe him to be the "inventor" of the Romans' fear, feel there was need to justify Rome's actions in 200 at all? These are questions Harris leaves unanswered but ones that must be answered in order to accept his argument.

A second assumption he makes concerns Roman knowledge of Eastern events when the decision to go to war was being made. Harris notes that the battle of Chios, while called a strategic victory for Philip, was actually a defeat for him. Therefore, the Romans knew that Philip was not a serious threat and did not feel any fear toward him.[22] Harris makes a serious error here, however, if we are talking about perceptions and not realities. For if we are really going to attempt to get into the minds of the Roman Senate in 200 (which, admittedly, may be a near impossibility without a direct firsthand account), then we must base our suppositions on what the Romans knew at the time, not what we know from the vantage of hindsight. Even Harris is aware of this, as he notes "Its [the Roman Senate's] information may admittedly have been defective. Senatorial opinion may have hardened to an important extent after the Pergamene-Rhodian embassies, if members lacked reliable news about the Aegean situation that resulted from the battle of Chios."[23] Harris treats the situation as if the Roman Senate before they made their decision was as fully informed as he – a dubious prospect at best.

The other major side of the divide on Roman imperialism (those who derive their views from the defensive school represented most strongly by

---

[21] Harris (1979) 214.
[22] Harris (1979) 214–215.
[23] Harris (1979) 215.

Holleaux)[24] would have no issue seeing this episode as a crisis. Clearly, the Romans were afraid of Philip, and they responded. Even if one does not accept Holleaux's preemptive war theory, others such as Badian,[25] have suggested that Rome was concerned about Philip's ambitions and the threat posed by him through Illyria (another position summarily dismissed by Harris). They as well would agree with Philip being perceived as a threat and, therefore, the trigger to a crisis.

I believe that we can take Livy's reports of fear among the Romans caused by the specter of Philip invading Italy as reflecting a genuine report of what he found in his sources. Even if we know from the vantage of hindsight that the threat was exaggerated, that does not mean that the threat was not felt. This would not be the first, nor the last, war to be fought because of exaggerated fears of nonexistent dangers based on unreliable intelligence and faulty information. The military build-up in 201, the year before the Romans actually decided to declare war, would point to rising Roman fears of a new military threat from the East. As yet another piece of evidence for the Roman attitude in 200, let us note what might seem to be a minor event but is rather important. After war was declared, the consuls had given notice that the third debt repayment, owed by the Roman state to those who had loaned it money back in 210 during the Second Punic War, could not be made because what funds were in the treasury were now necessary for the newly voted upon war.[26] In response to the demand of creditors, the senate made a compromise: they would not be able to repay the money owed now but would allow creditors to lease public land for a nominal rent of a single *as*, so that the state would be able to retain title. When the treasury was sufficiently replenished, repayment on the loans would be made.[27] That the senate was willing to give away public land practically rent-free in order to avoid draining the treasury of much-needed funds for the coming war demonstrates the seriousness of their apprehension about the battles to come.

The senate (spurred by the consuls, of course) decided that one of the consuls would have Macedon as his province and that that consul would bring a war vote before the people (Livy 31. 5. 9). Although the consul who was assigned to the war, P. Sulpicius Galba (previously *cos.* 211), failed to pass the war vote on the first attempt (31. 6. 1–4), it was eventually passed

---

[24] Holleaux (1921), esp. 276–331 for the events surrounding 200.
[25] Badian (1958) 61–66.
[26] For the original loan, see Livy 26. 36. 8. Repayment was first arranged in 204, to be made in three biennial installments (see 29. 26. 1). On the issue of Rome's finances at the time, see Buraselis (1996).
[27] Livy 31. 13. 2–9.

(31. 8. 1). Legions were voted for the consuls, and Sulpicius was authorized to enlist volunteers from Scipio's army returning from Africa, although otherwise the senate was attempting to discharge veterans from the Second Punic War (31. 8. 5–6). Further preparations were made by dispatching an embassy to Masinissa with a request for Numidian horsemen. The king offered 2,000; the Romans only accepted half (31. 11. 8–12, 19. 3–4).

Sulpicius gathered his army and fleet at Brundisium and embarked for Greece. Once there, he was met by Athenian ambassadors and sent his subordinate C. Claudius Cento with 20 ships and 1,000 soldiers to relieve Athens (31. 14. 1–5). The war did not proceed quickly; it dragged on through the next consulship, which saw P. Villius Tappulus replace Sulpicius as commander (32. 1. 1–3, 3. 2–7, 6. 1). Villius was also not particularly successful in seeing things through when his successor, one of the new consuls of 198 – the young T. Quinctius Flamininus, appeared on the scene to take over (32. 6. 4, 9. 6–11). At this point, Philip decided to send out peace feelers through the Epirotes; Flamininus made some counterproposals that only managed to anger Philip, so the two sides headed for battle (32. 10) near the Aous gorge, which saw Philip driven back into Thessaly (Livy 32. 11–2; cf. Plut. *Flamininus* 4. 2–3 offers a very slight variant). This battle was not a crisis terminator because Philip managed to escape with most of his army. The perception that Philip remained a threat continued.

As the next consular year opened, an attempt by the new consuls to have Macedon decreed as one of the new consular *provinciae* was quashed by two tribunes who suggested that the consuls allow the senate to decide the matter. The senate decreed that Flamininus would continue in Greece until the senate sent a successor (Livy 32. 28. 3–9). Back in Greece, there was another round of negotiations between Philip and his enemies (the Romans, Athenians, King Attalus, the Rhodians, the Aetolians, and now the Achaeans as well), but the negotiations did not go anywhere. It was finally decided that all parties would send ambassadors to Rome (Polyb. 18. 1–11; Livy 32. 32–36). At Rome, the Romans asked if Philip would evacuate the so-called fetters of Greece (Acrocorinth, Chalcis, and Demetrias), and his ambassadors replied that they had no instructions on the matter, so diplomacy again produced no results. The senate gave Flamininus full discretion in the matter, and he proceeded to plan for the war (Polyb. 18. 12; Livy 32. 37).

After the opening of consular year 197, Flamininus and his allies fought a decisive battle with Philip at the "dogs' heads" (Cynoscephalae) in Thessaly. It was a resounding victory for the forces arrayed against Philip (Polyb. 18. 19–26; Livy 33. 3–10). Immediately following the Battle of

Cynoscephalae, the crisis abated as Philip swiftly retreated back to his kingdom, stopping only at Larisa in Thessaly to burn his records; he also sent a herald to Flamininus asking for a truce to bury his dead, secretly requesting permission to send an embassy to treat for peace (Livy 33. 11; cf. Polyb. 18. 33–34[28]). With Philip's retreat, the perception of his remaining a threat receded, and all that remained was to arrange a peace. After further negotiation, terms of peace were laid out, and Philip was ordered to send embassy to Rome (Polyb. 18. 36–39; Livy 33. 13). Flamininus was eager to have things settled, as there was already a hint that Antiochus had his eye on a crossing to Europe (Polyb. 18. 39. 3; Livy 33. 13. 15). All sides converged on Rome, and although one of the new consuls for 196, M. Claudius Marcellus, attempted to wreck the peace (in order to have Macedon decreed for himself so that he could bring the war to a conclusion), the peace was approved with the customary (*more maiorum*) and by now normal appointment of ten commissioners to help Flamininus draw up the final peace settlements (Polyb. 18. 42; Livy 33. 24. 5–7, 25. 4–7). Thus ended the war between Philip and Rome (Livy 33. 35. 12).

For this crisis, again there is clearly a perceived threat and at the beginning a limited time in which to respond to the threat or at least the perception that time was a factor. What there is not is any indication that the Roman government and its decision makers saw any need to institute immediate emergency measures to respond to the threat. And there was no need to do so. Philip was not going to be knocking on Rome's door with an army as Hannibal did and Antiochus had threatened to do – at least in the minds of Rome's decision makers – which led to the declaration of a *tumultus* in Sicily and southern Italy in 192.[29] There was time enough for the regular machinery of war to provide the necessary tools to respond to the threat posed by Philip.

The Bacchanalian Affair of 186

Not every crisis is tied exclusively to war, although war, or the imminent prospect of it, often led to crisis. Our next situation that provoked an active, albeit unique, response was caused by the fear inspired by a religious cult that did not have the approval of the senatorial establishment. As there is substantial bibliography on this topic, there is little need for a lengthy introduction. One can consult the recent works by Pagán

[28] There is a small lacuna in Polybius at this point. See Walbank, *Polybius* 2. 592 and Briscoe, *Livy* 1. 266–267.
[29] See Chapter 3.

(2004), Takács (2000), and the now somewhat older but useful treatment of Gruen (1990).[30] Briscoe (2003) is concerned with the ultimate origin of the information found in Livy. Rasmussen (2001) looks at how contemporary figures (such as M. Antony and Cleopatra) may have affected Livy's narrative.[31]

I am in partial agreement with the line taken by Takács, which follows that of Gruen, in that the whole crisis was a staged event, part of a larger plan by the Roman Senate to assert and expand their authority over Rome's growing sphere of control in Italy. What was not staged was the perceived threat presented by the Bacchanalian followers themselves. Even if crisis itself was staged – a crisis deliberately triggered by the Roman authorities – we still have an actual crisis. For this event, we not only have Livy's complete and extant narrative; we also have the good fortune to have a preserved epigraphic copy of the senatorial decree that was passed in response to the crisis.[32]

As we have it according to our major source, Livy, there seems to be a short initial phase to the crisis. When Livy begins his report of the whole affair, it is already a full-blown crisis, as he notes at the opening of consular year 186 that the consuls were diverted from armies and war and provinces "to the suppression of an internal conspiracy" *ad intestinae coniurationis vindictam* (39. 8. 1).[33] After a brief summary of the origin of the cult in Italy (39. 8. 3–8), Livy begins to spin his dramatic tale of the young Aebutius and his prostitute "with the heart of gold," Hispala Faecenia (39. 9. 2–10. 9). We get the story of the young man being driven from his home upon refusal to be initiated into the cult and his seeking refuge with his aunt Aebutia. She advised the young man to speak to the consul. Aebutius goes to the consul Sp. Postumius Albinus[34] to inform him of the whole affair. The consul is initially skeptical and decides to see if the aunt, Aebutia, is trustworthy. So, he turns to his mother-in-law (!) Sulpicia to find out if Aebutia is someone whose word can be believed. Aebutia is brought to Sulpicia's house as a ploy to allow Postumius to interview her

---

[30] Gruen (1990) 72–77.

[31] Pagán (2004), even though focused on Livy's account as a conspiracy narrative, seems to be unaware of Takács (2000), Briscoe (2003), and Rasmussen (2001).

[32] Livy 39. 8–19, 41. 6–7; 40. 19. 9–10; *SC de Bacchanalibus* : *ILLRP* 511 (*CIL* 1² 581).

[33] The translation is from E. Sage's Loeb. Livy may not be correct, however, in his portrayal of the sudden appearance of the cult. Brennan (2000) 205, following up on an observation by Pailler (1988) 297 (cf. 299), notes that circumstantial evidence, the activity of praetorian commanders in the region between 190–187, "suggests that the explosion of Bacchic cult activity in 186 was not as spontaneous as it seems from Livy's account."

[34] For references on him, see *MRR* 1. 370–371.

in secret. From this interview, the consul believes that Aebutius is serious (39. 11. 1–7).

In the next phase of the drama, we have the consul interview the prostitute Hispala through the medium of his mother-in-law Sulpicia again. The freedwoman refuses to acknowledge anything beyond her own membership in the cult at first, but after application of pressure by the consul, she reveals all of the activities that take place during the nocturnal rites (39. 12–3). After divulging everything, the consul has Hispala moved into Sulpicia's house and has Aebutius lodged at the house of one of his clients (39. 14. 1–3). At this point, Postumius moves to trigger the crisis for the state by laying the entire matter before the senate (39. 14. 3). Livy records the reaction of that august body: *patres pavor ingens cepit* "a great terror seized the senators" (39. 14. 4). Again, this seems more like a drama than true history, but before we dismiss out of hand the idea that the senators were afraid, there is the matter of the inscription providing external proof that the crisis, regardless of its artificial nature, was real. Therefore, it is unreasonable to wave away the report that the senators were gravely alarmed by this situation, even if we wish to think that it is overstated.

Going back to Livy's narrative, in response to this dangerous situation, the senate, practically in a panic, decreed that the consuls begin an investigation into the whole affair, that the witnesses be placed in protective custody, and that rewards be offered to informers willing to provide further information (39. 14. 4–7). What is noteworthy here, as already noticed before by Gruen, is that the investigation was ordered *extra ordinem* (39. 14. 6) without any authorization beyond a decree of the senate.[35] Thus, the charge by later scholars that this was largely a power grab by the senate is probably correct.

As Livy reports it, the first business of the consuls was to investigate any persons who had engaged in either immorality (*stuprum*) or criminal acts (*flagitium*) (39. 14. 8). The consuls ordered the curule aediles to locate all priests of the cult and place them under watch; they ordered the plebeian aediles to prevent any secret celebrations of the rites (39. 14. 9). The *triumviri capitales* were ordered to place the city under guard (organize the vigiles, the night watch) and guard against any possibility of arson, with the assistance of the *quinqueviri uls cis Tiberim*, two boards of five (one on the nearer bank, one on the further bank of the Tiber) who normally had care of the banks of the river. In this respect, the way of managing the situation is reminiscent of the events of 213, with the minor magistrates being deployed to clean up the spread of foreign cults in the city, although

[35] As Gruen (1990) 40–41 notes, the lack of any popular sanction is odd.

their failure at that time forced the senate to decree the task to the city praetor instead (25. 1. 10–12).[36]

At this point, the consuls held a *contio* to address the Roman people. Postumius made a long speech to the crowd (39. 15. 1–17. 1), revealing the goals of the Bacchanalians, including their wish to control the state (39. 15. 3). The senate's decrees were then read, including rewards for informers and penalties for those who tried to help any fugitives escape (39. 17. 1–3). There followed a panic among those who were involved in the cult, as people were caught trying to leave the city in secret by the guards posted by the *triumviri capitales*. The ringleaders were captured and put on trial, and Livy records that over 7,000 men and women were implicated (39. 17. 4–7). So many were being brought before the praetors in the city (T. Maenius and M. Licinius) that cases began to fall through, and the senate compelled the praetors to adjourn all legal hearings for thirty days until the consuls could complete their investigations (39. 18. 1).[37] This task the consuls prosecuted vigorously, condemning to death most of the cult members they found, with female transgressors handed over to their relatives for punishment, with the state carrying out the death sentence only when a woman had no relatives who could undertake the task (39. 18. 2–6).

After the "witch hunt" was completed, the final measures were taken: the decree of the senate was passed that severely restricted the cult within Italy (the *SC de Bacchanalibus*, which is surely what Livy 39. 18. 8–9 refers to). It is implied that Postumius was responsible for the stamping out of the cult outside of the city of Rome, while Q. Marcius, the other consul of 186 stayed in the city (39. 18. 7–19. 1). Through these actions, the government could begin to breathe easier and see an end to the crisis. With the cult and its membership brought under control (for the most part) after the return of Sp. Postumius, decrees were passed that provided very generous rewards to Aebutius and Hispala: he was exempted from all military service, whereas she was given rights over her property and legal standing in the courts that practically put her on a level with a free-born woman (39. 19. 3–7). As for the Bacchanalians, a few scattered remnants apparently gathered in the south, and one of the praetors of 185, L. Postumius Tempsanus, who

---

[36] This incident is noted by Gruen (1990) 39–40 as a precursor to the current episode. Another possible precedent for this measure was the similar action taken during the slave tumult of 198 (see p. 92f.).

[37] Bauman (1990) 337 and 339 calls it a *iustitium*, which is possible, but Livy does not use the word at all, stating *cogerentur praetores T. Maenius et M. Licinius per senatum res in diem tricesium differre*. Note that it was only an adjournment of legal cases, not a complete cessation of public and private business, which occurred during a declared *iustitium*.

was given Tarentum as his *provincia*, was ordered to continue rooting out members of the cult (39. 41. 6–7). Finally, one of the praetors of 181, L. Duronius, was assigned the task of mopping up the last remaining "seeds" of the group in his assigned province of Apulia (40. 19. 9–10).[38]

In this episode, there was a need for force in order to suppress the cult. We have a reference from Cicero (*Leg.* 2. 37) that states that the consuls suppressed the cultists *exercitu adhibito*. Livy, however, makes no mention of employing an armed force, which has sparked some debate over who is correct. Bauman has proposed a possible solution to reconcile the seeming difference between the two authors: within Rome itself, where soldiers were not normally allowed unless special dispensation was granted, Postumius made use of an irregular levy, an *evocatio*. Once operations moved outside of Rome, the regular annual levy was likely completed, and Postumius would have had the use of those soldiers.[39] Bauman calls these soldiers *milites tumultuarii*, which could imply that a state of *tumultus* was declared, and it may be that the situation might have called for one, but it would be very strange, to say the least, for Livy to pass over this detail entirely, along with the report of soldiers being hastily enlisted by the consul, if a *tumultus* had actually been declared. Although I think Bauman is correct that the suppression of the Bacchic cultists in Rome was carried out by an irregular force, I am not sure that he is correct about calling them soldiers. As we see from the measures outlined in the decree that the senate passed and from Livy's narrative, the consuls and the senate preferred to view the entire matter as more a "public order" issue and not a military threat.[40] The evidence is in the details provided by Livy: there is no mention of an emergency levy or the use of sworn or unsworn soldiers. Instead, he reports clearly – and believably – that the *triumviri capitales* were ordered to station night watches (*vigiliae*) throughout the city to prevent nocturnal meetings and arson. The *quinqueviri uls cis Tiberim* were ordered to stand guard over buildings in their districts. There are no battle lines, no parades of troops. When we come to the actual action in suppressing the cultists,

---

[38] The praetors assigned to southern Italy from Tempsanus down to Duronius apparently had a double task in the region, both to round up the remains of the Bacchic cultists, who may have doubled as rebels against Roman authority, and to suppress uprisings by slave shepherds in Apulia. See Brennan (2000) 204–205.

[39] Bauman (1990) 343–345, which also contains references to the division among some scholars as to whether Cicero's notice should be given credence at all, and n. 35 with references to the *evocatio*.

[40] A position that I believe would be in accord with Bauman's interpretation of the senatorial response, as he noted that " . . . the whole point about the emphasis on common law crimes is that cultists' acts were not elevated to treason." See Bauman (1990) 343.

the only use of force appears to be the actions of the guards stationed at the city gates by the *capitales*, who seized and brought back people who tried to escape the city (*custodiis circa portas positis fugientes a triumviris comprehensi et reducti sunt* 39. 17. 5). In Rome itself, it appears that what was employed was more an irregular posse or volunteers who came forward to assist the *capitales* and other minor magistrates in their assigned tasks. This does not rule out Bauman's idea of an *evocatio*, certainly, but when we look at clear examples of *tumultus* from Chapter 3, we see many instances, even in minor affairs such as the slave tumult of 198, where Livy makes explicit mention of the sudden enlistments of soldiers. If that did occur in this case, it would be odd for him to omit a detail that might otherwise increase the dramatic tension of the episode, an effect he clearly wished to achieve.[41]

Once the focus of the investigation moved outside of Rome, there would be need for an armed force to back up the decisions of the consuls, especially as we know that within Rome, many of the accused cultists were executed (39. 18. 4). Outside of Rome, in potentially hostile communities, the army would be required to support the consul. This was without doubt an extraordinary, unique event in Roman history, and the measures taken to respond to the threat that was claimed to emanate from the Bacchanalians were extraordinary, but did not, apparently, include the declaration of a state of emergency of the normal kind, unless the suspension of the courts for thirty days was indeed a *iustitium*, although we have no firm evidence that it was, as there was no reference to all public business (and private business) being suspended. It may seem odd if the affair presented as dire a threat as Livy would have us believe. But if it is correct that Postumius and the senate wanted to have the matter seen more as a problem of public order than a military threat, then it makes sense that they would not declare a state of emergency but instead use measures tied more to law enforcement than war.

Political Impasse in 173–172: The Troublesome Laenates

So far in this study, we have focused almost entirely on situations where there was a palpable threat of physical violence to which Roman decision

---

[41] As Pagán (2004) 53 has noted, there is a "novelistic quality" to Livy's narrative, which certainly is embellished in many respects. But that would be a point in favor of my position, as mentioning the sudden raising of troops and the declaration of a state of emergency would only increase the drama of the situation.

makers had to formulate a response. Yet crises to the machinery of government that had the effect of rendering them in danger of overthrow, or at the
very least render it inoperative, could be created even in the absence of any
threat of physical harm being done to the state. The reason for this weakness in the Roman government before the creation of the Principate is that
it lacked any independent instrument, whether an institution or a person
invested with unchallengeable power, which could settle matters between
rival sources of authority within the governing system of the Romans. The
people were sovereign, but they had no independence of action. They could
only "wish and order" what a magistrate or tribune put before them. The
senate had *auctoritas*, but it again lacked initiative and was only powerful
when it had the active cooperation of a magistrate with sufficient power
to enforce its will. Although the magistrates had power and freedom of
action, they were not free to do as they liked, being bound by statute law,
custom, and the need to achieve consensus within the ruling stratum of the
senatorial class. If there was open competition between these groups, the
entire system could break down.

We already discussed one incident where this occurred, the "troublesome" ex-tribune C. Sempronius Gracchus, who was opposed by the consul L. Opimius. That episode, of course, ended in violence as both sides felt
sufficiently threatened by the other to resort to physical action to uphold
their political positions. Opimius and his supporters in the senate crafted
the so-called *senatus consultum ultimum* as a means of ending the political
impasse. But not every situation that could result in constitutional gridlock
necessarily gave rise to the sides feeling that violence was the only means
of holding to their position.

A famous example of a political impasse that sparked a crisis in
the machinery of government itself was caused by the brothers Popillii
Laenates, consuls in 173 (Marcus) and 172 (Gaius).[42] We have the story
only in Livy. The elder brother, Marcus, campaigned against the Ligurians
and ended his expedition there by committing an act that upset the *patres
conscripti* back in Rome: he sold the Ligurians into slavery and demol-
ished the town of the Statellates after they had surrendered themselves to
the Roman people without conditions (Livy 42. 7. 3–8. 3). When the consul's dispatch was read in the senate by the city praetor A. Atilius Serranus,

---

[42] For full references on both, see *MRR* I under their respective years. The prominence given to
this story is curious. In a private conversation, A. M. Eckstein suggested to me that the story
only appears here in order to highlight the arrogance of the Popillii Laenates, a family not in
the good books of Livy because a later member of the family was the murderer of Cicero (Dio
47. 11. 1–2), for whom we know Livy had a high regard (Livy's eulogy of Cicero from his lost
120th book is partly preserved in Seneca the Elder, *Suas.* 6. 17). A plausible supposition.

the senate reacted with outrage and a decree was passed – it must be noted, under the presidency of the praetor Serranus – to order the consul to free the Statellates immediately, restore their lands and arms, and pay back to the buyers who had purchased the enslaved Ligurians the price that they had paid for them (42. 8. 4–8).

M. Popillius Laenas, however, chose to ignore the decree. Coming to Rome in a huff, he instead upbraided the praetor (and fined him!) for passing a decree directed against his superior, when the praetor should have instead been moving for a *supplicatio* to reward him for his actions. Then Laenas asked the senate to repeal their earlier decree and instead pass the thanksgiving in his presence to do him honor (42. 9. 1–5). The response of the senators gathered there was a series of speeches attacking him that were no less harsh than when he had been absent (*nihilo lenioribus quam absens*). Neither of the consul's wishes was granted, and he returned to his province (42. 9. 6). Here we see clearly how powerless the senate, on its own, actually was. Although the praetor Serranus could pass a decree ordering the consul to follow the senate's will, there was no actual mechanism for Serranus to enforce the decree, for a praetor could not order a consul. On the other side, M. Laenas was consul, and in the absence of his colleague, would have had no one to oppose him in the exercise of his official powers; nevertheless, he could not just order the senate to pass an honorary decree to his liking and repeal a decree that he likely considered a personal affront. Customary law prevented a consul from simply declaring a thanksgiving for himself (the preliminary step toward a triumph), which also would have required senatorial permission. This is all of little consequence (other than for the haughty M. Laenas's large ego) compared with the more important matter of the status of the Statellates and the good name of Rome with regard to those whom the Romans had received *in fidem*.

The events of the following year, when M. Laenas was no longer consul and could not block the senate's wishes by himself, further demonstrated the impotency of the senate when it did not have the backing of the highest magistrates in office. Seeking to have the decree reenacted (which would be necessary because the original decree directed M. Laenas to restore the Statellates; one of the new consuls would have to carry out the restoration now), the senate asked the new consuls, P. Aelius and C. Popillius Laenas, to have it passed. Initially, P. Aelius was prepared to resubmit the decree to the senate, but C. Laenas threatened to veto it if it were passed and soon convinced his colleague to refuse to resubmit the decree for a vote (42. 10. 10–11). The senators in response refused to allot either of them the coveted province of Macedonia but instead decreed Liguria again for both and would not open the question of Macedonia being assigned unless the decree concerning M. Laenas were passed. When the consuls petitioned the senate for permission to enlist new armies or supplement the old ones, the senate refused to decree any reinforcement levies, even for the praetors destined for the two Spanish provinces (42. 10. 11–13). The consuls then announced that they would hold the Latin Festival at the earliest date possible and then leave for their provinces; before that, they would refuse to carry out any other business except what was related to their provinces (42. 10. 15). The two sides "punished" each other for their lack of "cooperation:" the consuls prevented the passage of the decree ordering the restoration of the Statellates, while the senate refused to agree to any of the proposals concerning the provinces referred to them by the consuls. Clearly, this was an insurmountable impasse for both sides, which had the effect of impeding necessary government action, such as the likely real need to recruit supplements to the Spanish armies. The decision-making machinery of the Republic was at an effective standstill so long as the consuls remained in Rome.[43]

In this situation where the power of the consuls was at variance with the authority of the senate, it is ironic, considering later events, that one of the anomalies of the Roman Republic's governing structure would come to its rescue at this time. The impasse that had threatened to prevent any major decisions being taken by the consuls and the senate for the administration of the state would only be broken by the actions of an outside party: the intercession of two tribunes of the plebs, M. Marcius Sermo and Q. Marcius Silla.[44] They threatened the consuls with a fine unless they left Rome for their provinces and further read in the senate a bill they were going to propose before the assembly that would give the senate the power to effect the restoration of the Statellates. With the senate's blessing, they promulgated the bill (42. 21. 4–5). The bill was passed (42. 21. 8).

Thus came an end to the impasse between the consuls and the senate, but the structural problem of the system – that it relied upon the mutual cooperation and agreement of senate and chief magistrates – was on display for all. Although the senators who strongly opposed the behavior of M. Popillius Laenas were ultimately successful in getting their way, they

---

[43] Which they did for some considerable time: Livy 42. 21. 1.

[44] No praetor, of course, could attempt to end the deadlock as the consuls very likely forbade them from calling the senate into session by virtue of their *maius imperium*. A precursor to this incident occurred in 210, when the consul M. Valerius Laevinus was at odds with the senate, and forbade the *praetor urbanus*, L. Manlius Acidinus, from acting. The impasse was ended only when a tribune of the plebs stepped in to push the measure through. For full details and references, see Brennan (2000) 113–114.

were unable to achieve this result on their own. They had to rely on the actions of two tribunes of the plebs, the sole officials who would be capable of operating outside of the consuls' ability to veto or obstruct any governmental action, in order to have their will expressed. The senate as a whole also only managed a qualified victory. The plebiscite passed by the tribunes allowed the senate to name an official to restore the Ligurians and to investigate the circumstances of their enslavement, and the senate named C. Licinius Crassus, the city praetor (who presided over the meeting at which the decision was made),[45] to hold the investigation (42. 21. 8). Licinius and the "foreign" praetor Cn. Sicinius were ordered to restore the Statellates (42. 22. 5). However, the attempt to punish M. Laenas for his behavior fell short: C. Licinius, overcome by the influence of the absent C. Laenas and the entreaties of the Popillian family, used a procedural maneuver to evade pronouncing sentence on M. Laenas, which in effect allowed the ex-consul to get off scot-free (42. 22. 7–8). So, once again, we see how the senate had to rely on magistrates to carry out their wishes and had little recourse available to them if the magistrates did not follow the expressed will of the senate.

The impasse of 173–172 over the Ligurian Statellates did not threaten the foundations of the Republic, certainly. And yet, had the impasse involving both consuls appeared in 173, not 172, with no quick resolution, it could have had serious and negative consequences. The year 173 was a rather busy one, for in this very same year, a swarm of locusts coming from the sea suddenly appeared in Apulia, covering large areas with the crop-destroying pests. The situation was of sufficient gravity that the Romans sent Cn. Sicinius, while still praetor designate for 172, with *imperium* to Apulia to deal with the swarm. He employed a veritable battle line of men (*ingenti agmine hominum*) to collect the locusts (Livy 42. 10. 7–8). It is interesting that it was felt necessary to send a man with military command authority (*imperium*) to take control of this local crisis, but considering the method that he used to deal with the pests, basically conscripting what was for all intents and purposes a "bug-catching army," we should not be surprised at all.[46] However, what if the consuls were

---

[45] In itself, this was unusual, as normally the highest magistrate available presided over any meeting of the senate, although in this case it was likely written into the statute, which ended the impasse. See Brennan (2000) 115.

[46] What is most curious of all is to consider the actions of this man in the near future. In his year of office in 172, although peregrine praetor, he was ordered to go to southern Italy again, but this time he was instructed to raise a regular army near Rome, march it to Brundisium, and prepare it for transport to Apollonia in preparation for the coming war with King Perseus of Macedon (Livy 42. 18. 2–3, 27. 3–8). With his *imperium* prorogued, he later crossed to Greece

sitting in Rome, blocking all measures that could come before the senate? In such a situation, the locust invasion could well have been allowed to proceed unchecked, causing serious damage to agriculture and livelihoods. As nature is unpredictable, no state can afford to have its ability to make decisions be held hostage for political reasons.

Similarly, what would have happened if there had been a continued impasse in the year afterward, when the senate was at loggerheads yet again with another consul? In this year, following close on the heels of the two Laenates, C. Cassius Longinus (*cos.* 171), who was assigned Italy as his province, conceived a rash plan to lead his army overland to Macedonia, in order to join his colleague P. Licinius Crassus, who was pursuing the war against King Perseus of Macedon. When the senate learned of this, they immediately passed a decree ordering the consul to return to Italy. Three envoys were sent to deliver the decree (Livy 43. 1. 4–12). Sadly, we do not know exactly how the embassy fared, but we do know that it was likely successful because for the next three years (170, 169, and 168), Cassius did not return to Rome but remained in the field as a tribune of the soldiers to various commanders.[47] Livy makes it clear from his first notice of Cassius's continued absence from Rome that he was remaining in the field *rei publicae causa* to avoid having to account for misdeeds he likely committed in relation to his venture to march to Macedonia (43. 5. 1–10). It would appear that the mission to stop him had succeeded, and Cassius was now sufficiently fearful for his future political life and position if he returned to face a wrathful senate. But what would the case have been if instead of his colleague being abroad as well, he were in Rome and aided Longinus by blocking the senate from acting? Or what if the city praetor were to take his part? It is true that hypotheticals do not carry any weight of their own, and of course, the aid of the tribunes of the plebs (as in the solution found to the problem with the Laenates) would have worked just as well with restraining Cassius Longinus. Nevertheless, the issue remains.

Crisis response measures aimed at countering the use of violence would be of no use in these situations. The incident involving the Popillii Laenates holds great importance when discussing crisis and the governmental response to crisis situations, as it represents a crisis that affected

---

with his forces from Brundisium and waited for the consul P. Licinius Crassus (*cos.* 171) to assume command (Livy 42. 31. 3; 36. 4, 8–9; 42. 49. 10 [Licinius relieves him]). It is interesting that for two years in a row this particular man was sent south in command of a sizable body of men.

[47] For references and details, see *MRR* 1. 421, 425, and 429.

the very ability of the government to decide on a response to a debilitating impasse, or anything else for that matter. One could, of course, argue that the situation was not so dire in the end, as a final arbiter between the two opposing sides was found in the Roman people, who were theoretically sovereign and could settle the matter through the formal enactment of their expressed will; the plebiscite passed by the two tribunes. But how practical was this mechanism for ending a political impasse that had the potential to prevent the proper functioning of the governing institutions of the Republic? Would the people be able to act quickly in a deteriorating situation that needed a response within a fixed time period? And how reliable was this method of crisis resolution? It is entirely possible that the Popillii could have found another one of the ten tribunes of the plebs who might be willing to support them and interpose his veto, which would have continued the stalemate. It is only because the other eight tribunes were either actively supportive or, at the very least, willing to stand aside so that the two Marcii were able to promulgate and pass their bill. And if a tribune were the one who was at loggerheads with a consul or the senate or both... we have already seen how that turned out twice before: the organized call for violence supported by the *senatus consultum ultimum*. This, however, was a later innovation, created by L. Opimius, most likely in light of the first experience the ruling element in the senatorial class had when a tribune acted in a provocative manner that went against the wishes of powerful interests within the senate.

THE FIRST TROUBLESOME TRIBUNE: TIBERIUS GRACCHUS

Tiberius Sempronius Gracchus *tr. pl.* 133 is a figure who continues to draw the attention of scholars for many reasons.[48] The events that led to his death at the hands of an upper-class lynch mob are of vital concern to us, as this is clearly a crisis where the government needed to take active measures to counter potential violence but utterly failed to do so. We are fortunate that we have full accounts of the episode from Plutarch (in his biography of Tiberius Gracchus) and Appian (1. 9. 35–16. 70 of his *Civil Wars*).[49]

---

[48] In recent years, there has been work by De Ligt (2004), Ossier (2004), Badian (2004), and Linderski (2002). A reappraisal of Scipio Nasica's role in this mess is offered by Binot (2001). For additional works, see those mentioned in the discussion of his brother Gaius Gracchus in Chapter 5.

[49] For a complete list of sources and cursory references, see Broughton, *MRR* 1. 494–495.

The origins of the crisis for the Roman state originated in the standoff between Tiberius and his fellow tribune of the plebs M. Octavius. As we have it in the accounts of Plutarch (*TG* 9–10) and Appian (*BC* 1. 9. 25–10. 50),[50] Tiberius attempted to have his law on reclaiming the *ager publicus* read before the popular assembly, and Octavius interposed his veto to stop the reading of the bill. Gracchus tried again, and again Octavius blocked it. At this point, when things could have moved to violence, two influential senators (named Manlius and Fulvius by Plutarch) successfully interceded with Tiberius to have the matter referred to the senate; this accomplished nothing, however, as the opponents of the bill held sway there (Plut. *TG* 11; cf. Appian 1. 12. 50–1).

At this point, Gracchus turned to a measure that Plutarch called οὐ νόμιμον οὐδὲ ἐπιεικές "neither lawful nor reasonable" (11. 4), by proposing to have his colleague deposed from office by vote of the plebeian assembly. According to Plutarch (11. 5–8; not mentioned by Appian), he first offered to allow Octavius to move for his (Gracchus's) removal, but Octavius refused, so Tiberius proceeded to propose the deposition of Octavius. Both Plutarch (12) and Appian (12. 51–54) agree that Gracchus hesitated during key parts of the vote to allow Octavius the opportunity to relent, but the latter refused. So the removal of Octavius from office was voted, and with his removal, the only roadblock to the passage of *lex agraria*. A commission of three was elected to administer the law, but the senate refused to vote the commissioners sufficient funds to provide for its expenses (Plut. *TG* 13; cf. Appian 1. 13. 55, who does not mention the senate's refusal to fund the commission fully).

The situation could have ended there, to some extent, except that Tiberius decided to take on a new project when notice of the death of King Attalus (III) of Pergamum came to Rome, accompanied by the news that Rome was to be the beneficiary of his will. Tiberius attempted to interfere with the senate's traditional role in overseeing matters of Rome's relations with foreign states by announcing that he would arrange for the disposal of the inheritance through acts of the assembly proposed by himself (Plut. *TG* 14; cf. Livy *Per.* 58).[51]

Although we do not have the details, it would appear that the insults to the group in the senate who opposed Gracchus were becoming insufferable.

---

[50] There are significant divergences in minor details between the two accounts (for example, Plutarch says there were two versions of the land bill, whereas Appian only mentions one; Plutarch states that Gracchus consulted many eminent men before proposing his measure, whereas Appian omits this), but they do not disagree about the important events, to which we will confine our discussion.

[51] See Stockton (1979) 67f., 81–83.

Livy's epitomator succinctly states *tot indignitatibus commotus graviter senatus* (*Per.* 58). Though it removes this clause from its original sense (and sentence), it could be said that "the senate was strongly moved by so many insults." The subtext, not clearly spelled out, was that Gracchus's action in bypassing the senate and working such matters directly through the assembly, although not illegal, was seriously undermining the power of the senate.

Sensing a threat from the opponents of the reforms, Tiberius's friends urged him to seek reelection to the tribunate in order to protect himself from the almost certain attacks against him that would be launched by his political opponents (Plut. *TG* 16; cf. Appian 1. 14. 58–59). It would be at the riotous and fateful electoral[52] assembly for the new tribunes who would take office on December 10 that matters would come to a head. At the electoral assembly on the capitol, disturbances broke out between the pro- and anti-Gracchan forces (Plut. *TG* 17–18; cf. Appian 1. 15. 64–66). Plutarch records that during the assembly, Fulvius Flaccus came to warn Tiberius that there was a movement afoot in the senate, led by P. Cornelius Scipio Nasica, the current *ponitfex maximus*, to come and put down Gracchus.

In the preserved accounts of the senate meeting, held at the Temple of Fides according to Appian (1. 16. 67; Plutarch does not say where the senate convened), confusing reports were apparently coming in. Appian reports that the senators were informed (wrongly) that all of the tribunes had been deposed by Gracchus (because the other tribunes could not be seen on the capitol) and other notices came in that Gracchus had declared himself tribune without holding any election (1. 15. 66). Plutarch says the senate was informed that Gracchus was trying to make himself king (19. 1–3). From these various reports, expectations rose among the senators that violence might occur, and a full-blown crisis came into existence.

Nasica, the *pontifex maximus*, called on the consul to immediately aid the state and put down the "tyrant" (Plut. *TG* 19. 3). The consul, Mucius Scaevola (the other consul, L. Calpurnius Piso Frugi, the later annalist, was out of town), refused to intervene, but preferred to wait on events and stated that he would consider any "illegal" (παρανόμος) acts of the assembly under Tiberius's control as not having any binding force (τοῦτο κύριον μὴ φυλάξειν Plut. *TG* 19. 5).

In his brief account of the senate meeting, Appian includes an interesting note. He wonders (or did he get this from his own source?) why the senate

---

[52] Here following Stockton (1979) 74 and n. 40, against the thesis proposed by L. R. Taylor (*Athenaeum* 51 [1963] 51ff.) that it was a legislative assembly.

did not think it right to appoint a dictator to deal with the situation, although he notes that the Romans had made use of this expedient "in such times of peril" (White's Loeb translation: Appian 1. 16. 67 ἐν τοιοῖσδε φόβοις). And we may wonder ourselves for a moment. This was clearly a serious internal crisis, and the consul Mucius Scaevola (whom, if we believe Plutarch [*TG* 9. 1], was on friendly terms with Gracchus) was not providing leadership that the majority of the senate was willing to follow. Would it not have been in the interests of the state to move for decisive leadership in this crisis? Not that the appointment of a dictator was necessarily the best measure that they could take to defuse the situation, and as Appian notes, by this time, it was a forgotten measure. As it was, Nasica was not satisfied with the consul's answer and called upon his supporters to raise what was, in effect, a lynch mob to deal out vigilante justice to Tiberius Gracchus and his supporters (Plut. *TG* 19. 5–6; cf. Appian 1. 16. 68–70).

The crisis ended very abruptly. The senatorial mob called for by Nasica gathered and charged the capitol. Tiberius Gracchus was slain (first struck with the leg from a bench by his fellow plebeian tribune P. Satureius, according to Plut. *TG* 19. 10) along with many of his followers. Their bodies were dumped into the Tiber. Even though the crisis was over, its resolution did nothing to settle the important issues that had given rise to the rift between Gracchus and many senators. In fairness, there was no precedent, no situation in their historical knowledge at the time that would have provided guidance. It was likely that very fact that pushed Opimius over a decade later to invent the *senatus consultum ultimum*. And that is the key and decisive difference between how the unrest surrounding Gaius Gracchus was handled compared with the events that led to his elder brother's death. In this situation, the consul did not provide decisive leadership. Although Scaevola was on firm legal ground, perhaps the only person in this entire debacle who was acting in accordance with the law, there was need for strong consular leadership in this situation, and Scaevola's inability to check Nasica and his fervent followers shows that he was not providing it. The Roman state had no means of responding to a situation where a tribune of the plebs was at variance with a large number of senators, and using brute force provided by a crowd of supporters to gain his objectives. A *tumultus* does not address the issue. The dictatorship was already forgotten, and one could question what help it might have provided on this occasion. A *iustitium*, by impeding public business, may have worked, but Tiberius might have ignored it or vetoed it before it could be officially proclaimed. A way to respond to this situation would have to be developed, and later it was.

THE MENACE FROM THE NORTH: THE CIMBRI AND TEUTONI

Already as early as 113, there was an encounter between the Romans and the Cimbri,[53] a Germanic grouping who invaded Illyria that year and defeated a Roman army under the command of the consul Cn. Papirius Carbo near Noreia (Strabo 5. 1. 8 [C 214]; Livy *Per.* 63; for other sources see *MRR* 1. 535). Whereas Q. Caecilius Metellus was beginning to turn around the ill-managed war in Numidia, his fellow consul of 109, M. Junius Silanus, was in Gaul to face the Cimbri, who had now allegedly (if we put any faith in the tale told by the imperial era epitomator Florus) come and demanded land from the Romans in exchange for offering their services as soldiers (Florus 1. 38. 2). Receiving a negative answer from the senate, a battle was fought either in 109 or 108, and Silanus was worsted (Livy *Per.* 65; Vell. Pat. 2. 12. 2; Florus 1. 38. 4). In 105 came the next major clash, when the Cimbri, joined by another group called the Teutoni or Teutones, defeated two Roman armies near Arausio on October 6, 105.[54] In this instance, the arrogant intransigence of one of the Roman commanders (the proconsul Q. Servilius Caepio) probably played a role in the disastrous outcome for Rome. In the immediate aftermath of the news, apparently all of Italy trembled, if we believe Sallust (*Iug.* 114. 1–2). We have no reason to doubt him. Although an immediate declaration of a state of emergency is not recorded, we do have record of an emergency measure that seems to fall just short of one: the other consul, P. Rutilius Rufus, extracted an oath from all of the *iuniores* (those of normally draftable age) that they would not leave Italy, and he issued an order sent to all of the ports along the shores of Italy that forbade anyone younger than thirty-five years old from being received on board a ship (Granius Licinianus 33. 25–27). From the reference only to men of normal draft age, and no reference to a suspension of exemptions from service (*vacationes*), it does not sound like a *tumultus* was declared, even though one might well have expected one in this situation. In addition to this extraordinary oath, Rutilius appears at some point (although this could have been much later in time) to have put his men through special military training, calling in gladiators to train the soldiers how to better avoid and give blows (Val. Max. 2. 3. 2).

---

[53] For a recent study of the encounter between the Romans and the Cimbri and Teutones, see Burns (2003) 42–87.

[54] Date from Granius Licinianus 33. 1–17; cf. Livy *Per.* 67, Florus 1. 38. 4, Dio 27 fr. 91. 1–4. For full references, see *MRR* 1. 555.

There was no immediate invasion of Italy, however, although the fear of one drove the Romans to take the unusual step of electing Gaius Marius *in absentia* to the consulship for 104.[55] He was given Gaul as his province, although he was fortunate that the Cimbri made a side trip to Spain (Livy *Per.* 67; Plut. *Marius* 14. 1; Obsequens 43), which gave him time to train his army (Plut. *Marius* 13–14; Vegetius *RM* 3. 10). Although there was a lengthy delay, the Cimbri, rejoining the Teutoni, finally made their descents upon Italy, taking different paths, in 102 (Plut. *Marius* 15. 5). Marius met the Teutoni; joined by another group, called the Ambrones, in battle; and overcame them at Aquae Sextiae (Aix-en-Provence; Plut. *Marius* 18–21; see *MRR* 1. 567 for full references). Marius's colleague for 102, Q. Lutatius Catulus, was unable block the Cimbri from entering Italy (Plut. *Marius* 23), and Marius, reelected again for 101, joined forces with Catulus (now proconsul) and annihilated the Cimbri at Vercellae (Plut. *Marius* 24–27; see *MRR* 1. 570 for full references).

This situation was certainly a crisis, as we have noted the clear perceptions of threat that the Roman sources have recorded. Yet as far as our sources tell us, at no point was a state of emergency proclaimed. Certainly, a case could be made that P. Rutilius might have had one proclaimed in 105, following the disastrous defeat at Arausio, but the evidence points to measures that just fall short of the declaration of a *tumultus*, even though we should reasonably expect one at this time. Broughton states that Rutilius "raised new legions,"[56] which could point to a tumultuary levy and thus a declaration of a *tumultus*. The source he cites in support, however (pseudo-Frontinus 4. 1. 12 and 4. 2. 2), does not clearly indicate that an emergency levy was held. The first reference is a mere anecdote that Rutilius forced his son to serve as a regular soldier when Rutilius junior could have been a *contubernalis* (tent mate) of his father, whereas the second records Marius's decision immediately after taking office in January of 104 to use the army Rutilius had the previous year instead of the one he had transported back from Numidia, as the senate had given him free choice in deciding which army he wished to command. The army of Rutilius reportedly had better discipline. Although it is certainly possible that Rutilius did not have any forces previously and raised a scratch force after October 6, does it not seem rather strange that Marius would choose a reportedly smaller army of men who had only been in service for less than three months over his own army of veterans? Granted, many of the men in the army from Numidia might have been worn out from their service, while

---

[55] For full source references for Marius during the year 104, see *MRR* 1. 558.
[56] *MRR* 1. 555.

Rutilius's army was fresh, but if Rutilius's force was a tumultuary levy, it is highly unusual that they would be retained for potentially extended duty, especially when a tumultuary levy often included men who might not otherwise be fit for such duty (during an emergency, every man who meets the bare requirements will be drafted) and were meant to be discharged as soon as the emergency was over. In no recorded *tumultus* is there an instance of tumultuary troops being retained after the immediate emergency was over. And by January of 104, the Cimbri were not on Rome's doorstep, and time could be taken to carry out a regular levy, choosing the best men for service.

It is also entirely possible that Rutilius had soldiers under his command from the beginning of the year. If the Romans were concerned enough to have two armies operate in the north (Caepio's retained from the previous year and a new one under the consul Mallius), is it out of the question to believe that a reserve force was kept at Rome? Of course, Rutilius could have supplemented it with a tumultuary levy after the news of Arausio came to Rome and discharged those men when it was apparent that the Cimbri were not suddenly to appear, handing over to Marius only the men who had been regularly conscripted. This would account for the difference in the size of the two armies offered to Marius, but if Rutilius had spent so much time training these men for the past three months, would Marius have wanted to let them go? Yet even if none of them were discharged and Marius took over Rutilius's entire force, are we to believe that in the "panic" following Arausio, Rutilius conscripted a force smaller than a normal consular army, which is what Marius had with him in Africa? Although the evidence does not rule out Broughton's interpretation, it does not support it without raising serious questions. As we have it, the only firm record of emergency crisis response measures taken by P. Rutilius was the oath extracted from the *iuniores* not to leave Italy and the order to ports to prevent ships from taking on men under age thirty-five as passengers. Extraordinary measures certainly but not ones we normally learn of in relation to an official state of emergency.

Once Marius had been entrusted with handling the crisis, it was no longer necessary to use measures such as a *tumultus*. By good luck, the Germanic tribes went in other directions. Marius was given time to prepare for the coming struggle. This cushion of time did not mean that it was no longer a crisis: there was certainly a perception that the Cimbri and Teutoni would come at some point and that their arrival could potentially cause serious damage to Roman core values (control over their land and protecting their Italian allies). But it was no longer an emergency. There was time to plan, time to deliberate, and time to craft the response using the normal procedures.

The Coming of the Mithridatic War and the Fall of the Roman Republic in 88

Of course, following precedent and expecting similar outcomes from seemingly similar situations has resulted in any number of errors in judgment, although those errors are recognized only in hindsight. One such situation where the decision-making elite of the Romans misjudged a situation (although one should not fault them for the choices they made at the time) was the mistaken approach employed in the face of aggressive moves by an Eastern king. There are many good modern discussions of the events that preceded the first war between Rome and Mithridates VI, king of Pontus, providing full details (with complete references to the sources) of the prosecution of the war and the aftermath.[57] Although it is always much easier to analyze matters with the greater knowledge of hindsight, it seems clear that what hampered the Romans most in this situation is that they did not perceive it to be a crisis for them. In many respects, they were correct to view the matter thus, as their knowledge of events in the east was not as complete as could be, and past experience proved to be a faulty guide this time. Mithridates VI, as powerful as he was, and his kingdom of Pontus could never present a survival-level threat to the Roman empire (I avoid using the capital letter merely to avoid confusion; although there was no "emperor," Rome was most certainly an empire in every other sense of the word by this time), and the Romans knew that. Yet as became clear in the aftermath, the Romans had miscalculated the situation gravely. It is unfortunate for them that one of the consequences of this miscalculation resulted in a genuine existential crisis that sprang from a fight over who got to lead the inevitable Roman triumph (in their minds, proven correct by events) over the Eastern monarch. We have already discussed that episode in full detail in Chapter 4 and will return to its unhappy aftermath later in this discussion.

After the death of the last Attalid king of Asia, Attalus III, in 133, Rome became the paramount power in the Anatolian peninsula, inheriting

---

[57] Most recently, see Kallet-Marx (1995) 250–260, 261f. for Sulla's settlement at the end; McGing (1986) 66–88 lead up to the war, 89–108 Mithridates' propaganda, 108–131 account of the First War; Sherwin-White (1984) 92–148. There are earlier accounts as well by Magie (see note 58), Mommsen and Reinach; see McGing (1986) 108 note 94 for full references.

the kingdom of the Attalids and the important role of playing arbiter between the various kingdoms and cities located there.[58] Whereas at first the Romans tried not to get too involved in the affairs of the various kings, the actions of King Mithridates VI of Pontus would cause them to intervene on occasion. An important precursor to the events that led to the First Mithridatic War was the Roman intervention in the kingdom of Cappadocia during the 90s. Sometime during the early part of that decade, Ariobarzanes, the king of Cappadocia, was driven from his kingdom by Mithridates through the agency of a usurper, Gordius, with support from Tigranes, king of Armenia. Sulla (the later dictator), who was likely praetor in 97,[59] was assigned the task of restoring/safely installing Ariobarzanes upon his throne. This was merely a practice run for what would come later.

The immediate trigger for the crisis was another attempt by Mithridates to take control of Cappadocia and Bithynia. Around 92, a usurper, Socrates Chrestus, backed by Mithridates, seized control of Bithynia from the Roman-recognized King Nicomedes IV, who had just succeeded to the throne. At the same time, Mithridates's newly acquired son-in-law Tigranes, king of Armenia, expelled Ariobarzanes from his kingdom in Cappadocia and attempted to reinstall the Mithridatic usurper Ariarathes IX. Confronted with a heightened expectation of the possibility of military hostilities breaking out (the sign of the onset to a crisis), the Roman response relied on employing basically the same approach as they did the last time. This time, instead of an ex-praetor, a commission of three headed by M.' Aquillius, consul of 101, was sent to restore both Ariobarzanes and Nicomedes IV to their thrones. With token Roman forces under the command of the (praetorian) proconsul of Asia, C. Cassius, the kings were restored. It would appear that the decision to follow the pattern of Sulla's earlier intervention was the correct response to the situation.

---

58 For discussions of Rome in Asia, see works in note 57. Although older, still very useful is Magie (1950).

59 There is contention over this dating. The original *MRR* 2 has Sulla's praetorship listed under the year 93, with the promagistracy in Cilicia in 92. In *MRR* 3 Supp. (1986) 73–74, Broughton has provided some discussion of the attempts to change that date, noting the earlier chronology advanced by Badian, placing the praetorship in 97 and the mission to Asia in 96. Broughton himself, after wavering a bit, seems to side with Sherwin-White, who has Sulla restoring Ariobarzanes in 94, with the praetorship coming shortly before then (see Broughton for full references). More recently, Brennan has provided a detailed analysis of the issues, holding to Badian's early date for the praetorship (97), followed by prolonged service in Asia, lasting to as late as 93/92; see Brennan (1992) 103–158. [Brennan holds to this dating in Brennan (2000) 358, 765n. 9]. Kallet-Marx (1995) 355f. (appendix H) also supports Badian's date.

It is at this point that apparently our sources fail us. Our main source is Appian, who provides us with a highly unbalanced account pinning the blame for the start of the war on the legate Aquillius, who allegedly impelled Nicomedes (holding the large debts that he owed to Roman moneylenders over his head) into raiding Mithridates's territory, which resulted in Mithridates responding with a new incursion into Cappadocia (reinstalling the usurper Ariarathes IX again) and an embassy to the Roman commission, complaining of Nicomedes's attacks. The Roman commissioners ordered Mithridates to withdraw from Cappadocia again and stated that they wished both kings not to suffer any harm. At this point, the Romans prepared their forces to restore Ariobarzanes, and Mithridates readied for war.

Appian's account (which many scholars have accepted to a greater or lesser extent) receives a fairly convincing rebuttal by Kallet-Marx, who exposes the bias in Appian's likely source, and provides a reasonable explanation for why Nicomedes may have engaged in the raiding of Mithridates' territory on his own, which started the war.[60] In these circumstances, it is probably counterproductive to "assign blame" and more useful to report events in the most likely order. At this point, it became clear to the Roman commissioners that Mithridates was not going to submit "meekly."[61] Whatever the truth, whether Nicomedes was impelled by Aquillius or conducted the raid on his own, that action served as the trigger to escalate the crisis significantly for Mithridates, as either Mithridates would have to give in or be forced to respond by launching military action of his own. The perception of threat to Roman interests by the chief Roman officials, Aquillius and Cassius, concerned with maintaining their prestige and authority over others in the region being paramount and the near certainty of military hostilities (should Mithridates fail to concede) were manifest.

Mithridates, as mentioned earlier, attempted negotiations to head off a full-scale conflict, but the Romans on the scene expected Mithridates to submit to their authority, as he had done in the past. Still, Aquillius and the other Roman officials were not taking chances, and they prepared military forces, but their armies largely consisted of scratch levies from the Asian cities and the royal forces of Nicomedes.[62] Overconfidence, however, would take a heavy toll on Roman interests. Mithridates defeated the

---

[60] Kallet-Marx (1995) 251–256.
[61] Here I borrow Kallet-Marx's characterization of Mithridates's behavior. See Kallet-Marx (1995) 255.
[62] For the Romans' strategy and forces, see Kallet-Marx (1995) 258.

numerically superior forces of Nicomedes and followed that up by routing Aquillius's force of raw recruits. Cassius, seeing the futility of facing the Pontic king, dismissed his army and retired to Rhodes. The other Roman commander, Q. Oppius, the (praetorian) proconsul of Cilicia, was besieged and captured at Laodicea. Mithridates overran all of Roman Asia. Herein lay the mistake made by Aquillius, expecting Mithridates to submit to Rome no matter what action Rome, or its allies, took against the Pontic king.

In the aftermath, we can see that the decision makers in Rome also made a mistake, although we can hardly blame them for it: at the very beginning, they thought that the situation in 90/89 would merely repeat the situation when Sulla was able to push Mithridates's proxy out of Cappadocia and restore the balance of power in the region in the previous decade with little effort. Their mistake was to send *auctoritas* in the guise of M.' Aquillius, an ex-consul, without the necessary military force to back up that authority. It is entirely understandable, however, as Mithridates had backed down in the previous instance when Sulla also had led a "Roman" army that was more a collection of allied local forces than a strong body of legionaries. It was unfortunate for the Romans that they did not get any sense that things would be different this time around. For while the Mithridatic War itself did not present a survival-level threat to Rome, it contributed to an internal crisis in the Roman state, the first internal crisis that the Republic was not able to withstand. This was the dispute between the tribune P. Sulpicius Rufus and the now-consul Sulla, with the added involvement of C. Marius, which we have recounted in Chapter 4 and will now revisit by proceeding to the aftermath, which represents another example of a crisis for which no adequate response was made.

Sulla marched his army against his own native city, intending to use force to settle what was a political dispute. Chapter 9 of Plutarch's *Sulla* and Appian *BC* 1. 57 are largely in agreement about the broad outline of events, although each author recounts slightly different details. According to Plutarch, after the military tribunes sent by Marius were murdered by Sulla's men, there was movement of individuals between the two camps. We may get a complementary version of this from Appian, who notes that all of Sulla's ἄρχοντες, which should likely refer to his senior staff officers, his legates, and the six military tribunes assigned to each legion, left him except for his quaestor (L. Licinius Lucullus). Returning to Plutarch's account, when news of Sulla's march was reported at Rome, the senate – said to be under the control of Marius and Sulpicius (but where is the other consul, Pompeius Rufus, in all this?) – sent two praetors, Brutus and Servilius, to forbid Sulla's advance on Rome. They met with a hostile reception as Sulla's soldiers, who had worse in mind, contented themselves with breaking the praetors' fasces and sending them back humiliated to Rome. The spectacle of the humbled praetors caused dejection back in Rome.

Appian mentions three embassies, although no details of their composition. After the praetors were turned back, Plutarch recounts that Pompeius Rufus had joined Sulla from Nola, and they continued their march on Rome. At Pictae, another delegation from the city came, stating that the senate had voted that Sulla would have all his rights, and Sulla agreed to stop and encamp where he was, although this was a ruse. Here we encounter a substantial discrepancy between Appian and Plutarch, as Appian states that it was only at this point (as Sulla was approaching Rome) that Pompeius Rufus came to greet him and give him his full support. Regardless of when he joined Sulla, however, it is clear that Pompeius Rufus was not in Rome and not in control of the senate's deliberations. Unlike Plutarch's account of Sulla being promised his full rights if he moved no closer to Rome, Appian reports that Marius and Sulpicius sent messengers, under the guise of envoys from the senate, to order Sulla not to move his camp nearer than forty stades from Rome. Both accounts, however, are in agreement that this incident, when Sulla apparently agreed to camp away from the city, was a ruse on Sulla's part, as he quickly broke camp and marched upon Rome immediately, leaving Marius and Sulpicius no time to organize a credible defense. Sulla seized Rome.

As it stands, forming a precursor to both the march on Rome by Julius Caesar in 49 and the situation with Octavian and the senate in later 43, the response of the state to Sulla was not a good precedent. Granted, it was never going to be. As consul, Sulla was the man who was supposed to protect the state, not lead an army against it. Pompeius Rufus, the other consul, also apparently was not in any position to stand by the state. Yet if Sulpicius and Marius represented such a great threat to the government's continued operation, why did neither of the consuls demand the passage of the *senatus consultum ultimum* earlier when they had the chance to approach the senate, especially right after the death of Pompeius Rufus's son? When Sulla had resorted to his army and then convinced his men to march on Rome to vindicate his rights as consul, he was trampling all over the very laws and principles that gave him those rights. In 88, sadly, we have just about everything that could go wrong doing so. A tribune of the plebs and a private citizen, with the support of armed gangs, succeeded in driving out the consuls from Rome. Then the consuls, especially one consul, turned a formally enrolled Roman army against them. People can, and have, argued over who committed the greater wrong, but in terms of response, the Roman state, as an institution, was completely incapable of mounting any proper response to this. But we can remain surprised at what did not occur. Just as one wonders why Sulla and Pompeius did not convene the senate and pass the *senatus consultum ultimum* to "authorize" the use of force against Sulpicius and Marius, one is then also surprised that we have no mention of Sulpicius and Marius invoking the decree, or calling for the passage of a *tumultus* declaration, in order to authorize them to gather together, as best as they could, an armed force to match Sulla's army. The year 88 then really does go down as the year when the wheels fell off for the Roman governing class and the machinery of politics. The Romans, for good reasons, underestimated the situation in the east and through the poor judgment of their representatives on the scene, ended up with a more serious war than they had likely intended. Far worse, and for bad reasons, the Eastern war caused a crisis that did wind up overthrowing the Roman Republic.

Crises that Did Not Result in Employment of the Usual Crisis Response Mechanisms

Looking back over the various crises that we have recounted in this chapter, we can see that they fall into three broad categories: crises that were not emergencies, crises that were emergencies but that did not evoke the usual emergency measures, and crises in the face of which the state proved itself incapable of mounting a coherent response. In clear-cut cases of the second type, such as Hannibal's march on Rome and the panic in Rome following the disaster at Arausio in 105, we are surprised that we have no record of the usual emergency responses being used, although we have indications that extraordinary measures were put in place. It is also not unreasonable to assume that the normal emergency response, a *tumultus* and a *iustitium* followed by a tumultuary levy, occurred, although from the evidence we have, this can only remain an assumption. It is just as obvious that situations of the first type, when there was no sudden threat hanging over the heads of the Romans, they preferred to make use of the usual operating procedures of the Roman government, thus no state of emergency for Saguntum or against Macedon or later against the Cimbri and Teutoni after the initial wave of concern and it became clear that they were not at Rome's doorstep. The Bacchanalian cult was viewed more as a public order matter, requiring a judicial response rather than a military threat.

The most intriguing cases are the ones in which the government failed to mount a response – not the Mithridatic conflict, when the Romans merely underestimated the resolve and goals of their opponent at the start, but the two cases when the machinery of government itself failed: the unrest surrounding Tiberius Gracchus in 133 and the complete breakdown of the institutions of the Republic in 88. In both cases, an internal political impasse was ended through violence. In the earlier episode, a private citizen, P. Cornelius Scipio Nasica, the *pontifex maximus*, took it upon himself to raise an extra-legal (which is merely a polite way of saying illegal when the side wins and is seen as acting in a legitimate manner later) armed force to crush Gracchus and his supporters. Although Gracchus and his supporters may not have been acting within strict legality themselves, only Mucius Scaevola the consul behaved in line with the traditions and laws of the Romans by declaring that he would not accept any illegal actions undertaken by Gracchus and his supporters. Our perspective might well be different if Scaevola had put himself at the head of the mob, covering Nasica's illegal action with the cloak of consular authority. But that did not happen, and it would await for another consul to give official sanction to the senate declaring that the activities of a troublesome tribune were in need of violent suppression.

In comparison, the situation was far worse in 88. A new tool of dealing with a plebeian tribune, even one with armed supporters, had been invented between 133 and 88, yet the consuls, Sulla and Pompeius Rufus, did not make use of it. Interestingly, the sources do not seem to ask why, although one would really like to have been able to read Sulla's memoir on this point to see whether he contemplated calling for the *senatus consultum ultimum* or had already decided on using armed force without the pretence of the senate's *auctoritas*. Sulla might argue that Sulpicius and Marius had already between them overthrown the Republic, as they had used brute force to overturn the action of the consuls in attempting to stop laws from being passed by declaring a cessation of business. However, that would be a gross overstatement as Sulpicius would be out of office at the end of the year and Marius would be in Asia minor. If Sulpicius had tried for reelection, he would immediately invite comparison to the Gracchi. If there had been reluctance on the part of the senate to consider the *senatus consultum ultimum* for some reason, such behavior may well have changed minds.

7

THE WINTER OF DISCONTENT
AND THE SUMMER THAT LED
TO A FALL

Now we may return to the question that began this inquiry: what knowledge of crisis response did the ruling class in Rome have available to them in the winter of 44/43 as they faced the prospect of an armed force engaging in an attack on a Roman governor in the province immediately to the north of the Italian heartland? This situation was not just a military crisis but also a political one, as the attacker was himself a Roman and would portray himself as acting legally and properly in his attempt to seize Cisalpine Gaul. Mark Antony, however, was no longer consul and, therefore, could not guide the policy of the Roman state. That was the job of the new consuls, A. Hirtius and C. Vibius Pansa.[1] Under their guidance, and later under that of the City Praetor M. Caecilius Cornutus when the consuls had left the city, the crisis response of the Roman government would be managed. Let us now turn to the course of events.

THE WINTER OF DISCONTENT: THE FIRST

TUMULTUS OF 43

Of course, one could argue that these two final crises do not belong in this examination of crisis and response during the Roman Republic. The events that followed Caesar's death on the Ides of March of 44 cannot count as a true case study in crisis and response during the Roman Republic for the simple reason that the Republic was dead. Here I will quote the words of Cicero, a contemporary and major player in the events that are to be discussed. Cicero *Att.* 14. 13. 6, written c. April 26, 44: *Redeo enim*

---

[1] For full ancient references to these two men and all other magistrates and promagistrates for the year 43, please consult their individual entries in *MRR* 2. 334f.

ad miseram seu nullam potius rem publicam. "So now I return to the pathetic, or rather, non-existent Republic." At this point, as far as Cicero was concerned, there was *nulla res publica.* The Republic was dead.[2] Alternatively, during the period between the death of Caesar and the march of Octavian[3] on the city of Rome in August of 43, we have a return to the institutions and processes of the Republic, as can be seen from the events as we have them recorded. Because one of our main sources concerning how a *tumultus* even functioned comes from the work of Cicero that was created during this tumultuous period, it is proper that we end our look at crisis responses with the two final occasions upon which a *tumultus* and the various other crisis responses were put to use.

There is, of course, a rather large bibliography on this watershed period in Roman history, far too much to list. The classic account, despite certain flaws in its perspective, is still that of Syme.[4] A recent, if somewhat brief, survey of the time period is provided by Osgood, who tries to bring in perspectives other than that of the governing elite.[5] As for the sources for these two final crises, we have much in the way of good firsthand material from Cicero in his correspondence and his famed speeches that he called *Philippics*, inspired by the speeches the Greek orator Demosthenes launched against Philip of Macedon about three centuries before these events. I will draw on the contemporary sources as much as possible for events. It is necessary, of course, to supplement Cicero's and his correspondents' limited perspectives with that of the later historical accounts written in the decades and centuries that followed. Sadly, we only have the summaries from the monumental history of Livy, although that does not mean that we are bereft of fuller accounts; we have the complete narratives of Appian and Dio Cassius for these events, along with important biographies by Plutarch, as we learn vital information from his works on Caesar, Cicero, Brutus, and Antony.[6]

---

[2] Cf. Cic. *Fam.* 12. 23. 3 to Q. Cornificius, sent sometime in October of 44: *habes formam rei publicae, si in castris esse res publica; in quo tuam vicem saepe doleo, quod nullam partem per aetatem sanae et salvae rei publicae gustare potuisti* "you have the state of the Republic, if [there is able] to be a Republic in an armed camp; concerning which I often deplore your turn [at handling public affairs], since you were not able, because of your age, to taste any part of a safe and sound Republic."

[3] I follow common practice in referring to him as Octavian, even though he never used the name and preferred to be called C. Iulius Caesar, as was his right by being adopted by his great-uncle. The common practice, however, avoids any confusion.

[4] Syme (1939).

[5] Osgood (2006) 12–61.

[6] I agree with opinions expressed in the brief summary of the nature of our written sources for the time period by Osgood (2006) 7–10.

The death of Caesar the Dictator made possible a return to life for the *libera res publica*, and in the days immediately following the assassination there was a struggle to see whether the Republic would be revived. The most important day was not actually March 15 or 16 but March 17, when the senate was called together by Antony, for the moment the sole legal consul (Dolabella's arrogation of the consulship that Caesar intended for him had yet to be acquiesced in or formally confirmed) and highest magistrate in Rome. The Master of the Horse M. Aemilius Lepidus had troops at his disposal, but with the death of his superior, his position was much less secure for any attempt at seizing power.

The meeting was held at the Temple of Tellus (Appian tells us the choice was dictated because it was near Antony's house), and much needed to be discussed. The so-called Liberators had seized the capitol and would not come down. The debate centered on whether Caesar would be mourned and his doings honored as legal and whether the Liberators would be absolved – even thanked – or would the assassins be condemned and prosecuted. In the end, as is usual when the sides seem somewhat balanced, a compromise was worked out. Caesar would not be branded a tyrant, and his *acta* were to be ratified. Yet Brutus and the "Liberators" were to be given a free pass for their deed. The now rather senior ex-consul M. Tullius Cicero proposed that the Romans follow the model of the Athenians and declare an "amnesty," a literal "forgetting" of the actions that had occurred over the past couple of days. This was decreed. It was finally voted that Caesar's will should be openly read and that he receive a public funeral. (Cic. *Att.* 14. 10. 1; *Phil.* 1. 1; Appian *BC* 2. 126. 525–136. 563; Plut. *Cicero* 42; *Brutus* 19–20. 1; cf. *Caesar* 67; *Antony* 14; Dio 44. 22–34). So the initial crisis that immediately followed Caesar's death, when it was possible that civil war and violence would break out inside Rome itself, was weathered fairly well by the Roman state, and the senate, according to one report, even passed a formal vote of thanks to Antony the next day (March 18), praising him for stopping a new civil war (Plut. *Brutus* 19. 4).

The origins of the *tumultus* of 43 were in the events after everyone had breathed a sigh of relief and thought that the worst part was over. The problem for those who wanted the status quo was the consul Antony. In the immediate aftermath of Caesar's death, Antony, even though he was in charge of Caesar's papers (cf. Plut. *Antonius* 15; Dio 44. 53. 2–3), did not act in a manner that offended "senatorial" opinion (Cic. *Phil.* 1. 2–5).[7] Yet

---

[7] It is not, I believe, unreasonable to take Cicero and the views he expresses as representative of the thinking of many "middle of the road" senators, neither beholden to Caesar nor bold enough to have joined in the conspiracy that murdered him.

already by April, we have hints that Antony began to strike out on his own. In a letter to Atticus dated firmly April 22, 44, Cicero (currently in Puteoli) noted that Antony apparently posted a law that made the Sicilians into Roman citizens, claiming the measure had been passed by Caesar through the assembly (Cic. *Att*. 14. 12. 1). More unsettling news of Antony's behavior began to reach Cicero on his trip, as revealed in another letter to Atticus, written sometime in late April. In it he wrote: *sublato enim tyranno tyrannida manere video, nam quae ille facturus non fuit eas fiunt* "For while the tyrant was removed, I see the tyranny remains. For the things which that man [Caesar] would never have done, these are being done" (*Att*. 14. 14. 2). In the same paragraph, Cicero sarcastically added *cui servire ipsi non potuimus, eius libellis paremus* "to the man whom we were unable to be slaves, we are obedient to his notebooks."

The same letter provides us as well with a very important piece of information, the trigger to the opening stage of the crisis: in §4, Cicero records that Atticus had informed him of a senate meeting being called on June 1 by Antony, with the consul planning to make a motion to redistribute the provinces, with Cisalpine Gaul being removed from D. Brutus, *cos. design.* for 42, and given instead to Antony himself. Cicero had doubts that there would be a "free vote." Still, he was planning on attending himself, in order to raise other issues, including some measure that Atticus himself desired (14. 14. 6).

By early May, Cicero began to be seriously upset with the way that Antony was managing affairs. In a letter to C. Cassius Longinus, the "Liberator," written on May 3, 44, Cicero complains how *interfecto enim rege regios omnis nutus tuemur* (*Fam*. 12. 1. 1). The king may be dead, but the royal commands are not. What made it outrageous to Cicero, however, was not that Caesar's *acta* were to be upheld but that Antony had used the nebulous status of some of Caesar's plans to include pet projects of his own, things that Caesar would not have done. In the same passage, he wrote: *Tabulae figuntur, immunitates dantur, pecuniae maximae discribuntur, exsules reducuntur, senatus consulta falsa referentur* "tablets [containing laws] are being posted up [which signifies their validity], exemptions are being granted, huge amounts of money are being allocated, exiles are being recalled, fake decrees of the senate are being passed." In the uneasy days following Caesar's death, the senate had agreed to ratify his actions, *sed immoderate quidam et ingrate nostra facilitate abutuntur* "but they [Antony and his friends] are taking advantage of our obliging nature without restraint or gratitude" (*Fam*. 12. 1. 2).

Already at this early stage, Cicero saw a threat to the peace, as he wrote in a letter to Atticus from May 11: *causam armorum quaeri plane video*

"I clearly see that a pretext for arms is being sought" (*Att.* 14. 20. 4). In another letter from the same day, Cicero thinks the appeal to arms is inevitable: *mihi autem non est dubium quin res spectet ad castra* (*Att.* 14. 21. 3). Cicero was not the only senator out of Rome hearing about trouble brewing in Rome. In a letter sent on May 24 by C. Trebonius, one of the Liberators, now at Athens on his way to govern the province of Asia, Trebonius tells Cicero that he was hearing disturbing reports from Rome (*audiebam quaedam turbulenta*–*Fam.* 12. 16. 3).

The day that Antony planned to make his move was on June 1. Cicero was already informed that Antony planned to have Cisalpine Gaul voted to him that day (*Att.* 14. 14. 4; 15. 4. 1). Cicero, Brutus, and Cassius were also aware that Antony had planned to bring in a large crowd of Caesarian veterans into the city (*Att.* 14. 21. 2; 14. 22. 2; letter of Brutus and Cassius to Antony, *Fam.* 11. 2. 1). In the event, Antony did carry through his plan to have Cisalpine Gaul transferred to his control, but it was done through the popular assembly and not the senate (Cic. *Phil.* 1. 6; cf. 1. 25–26; Appian *BC* 3. 30. 115–119). Tensions continued to rise throughout the summer (see *Att.* 15. 18. 2; 15. 19. 1; 15. 20. 2); the first attack on Antony's actions came not from Cicero but from Julius Caesar's father-in-law, L. Calpurnius Piso Caesoninus (*cos.* 58). This event brought Cicero back to Rome from his planned trip to visit his son at Athens (*Phil.* 1. 10). On September 2, Cicero delivered before the senate (Dolabella was presiding) the first of his extended attacks on Antony, his first *Philippic*. In response, Antony may have considered killing his opponents (*Fam.* 12. 2. 1 specifically mentions September 19 as the date for their removal) but in the end decided against that course of action, preferring instead to engage in a propaganda campaign, as he had the statue of Caesar located near the Rostra inscribed with the words *parenti optime merito* "to the parent deserving most well [from his children]," to which Cicero remarked *ut non modo sicarii sed etiam parricidae iudicemini* "so that we are judged not only murderers, but parricides" (letter to Cassius, *Fam.* 12. 3. 1). Cicero notes that Antony was now trying to lump him into the company of the "assassins."

The war of words subsided for the moment when Antony left Rome for Brundisium to take control of the legions his brother C. Antonius had brought over from Macedon (cf. Appian *BC* 3. 27. 102–28. 105). He left on October 9 (*Fam.* 12. 23. 2; cf. Dio 45. 12. 1). It was around this same time that Cicero began to place hope in a young adventurer in town who had his own private armed following: the young Caesar, Octavian. Of him, Cicero notes in the same passage: *magna spes est in eo* (this phrase could very loosely but to better catch the sense be translated as "our best hope lies in this man"). While Antony was on his way to Brundisium, Octavian, in late October,[8] went around parts of Campania gathering an armed following among Caesar's veterans who had been settled on lands there (*Att.* 16. 8. 1; 16. 9. 1; cf. Dio 45. 12. 2). At Brundisium, Antony had trouble with the legions, as the monetary gift he offered them seemed too low. He responded by having the leading malcontents executed, which made the legions unhappy (Dio 45. 13. 1–2; cf. Cic. *Phil.* 3. 4; 5. 22).

Antony's rough treatment of his soldiers would come back to haunt him. In early November, Antony set out for Rome at the head of the Alaudae legion (*Att.* 16. 8. 2; cf. Appian *BC* 3. 40. 166). He reached Rome, but Octavian was already there with a large armed force (*Phil.* 3. 4; cf. *Fam.* 12. 25. 4). In late November, Antony planned to call the senate into session under his presidency, but both of his meetings did not go as planned. His first summons was for November 24, but he did not actually show up (*Phil.* 3. 19). His plan was to denounce Octavian's actions, but he did not carry through with his plan when he was informed that one of his legions from Macedon, the Martian legion, had refused to obey his orders any further and had instead halted at Alba and proclaimed themselves to be under Octavian's command (*Phil.* 3. 6; 4. 5; cf. Appian *BC* 3. 45. 185; Dio 45. 13. 3). The meeting of the senate was then postponed to November 28, when Antony planned again to launch an attack on Octavian, but he was already showing signs of worry. To be held at the Capitoline Temple, Antony entered by an underground tunnel (*Phil.* 3. 20). Instead of immediately attacking Octavian, however, Antony spent the beginning of the meeting calling for a *supplicatio* for Lepidus, which Cicero considered odd, as Antony had taken the trouble to scare away many of his political opponents, such as the tribunes L. Cassius and Ti. Cannutius, from attending this session (*Phil.* 3. 20–23).

Finally, Antony was planning to make a motion *de re publica* (concerning affairs of state), but he apparently lost his nerve when news came that another one of the Macedonian legions, the Fourth Legion, had also defected from him to Octavian (*Phil.* 3. 24; cf. 4. 6; Appian *BC* 3. 45. 185–186; Dio 45. 13. 3). So all Antony managed to accomplish was to call a formal division (*discessio*) of the senate for the *supplicatio*, a procedure that Cicero found unusual (*Phil.* 3. 24: *cum id factum esset antea numquam*). Antony quickly left the senate and traveled to Alba to try to win back the deserters, but he was repelled from the camp (*Phil.* 3. 24; cf. Appian *BC* 3. 45. 186–187).

---

[8] Cicero received a letter from Octavian on November 1 (*Att.* 16. 8. 1), so we can date Octavian's activity in this time period with confidence.

In late November to early December, Antony, repelled in his attempts to stifle Octavian and weakened by the defections of two veteran legions, decided to cut his losses and undertake his main task: head northward to remove D. Brutus from Cisalpine Gaul, with an eye to strengthen himself by gaining the support of the Caesarian military commanders in the north, M. Lepidus with four legions (in Narbonese Gaul and Near Spain), L. Munatius Plancus with three (*cos. desig.* 42 and governing Transalpine Gaul), and C. Asinius Pollio with two legions (governing Further Spain). Antony himself set out from Tibur with four seasoned legions, as well as some fresh levies, and made for Brutus (Appian *BC* 3. 45. 187, 46. 189–190; cf. Cic. *Fam.* 11. 5. 2–3; cf. Dio 45. 13. 5).

The news reached Rome that D. Brutus was under siege by Antony in the town of Mutina (modern Modena), providing the spectacle of a consul of the Roman Republic laying siege to a promagistrate who refused, with good reason, to hand over his province to said consul (for the run up of events, see Appian *BC* 3. 49. 198–201 and Dio 45. 14. 1). Here is where the crisis for the Roman government began. It was not just the outbreak of hostilities; there was also a political crisis. The provincial assignments of magistrates and promagistrates were usually a preserve of the senate.[9] In this case, however, the change had been accomplished by violence through the assembly (see previous mention of June 1), which provided grounds for resistance to Antony's designs by D. Brutus. Early on December 20, a manifesto from D. Brutus was read in Rome, announcing that he would hold the province for the senate and people of Rome (*Fam.* 11. 6a. 1; *Phil.* 3. 8). On this same day, Cicero decided to act boldly for a change. He delivered two speeches, one in the senate (*Philippic 3*) and one before a public meeting (*Philippic 4*), inveighing against Antony and demanding that the consul be branded a public enemy (*hostis*).[10] Although Cicero did not achieve this aim, he did manage to get two important matters through: first, he did convince the senate, which was meeting under the presidency of the tribunes of the plebs, to pass a vote publicly praising D. Brutus, Octavian, and the Martian and Fourth Legions for their actions; second, and more importantly, Cicero had the senate pass a resolution that D. Brutus, L. Plancus, and all other provincial governors under the *lex Iulia*

---

[9] Not even Gaius Gracchus had sought to remove the senate's customary authority in this matter, as his *lex Sempronia* merely forced the senate to name the consular provinces for the next year's consuls in advance of the elections being held. On the *lex Sempronia*, which was later superseded by the *lex Pompeia* of 52, see Stockton (1979) 129–131; Lintott (1999) 101–102.

[10] For this attempt to declare a Roman an external enemy and thus a valid military target, see the previous discussion on its first usage during the Marian-Sullan conflict.

be retained until a successor could be appointed by decree of the senate (*Phil.* 3. 38; *Fam.* 12. 22a. 1; cf. *Fam.* 12. 25. 2). This latter decree provided D. Brutus with the legal cover to refuse to give way to Antony, who could claim to be acting in accordance with the law he had passed during his consulship granting him the province.

The next critical day in the affair was January 1, 43, when the new consuls, A. Hirtius and C. Vibius Pansa, entered office. On that day, a meeting of the senate was held under guard (as had also been arranged at the senate meeting of December 20), and the question of what to do about Mutina was put before the chamber. Q. Fufius Calenus, a close friend of Antony, proposed sending a delegation to talk to Antony. Cicero responded that at this time, D. Brutus was under siege from Antony (*Phil.* 5. 24). The current situation was that of a grave internal crisis, if not outright civil war. Cicero's view was that "not only in every crisis of the state, but even in war and especially in civil war" (*Phil.* 5. 26: *cum in omni casu rei publicae tum in bello et maxime civili*), there was need for far stronger measures.

Therefore, he called for an immediate declaration of a state of emergency, a *tumultus*, and for all-out war to be waged against Antony. In his own words: *tumultum decerni, iustitium edici, saga sumi dico oportere, dilectum haberi sublatis vacationibus in urbe et in Italia praeter Galliam tota* "I say that it is necessary that a state of emergency be declared, a suspension of business be announced, military cloaks be worn, [and] that a levy be held in all of Italy except [Cisalpine] Gaul, with exemptions from military service being removed" (*Phil.* 5. 31). He went even further, asking for the senate to pass the so-called *senatus consultum ultimum*, entrusting the safety of the state to the consuls (*Phil.* 5. 34). Another important measure was a proposal that Octavian, sitting at Alba with a large armed force (two veteran legions, one freshly levied, and two with some recalled veterans mixed with recruits: Appian *BC* 3. 47. 191–192), have his status legitimized by voting him *imperium pro praetore* (*Phil.* 5. 45).

Nothing was resolved the first day, however. On January 2, Cicero seemed to be gaining his point before a tribune of the plebs named Salvius vetoed the session (Appian *BC* 3. 50. 206). Finally, by the third or fourth, the senate took some measures but not all as Cicero envisioned: an embassy was sent to Antony to consist of Ser. Sulpicius Rufus, L. Marcius Philippus, and L. Calpurnius Piso, all ex-consuls, although Cicero did manage to have *imperium* voted to Octavian, as well as a decree thanking D. Brutus for not abandoning his province (*Phil.* 5 and 6; cf. *Fam.* 11. 8. 1, 12. 24. 2; cf. Appian *BC* 3. 50. 202–206, 51. 209–210, cf. 61. 250–251; Suet. *div. Aug.* 10. 3; Plut. *Cicero* 45. 4; *Antonius* 17. 1; Dio 45. 17–47,

46. 1–29). Here we are in the heart of the crisis, as Cicero turned up the rhetoric. In his address to the Roman people on January 4, Cicero states that *res in extremum est adducta discrimen* "the state of affairs has been brought into extreme crisis" (*Phil.* 6. 19).

Speaking in the senate again later in January, Cicero notes the he cannot focus on the matter at hand because *adducta est enim, patres conscripti, res in maximum periculum et in extremum paene discrimen* "For, Conscript Fathers, the state of affairs has been brought into the greatest danger and almost into extreme crisis" (*Phil.* 7. 1). All of his strident rhetoric must have had some effect, as not too long after the series of senate meetings at the beginning of the year, it had finally been decided to send the consuls to fight Antony; Hirtius was already in the field, and the levy was being held throughout Italy without any exemptions from service (*vactiones*) being recognized (*Phil.* 7. 11–13). From this, it would appear that the senate had declared a *tumultus* before Antony's response had even been received. We have a consul sent to war and a levy being held without any *vacationes* being honored, which only occurred during a *tumultus*. The sole notice we get of a *tumultus* being declared at this time is from Dio, but it is spelled out explicitly: Dio 46. 29. 5 states that shortly after the senate meetings of the first several days of January, and even before Antony's reply was learned (in early February), ταραχήν τε εἶναι ἐψηφίσαντο καὶ τὴν ἐσθῆτα τὴν βουλευτικὴν ἀπεδύσαντο, τόν τε πόλεμον τὸν πρὸς αὐτὸν καὶ τοῖς ὑπάτοις καὶ τῷ Καίσαρι, στρατηγοῦ τινα ἀρχὴν δόντες, προσέταξαν "they voted that there was a state of *tumultus*, and they put aside senatorial dress, and they assigned the war against Antony to the consuls and to Caesar (Octavian), giving him the authority of a praetor."[11]

After the embassy returned around February 1, debate opened again. Apparently Antony had counterproposals, and the senate rejected them outright (Cic. *Fam.* 12. 4. 1; cf. Dio 46. 31. 1) At this point, during the senate meeting held on February 3 under the presidency of Pansa – for Hirtius, we learn, was already in the field at Claterna – a debate was held over formally declaring a state of war to be in existence. Cicero pushed hard for this to be decreed, but there was opposition from those who still had ties to Antony. In the end, Cicero's *sententia* was rejected with the consul's approval, whereas the motion of L. Julius Caesar (*cos.* 64), Antony's maternal uncle, calling for a declaration of a state of *tumultus* was formally passed (*Phil.* 8. 1–6; cf. Dio 46. 31. 2–3). Cicero mocks this trifling over words in his speech the next day (the *Eighth Philippic*),

---

[11] On the grant of praetorian *imperium* to Octavian, cf. Livy *Per.* 118, which further notes that he was given consular *ornamenta* and senatorial status.

but regardless of anything else, there most certainly was a formal state of *tumultus* declared, and it was to be full-scale war against Antony.[12]

While the Republic's armies marched north to free D. Brutus (*Phil.* 8. 6; cf. Dio 46. 36. 2–3), there was one last attempt at diplomacy. Apparently, Antony's friends in Rome spread the story that Antony was willing to come to terms, and there was an attempt to decree that a second embassy be sent, consisting of just about all of the ex-consuls in the senate. Cicero reports that Calenus and Piso (*Phil.* 12. 3) brought the hope of an "honorable peace" and that envoys, including himself, had been named to go to Antony (*Phil.* 12. 5). Cicero refused to go, however, as he stated that he would be the person least suitable for negotiating with Antony (*Phil.* 12. 17). Cicero's refusal must have put an end to this attempt to stop the war, as Dio notes that when Cicero refused to go, none of the other envoys would agree to go either (46. 32. 3–4).

The height of the crisis for the Roman Republic was reached in early April, as Pansa's army was entering the war zone. On March 30, 43, Cicero wrote to L. Plancus, who happened to be an old family friend, saying that he expected the *omnis fortuna rei publicae* to be decided by a single battle, whose result would already be known by the time Cicero received a response from all the way in Gaul (*Fam.* 10. 10. 1). Writing to Cassius the "Liberator" at around the same time, Cicero noted *res, cum haec scribebam, erat in extremum adducta discrimen* "matters, while I was writing, had come to the furthest point of crisis" (*Fam.* 12. 6. 2), echoing the same usage I have previously noted. He uses a similar phrasing while writing to M. Brutus in Macedon (*ad Brut.* 1[2. 1]. 1). Finally, on April 14, 43, there was a pair of battles near Forum Gallorum, close to Mutina.

We have a firsthand account, written the next day, from Ser. Sulpicius Galba, a friend of Cicero's who was serving in the army of the consul Pansa and wrote a letter to Cicero detailing the battles (*Fam.* 10. 30). In the first battle, Antony attempted to slip away from his siege of D. Brutus in order to intercept Pansa and his force of raw recruits before they could join the veteran army of Hirtius and Octavian. His plan was not a complete success because Hirtius and Octavian had suspected that Antony might make such an attempt and had sent to Pansa's aid the Martian legion and

---

[12] Dio further records the passage of the so-called *SC ultimum* against Antony (46. 31. 2), which is not mentioned by any other source, although perhaps we have a hint of this from Cicero's discussion of the uses of the "ultimate decree" in *Phil.* 8. 14–15. The *tumultus* is further confirmed by Livy *Per.* 118: *populus Romanus saga sumpsit* and from a direct and explicit reference to the state of tumult in a letter from Cicero to M. Brutus around the beginning of April 43 (*Ep. ad Brut.* 1[2. 1]. 1): *omnia quae severe decreta sunt hoc tumultu.*

Octavian's praetorian cohort in order to provide some protection for the consul's force. Antony's plan, however, turned out to be successful enough, as his veteran force of two seasoned legions cut Octavian's praetorian cohort to pieces and inflicted heavy casualties on the Martian legion, while Pansa himself, gravely wounded, and his force of recruits retreated to Bononia (*Fam.* 10. 30. 1–4; cf. Appian *BC* 3. 66. 272–69. 284; Dio 46. 37. 3–6).

Antony, however, was robbed of complete victory on his way back to Forum Gallorum, when Hirtius led out twenty-two veteran cohorts and routed Antony's army, which was exhausted from their battle earlier in the day (*Fam.* 10. 30. 4–5; cf. Appian *BC* 3. 70. 285–289; Dio 46. 37. 7). In the days following, Hirtius and Octavian pressed the attack and even managed to take Antony's camp near Mutina, but at a heavy cost, as Hirtius fell there (Appian *BC* 3. 71. 290–294; Dio 46. 38. 5). Pansa as well, at Bononia, succumbed to his wounds, and the state was left without consuls (Appian *BC* 3. 75. 305–76. 311 [containing a dubious, at best, death scene of Pansa urging Octavian to patch up things between himself and Antony, in order to provide a Caesarian "united front" against the "Pompeian" senate]; Dio 46. 39. 1). Antony, however, was defeated and decided to make a run for it to try to join Lepidus in Gaul (Appian *BC* 3. 72. 295–297).

At Rome, on the other hand, everything seemed to be well. The news of the victory at Forum Gallorum reached the city on April 20, and the city populace apparently gave Cicero an impromptu "triumphal" procession of sorts, from his house up to the capitol (*Phil.* 14. 12; cf. *ad Brut.* 9[1. 3]. 2). The next day, the Parilia (April 21), Cicero made a speech in the senate (*Phil.* 14) mentioning the dispatches about the victory (§1), but resisting P. Servilius's call for a return to civilian dress (§2) until D. Brutus was known to be safe. A *supplicatio* was voted for fifty days (*Phil.* 14. 29, 37; cf. Appian *BC* 3. 74. 302; Dio 46. 39. 3 wrongly has sixty days). Dio alone records that the senate returned to civilian dress at this time, which might mark the end of the formal state of tumult (46. 39. 3). A few days later, however, probably on the twenty-fifth,[13] the sad news reached Rome that Hirtius had died fighting at Mutina and Pansa had succumbed to his wounds. Around this time, Cicero reports that the senate passed a decree branding anyone who fled with Antony as public enemies (*ad Brut.* 10[1. 3a][SB 8], 13[1.5].1[SB 9]; cf. Dio 46. 39. 3).

---

[13] This is the suggestion of Shackleton Bailey; see commentary to *ad Brut.* 10(1.3a) [SB *ad Brut.* 8, p. 233].

THE SUMMER THAT LED TO A FALL: THE FALL OF THE "FREE" ROMAN REPUBLIC

Although it might seem that the crisis was over, with Antony in full retreat and D. Brutus relieved from siege at Mutina, there was actually a second crisis that occurred in 43, which followed closely on the heels of the *tumultus* that lasted from February 3[14] to roughly April 21 or shortly thereafter. Antony's defeat at the hands of the armies loyal to the senate made it appear to some that the Republic would arise anew, like the mythical phoenix, from the proverbial ashes. Yet two serious problems arose in the immediate aftermath. First, Antony had escaped, and the threat from him was not over. That in itself promised future disruption. As D. Brutus, writing to Cicero at the end of April, noted, M. Aemilius Lepidus, governing Narbonese Gaul and Near Spain, could ruin everything if he decided to join with Antony (Cic. *Fam.* 11. 9. 1). D. Brutus also had doubts about Cicero's friend L. Munatius Plancus, governing all of Gaul over the Alps except Narbo (*Fam.* 11. 9. 2). Plancus himself, writing to Cicero, made similar remarks to those of Brutus about where refuge lay for Antony: in Lepidus's army (*Fam.* 10. 11. 2).

The other major problem facing the revived Republic was the loss of both its chief magistrates. In other crises, especially internal ones, I have noted how the consuls were often the chief "point men" for the senate and were trusted to carry through the defense of the state on their own by virtue of their magisterial powers.[15] Now Rome had no consuls to guide her. We have already noted the deaths of the consuls in late April. The ruling element at Rome was not completely stagnant in this situation. A debate on the military situation and what should be done about those who had been declared public enemies (*hostes*) was held in the senate on April 27 according to Cic. *ad Brut.* 13(1. 5). 1[SB 9]. The senate could function quite normally under the presidency of the city praetor (at this time, M. Caecilius Cornutus[16]), *qui, quod consules aberant, consulare munus sustinebat more maiorum* "who, since the consuls were absent, was undertaking the consular burden following ancestral custom" (Cic. *Fam.* 10. 12. 3). But from no source do we hear that Cornutus made any attempt to

---

[14] Whereas the *tumultus* may have been declared earlier if Dio's first notice before February 3 was correct, there is absolutely no doubt that the state of emergency was formally voted and approved on February 3.

[15] No greater expression of this can be found than the whole point of the *senatus consultum ultimum*, which entrusted the safety and defense of the state to the consuls, if available.

[16] For full references to him, see *MRR* 2. 338.

provide strong leadership or executive direction during the vacuum caused by the death of the consuls. Instead, we have the words of D. Brutus writing to Cicero in early May, again to inform us of the situation: *Primum omnium quantum perturbationem rerum urbanarum adferat obitus consulum, quantumque cupiditatem hominibus honoris iniciat vacuitas, non te fugit* "First of all, it does not escape you how much confusion the death of the consuls has brought into city affairs, or how much desire for office the vacuum has stirred up in men" (Cic. *Fam.* 11. 10. 2).

On both fronts, the situation would get worse for the Republic. First, there came the news that Antony had been joined by his friend P. Ventidius at Vada near the Alps, leading three legions (Cic. *Fam.* 11. 10. 3). According to D. Brutus, the fault lay with Octavian, who did not act in concert with him to stop Antony (*Fam.* 11. 10. 4).[17] More worrisome, in the same passage, D. Brutus notes: *sed neque Caesari imperari potest nec Caesar exercitui suo.* Octavian is not to be ordered, but his army is not following orders either. D. Brutus himself, who had been voted by the senate to command the war (Dio 46. 40. 1), was slow to follow Antony (he makes his excuses in a letter to Cicero, *Fam.* 11. 13), which gave Antony the opportunity he needed to reach Lepidus. Lepidus himself sent letters to Cicero (there were doubtless ones to others in Rome as well) protesting his loyalty (*Fam.* 10. 34a, 10. 43). Regardless, no one else seemed to put much faith in Lepidus (see Cic. *Fam.* 10. 21. 1 [Plancus], 11. 23. 1 [D. Brutus], 10. 20. 1 [Cicero]).

The second crisis of 43, the final crisis that would see an end to the free workings of the tangled web of law, custom, and unspoken agreement that comprised the "constitution" of the Republic, can be precisely dated to start from May 30, when Lepidus wrote an official dispatch to the *Senatus Populusque Romanus*, claiming that his army had mutinied and that the decision (on whether to fight Antony or not) was taken out of his hands (Cic. *Fam.* 10. 35. 1). Lepidus called on the senate to put aside public quarrels and think about the best interests of the state (§2). Whether he was telling the truth or lying through his teeth (cf. Appian *BC* 3. 83. 340–84. 348 and Plut. *Antonius* 18. 1–6 –both seem to subscribe to the idea that the suborning of the army was the work of Antony, and Lepidus was forced to bend to circumstances or be forcibly removed) does not matter. Antony was now in command of a sizable army. The threat perception and fear perception among the decision makers of the Republic are clearly apparent in our contemporary source, the correspondence of Cicero. D. Brutus, writing to Cicero on June 3, by which date he had certainly heard

---

[17] Cf. Appian *BC* 3. 80. 325–329.

the news about Lepidus's army, stated *Crede mihi, nisi ista omnia ita fiunt quem ad modum scribo, magnum nos omnis adituros periculum* "Trust me, unless everything is done as I write [earlier in the letter, D. Brutus suggests recalling the legions from Africa and Sardinia, summoning M. Brutus and his army from Macedon, and voting pay for his own army], all of us are going to be heading into great danger" (Cic. *Fam.* 11. 26).

On another front, another danger presented itself to the Republic. Already following Antony's rout from Mutina, doubts began to surface about the reliability of Octavian. More than his refusing to help D. Brutus corner Antony near the Alps, Appian reports immediately after that incident that Octavian had opened up communication with Lepidus and Pollio, offering to join them in suppressing the "Pompeians" (Appian *BC* 3. 81. 330–332). M. Brutus in Macedon must have been receiving troublesome reports, as he wrote to Cicero on May 15 (which means the letters coming to him were likely from the end of April to early May) that he had serious fears of Octavian and his desire for the consulship. He went on to note that Cicero would receive a serious measure of blame if things turned sour because Cicero had been so instrumental in the many honorific decrees the senate had passed to favor the young Caesar (ad Brut. 12[1. 4a]. 2–3 [SB 11]).

Again, from the other Brutus, Decimus, word came to Cicero that Octavian was now becoming less than pleased with Cicero: apparently, people had been telling Octavian that Cicero's plans for the youth could be summed up as *laudandum adulescentem, ornandum, tollendum* "...the youth must be praised, decorated and then lifted up [and out of the picture]" (*Fam.* 11. 20. 1). Apparently, Octavian had already made his response. Octavian said (as reported by D. Brutus in the same passage): *se non esse commissurum ut tolli possit* "he would see to it that he could not be removed." At the same time, Octavian's behavior was also a sign of future trouble, as he refused to send to Brutus the legion from Pansa's army that Octavian had taken over after the consul's death (§4).

The most significant problem, however, for those who wanted to restore the free working of the political system, free from the influence of men such as Antony, arose from the soldiers, especially from the Caesarian legions. In early June, Cicero reports that the Martian and Fourth Legions had refused to serve under D. Brutus (*Fam.* 11. 14. 2). This news, combined with the shock of Lepidus's turnabout, had taken everyone at Rome by surprise. They had thought the war was over, but now they faced *hi novi timores* (§3). The Republic was not finished yet, as Plancus was still loyal to the senate and even joined D. Brutus's army in Gaul to face off against Antony and Lepidus (Cic. *Fam.* 10. 23, 11. 13a, 11. 25, 10. 26, 12. 10, *ad Brut.* 18(1. 10) [SB 17]. 2). On June 30, Lepidus was added to the list of public enemies, but the senate was not beyond compromise, as they set a deadline of September 1 for all of those who had turned against it to come to their senses (Cic. *Fam.* 12. 10. 1). However, Octavian had become utterly unreliable.

Cicero wrote to M. Brutus, urgently calling on him to come because Octavian was now of no help to the state: *exercitus autem Caesaris, qui erat optimus, non modo nihil prodest sed etiam cogit exercitum tuum flagitari* (ad Brut. 22[1. 14][SB 22]. 2). The last dated letter from the Ciceronian corpus that refers directly to events is a letter from Plancus, camped in Gaul with D. Brutus, sent on July 28, 43. He reports that the situation is currently a stalemate, with the Republic's army encamped facing Antony and Lepidus, neither side making a move (Cic. *Fam.* 10. 24. 3). He states that they would be in a position to attack if they could be reinforced by either the legions from Africa or Octavian's army. He had sent messengers to Octavian asking him to come and said that Octavian had even promised to do so – but had not (§4). He blames the situation on Octavian's desire to have the consulship for the rest of the magisterial year (§§5–6). He and D. Brutus will not attempt a decisive engagement without the African legions or Octavian (§8).

At this point, exact dates are harder to come by, so a brief summary of events will follow. We are also forced to rely on the later narrative sources, as we no longer have Cicero's correspondence to guide us. With the decline in trust of Octavian, the senate attempted to woo his army away from him, a plan that utterly backfired (Appian *BC* 3. 86. 353–357; Dio 46. 40. 4–6). Octavian's response was to rouse his soldiers against the senate (Appian *BC* 3. 87. 358–360; Dio 46. 42. 4–43. 1). Although the senate tried various measures to soothe him, giving him command in the war against Antony and Lepidus (Appian *BC* 3. 85. 352; Dio 46. 42. 1) and granting him still more honors (Dio 46. 41. 3), nothing worked. Octavian's soldiers then demanded the consulship for him, which the senate refused, leading to Octavian marching on Rome (Appian *BC* 3. 88. 361–366; Dio 46. 42. 2–43. 6).

The senators dithered between resistance and appeasement. Their last stand came when the legions from Africa arrived, and combined with one legion left by Pansa, they attempted to make one last stand against Octavian's army (Appian *BC* 3. 91. 373–376; Dio 46. 44. 2–5). Dio records one last use of the so-called *senatus consultum ultimum*, with the care of the city entrusted to the praetors, as there were no consuls, and apparently one last declaration of a *tumultus*, as he records that the senators changed their dress: Dio 46. 44. 4 καὶ αὐτοὶ τήν τε ἐσθῆτα αὖθις ἠλλάξαντο καὶ τοῖς στρατηγοῖς τὴν φυλακὴν τῆς πόλεως ἐνεχείρισαν, ὥσπερ εἴθιστο. It is curious that here, as elsewhere, the Greek accounts have no special terminology to designate an *SC ultimum*. We must infer its existence (but do so with confidence) from the order concerning the protection of the city.

However, this crisis – the final one for the Roman Republic – would end mostly with a whimper, not a great battle. The final usage of the *SC ultimum* would not serve to deter Octavian from his goal. The senate's army quickly decided to go over to Octavian (Appian *BC* 3. 92. 377–382; Dio 46. 45. 1–2). In an act perhaps more worthy of another age (or did he see what was coming inevitably ahead?), the city praetor, M. Caecilius Cornutus, committed suicide (Appian *BC* 3. 92. 381). The crisis was now over. The legitimately chosen leadership of the Republic had been replaced by a temporary commander with an irregular command. No greater proof needs be offered for the change in affairs than to recount the events that immediately followed. In a strange, but not implausible, notice from Dio, we hear of the "irregular" procedures that followed Octavian's coup. As it was not possible to follow normal custom and seek the appointment of an *interrex* (apparently, all holders of patrician magistracies needed to resign their offices in order to allow the auspices to return to the *patres* [in this special sense, the patrician members of the senate], an impossible situation because at least one patrician magistrate, P. Ventidius the praetor, was currently with Antony in Gaul[18]), two men were appointed *pro consulibus* in order to hold the elections (δύο τινῶν ἀντὶ ὑπάτων πρὸς τὰς ἀρχαιρεσίας αἱρεθέντων), a highly irregular procedure without precedent at any point in Roman history (Dio 46. 45. 3).

And so, at the age of nineteen, C. Julius divi f. Caesar (Octavianus) became consul with his relative Q. Pedius (Appian *BC* 3. 94. 387–388; Dio 46. 46. 1; Livy *Per.* 119; Suet. *div. Aug.* 12; *RGDA* 1. 4). The date of his inauguration was August 19, 43 (Dio 56. 30. 5; cf. Tac. *Ann.* 1. 9).[19] A system of institutions that had managed to govern Rome for several centuries was finally overthrown by the power of the soldiers and an unscrupulous youth.

We may now return to where we began this examination by asking what means the Roman state had to counter threats to the existence of the legitimate government and the entire governing system. We can see that Cicero and the Romans of his time had a series of measures that could be

---

[18] A problem that had already been noted back in May by Cicero was *dum enim unus erit patricius magistratus, auspicia ad patres redire non possunt* "for so long as there is one patrician magistrate, the auspices cannot return to the *patres*" *ad Brut.* 13(1. 5)[SB 9]. 4.

[19] For full references with regard to Octavian's first consulship, see *MRR* 2. 336.

employed in an emergency such as the one presented by Mark Antony's siege of D. Brutus in Mutina. The declaration of a state of emergency, a *tumultus*, facilitated the quick enrollment of an army to relieve the besieged Brutus. It may also have smoothed the passage of the decree regularizing the "irregular" armed force under the command of Octavian. In the emergency, there was need for immediate mobilization of every experienced soldier, and Octavian already had a large group of them following his orders. In this case, it happened that the crisis response was adequate to the task.

In the end, however, the emergency measures that the Romans had available to them were insufficient for successfully countering the threats that brought the system down. When Octavian, at the head of a large and experienced army, marched toward Rome, a *tumultus* and even the *senatus consultum ultimum* were of no avail. As had happened in the case of Caesar six years previously, the decision makers of the Roman Republic were incapable of finding a crisis response that could counter the threat that was presented against them.

8

THE EVOLUTION OF CRISIS RESPONSE DURING THE ROMAN REPUBLIC

The Romans and Crisis through Time

As we have just recounted, Cicero and the other leaders within the Roman Senate during the winter of 44/43 had good knowledge of how their ancestors reacted to crisis situations, which presented similar dangers to the safety of the Roman state and the preservation of its core values, including the "free" workings of the complicated interplay of statute law, ancestral custom, and unwritten agreements that together formed the structure of the *libera res publica*, the system that we mean when we, modern students of the ancient past, say "the Roman Republic." They knew that when a hostile, armed force threatened the safety of Rome and the governing apparatus, there were measures available: the *tumultus* and the so-called *senatus consultum ultimum*, which could be employed to put Rome on an emergency alert status and mobilize all available resources to come to the state's defense.

We have also seen, however, how inadequate these measures were in the end. We may ask the question why. Why were measures that had proven capable of seeing off threats as diverse as Hannibal and the Gracchi incapable of handling several of the final crises (Sulla's march, Caesar's march, Octavian's march), the last one of which resulted in the end of the "free" Republic? To explore that issue more fully, it would be useful to examine Roman crisis response over the lifetime of the Republic, as well as the nature of the military security and political crises that the governing institutions faced. We need to see whether there was any change, or continuity for that matter, in the overall way that the Romans responded to crises. Was there a method behind their chosen responses to crises throughout time? Is it that the nature of the crises themselves changed in some fundamental way that rendered their methods of response obsolete?

The early records of the Roman state, as we have them, point very strongly to the primary role of executive leadership in the resolution of serious crises in the early period of the Republic. Strong evidence for this is provided by looking at how often the Romans resorted to the use of the extraordinary office of dictator during the early period of the Republic.[1] Clearly, the Romans felt the need for unified executive authority in the face of urgent military threats. A change occurred, however, during the course of the third century. In that important century when Rome began to expand beyond its immediate environs and even started what would be a long process of projecting Roman power far from its Italian heartland, there is a marked decline in the employment of the dictatorship for military purposes. Although explanations for the gradual disappearance of the dictatorship vary,[2] the reasoning put forward by Hartfield makes a certain amount of sense. She notes several important factors in the gradual disappearance of the use of the extraordinary magistracy: the creation and rise in the number of promagistracies, the greater flexibility and control that promagistracies gave the senate, and the limitations of the dictatorship as an office (six-month term of office; generally restricted to Italian soil; it was an extraordinary office and thus went against a preference for adhering to the "normal" governmental structure).[3] In general, this theory seems sound and can be seen as a parallel development to where the primary responsibility for crisis management moved during the course of this century, away from a single executive official and toward a larger group of members of the ruling class. It is during this century that the senate began to assert itself more as a primary crisis decision-making authority and not a body that handed off responsibility to deal with crises to an executive officer who was free to do as he wished.

This change in decision making can already be seen at work during the critical situation where Rome faced off against King Pyrrhus of Epirus, who had been called in by the Greek city of Tarentum in southern Italy to defend it from Rome.[4] Unfortunately, our main source, Plutarch's biography of the Epirote king, does not tell us as much about internal Roman deliberations as we might like, but it still is apparent that the senate took

---

[1] The importance of the use of a dictator as a means of response by the Roman state is discussed in Chapter 2.

[2] One of more recent attempts is Morgan (1991), claiming that many senators did not like how holding the office gave too much precedence to a select few men over other ex-magistrates and, therefore, decided to appoint no more. I am not convinced by his argument. For earlier attempts to explain its disappearance, see Hartfield (1982) 249, 265 n. 4.

[3] Hartfield (1982) 247–255.

[4] On the outbreak of war between Rome and Tarentum, see Barnes (2005).

the lead in responding to the situation, sending embassies and deciding how the state would respond to the threat from Pyrrhus. It should be noted that the Romans did not resort to the naming of a dictator even once to lead their forces in their encounter with Pyrrhus.[5] Of course, one may counter that the threat posed by Pyrrhus was not an existential threat, quite different from the crises that are discussed in detail in the preceding chapters. It may not have been an existential crisis, but it was a significant military threat, and again I repeat that the senate, which could have appointed a dictator to lead Roman forces against the Epirote king, especially after the serious defeats at Heraclea and Asculum, chose not to do so. Likewise, during the First Punic War, a dictator was only appointed once for war-related duties: A. Atilius Caiatinus, who was named to replace the disgraced consul P. Claudius Pulcher (*cos.* 249).[6] On the contrary, from Polybius's account of the war, it seems that the senate played a major role in decision making in every critical moment, as far as we can tell.

The importance of the senate as the prime responder to a crisis situation, however, comes sharply into focus when we examine their active role in deciding policy during the Second Punic War. I have already discussed in detail the senate's role in managing the Saguntine Crisis.[7] After the war was underway, the senate was the primary crisis manager during periods of severe crisis. As discussed in Chapter 2, when the Roman state was faced with one of its darkest days following the consul C. Flaminius's defeat and death at Lake Trasimene, the senate and the magistrates on hand (two praetors) deliberated what to do. They decided on the selection of a dictator even though the normal means of appointment (naming by a consul) could not be carried through. Again, in the aftermath of the horrific defeat at Cannae, it would be the senate that would decide what measures to take in response to the crisis. In many respects, the period between 218 and 207, when Hasdrubal's death and defeat at the Metaurus put an end to the imminent threat to Roman survival posed by Hannibal's presence in Italy, could be considered one long sequence of continuous crises (Saguntum, Trebia, Trasimene, Cannae, the defection of Capua, the defection of Tarentum, the non-compliance of several Latin colonies, the

---

[5] Cn. Domitius Calvinus was named in order to hold the elections (*comitiorum habendorum*) in 280 (see *MRR* I. 191), but otherwise, no other dictators were named at all during the war against Pyrrhus.

[6] See *MRR* I. 215 for sources; Hartfield (1982) 480–484 for discussion of this man, and his curious predecessor M. Claudius Glicia, who was appointed, but never acted, as dictator immediately before Caiatinus. For recent work on the First Punic War, see Hoyos (1998) and Lazenby (1995). Still fundamental are the notes in Walbank's commentary on Polybius.

[7] See Chapter 6.

threat from Philip V of Macedon, and finally, the Metaurus). Throughout this period, the leadership of the senate was clear.

The turning point – the time at which the pendulum begins to swing away from the senate's predominance in managing the Roman state during crises – is one that is probably well known to most and will come as no surprise: the turbulent tribunate of Tiberius Sempronius Gracchus.[8] This episode is, of course, the point at which many scholars begin to speak of what is called "The Crisis of the Republic."[9] In reality, the so-called Crisis of the Republic is not a true crisis as I defined in Chapter 1. The growing tensions within the ruling class were most certainly a problem, but it was not a crisis because there was no finite time for response. It was instead an open-ended problem for which there was plenty of time for a response to be developed. This is in sharp contrast to the actual crisis that Tiberius Gracchus presented. When a false perception that Tiberius was contemplating the use of force to seize power for himself was spread among the senators gathered to discuss the "problem" of Gracchus, who had made himself a thorn in the side of senatorial prerogatives, the fact is that at heart, this was mainly a political dispute, a political impasse. We have discussed some other political impasses, especially the dispute between the majority of the senate and the Popillii Laenates in Chapter 6. That stalemate eventually ended with the intervention of tribunes of the plebs who were amenable to ensuring that the will of the majority of the senate was followed. In this case, however, the one who was thwarting the senate's will *was* a tribune of the plebs.

This was also not the first time that a political impasse had arisen because of a land reform program. The consul C. Laelius in 140 had also attempted to relieve the problems of the Roman "yeomanry" and get them back on the land (which served the twin goals of requalifying them for military service and encouraging them to procreate to produce the next generation of Roman legionaries) but had faced the stiff opposition of the "powerful" as Plutarch tells us.[10] In that situation, Laelius decided to give in, abandoning his attempt and earning for himself the sobriquet *Sapiens* – the wise or prudent (σοφὸς ἢ φρόνιμος) as Plutarch spells out for his non-Latin–speaking readers. It may indeed have been both wise and prudent to hold off from challenging the wealthiest and most powerful among the Roman ruling class, but Gracchus refused to stand down. As

---

[8] See Chapter 6.

[9] A very good recent summary of the topic, with references to ancient and modern discussions, is von Ungern-Sternberg (2004).

[10] Plut. *TG* 8. 3–4.

they did not have the help of another plebeian tribune to counter Gracchus (the one who had tried to help them, Octavius, had been cashiered for his troubles), another means of solving the impasse in their favor would have to be found. However, the senate never managed at this time to develop a response. Neither did the consul Mucius Scaevola. Instead, in an action that was without any true sanction of law, the Pontifex Maximus Scipio Nasica led a lynch mob to suppress Tiberius and his supporters.

Both executive authority (embodied in the consul Scaevola) and the senators as a corporate decision-making body failed to devise a response to Tiberius Gracchus. When the particular crisis presented by Tiberius was repeated, this time by his younger brother Gaius Gracchus, a response was finally devised, but not one that would address the "Crisis of the Republic" – the growing tensions and lack of unity within the ruling class. What they came up with was only a response to the immediate threat presented by Gaius: the so-called *senatus consultum ultimum*.[11] The legacy of the *SC ultimum* would prove, however, to be mixed, at best, for the senatorial aristocracy. When it was first passed in 121, it gave the consul L. Opimius the legal, or at least the political, cover to use violence to put down a turbulent tribune whose political program was not to the liking of the majority of the senate. From the standpoint of the senators who passed it, it must have seemed to have been a success: Gaius Gracchus and his supporters were crushed, the authority of the senate was respected, and there was peace.

Yet what they created that day set two very important and lasting precedents that they might not have approved of, had they been aware of them. First of all, the passage of the *SC ultimum* provided an institutional basis for resorting to violence in order to resolve an internal political dispute. The senators had irrevocably brought violence into the system. What Nasica had done in 133 was appeal to ideas and concepts that transcended the "constitution" of the Republic. What Opimius and his supporters in 121 did was to use the machinery of the Republic to authorize those very same actions. Secondly, and more significantly for the future of the "free" Roman Republic, the senate abdicated the decision-making power for resolving a crisis and instead handed that power back to the executive, this time in the form of the consul(s) who asked the senate to pass the decree. Although they might not have thought about it, what the senators had done was to return to the old way of crisis management of the early Republic: handing power over to the executive and having the executive make all of the decisions about resolving the crisis. From

---

[11] Discussed in detail in Chapter 5.

this point forward, the senate would turn toward the executive to handle serious crises.

Although it did not have to be this way, sadly, the Romans of the ruling class may have been culturally constrained and shaped by their mentality to the point where no other solution than violence orchestrated by the executive was possible. In the modern world, we have other methods available to resolve political impasses within a state, and even states that do not have a written constitution (such as Rome) make use of these methods. There are the courts. There is the ballot box. It would appear, however, that the Romans could not think in those terms. Whereas the courts could be used for political purposes to strike out against one's enemies, that may well have made them unsuitable to act as an impartial arbiter in internal political impasses. As for the ballot box, although there has been debate about the nature of the Republic and how "democratic" or not it was, I believe most scholars would agree with me that the senatorial class would likely have recoiled from the concept that a political dispute among themselves should be decided by the urban mob. Instead, the Romans of the ruling class chose to institutionalize violence.

The effect of this choice would be profound. Although the next threat from a tribune of the plebs would be easily seen off, a little more than thirty years after the younger Gracchus, yet another troublesome tribune would cause problems for the consuls in office. In this case, the consuls of 88, L. Cornelius Sulla and Q. Pompeius Rufus, faced P. Sulpicius Rufus, a man with ambitions.[12] The consuls attempted a novel maneuver in order to block his legislation, declaring a *iustitium*, but it ended in failure when Sulpicius and his supporter C. Marius resorted to violence and forced Sulla to rescind the suspension of business. Violence had become the norm for achieving political goals. At this point, one can ask: why did Sulla and Pompeius choose not to call upon the senate to pass the *SC ultimum* against Sulpicius and Marius? How could they be unaware of the response method available, when C. Marius himself had made use of it?

In fairness to them, it is entirely possible that they sought to follow that route. There are probably good reasons why it did not happen. The senate itself may have been divided on the issues. It is a great mistake to look at it as a monolithic body with a single mind. The senate was a collection of individuals with divided loyalties and interests. In addition, Sulpicius, perhaps all too aware of the tools that could be deployed against him, might have been more capable in preventing the passage of a decree against him than previous turbulent tribunes. Whatever the reason, the fact

---

[12] See Chapter 4.

is that the SC *ultimum* was not resorted to in this instance, when previous precedent would suggest that this was an optimal time for a consul, being faced with a tribune who resorted to violence, to move for its passage.

Instead, the consul Sulla decided to resort to unauthorized and extreme violence, of a kind never contemplated before by any other magistrate faced with political opposition at home: he went to the army stationed at Capua, which had been previously assigned to him for the war with Mithridates (but had now been taken away from him by Sulpicius's legislation), and suborned the soldiers into marching upon the city of Rome. Sulla decided to use the ultimate level of force available to settle this political dispute in his favor. However, it can be noted that his use of a Roman army to end a political fight was not entirely out of keeping with the methods that the senate itself had sanctioned for the resolution of political disputes within the city when they first passed the SC *ultimum* thirty-three years previously. The difference is that Sulla made no attempt to provide even a legal fig leaf for his actions. Sulla's march would in fact have been an entirely different matter had he first been able to pass the SC *ultimum* before he marched against his own homeland.

Here was the real crux of the so-called Crisis of the Republic, the issue that the Romans of the ruling class never addressed until a solution was imposed upon them. There was no final arbiter within the system whose judgment would be acceptable to all sides in a political impasse. It could be argued that the senate should have served in the role of final arbiter within the system, as they had increasingly taken on that role in responding to state crises since the Second Punic War. The senate, however, suffered institutional shortcomings that made it possible for the senate itself to be thrown into crisis, with its own authority and survival being threatened, which rendered it incapable of formulating a peaceful response to internal political impasses. When the state crisis was a threat from the outside, the senate could be an effective body through which to deliberate and determine the correct response. As is common among all peoples when threatened from outside, even political enemies who would as soon stick a knife in their opponent's back as greet them with a handshake would "circle the wagons" in the face of an external danger. Nevertheless, when the threat was internal, when the senate's own membership was part of the threat to the workings of the system, the body could be rendered powerless and incapable of formulating a response.

Even when working in close cooperation with a magistrate, that response more and more reflected the leadership of the magistrate, not the collective will of the senate. The senate in 121 had decided that the use of force would be the final arbiter for political disputes within the Roman

Republic. In that sense, what Sulla did was appeal to the final arbiter but to an extent that was unimaginable to the vast majority of Romans of the political class of that time. It should be remembered, after all, that all of Sulla's officers (save one), most of them coming from the senatorial and equestrian orders, refused to join him on his march, and the senate, even if it may have been intimidated by Sulpicius and Marius, did send two praetors to intercept Sulla and stop his march upon the city. Regardless of political views, the majority of the senate certainly did not want armed soldiers to decide what was an internal political matter.

Although the Republic would be restored eventually, the problem of resolving political disputes without resorting to violence did not disappear. As we saw again in 63, during M. Tullius Cicero's consulship, a spurned noble (L. Sergius Catilina) decided to turn to armed force in order to defeat his political opponents.[13] The consul Cicero had the "final decree" passed. This time, the main violence would be restricted to outside the city, but Cicero was prepared to use armed force on a large scale within the city if necessary. The deaths of the conspirators, including an ex-consul, were certainly a resort to violent force to suppress the threat. This would be the last successful use of the *SC ultimum*. The power of the executive in resolving internal political crises was now more firmly established than ever. The state had institutionalized the use of force to crush political opposition to those who currently held the levers of power. Armed force required strong and centralized leadership. Future challengers decided that they would need to match force with force.

With Julius Caesar and the crises that brought an end to the "free" Roman Republic,[14] the twin legacies of the *SC ultimum*, the handing off of crisis management into the hands of the executive, and the institutionalization of the use of force to settle political disputes, would set the pattern for the final resolution of the Crisis of the Republic. For with the victory of Caesar in the Civil War of 49, a final arbiter was created: namely Caesar. In fact, the "free" Roman Republic would be plunged into its final crises when that arbiter was assassinated in March of 44. After nearly fifteen more years of turmoil and intermittent civil war, the Roman state did, at last, develop a final arbiter who would decide all political disputes, and for that matter, all political decisions of any kind: the *princeps*. The *princeps* embodied the legacy of the decision made in 121. He was an executive officer acting in the name of the senate, and he had a monopoly on the deployment of force within the state against enemies both within

---

[13] See Chapter 5.
[14] See Chapters 5 and 7.

and without. So, we can see that the decision made by L. Opimius and the senate in 121 had a much more profound impact than many might have thought – it set the course for the "Roman Revolution"[15] that would result in the "new" governing structure of the Roman state. For while there would still be consuls and praetors and tribunes of the plebs and a senate, one man – in the words of a later historian looking back at the changes that occurred – had seduced the army with gifts and the populace with grain and enticed everyone with the sweetness of peace. Only then did he proceed to assume all the powers of the senate, the magistrates, and even the law for himself.[16]

[15] The term coined, of course, by Syme (1939).
[16] Tac. *Ann.* 1. 2: *ubi militem donis, populum annona, cunctos dulcedine otii pellexit, insurgere paulatim, munia senatus magistratuum legum in se trahere.*

FINAL THOUGHTS

The aim of this work has been two-fold from the start. It is a study of Roman crisis behavior, an important topic in and of itself. There was, however, always a further goal in studying this subject: to see what Roman crisis response can tell us about how the Roman Republic functioned in practice, not theory. When a system is placed under stress, it is possible to see, as the cracks begin to develop, how the structure was built and where power ultimately resided. Looking back on the subject as a whole, we see a number of interesting observations come to light.

One is that the Republic never developed an institution or an institutional response to deal with internal political crises – situations where competing power centers within the structure were unable, or unwilling, to resolve policy or personality disputes, which fell into a state of impasse. The Roman Senate as a body attempted to assume this role for itself, with the notion being that it spoke for the entire ruling class of Rome. It sought to assume the role of final arbiter in political and policy disputes. When the crisis, however, involved someone with independent authority challenging the senate's right to act as final arbitrator in a dispute, it often provoked a far more severe crisis. In such situations, the senate, having certain institutional limitations to its ability to enforce its will, was unable to resolve matters. In severe situations, where violence was contemplated by the opposing sides in the dispute, recourse was eventually made by the executive to a novel decree of the senate, whereby it "advised" the executive authorities of the Republic to use any and all means to end the impasse: the *senatus consultum ultimum*. The *SC ultimum*, however, was not a true institutional response that could peacefully resolve an internal political dispute by appealing to law or custom, the foundations of the system we call the Republic. Instead, it handed matters off to the executive, with the senate's blessing to do "whatever the magistrate saw fit." How else can one interpret *uti rem publicam defenderet et ne quid detrimenti rem publicam capiat?* One can argue whether *carte blanche* was being offered to the magistrate who was calling for the passing of the *SC ultimum*, but it is clear that the power to resolve the dispute was now being handed over to the magistrate and not for the senate as a group any more to decide. The failure of the Romans to create a peaceful institutional mechanism that could resolve internal political impasses to the satisfaction (or at the very least, grudging acceptance) of everyone in the state was a serious weakness and eventually opened the door to the aristocratically inclined senatorial class being overshadowed by a group that the ruling class had never expected to be subject to: the soldiery.

It is unfortunate that they were not able, or not willing, to develop a peaceful means of resolving internal policy disputes when neither side was amenable to backing down from their position. This brings us to a second observation: perhaps it was not in their nature. I am reminded of a statement by Polybius, a keen observer of the Romans. Perhaps it serves as something of a guide about their attitude toward problem solving. After recounting the disaster at sea suffered by the consuls of 255, M. Aemilius Paullus and Ser. Fulvius Nobilior, whose fleet was shipwrecked off the coast of Sicily at Camarina bringing home the survivors of the equally disastrous land expedition of M. Atilius Regulus (*cos. suff.* 256), Polybius takes the occasion to comment about the character of the Romans as a people.[1] Among the many things he notes about the Romans, he states: καθόλου δὲ Ῥωμαῖοι πρὸς πάντα χρώμενοι τῇ βίᾳ, which can roughly be rendered as, "In general, the Romans in all things make use of force."[2] Whereas Polybius was discussing their attitude toward naval affairs – which, according to him, they later adapted to fit the realities of the situation – the statement could apply equally well to their approach to crisis. We see the same thought echo centuries later in the mind of another Greek writer, Plutarch, as he places this memorable phrase in the mouth of Licinia, the wife of Gaius Gracchus, who tried to stop her husband from venturing forth on the fateful day that would see his death: κεκράτηκεν ἤδη τὰ χείρω· βίᾳ καὶ σιδήρῳ τὰς δίκας πράττουσιν "the lesser has now prevailed; by violence and the sword do they decide matters of debate."[3]

In military security crises, when an enemy was at the gates ready to harm the state, we fully expect the Romans to employ force to achieve their ends. Their diplomacy with other nations was also based on this principle. For instance, it was the very real threat of force that headed off war

[1] Polyb. 1. 36. 10–37.
[2] Polyb. 1. 37. 7.
[3] Plut. C. *Gracchus* 36. 4.

between Antiochus IV of Syria and the kingdom of the Ptolemies in Egypt in 168.[4] C. Popillius Laenas (*cos.* 172), whose role in an internal impasse we have recounted before, showed equal stubbornness and inflexibility in his dealings with the Seleucid King: he drew a circle in the sand around King Antiochus's feet and ordered him to make an answer to the senatorial decree that Laenas had handed him, which threatened what amounted to war on the party who refused to cease hostilities. In this case, Antiochus complied, and one might argue that here we have an example of a potential crisis defused by peaceful means: negotiation. That is true, but it was negotiation with the heavy shadow of force hanging over all. It is perhaps less expected that the Romans would be so inclined to employ violence on a regular basis to solve internal political disputes as well.

Besides noting that the Romans never developed an institutional response to internal political crisis and their common use of force to resolve an impasse (which is not at all a particularly Roman character trait: even today we hear reports of fistfights breaking out on the floors of modern parliamentary states in disputes over legislation), we may note another important observation about the nature of the Roman Republic. It relied very strongly on magistrates and tribunes, who had fundamental powers that were in theory unlimited, being willing to restrain themselves from using those powers in their raw form. We see the importance of that restraint most in internal disputes over policy. For when internal disputes involved individuals whose power within the system was grounded on a more fundamental basis than the shadowy *auctoritas* of the senate, these disputes often had to be settled by the use of force if neither side in the dispute was willing to back down or compromise.[5] If the dispute was between the senate and one of these fundamental power wielders, there was a path to resolution by the employment of another. As recounted before, this happened in the incident with the Popillii Laenates in the late 170s in Rome, where two tribunes of the plebs were able to make use of their powers that could not be blocked by the consuls to force through a resolution to the impasse between the senate and consuls over the status of the Statellates.

---

[4] Polyb. 29. 2, 27; Livy 44. 19. 6–14, 29. 1–5, 45. 10. 2–12. 8, 13. 1.

[5] Here is where the role of the senate as mediator was important, so long as the holders of fundamental powers – consuls and tribunes – were willing to abide by the senate's decision. See Eder (1996) 447, who discusses the impact the failure of the senate to act as mediator had on the impasse between Tiberius Gracchus and M. Octavius. Where I would differ with Eder is that he thinks the senate's failure lies in its unwillingness to intercede. I would argue that the senate was not capable of interceding as it had become a party to the dispute or at least a large and influential bloc of its members had, which made it incapable of serving as a neutral mediator or even coming to a consensus within itself as to how to resolve the impasse.

In this situation, a peaceful end to the dispute resulted. However, when the dispute pitted two holders of fundamental power against each other – a consul versus a tribune – unless one backed down, there was no other means of resolution than force.

We may note further points about the nature of the Roman political system in light of the observation about the use of force to settle internal political disputes where one party or both were fundamental parts of the governing system. One, internal crisis, beyond doubt demonstrated the central importance of the executive (the magistrates) in the functioning of the Roman Republic, whose role has sometimes been overshadowed in both the ancient sources and the modern literature by an overemphasis on the role of the senate.[6] Magistrates mattered. I do not in any way believe that the senate was not an important and vital part of the machinery that governed the Roman state, but to believe that the magistrates, especially the consuls, had been "turned into a kind of executive instrument of the Senate"[7] goes against the evidence of the actual working of the Roman state, even during the period where it is clear that the senate had become a key center for decision making during critical situations. Let us recall the limitations under which the senate operated: it could not be called into session without a magistrate (and later, the tribunes of the plebs, who are not strictly magistrates but increasingly began to function as ones by the end of the Republic, as they had gained the ability to consult the senate). The magistrate calling the senate into session could, if he did not like the "advice" being offered, dismiss the gathering. Further, even if the will of the senate was formally pronounced, if an equal or higher magistrate did not wish the decree to be acted on by the magistrate who consulted the senate, he could block its implementation. The senate during the Republic was dependent on a magistrate to carry out its will, unlike statute laws, which forced compliance on everyone alike, regardless of position or authority.

We can recount other ways in which magistrates were central to the system. The assemblies could neither conduct elections nor pass laws without a magistrate present to convene and preside over them. The selection of the senate itself (before the *dominatio* of Sulla) depended on the censorship, a magistracy. And in facing internal crises, where the use of force was necessary to put down a physical threat to the safety and continued

---

[6] For example, Hölkeskamp (2010) 25–30 echoes the whole line of scholars who would hold up the senate as "the central organ of Roman Republican government" (quoted from Meier (1997) 50).

[7] Hölkeskamp (2010) 27.

survival of the Roman Republic, the need for strong executive leadership was paramount. Magistrates were neither tyrants nor kings. They were normally constrained by heavy bonds of social convention and unwritten agreements among the ruling the class, along with some statutory limitations. This, as previously mentioned, was absolutely necessary to keep the system operating smoothly. Instances where the consuls and the tribunes were determined to stand on their fundamental rights and not give way to compromise led to the breakdown of the system and demonstrated the senate's ultimate impotence in the face of the employment of raw, unrestrained power.

The other important point is that the lack of any accepted final arbiter within the system, combined with the central role of executive officials (magistrates, and in some ways tribunes) in the system that comprised the Republic, demonstrated the path the Romans would tread in the future. It could have been different if the Romans had developed an institutional means of resolving internal political crises peacefully, a body or person whose judgments would be accepted as final (even if only grudgingly) by all parties without exception.

When political crises develop in modern constitution-based polities (such as the United States), the constitution (usually a written document) serves as the final arbiter of all disputes.[8] Thus, when an impasse occurs in the United States, both sides can make an appeal to the written document, and although the dispute can then morph into one about interpretation, a method of determining which interpretation is correct can be employed to settle the matter, to the acceptance (if not satisfaction) of both sides.[9] Once that ruling is made, the different sides agree to respect it. Turning to a country without a written constitution, such as the British system, the final arbiter in theory is the monarch, even if in reality, power resides in the House of Commons representing the British people. This theoretical supremacy of the monarchy is still necessary for settling potential impasses between the House of Commons and the upper house (the now modified House of Lords). For if the Lords refuse to agree to a bill put through the Commons, their refusal can ultimately be overridden by a threat from the monarch to appoint extra peers to the House of Lords until a majority is

---

[8] See Finer (1997) 3. 1570–1571: "... constitution ... supreme law of the land, all other acts of government having to comply with these rules."

[9] Although the United States Constitution already proclaims itself as the "supreme law of the land" in Article VI, it would be the establishment of judicial review by the Supreme Court that provided the method for deciding upon questions of interpretation and the Court's status as the decision-making body in that respect. See Finer (1997) 3. 1510–1512.

reached to give assent.[10] Although it may be ironic, in their system, the monarch is the ultimate guarantor of democracy.[11]

There is no such clear-cut group or institution within the Roman system with unquestioned authority to end disputes. It potentially existed in the early Republic, where use could be made of the Roman dictatorship, and actually, that was an institutional response to severe crises, both internal and external. The dictator's word was meant to be the last word, at least while he was in office. The use of this extraordinary office reveals a key foundation in Roman thinking about crisis response and government power, as it left crisis management in the hands of a powerful executive officer who would be entrusted to resolve the crisis. Especially in an internal dispute, the dictator's superior position, power, and *auctoritas* backed up any settlement that he might impose to resolve even severe internal crises.[12] The use of the dictatorship, however, was abandoned by the end of the Second Punic War, and thus, it did not live to see itself become the final institutional arbiter.[13] When "revived" by Sulla and Caesar at the end of the Republic, its use was a complete anomaly, not in keeping with the traditions and customs of the Roman state. Their positions as "final arbiter" within the Roman state did not rest on law, tradition, or their office. It was enforced by the points of their soldiers' swords. Unfortunately, the system never gave rise to a final arbiter whose decision would be acceptable to all parties. Political disputes were often resolved in the senate, it is true, but when the senate itself was the ground of contention or one of the parties involved in the dispute, the Romans resorted to force.[14]

In the late Republic, it can be claimed that the *SC ultimum* was developed as an institutional response to severe internal threats, a means by which a resolution could be forced through in situations that looked to

---

[10] See Finer (1997) 3. 1594.

[11] Although this measure may never have to be resorted to in the future. The recent modification of the House of Lords (removing the hereditary peers) is likely a first step in moving toward an upper house chosen in another manner, which would have then a different source of legitimacy and potentially different powers.

[12] There are numerous examples, such as the dictatorships of M'. Valerius in 494 (see *MRR* 1. 14) and Q. Hortensius in 287 (see *MRR* 1. 185), which were instrumental in ending the famed "Secessions" of the plebs. We can doubt the historicity of the first one all we wish, but what is important is that the principle of unitary executive authority to resolve internal political crises was part of the Roman mindset; it was not a foreign concept and it is not anachronistic to see the Romans thinking in these terms.

[13] See Chapter 2 and Chapter 8.

[14] As noted in the events of 133 by Eder (1996) 447. "In this case the weight of *dignitas* in a Roman noble's life left open only the way to violence" is a statement that could be applied to any of the holders of fundamental power in the various internal crises discussed in the preceding chapters.

be headed into permanent impasse, where the only solution would be a literal struggle to determine the winner. And it was, but not one of a very complex nature. For the *SC ultimum* merely brought back the primacy of the executive in crisis management. The senate, after all, did not tell the consul or other executive officer(s) in the absence of consuls what means were to be used to "defend the state and see that it takes no harm." That was given over entirely to the discretion of the executive. As the executive, in every case where the *SC ultimum* was passed, decided to use armed force to defend the state, the end result is that it actually institutionalized violence, providing political cover to the executive's decision to employ armed force even in situations where it would normally be unacceptable and illegal. The experiment of L. Opimius succeeded when he was acquitted at his trial the next year for his actions undertaken following the first historical passage of the *SC ultimum* in 121. We should not forget that there were those who tried to bring him to trial for it, which shows that there was no consensus even among the political classes (while not always the cream of the crop, as it were, the tribunes were men of some means and part of the class that governed the Roman state) about the status of the decree and what protection it offered to the magistrate who acted under its "guidance." The use of the *SC ultimum* was successfully repeated in 100, when Marius put down Saturninus without any personal repercussions. It might be thought that it was established at this point as the institutional response to internal crisis, but the following two cases will show that it was not clearly so.

First, the sources without reservation tell us that there was a tribune in 88 passing laws through unacceptable means (the use of mob violence and intimidation). Why did the consuls Sulla and Pompeius not seek an *SC ultimum* to put down Sulpicius and his supporters (including Marius)? It may be that the senate was deeply divided and Sulla and Pompeius lacked the support or influence to push through its passage. The consuls' attempt to forestall matters by declaring a *iustitium* was a legal and novel way of handling the situation, but it failed in the end because of the violent means used by Sulpicius and Marius to have it lifted. As violence had been used against the consuls of the Roman Republic, why did Sulla and Pompeius not demand an *SC ultimum* from the senate at this point? That is an interesting question for which I cannot offer any answer. Instead, Sulla suborned a Roman army and brought down the Republic.

For the other case, let us look again at M. Tullius Cicero. He had a *senatus consultum ultimum* passed in response to the troubling information coming out of Etruria but then made use of the political cover provided to take extra-legal action against the Catilinarian conspirators in the city.

The decree, however, gave him no comfort when P. Clodius became tribune in 58 (December 10, 59). Cicero was forced to seek safety in exile largely because the necessary political support that the "ultimate decree" should have provided seems to have eroded in the years between 62 and 59. When Clodius passed his new law, the senators (had they and the magistrates in office wished) could have extended the threat of action against anyone who would question the events of 63 to any who sought to make use of Clodius's new law. They did not. The political cover offered by the *SC ultimum* lasted only as long as the senatorial consensus that brought it into being. If that consensus faded, a former consul who took illegal or extra-legal action to put down an internal threat, even if he had "saved" the state, became a viable target. And we should not forget that Opimius was later brought down for other reasons, with his handling of Gracchus as a major factor in his downfall.[15]

Clearly, the *SC ultimum* may represent an attempt at formulating a response to internal crisis but one that was not based on law, human or divine, as it was simply a resort to brute force to resolve the dispute. It does, however, clearly demonstrate to us the central role of magistrates in the functioning of the Republic and especially in the protection of the system from any threat. For the senate did not, and frankly could not, take any powers unto itself to attempt to resolve an internal political dispute. It could only act as a place where the parties could meet and discuss their differences, hopefully resulting in a resolution. If one side was unwilling to accept the debating space offered by the senate, it did not have the authority under law to force a resolution. When the senate saw its will being thwarted by someone it could not convince or cajole, the only option left was to turn to the executive to use its powers to attempt to carry through the senate's will.

One of the key answers in any explanation of the fall of the Roman Republic must address the issue of the Romans' inability to resolve internal political disputes successfully without, in the end, resorting to force. There is no need to cite in detail the great political impasses that shattered the Republic to its core – the problems of Sulla, Caesar, and then the Caesarian party (Antony and Octavian). It is clear that the Romans needed to have a final arbiter whose judgment would be final to bring an end to the violence. As the senate itself increasingly turned to the executive to handle serious crises that arose within the Roman state, which was consistent with Roman thinking about how one responds to a severe internal crisis, it comes as

---

[15] He was condemned by the Mamilian Commission created to investigate those who had colluded with Jugurtha, king of Numidia. See Cic. *Brutus* 128; Sallust *Iug.* 40.

no surprise that the end result of those cataclysmic contests for control of the Roman state in its last decades resulted in the creation of a new "executive official," one who brought together the fundamental powers of the consuls' *imperium* and the tribunes' *potestas*, as the final arbiter who could render binding judgments in political disputes: the *princeps*.

We may end with a few lingering questions. First, why did the Roman Republic fail to develop any institutions or institutional responses to settle internal impasses? In modern states, governments have developed professional policing forces and emergency law to cope with internal crises. When a peaceful protest turns into a violent uprising, the riot police are called out, and the use of force is permitted to an extent that would not be considered lawful during "normal" conditions. This is not the same as the conditions following the passage of a *senatus consultum ultimum*. The consul and what we could call his *comitatus* (perhaps the Romans might say *subitarii milites*) did use force beyond what was normally permitted, but there was no similar suspension of the normal law as occurs in modern states. And for the political operators (the executive officers, legislators, administrators) in the majority of modern civilized states, the use of deadly force to win a political dispute is increasingly becoming unthinkable. When intractable disputes arise, recourse to the courts has become the norm. Although the Romans were no strangers to the courtroom, they never even considered employing the courts as a forum for resolving political disputes (personal vendettas, certainly; political policy debates, no).

So the question may be restated: why did the Romans never settle on a final arbiter until the destruction of the Republic created one? In the end, it may be that the reason why the Romans never established such a mechanism is simply that the nature of the Republic was far more simple and less complex than would have required a final arbiter. The true nature of the Roman Republic was really nothing more than a "gentleman's agreement." The most wealthy and socially powerful individuals in the Roman state agreed to abide by a certain set of codified rules (*lex*) and traditions (*mos*) in governing the Roman state.[16] This is not in any way to disregard the aspects of democracy and popular participation in the process that have recently been articulated by the work of Fergus Millar.[17] In fact, the limited participation of the Roman people is one of the rules by which the senatorial class agreed to abide. But like all gentlemen's agreements, its ability to survive was dependent on cooperation and all members of

---

[16] See Eder (1996) for a good discussion of this view.
[17] Several works published separately, but now conveniently collected in Millar (2002) 85–182. Strongly opposed (with too much animus) by Hölkeskamp (2010).

the agreement behaving "honorably." When disputes occurred and parties to the agreement refused to abide by it, the system, lacking a final arbiter with unchallenged authority (not the nebulous *auctoritas* of the senate), collapsed.

It could be said that what hampered the Romans was that there was no Roman "constitution." This has been touted as a virtue by some scholars, pointing to the flexibility that existed within the Roman system.[18] From the perspective of internal political crises, however, this was a shortcoming. It is an old maxim commonly ascribed to Napoleon that constitutions should be "short and obscure."[19] The Romans would likely get high marks from Napoleon on both counts, but then one must think about what kind of a political system a megalomaniacal military dictator would want. The actual amount of fixed statute law and formal descriptions of powers held by various offices of state was relatively short compared with the long and constantly growing body of known rules that comprised the gentlemen's agreement of the political class, which they claimed to be tradition handed down by their ancestors (*mos maiorum*).[20] Although the rules were not exactly obscure – they could be quite specific about certain matters, such as the ages required for holding magistracies – they had a level of uncertainty that sometimes led the Romans to desire nailing them down, as they did with the ages for office that were finally written into formal statute law by the *lex Villia* of 180.[21] Among the areas of obscurity, however, was who got to have the final say when competing centers of power within the system had strongly opposing views on policy or action. There was no mechanism or institution set up to arbitrate between the competing powers of magistrates and tribunes. The Roman Senate often tried to act as the final arbiter, but it was not accepted by all that it had the right or the authority to do so, and this became increasingly the case during the last century of the Republic.

Because there was no "constitutional court," written constitution, or universally accepted arbiter who could pass final judgment on a political dispute within the Roman Republic, such situations were decided by a literal contest of strength. Such was the case with Sulla and thus, Caesar. It would be Augustus who would put a final end to the dispute by creating a single authority who would be respected by all within the Roman

---

[18] For the thoughts of earlier scholars on flexibility, see Eder (1996) 448.
[19] In fact, this is a misattribution. According to Rose (1901) 323 n. 1, it was actually Talleyrand who made the remark.
[20] On the nature of the "constitution" of the Roman state, see Lintott (1999) 1–8.
[21] See Livy 40. 44. 1. For detailed discussion, see Astin (1958).

state as the final arbiter: himself. However, the creation of the Principate would be accomplished only by force, to return to Polybius's observation, although it would also have the beneficial side effect of largely destroying the bitter internal political clashes that brought down the Republic. Why did the Roman political class not establish a much-needed arbiter? It may be that they wanted it this way. The senatorial class may have preferred a free hand and not be tied down by explicitly spelled-out rules and regulations.[22]

From our full perspective on crisis response, we know well that the Roman Republic did have a series of institutional measures for dealing with external threats: states of emergency (or functional equivalents of them) such as the *tumultus* declaration, the *iustitium* edict, authorizations to magistrates by the senate for emergency levies during declared states of emergency, empowering of former magistrates to resume magisterial powers to provide more officers of state (Hannibal's march on Rome, Caesar's march on Rome), formally instituting the Night Watch (*vigiliae*), and stationing guards in the city (*praesidia, custodes*). Why did the Republic never transfer these measures to their handling of internal threats (that is, threats within the city itself)? Why did the senate not simply declare a *tumultus* when the Gracchans seized the capitol? When domestic enemies raised forces outside the city of Rome, the Romans were not reluctant to declare a *tumultus* (as happened in response to Lepidus in 78, Catiline in 63, and Antony in 43), but they seemed loath to use the emergency decree if the enemy was already within the boundaries of the city itself.

The only times where it appears that these states of emergency were employed in purely internal domestic circumstances were in 88, when Sulla and Pompeius Rufus attempted to declare a *iustitium* in order to prevent the tribune P. Sulpicius Rufus from passing his measures through the assembly, and in 52, when it appears that a *SC ultimum* was passed instructing an *interrex* (!) to institute a state of emergency, and then the *interrex* called upon the proconsul Cn. Pompeius to enter the city with armed soldiers to put down the violence in Rome between rioting supporters of the dead tribune Clodius and his rival Milo. As is clear, however, both of these examples are highly anomalous and come very late in the life of the Republic, the latter just a few years before the final crises that put an end

---

[22] On the resistance to institutionalizing explicit rules and regulations, which does not mean that it did not occur at all, but that it was not carried through to anywhere near the same extent as today, see the interesting piece on Roman political behavior by Brennan (2004) 31–58. The Romans' preference for allowing the senate to remain unrestrained by rules and regulations is also noted by Hölkeskamp (2010) 26.

to the *libera res publica*. As highly anomalous situations, it may be that they had little value as precedents.

As a final question, we may ask where did authority lie for dealing with crisis within the Roman state? How did the Romans successfully address crisis situations? I pair these two questions together because their answer is closely intertwined. The people were sovereign. The consuls held *imperium*. The senate had *auctoritas*. When one takes a long-term chronological view, it becomes clear that the Romans themselves turned to the executive for the resolution of crises. In the early Republic, resort to a dictator was a fairly common occurrence.[23] As the state grew and matured, the senate did rise in prominence in managing crises. Yet although the Second Punic War may be hailed as a high point in the senate's role in directing governmental policy, it should not be forgotten that that same senate, when faced with the overwhelming problems caused by the Romans' horrific defeats at Lake Trasimene and Cannae, did not shrink from turning to an all-powerful executive, the dictator, to take control of the Roman state's crisis response. Later on, the senate would begin to abdicate decision making for serious internal crises altogether, by empowering the executive, through the *SC ultimum*, to take whatever steps the executive saw fit "to see that the state takes no harm." As we come back to the events that began this work, the winter of 44/43, we can see that Cicero was eagerly awaiting the coming of January 1 and the beginning of the new magisterial year, with the new consuls taking office. Without them to provide teeth to any decision taken by the body, the senate itself was not fully capable of managing the crisis.

To conclude: a close examination of the phenomenon of crisis in the Roman Republic yields interesting insights into the nature of the Roman political system, as well as information about their conceptual categories related to law, states of emergency, and where authority lay in the Republic. With regard to the political system of the Roman Republic, crisis demonstrates the central role of magistrates in the functioning of the Roman State. From early in Roman history, this is clearly demonstrated by the use of the extraordinary office of *dictator*. When disputes arose and no side was willing to back down, and if the parties to the dispute were in positions of power (the consuls, the plebeian tribunes) that could not be overridden by the influence of the ruling class as a body (the senate), thereby lacking an institutional mechanism to resolve the dispute, there was left only the use of force to decide the matter. The Romans were unable either to create or to agree to the designation of a final arbiter to whom recourse could

---

[23] See Chapter 8.

be made when political impasses had proved incapable of being resolved through negotiation between the parties. The senate could play this role on occasion, but this was reliant on both sides accepting the senate as a neutral and fair arbiter. When the senate itself was a party to an internal dispute (as in the case of Tiberius Gracchus), bloodshed followed. Here we may reiterate Polybius's observation that the Romans commonly resorted to force. In the end, that problem would be solved by the radical step of practically removing debate completely from the hands of the ruling class and depositing all authority into the hands of a single man, the *princeps*, who would resolve all future political debates. When faced with one of its gravest crises ever, the Romans turned to the executive again, but this time permanently. Of course, this also meant the end of the Roman Republic as a system of institutions that allowed for a larger number of citizens to be involved in decision making for their state.

BIBLIOGRAPHY

Astin, A. E. 1958. *The Lex Annalis before Sulla*. Brussels.

———. 1967. "Saguntum and the Origins of the Second Punic War," *Latomus* 26:577–596.

Badian, E. 1958. *Foreign Clientelae (264–70 B.C.)*. Oxford.

———. 1959. "Rome and Antiochus the Great: A Study in Cold War," *CP* 54:81–99.

———. 1982. "'Crisis theories' and the beginning of the Principate," in Wirth 1982:18–41.

———. 1984. "The death of Saturninus: Studies in chronology and prosopography," *Chiron* 14:101–147.

———. 2004. "The pig and the priest," 263–272 in ed. H. Heftner and K. Tomaschitz. *Ad fontes !: Festschrift für Gerhard Dobesch zum 65. Geburtstag am 15. September 2004, dargebracht von Kollegen, Schülern und Freunden*. Vienna.

Bandel, F. 1910. *Die römischen Diktaturen*. Breslau.

Barnes, C. L. H. 2005. *Images and Insults: Ancient Historiography and the Outbreak of the Tarentine War*. Stuttgart.

Baronowski, D. W. 1995. "Polybius on the causes of the Third Punic War," *CP* 90:16–31.

Bassett, E. L. 1964. "Hannibal at the Tutia," 209–233 in *Studi Annibalici. Atti del Convegno svoltosi a Cortona, Tuoro sul Trasimeno, Perugia, ottobre 1961*. Cortona.

Bauman, R. A. 1973. "The *hostis* declarations of 88 and 87 B.C.," *Athenaeum* 51:270–293.

———. 1990. "The Suppression of the Bacchanals: Five Questions," *Historia* 39:334–348.

Beard, M. 2007. *The Roman Triumph*. Cambridge, MA.

Bellen, H. 1985. *Metus Gallicus-Metus Punicus: Zum Furchtmotiv in der römischen Republik*. Wiesbaden.

Bender, P. 1997. "Rom, Karthago und die Kelten," *Klio* 79 (1):87–106.

Beness, J. L. 2000. "The punishment of the Gracchani and the execution of C. Villius in 133/132," *Antichthon* 34:1–17.

_____. 2005. "Scipio Aemilianus and the crisis of 129 B. C.," *Historia* 54:37–48.

Beness, J. L. and T. W. Hillard. 1990. "The death of L. Equitius on 10 December 100 B.C.," *CQ* n.s. 40:269–272.

_____. 2001. "The theatricality of the deaths of C. Gracchus and friends," *CQ* n.s. 51:135–140.

Bickerman, E. J. 1945. "*Bellum Philippicum*: Some Roman and Greek views concerning the causes of the Second Macedonian War," *CP* 40:137–148.

Billows, R. A. 2009. *Julius Caesar: The Colossus of Rome*. London and New York.

Binot, C. 2001. "Le rôle de Scipion Nasica Sérapion dans la crise gracquienne, une relecture," *Pallas* 57:185–203.

Bonnefond-Coudry, M. 1989. *Le sénat de la République romaine de la guerre d'Hannibal à Auguste. Pratiques délibératives et prise de décision*. Rome.

Bradley, K. R. 1978. "Slaves and the Conspiracy of Catiline," *CP* 73:329–336.

_____. 1989. *Slavery and Rebellion in the Roman World, 140 B.C.–70 B.C.* Bloomington.

Brecher, M. 1993. *Crises in World Politics: Theory and Reality*. Oxford.

Brecher, M. and J. Wilkenfeld. 1997. *A Study of Crisis*. Ann Arbor.

Brecher, M., J. Wilkenfeld, and S. Moser. 1988. *Crises in the Twentieth Century*. Oxford.

Brennan, T. C. 1992. "Sulla's career in the Nineties: Some reconsiderations," *Chiron* 22:103–158.

_____. 1993. "The Commanders in the First Sicilian Slave War," *RFIC* 121:153–184.

_____. 1996. "Triumphus in Monte Albano," in Wallace, Harris 1996:315–337.

_____. 2000. *The Praetorship in the Roman Republic*. 2 vols. Oxford.

_____. 2004. "Power and process under the Republican 'Constitution,'" in Flower 2004:31–65.

Briscoe, J. 1964. "Q. Marcius Philippus and *Nova Sapientia*," *JRS* 54:66–77.

_____. 1973. *A commentary on Livy, Books XXXI–XXXIII*. Oxford. [=Briscoe, Livy 1]

_____. 1974. "Supporters and opponents of Tiberius Gracchus," *JRS* 64:125–135.

_____. 1981. *A commentary on Livy, Books XXXIV–XXXVII*. Oxford. [=Briscoe, Livy 2]

_____. 2003. "A. Postumius Albinus, Polybius and Livy's account of the «Bacchanalia»," 302–308 in *Hommages à Carl Deroux. 4, Archéologie et histoire de l'art, religion*. ed. by P. Defosse. Brussels. [*Collection Latomus* 277]

_____. 2008. *A commentary on Livy, Books 38–40*. Oxford. [=Briscoe, Livy 3]

Broughton, T. R. S. 1951–1986. *The Magistrates of the Roman Republic*. 3 vols. Atlanta [rpt. 1986] [=*MRR*]

Brunt, P. A. 1965. "Italian aims at the time of the Social War," *JRS* 55:90–109.

_____. 1971. *Italian Manpower, 225 B.C.–A.D. 14*. Oxford.

Büchner, K. 1982. *Sallust*, second edition. Heidelberg.

Buraselis, K. 1996. "*Vix aerarium sufficerent*. Roman Finances and the Outbreak of the Second Macedonian War," *GRBS* 37:149–172.

Burns, T. S. 2003. *Rome and the Barbarians, 100 B.C.–A.D. 400*. Baltimore.

Butler, H. E. and M. Cary. 1982. *Suetonius: Divus Julius*, with new intro., bibl. and additional notes by G. B. Townend. Bristol [original: Oxford, 1927].

Carey, W. L. 1996. "*Nullus videtur dolo facere*: The Roman seizure of Sardinia in 237B.C.," *CP* 91:203–222.

Carney, T. F. 1962. *A biography of C. Marius*. Salisbury. [Proceedings of the African Classical Association, Suppl. I].

Carter, J. 1996. Review of Evans (1994) in *CR* n.s. 46:313–315.

Chaplin, J. 2000. *Livy's Exemplary History*. Oxford.

Charles, M. B. 2006. Review of Keaveney (2005) [1982]. *BMCR* 2006.01.13.

Christ, K. 1979. *Krise und Untergang der römischen Republik*. Darmstadt.

_____. 2002. *Sulla. Eine römische Karriere*. Munich.

Chrol, E. Del. 2006. *Countercultural responses to the crisis of masculinity in late republican Rome*. Ph.D. diss., University of Southern California.

Cornell, T. J. 1995. *The beginnings of Rome: Italy and Rome from the Bronze Age to the Punic Wars (c. 1000–264 BC)*. London and New York.

Cornell, T. J., B. Rankov, and P. Sabin. 1996. *The Second Punic War: A reappraisal*. London. [*BICS* Supplement 67]

Crawford, M. H. ed. 1996. *Roman Statutes*. London. [*BICS* Supplement 64]

Crifò, G. 1964. "Il dilectus del 216 a. C. e l'editto di M. Iunius Pera," 387–395 in *Synteleia Vincenzo Arangio-Ruiz, I; II /* a cura di A. Guarino and L. Labruna. Naples.

Criniti, N. 1969. "M. Aimilius Q. f. M. n. Lepidus, *ut ignis in stipula*," *MIL* 30:319–460.

Crook, J. A., A. Lintott, and E. Rawson, eds. 1994. *The Cambridge Ancient History*, second edition, vol.ix: *The Last Age of the Roman Republic, 146–43 BC*. Cambridge.

Daly, G. 2002. *Cannae: The Experience of Battle in the Second Punic War*. London.

D'Arms. J. H. 1970 [2003]. *Romans on the Bay of Naples and Other Essays on Roman Campania*. Bari. [Reprint of *Romans on the Bay of Naples: A Social and Cultural Study of the Villas and Their Owners from 150 BC to AD 400*, Cambridge, MA, 1970, plus additional essays].

Davis, E. W. 1959. "Hannibal's Roman campaign of 211 BC," *Phoenix* 13:113–120.

De Ligt, L. 2004. "Poverty and demography: The case of the Gracchan land reforms," *Mnemosyne* 57:725–757.

De Martino, F. 1951–1967. *Storia della costituzione romana*. Naples.

Derow, P. S. 1991. "Pharos and Rome," *ZPE* 88:261–270.

Develin, R. 1977. "*Lex curiata* and the competence of magistrates," *Mnemosyne* 30:49–65.

————. 1978. "Scipio Aemilianus and the consular elections of 148 BC," *Latomus* 37:484–488.

Devijver, H. and E. Lipinski, eds. 1989. *Punic wars: Proceedings of the conference held in Antwerp from the 23rd to the 26th of November 1988 in cooperation with the Department of History of the Universiteit Antwerpen (U.F.S.I.A.).* Leuven.

Domínguez Pérez, J. C. 2005. "El potencial económico de Saiganthé como « casus belli » en el estallido de la segunda Guerra Púnica," *Latomus* 64:590–600.

Dorey, T. A. 1959. "Contributory causes of the Second Macedonian War," *AJP* 80:288–295.

————. ed. 1971. *Livy*. London.

Duverger, M. ed. 1982. *Dictatures et légitimité*. Paris.

Dyson, S. L. 1985. *The Creation of the Roman Frontier*. Princeton.

Earl, D. C. 1961. *The Political Thought of Sallust*. Cambridge.

————. 1967. *The Moral and Political Tradition of Rome*. Ithaca, NY.

Eckstein, A. M. 1980. "Polybius on the rôle of the Senate in the crisis of 264 BC," *GRBS* 21:175–190.

————. 1982. "Human sacrifice and fear of military disaster in Republican Rome," *AJAH* 7:69–95.

————. 1984. "Rome, Saguntum and the Ebro Treaty," *Emerita* 55:51–68.

————. 1987. *Senate and General: Individual Decision-making and Roman Foreign Relations, 264–194 BC*. Berkeley and Los Angeles.

————. 1994. "Polybius, Demetrius of Pharos, and the origins of the Second Illyrian War," *CP* 89:46–59.

————. 1999. "Pharos and the question of Roman treaties of alliance in the Greek East in the Third Century BCE," *CP* 94:395–418.

————. 2006. *Mediterranean Anarchy, Interstate War, and the Rise of Rome*. Berkeley and Los Angeles.

Eder, W. 1996. "Republicans and sinners: The decline of the Roman Republic and the end of a provisional arrangement," in Wallace, Harris 1996:439–461.

Ehrenberg, V. 1953. "*Imperium maius* in the Roman Republic," *AJP* 74:113–136.

Elwyn, S. 1993. "Interstate kinship and Roman foreign policy," *TAPA* 123:261–286.

Errington R. M. 1970. "Rome and Spain before the Second Punic War," *Latomus* 29:25–57.

Evans, R. J. 1994. *Gaius Marius: A political biography*. Pretoria.

————. 2003. *Questioning Reputations: Essays on Nine Roman Republican Politicians*. Pretoria.

Feldherr, A. 1998. *Spectacle and Society in Livy's History*. Berkeley and Los Angeles.

Finer, S. E. 1997. *The History of Government from the Earliest Times*. 3 vols. Oxford.

Flower, H. I. ed. 2004. *The Cambridge Companion to the Roman Republic*. Cambridge.

_____. 2006. *The Art of Forgetting: Disgrace & Oblivion in Roman Political Culture*. Chapel Hill.

Forsythe, G. 1994. *The Historian L. Calpurnius Piso Frugi and the Roman Annalistic Tradition*. Lanham and London.

_____. 2005. *A Critical History of Early Rome: From Prehistory to the First Punic War*. Berkeley and Los Angeles.

Frank, T. 1927. "The Bacchanalian Cult of 186 BC," *CQ* 21:128–132.

Franke, P. R. 1989. "Pyrrhus," in Walbank, et al. 1989:456–485.

Fronda, M. P. 2010. *Between Rome and Carthage: Southern Italy during the Second Punic War*. Cambridge.

Gabba, E. 1991. *Dionysius and the History of Archaic Rome*. Berkeley and Los Angeles.

_____. 1994. "Rome and Italy: The Social War," in Crook et al. 1994:104–128.

Gelzer, M. 1968. *Caesar: Politician and Statesman*. trans. P. Needham. Oxford.

Goldsworthy, A. 2001. *Cannae*. London.

_____. 2006. *Caesar: Life of a Colossus*. New Haven.

Gowing, A. M. 1992. *The Triumviral Narratives of Appian and Cassius Dio*. Ann Arbor.

Grainger, J. D. 2002. *The Roman War of Antiochos the Great*. Leiden.

_____. 2003. *Nerva and the Roman succession crisis of AD 96–99*. London.

Green, P. 2006. *Diodorus Siculus: Books 11–12. 37. 1. Greek History 480–431 BC: The Alternative Version*. Austin.

Greenidge, A. H. J. and A. M. Clay. 1960. *Sources for Roman history, 133–70 BC* 2nd ed. rev. by E. W. Gray. Oxford.

Gruen, E. S. 1969. "Notes on the 'First Catilinarian Conspiracy,'" *CP* 64:20–24.

_____. 1974. *The Last Generation of the Roman Republic*. Berkeley and Los Angeles.

_____. 1975. "Rome and Rhodes in the Second Century BC: A historiographical inquiry," *CQ* n.s. 25:58–81.

_____. 1976. "The origins of the Achaean War," *JHS* 96:46–69.

_____. 1984. *The Hellenistic World and the Coming of Rome*. 2 vols. Berkeley and Los Angeles.

_____. 1990. *Studies in Greek culture and Roman policy*. Leiden.

Gusso, M. 1990. "Appunti sulla notazione dei Fasti Capitolini interregni caus(sa) per la (pro-) diattatura di Q. Fabio Massimo nel 217 a. C.," *Historia* 39:291–333.

Hammond, N. G. L. 1968. "Illyris, Roman and Macedon in 229–205 BC," *JRS* 58:1–21.

Hammond, N. G. L., and F. W. Walbank. 1988. *A history of Macedonia*, Vol. III: 336–167 BC. Oxford.

Harris, W. V. 1979. *War and imperialism in Republican Rome 327–70 BC*. Oxford.

Hartfield, M. E. 1982. *The Roman Dictatorship: Its Character and Its Evolution*. Ph.D. Diss. Berkeley.

Haselberger, L., D. G. Romano, and E. A. Dumser. 2002. *Mapping Augustan Rome*. Portsmouth, RI. [*JRA* Supplementary Series 55; reprinted with corrections 2008].

Hayne, L. 1972. "M. Lepidus (Cos. 78): A reappraisal," *Historia* 21:661–668.

Hekster, O., G. de Kleijn, and D. Slootjes, eds. 2007. *Crises and the Roman Empire: Proceedings of the Seventh Workshop of the International Network Impact of Empire (Nijmegen, June 20–24, 2006)*. Leiden.

Henderson, M. I. 1957. "Potestas Regia," *JRS* 47:82–87.

Hill, H. 1961. "Dionysius of Halicarnassus and the origins of Rome," *JRS* 51:88–93.

Hinard, F. ed. *Dictatures. Actes de la table ronde réunie à Paris les 27 et 28 février 1984*. Paris.

Hölkeskamp, K. J. 2010. *Reconstructing the Roman republic: An ancient political culture and modern research*. Princeton.

Hölkeskamp, K. J., and E. Stein-Hölkeskamp. 2000. *Von Romulus zu Augustus: Grosse Gestalten der römischen Republik*. Munich.

———. 2000b. "Lucius Cornelius Sulla: Revolutionär und restaurativer Reformer," in Hölkeskamp 2000:199–218.

Holleaux, M. 1921. *Rome, la Grèce et les monarchies hellénistiques au IIIe siècle avant J. C. (273–205)*. Paris.

Hough, J. N. 1930. "The *lex Lutatia* and the *lex Plautia de vi*," *AJP* 51:135–147.

Hoyos, B. D. 1998. *Unplanned Wars: The Origins of the First and Second Punic Wars*. Berlin.

———. 2003. *Hannibal's Dynasty: Power and Politics in the Western Mediterranean, 247–183 BC*. London and New York.

Jaeger, M. 1997. *Livy's Written Rome*. Ann Arbor.

Kallet-Marx, R. M. 1995. *Hegemony to Empire: The Development of the Roman Imperium in the East from 148 to 62 BC*. Berkeley and Los Angeles.

Kaplan, A. 1973. "Religious dictators of the Roman Republic," *CW* 67:172–175.

Kaufman, D. B. 1932. "Poisons and poisonings among the Romans," *CP* 27:156–167.

Keaveney, A. 1982. *Sulla: The Last Republican*. London. [2nd ed. 2005]

———. 2003. "The tragedy of Caius Gracchus: Ancient melodrama or modern farce?" *Klio* 85:322–333.

Konrad, C. F. 1994. *Plutarch's Sertorius: A historical commentary*. Chapel Hill and London.

Kramer, E. A. 2005. "Book One of Velleius' *History*: Scope, levels of treatment, and non-Roman elements," *Historia* 54:144–161.

Kramer, F. R. 1948. "Massilian diplomacy before the Second Punic War," *AJP* 69:1–26.

Kraus, C. S. 1991. "*Initium turbandi omnia a femina ortum est*: Fabia Minor and the Election of 367 BC," *Phoenix* 45:314–325.

———. 1994. Livy: *Ab urbe condita. Book VI*. Cambridge.

Kunkel, V. W. 1995. *Staatsordnung und Staatspraxis der Römischen Republik*. Munich.

La Penna, A. 1968. *Sallustio e la 'rivoluzione' romana*. Milan.

Laurence, R. 1994. "Rumour and communication in Roman politics," *GR* 2nd ser. 41:62–74.

Lazenby, J. F. 1995. *The First Punic War*. Stanford.

Lefkowitz, M. R. 1959. "Pyrrhus' negotiations with the Romans, 280–278 BC," *HSCP* 64:147–177.

Le Gall, J. 1987. "*Tumultus* et *Vigiliae*: la «garde nationale» de la Réplic romaine," *Pallas* (special issue): *Melanges offert à Monsieur Michel Labrousse*, 41–47.

Lenaghan, J. O. 1969. *A Commentary on Cicero's Oration: De Haruspicum Responso*. The Hague.

Letzner, W. 2000. *Lucius Cornelius Sulla: Versuch einer Biographie*. Münster

Levene, D. S. 1993. *Religion in Livy*. Leiden.

———. 2010. *Livy on the Hannibalic War*. Oxford.

Levick, B. 1982. "Sulla's March on Rome in 88 BC," *Historia* 31:503–508.

———. 1983. "The *senatus consultum* from Larinum," *JRS* 73:97–115.

Lewis, R. G. 1998. "P. Sulpicius' law to recall exiles, 88 BC," *CQ* n.s. 48:195–199.

Linderski, J. 1984. "Rome, Aphrodisias and the *Res Gestae*: The *genera militiae* and the status of Octavian," *JRS* 74:74–80.

———. 2002. "The pontiff and the tribune: The death of Tiberius Gracchus," *Athenaeum* 90:339–366.

Lintott, A. W. 1968. *Violence in Republican Rome*. Oxford.

———. 1971. "The Tribunate of P. Sulpicius Rufus," *CQ* n.s. 21:442–453.

———. 1994. "The crisis of the Republic: Sources and source-problems" in Crook, Lintott, Rawson 1994:1–15.

———. 1999. *The Constitution of the Roman Republic*. Oxford.

Lovano, M. 2002. *The Age of Cinna: Crucible of Late Republican Rome*. Stuttgart.

Luce, T. J. 1970. "Marius and the Mithridatic Command," *Historia* 19:161–194.

———. 1977. *Livy: The Composition of His History*. Princeton.

———. 1989. "Ancient views on the causes of bias in historical writing," *CP* 84:16–31.

Ma, J. 2000. *Antiochos III and the Cities of Western Asia Minor*. Oxford.

MacMullen, R. 1976. *Roman Government's Response to Crisis, AD 235–337*. New Haven.

Magie, D. 1950. *Roman Rule in Asia Minor, to the end of the third century after Christ*, 2 vols. Princeton.

Mandell, S. 1989. "The Isthmian proclamation and the early stages of Roman imperialism in the Near East," *CB* 65: 89–94.

Mattingly, H. B. 1969. "Saturninus' corn bill and the circumstances of his fall," *CR* n.s. 19:267–270.

McGing, B. C. 1986. *The Foreign Policy of Mithridates VI Eupator, King of Pontus*. Leiden.

McGushin, P. 1992. *Sallust: The Histories. Translated with Introduction and Commentary*. Oxford.

Meier, C. 1982. *Caesar*. Berlin [also in English translation 1995 New York].

——. 1997. *Res publica amissa: Eine Studie zur Verfassung und Geschichte der späten römischen Republik*. 3rd ed. Frankfurt.

Messer, W. S. 1920. "Mutiny in the Roman Army: The Republic," *CP* 15:158–175.

Meyer, E. 2004. *Legitimacy and Law in the Roman World*: Tabulae *in Roman Belief and Practice*. Cambridge.

Miles, G. B. 1995. *Livy: Reconstructing Early Rome*. Ithaca, NY.

Millar, F. G. B. 1964. *A study of Cassius Dio*. Oxford.

——. 2002. *Rome, the Greek World, and the East, vol. 1: The Roman Republic and the Augustan Revolution*. ed. H. Cotton and G. Rodgers. Chapel Hill.

Mitchell, T. N. 1975. "The *volte-face* of P. Sulpicius Rufus in 88 BC," *CP* 70:197–204.

——. 1991. *Cicero: The Senior Statesman*. New Haven and London.

Mommsen, Th. 1887. *Römisches Staatsrecht*. 3rd ed. 3 vols. Leipzig.

Morgan, M. G. 1972. "The defeat of L. Metellus Denter at Arretium," *CQ* n.s. 22:309–325.

——. 1991. "Q. Metellus (cos. 206), *Dictatorii* in the pre-Sullan Senate and the end of the dictatorship," *Athenaeum* 79:359–370.

Morgan, M. G., and J. Walsh. 1978. "Ti. Gracchus (tr. pl. 133 BC), the Numantine Affair, and the deposition of M. Octavius," *CP* 73:200–210.

Mortensen, D. E. 1999. *Wine, drunkenness, and the rhetoric of crisis in ancient Rome*. Ph.D. diss., The University of Wisconsin-Madison.

Münzer, F. 1920. *Römische Adelsparteien und Adelsfamilien*. Stuttgart.

Nippel, W. 1995. *Public order in ancient Rome*. Cambridge.

Oakley, S. P. 1997–2005. *A commentary on Livy, Books VI–X*, 4 vols. Oxford. [=Oakley, *Livy*]

O'Connell, R. L. 2010. *The ghosts of Cannae: Hannibal and the darkest hour of the Roman republic*. New York.

Ogilvie, R. M. 1965. *A commentary on Livy, Books 1–5*. Oxford. [=Ogilvie, *Livy*]

Ormanni, A. 1990. *Il "regolamento interno" del senato romano nel pensiero degli storici moderni sino a Theodor Mommsen: Contributo ad una storia della storiografia sul diritto pubblico romano*. Naples.

Osgood, J. 2006. *Caesar's Legacy: Civil War and the Emergence of the Roman Empire*. Cambridge.

Ossier, J. F. 2004 "Greek cultural influence and the revolutionary policies of Tiberius Gracchus," *SHHA* 22:63–69.

Pagán, V. E. 2004. *Conspiracy Narratives in Roman History*. Austin.

Pailler, J. M. 1988. *Bacchanalia: La répression de 186 av. J. C. à Rome et en Italie: Vestiges, images, tradition*. Paris.

Patterson, M. L. 1942. "Rome's choice of magistrates during the Hannibalic War," *TAPA* 73:319–340.

Paul, G. M. 1984. *A Historical Commentary on Sallust's Bellum Jugurthinum*. Liverpool.

Peacock, D. P. S. 1986. "Punic Carthage and Spain: The evidence of the amphorae," *CEA* 18:101–113.

Pelling, C. B. R. 1979. "Plutarch's method of work in the Roman Lives," *JHS* 99:74–96.

———. 2002. *Plutarch and History. Eighteen Studies*. Swansea and London.

Perelli, L. 1993. *I Gracchi*. Rome.

Powell, J. G. F. 1990. "The Tribune Sulpicius," *Historia* 39:446–460.

Ramsey, J. T. 1984. *Sallust's Bellum Catilinae*. Atlanta. [2nd ed. rev. 2007 New York]

———. 2001. "Did Mark Antony contemplate an alliance with his political enemies in July 44 BCE?" *CP* 96:253–268.

Rasmussen, C. M. 2001. *Livy's Bacchanalian Affair: Contemporary issues and influences*. Ph.D. diss., University of Southern California.

Reid, J. S. 1912. "Human sacrifices at Rome and other notes on Roman religion," *JRS* 2:34–52.

Rich, J. W. 1996. "The Origins of the Second Punic War," in Cornell, Rankov, and Sabin, 1996:1–38.

Richardson, jr., L. 1992. *A New Topographical Dictionary of Ancient Rome*. Baltimore.

Richardson, J. S. 1980. "The ownership of Roman land: Tiberius Gracchus and the Italians," *JRS* 70:1–11.

Ridley, R. T. 2000. "Leges Agrariae: Myths Ancient and Modern," *CP* 95:459–467.

———. 2003. "The contradictory revolution: The Italian war (91–89 BC)," *AH* 33:31–57.

Rigsby, K. J. 1988. "Provincia Asia," *TAPA* 118:123–153.

Rose, J. H. 1901. *The Life of Napoleon I*. London.

Rosenberger, V. 2003. "The Gallic Disaster," *CW* 96:365–373.

Rosenstein, N. S. 1990. *Imperatores victi: Military Defeat and Aristocratic Competition in the Middle and Late Republic*. Berkeley and Los Angeles.

———. 2004. *Rome at War: Farms, Families, and Death in the Middle Republic*. Chapel Hill.

Ruoff-Väänänen, E. 1978. "The Roman Senate and criminal jurisdiction during the Roman Republic," *Arctos* 12: 125–133.

Sage, E. T., and A. J. Wegner. 1936. "Administrative commissions and the official career, 218–167 BC," *CP* 31:23–32.

Salmon, E. T. 1957. "Hannibal's march on Rome," *Phoenix* 11:153–163.

Scalia, L. 1999. "Osservazioni su due iustitia repubblicani (Cic. *Planc.* 33 e Plut. *Tib.* 10, 4)," *Med. Ant.* II, 2:673–695.

Schwarte, K. H. 1983. *Der Ausbruch des zweiten Punischen Krieges: Rechtsfrage und Überlieferung*. Wiesbaden.

Scullard, H. H. 1981. *Festivals and Ceremonies of the Roman Republic*. Ithaca, NY.

Seager, R. 1967. "The Date of Saturninus' Murder," *CR* n.s. 17:9–10.

———. ed. 1969. *The Crisis of the Roman Republic*. Cambridge.

Shackleton Bailey, D. R. 1965–1970. *Cicero's Letters to Atticus*. 7 vols. Cambridge.

———. 1977. *Epistulae ad Familiares*. 2 vols. Cambridge.

———. 1980. *Epistulae Ad Quintum Fratrem et M. Brutum*. Cambridge.

———. 1986. *Cicero. Philippics*. Chapel Hill.

Shaw, B. D. 2001. *Spartacus and the Slave Wars: A Brief History with Documents*. Boston.

Sherwin-White, A. N. 1973. *The Roman Citizenship*, second edition. Oxford.

———. 1977. "Roman involvement in Anatolia, 167–88 BC," *JRS* 67:62–75.

———. 1984. *Roman Foreign Policy in the East, 168 BC to AD 1*. Norman, Okla.

Smith, C. J. 2006. *The Roman Clan: The Gens from Ancient Ideology to Modern Anthropology*. Cambridge.

Smith, R. E. 1958. *Service in the post-Marian Roman Army*. Manchester.

Starr, jr., C. G. 1943. "Coastal defence in the Roman world," *AJP* 64:56–70.

Stewart, R. 1995. "Catiline and the crisis of 63–60 BC," *Latomus* 54:62–78.

Stockton, D. 1979. *The Gracchi*. Oxford.

Stone, A. M. 1998. "A house of notoriety: An episode in the campaign for the consulate in 64 b.c.," *CQ* n.s. 48:487–491.

Sumi, G. S. 1997. "Power and ritual: The crowd at Clodius' funeral," *Historia* 46:80–102.

Sumner, G. V. 1968. "Roman policy in Spain before the Hannibalic War," *HSCP* 72:205–246.

———. 1972. "Rome, Spain, and the outbreak of the Second Punic War. Some clarifications," *Latomus* 31:469–480.

———. 1975. "Elections at Rome in 217 BC," *Phoenix* 29:250–259.

Swan, P. M. 2004. *The Augustan Succession: An Historical Commentary on Cassius Dio's ROMAN HISTORY Books 55–56 (9 BC–AD 14)*. Oxford, New York.

Syme, R. 1939. *The Roman Revolution*. Oxford.

———. 1964. *Sallust*. Berkeley and Los Angeles. [reprinted with a new foreword by Ronald Mellor 2002]

Takács, S. 2000. "Politics and religion in the Bacchanalian Affair of 186 BCE," *HSCP* 100:301–310.

Talbert, R. J. A. 1984. *The Senate of Imperial Rome*. Princeton.

Tamura, T. 1990. "The political trends at Greek city-states in Asia Minor during the first Mithridatic war," *JCS* 38:61–72.

Tatum, W. J. 1999. *The patrician tribune: Publius Clodius Pulcher*. Chapel Hill.

———. 2004. Review of Evans (2003). *CR* 54:490–491.

Taylor, L. R. 1962. "Forerunners of the Gracchi," *JRS* 52:19–27.

————. 1966. *Roman Voting Assemblies from the Hannibalic War to the Dictatorship of Caesar.* Ann Arbor.

Taylor, P. J. and I. Donald. 2004. "The structure of communication behavior in simulated and actual crisis negotiations," *Human Communication Research* 30:443–478.

Thommen, L. 1989. *Das Volkstribunat der späten römischen Republik.* Wiesbaden.

Thonemann, P. J. 2004. "The date of Lucullus' quaestorship," *ZPE* 149:80–82.

Toye, D. L. 1995. "Dionysius of Halicarnassus on the first Greek historians," *AJP* 116:279–302.

Treggiari, S. 1991. *Roman marriage:* Iusti Coniuges *from the time of Cicero to the time of Ulpian.* Oxford.

Twyman, B. L. 1984. "The consular elections for 216 BC and the *lex Maenia de patrum auctoritas*," *CP* 79:285–294.

————. 1989. "The day Equitius died," *Athenaeum* 67:493–509.

Untermann, J. and F. Villar, ed. 1993. *Lengua y cultura en la Hispania prerromana: Actas del V coloquio sobre Lenguas y culturas prerromanas de la Península Ibérica (Colonia, 25–28 de Noviembre de 1989).* Salamanca.

Valditara, G. 1988. "Perché il dictator non poteva montare a cavallo," *SDHI* 54:226–238.

————. 1989. *Studi sul magister populi, dagli ausiliari militari del rex ai primi magistrati repubblicani.* Milan.

Verbrugghe, G. P. 1972. "Sicily 210–70 BC: Livy, Cicero and Diodorus," *TAPA* 103:535–559.

Vishnia, R. F. 1996. *State, society, and popular leaders in mid-Republican Rome.* London.

von Ungern-Sternberg, J. 2004. "The Crisis of the Roman Republic," in Flower 2004:89–109.

Walbank, F. W. 1940. *Philip V of Macedon.* Cambridge.

————. 1941. "A note on the embassy of Q. Marcius Philippus, 172 BC," *JRS* 31:82–93.

————. 1949. "Roman declarations of war in the Third and Second Centuries," *CP* 44:15–19.

————. 1963. "Polybius and Rome's Eastern Policy," *JRS* 53:1–13.

————. 1970. *A historical commentary on Polybius.* Vol. 1. Oxford. [Originally published 1957; corrected and republished 1970] [=Walbank, Polybius]

————. 2002. *Polybius, Rome, and the Hellenistic World: Essays and Reflections.* Cambridge.

Walbank, F. W., A. E. Astin, M. W. Frederiksen, and R. M. Ogilvie, eds. 1989. *The Cambridge Ancient History,* second edition, vol. VII.2: *The Rise of Rome to 220 BC.* Cambridge.

Wallace, R. W. and E. M. Harris, eds. 1996. *Transitions to Empire: Essays in Greco-Roman History, 360–146 BC, in honor of E. Badian.* Norman, OK.

Walsh, P. G. 1961. *Livy: His historical aims and methods.* Cambridge.

———. 1996. "Making a drama out of a crisis: Livy on the Bacchanalia," *GR* 2nd ser. 43:188–203.

———. 1996b. *Livy: Book XL*. London.

Ward, L. H. 1990. "Roman population, territory, tribe, city, and army size from the Republic's foundation to the Veientane War, 509 BC–400 BC," *AJP* 111:5–39.

Warrior, V. M. 1996. "Evidence in Livy on Roman policy prior to war with Antiochus the Great," in Wallace, Harris 1996:356–375.

Waters, K. H. 1970. "Cicero, Sallust and Catiline." *Historia* 19:195–215.

Watson, A. 1993. *International Law in Archaic Rome: War and Religion*. Baltimore.

Welch, K. and A. Powell, eds. 1998. *Julius Caesar as Artful Reporter: The War Commentaries as Political Instruments*. London. [Reissued, Swansea 2009].

Willeumier, P. 1939. *Tarente: Des origines à la conquête romaine*. Paris.

Williams, J. H. C. 2001. *Beyond the Rubicon: Romans and Gauls in Republican Italy*. Oxford.

Wirth, G., K. H. Schwarte, and J. Heinrichs. 1982. *Romanitas-Christianitas: Untersuchungen zur Geschichte und Literatur der römisches Kaiserzeit*. Berlin.

Wiseman, T. P. 1971. *New Men in the Roman Senate, 139 BC–AD 14*. Oxford.

———. 1979a. "Topography and rhetoric: The trial of Manlius," *Historia* 28:32–50.

———. 1979b. *Clio's Cosmetics: Three Studies in Greco-Roman Literature*. Leicester.

———. 1994. *Historiography and Imagination*. Exeter.

———. 1998. *Roman drama and Roman history*. Exeter.

Wooten, C. W. 1983. *Cicero's Philippics and Their Demosthenic Model: The Rhetoric of Crisis*. Chapel Hill.

Wyke, M. ed. 2006. *Julius Caesar in Western culture*. Oxford.

Yavetz, Zvi. 1963. "The failure of Catiline's Conspiracy." *Historia* 12:485–499.

INDEX